THE BLUE GUIDES

Domestic building in Gjirokastra

BLUE GUIDE

Albania

James Pettifer

A & C Black
London

WW Norton
New York

Second edition 1996

Published by A & C Black (Publishers) Limited
35 Bedford Row, London WC1R 4JH

A CIP catalogue record of this book is available from the British Library.

ISBN 0-7136-3785-4

Published in the United States of America by
WW Norton and Company, Inc
500 Fifth Avenue, New York, NY 10110

Published simultaneously in Canada by
Penguin Books Canada Limited
10 Alcorn Avenue, Toronto, Ontario M4V 3B2

ISBN 0-393-31056-6 USA

The author and the publishers have done their best to ensure the accuracy of all the information in Blue Guide Albania; however, they can accept no responsibility for any loss, injury or inconvenience sustained by any traveller as a result of information or advice contained in the guide.

James Pettifer is a writer and journalist specialising in the southern Balkans. He has reported on events for the *Times*, the *Economist*, the *Wall Street Journal*, and many other publications in Britain and abroad. He is a member of the Royal Institute of International Affairs and a Senior Associate member of St Anthony's College, Oxford. His most recent book, *The Greeks: Land and People since the War*, was published in 1993. He is working on the first Blue Guide to Bulgaria.

Maps and plans by Terence Crump. © A & C Black.
Illustrations on pp. 2, 112, 140, 143, 147, 156, 161, 164, 171, 183, 193, 208, 210, 219, 231, 233, 240, 261, 278 © Beatrix Blake

Aspects of Medieval Albania, by Stephen Hill, was first published as *Byzantinium and the Emergence of Albania in Perspectives on Albania*, edited by Tom Winnifrith. © Tom Winnifrith 1992. The publishers are grateful to Macmillan Academic and Professional Ltd and St Martin's Press, Incorporated for permission to reproduce a shortened version of the original article.

The publishers invite readers to write in with comments, suggestions and corrections for the next edition of the Blue Guide. Writers of the best letters will be awarded a free Blue Guide of their choice.

Printed and bound in Great Britian by William Clowes Limited, Beccles and Clowes

INTRODUCTION

Albania is a Balkan country of dramatic natural beauty, with a wealth of historic buildings and ancient archaeological sites that can compare for interest and variety with any in the Mediterranean world. It is about the size of Wales, with a population of approximately 3.4 million people. It lies south of the Dinaric Alps, inside what for centuries were often almost impassable mountains bordering Montenegro to the north, with the Vikut, Mal i Korabit and Jabllanica mountains adjoining Macedonia to the east, and the equally intimidating Grammoz and Buret mountains on the border with Greece.

It has notable and historic lowland cities on the Adriatic sea, in Durres, Shkodra and Vlora, the Classical sites of Butrint and Apollonia, and the famous Ottoman cities of Elbasan, Berat and Gjirokastra. The Adriatic coast has some fine sandy beaches and tranquil pine forests growing on reclaimed marshlands, and Albania has the largest range of wild flowers in the Mediterranean. But it is the variety and grandeur of the remote mountain landscapes that attract many visitors to Albania, with scenery of extraordinary beauty and scale, including some of the last wild habitats in Europe for mammals such as wolves, jackals, bears and lynx. Albania is also noted for birds of prey, particularly eagles, which soar on the thermals above the mountain valleys. The name of the country in the Albanian language, *Shqipëria*, is believed by some scholars to derive from the word for eagle, *Shqiponja.*

The isolation engendered by the geography of Albania has meant that for centuries the country was cut off from much of the mainstream of European life, and remained backward under the Ottoman occupation of 500 years. But the customs and traditions of the Albanian people always survived, and in the late 19C the movement for national independence grew under the Ottomans to the point where it could no longer be resisted and Albania became an independent state in 1913, after the Second Balkan war.

The country was the home of the Illyrian tribes in antiquity, some of the earliest inhabitants of the Balkans, and the coast was colonised by ancient Greek settlers in the Classical period. After Roman occupation it became an important province under the Republic and Empire, and a stronghold of Christianity as the new religion spread along the Egnatian Way which linked the Adriatic port of *Dyrrachium*, modern Durres, with Macedonia and Constantinople. Albania played an important part in the military planning of Justinian and the later emperors against the barbarian invaders. After the Slavs destroyed the Eastern Empire provinces, the territory of modern Albania became subject to various feudal lords, and was then taken by the Turks in the 15C, after which most of the lowlands converted to Islam. Many beautiful churches and mosques can be seen, and the domestic architecture of Berat and Gjirokastra are often considered to be the best preserved examples of Ottoman towns of their period that have survived anywhere in the ex-imperial territories.

Travel in Albania

For 50 years, until the end of communism in 1991-92, it was very difficult for Britons and Americans to visit Albania, except in closely supervised guided tours that only visited a few parts of the country; it is now possible to travel freely, and the wealth of ancient sites, historic cities and the magnificence of its coastal and mountain scenery can be appreciated. The end of communism in 1991–92 has not, however, brought an easy future to Albania as yet, and thanks to social chaos between 1990 and 1992, and the subsequent effects of the war in neighbouring ex-Yugoslavia, tourist numbers are fewer under pluralism and democracy than they were under communism. There are still very many practical difficulties in transport and material life facing the people and in the first edition of this Blue Guide to the country I concentrated on what was easiest to visit and places where reasonable accommodation could be found, bearing in mind the very difficult social and economic conditions of the 1990–92 period in which most of the research was done.

This second edition offers wider itineraries in some parts of the country, and includes a full account of a number of places which it was not possible to visit at that time, particularly in the Central Highlands, and the north and north east. It also includes museums, such as those at Shkodra, which existed three years ago but were closed to visitors and where it was impossible to make an inventory of the contents. A more systematic approach to the problems of spelling Albanian place names has been adopted and the prevailing genitive forms of spelling derived from the *Harta e Rrjetit Rrugor te Republikes se Shqiperise* omitted.

It should still be borne in mind, though, that Albania is still by far the poorest country in Europe, and travel outside the lowland cities requires preparations similar to those which are needed for the some Third World countries. It is my personal opinion that all first-time visitors, however experienced as travellers, should still seriously consider taking an organised tour, particularly if they do not have friends in Albania to assist them. If individual travel is contemplated, the relevant sections in the Guide on practical matters should be studied very carefully. Security in the cities has improved in the last two years, but there are still major problems for the visitor in some areas, associated with the side effects of the prolonged war in ex-Yugoslavia, political tension with Greece, the growth of organised crime and the imposition of economic sanctions on Serbia by the United Nations. This applies particularly if the visitor has limited means, as traditional methods of economy travel like backpacking involve very real difficulties in Albania at the moment, and in the foreseeable future. At the time of writing it appears that UN sanctions on ex-Yugoslavia may be lifted, but an improvement in border security may not necessarily follow.

I referred in the first edition of the Guide to the difficulties, in providing a full and up-to-date picture of the museums the visitor is able to see. This remains the case in many places although the situation has improved in Tirana and the larger towns. I would welcome any comments visitors or readers may have, particularly in the light of the fact that the political situation in Albania has changed so rapidly in the last three or four years, and this has affected everybody's situation in quite fundamental ways. Property restitution disputes affect access to some museums.

I would like to thank most sincerely the many correspondents who have written to me with information, advice and records of personal travel experiences. I have tried to incorporate their observations wherever possible.

I regret that a few readers, especially in Albania, have felt that there were historical mistakes in the first edition. I should point out, though, that often what was regarded as error of fact actually turned out to be difference of ideology or historical interpretation.

Acknowledgements

I would like to thank the following for their help with the preparation of the second edition, viz. the late and much missed Harry Hodgkinson for information on pre-war Albania, Major Bob Churcher FRGS for ever generous and invaluable help in the north east, Professor Sir Dimitri Obolensky and Mary Allen Johnson for drawing my attention to the monastery of St John Vladimir, Miranda Vickers for teaching me so much about Mirdita history, Professor Basil Kondis on the Greek minority, Paddy Leigh Fermor on the 1940 military struggle in Albania, and on the Korça *tekké*, Professor Nicholas Hammond for comments on the Via Egnetia archeology, Andrew David for his photographs, Professor Frank Walbank on the Roman fort at Grazidhni, Betullah Destani for documents, Stephen Nash for a wonderful journey to Voskopoja and Korca, His Holiness the Euchumical Patriarch Bartholemos and the Rev. Stephen Parsons for material on Orthodoxy, Sir Reginald Hibbert GCMG for further material about the Second World War period, Professor Karl M. Petruso of the University of Texas at Arlington for details about his excavations at Konispol, Nick Hunter on the mining industry, Peter Oosterhuizen of Eastern Books for the loan of engravings, Larry Luxner for information on Jewish matters, Gjergj Bakallbashi on the history of Polena, Marijana Dworski and Gabriel Beaumont for help with rare books, Menduh Thaci and Arben Xhaferi, on the Albanians in FYROM, Gent Kadare for help with linguistic matters.

I am also very grateful to the following friends and colleagues for other various local information, hospitality, informal discussions, letters and documents viz Charles Meynell, His Excellency Joseph Lake, Alex Standish, Antonia Young, Dennis McConnell, Joanna Hanson, Professor Richard Crampton, Nigel Clive, Janet Gunn, Dr Karim Arafat, Dr Catherine Morgan, Guy Roberts, Michael Kaser, Richard Owen of *The Times*, Bektash Kollasi, Guy Dunn, Primrose Peacock, Robert Mickey, Dr Grammoz Pashko, Jenny Little, His Excellency Pavli Qesku, Gareth Crooker, Noel Malcolm, Neil Taylor, Frank Dalton, Dr Shahin Kadare, Kyril Drezov, Sir John Thompson GCMG, Xhervat Lloshi, Bill McAllister of the *Soros Foundation*, Lida Kita, Veton Surroi, Dr Neritan Ceka, Tanya Barron, David Alford, Paul Calverly, Alan Charlton, Dr Pascal Milo, Professor Arben Puto, Christopher Cviic, Andrew Lance, Anri Moçi, Dr John Moreland Dr James Gow, Ilir Cagi, Astrit Mulita.

Professors Archie Brown and Alex Pravda of the Russian Centre seminar at St Antony's College, Oxford have kindly enabled me to explore ideas on Albania in their forum, as has Professor Averil Cameron of King's College, London. Judy Tither of A&C Black has been a patient and expert editor.

All errors are my own responsibility.

For permission to reproduce the photographs in this book the publishers would like to thank Philip Green (p. 121), James Pettifer (pp. 12, 40, 88, 220), Jani Restani (pp. 43, 91, 109), Miranda Vickers (p. 57).

CONTENTS

Routes

Maps and plans

EXPLANATIONS

The book is organised into seven chapters, each covering a geographical region of the country, and divided into a total of 18 routes. Excursions, diversions and background information are presented as indented text.

Asterisks indicate points of special interest or excellence.

Distances are given throughout the route or sub-route in kilometres. In some cases, particularly in mountainous regions, they should be taken as approximate estimates rather than exact figures. Heights of mountains are generally accurate, and are given in metres.

Main roads. There is no generally recognised road numbering system in Albania. It is proposed that the European numbers will be adopted for a few major routes but this has not yet taken place. The itineraries in the guide are mostly following the Class I routes as designated on Albanian Ministry of Transport maps.

    Minor roads. The use of minor roads is not recommended, unless unavoidable, and a four-wheel drive or tracked vehicle is essential, even in summer.

Population figures and other statistics have been given from the latest official figures available. They should not be regarded as more than approximate estimates, as census figures are out of date and there have been considerable changes in some areas due to emigration from, and within, the country since the end of communism in 1990–91. Some statistics, on the size of particular ethnic minorities, for instance, are politically controversial, and are difficult to establish objectively. Most data from the communist period was subject to political manipulation, particularly figures concerning the economy.

Place names spelling is in the standard Albanian form, i.e. Korça, rather than the Greek *Koritsa*, Gjirokastra not *Agyrocastro* or Gjirokaster, Voscopoi not *Voscopolis*, although visitors may find the alternative names used on occasion, particularly by Tosk Albanians or members of the Greek minority. Many Albanian place names have an i as a suffix which is not always used in conversation, i.e. Berati or Berat. Some major cities have long established older names, i.e. Shkodra used to be called *Scutari*, Vlora was *Valona*, Durres was *Durazzo*.

    The latter are widely used in historical works and pre-1944 travel books but have generally disappeared from everyday use. Some Albanian places in the south have retained their Greek forms, i.e. *Himara*, in written texts and everyday verbal usage. There are also place names of Slavonic origin, particularly in the south and southeast of the country, i.e. *Boboshtica, Kapshtica*. Some regions, particularly in the northern highlands, are generally known by the name of the dominant tribe or clan originally living there, i.e. *Mirdita, Dukagjin, Hoti*. Some of the names of the administrative regions under communism are falling into disuse, and some places named after communist heroes have reverted to older forms, i.e. *Qyteti Stalin* (Stalin City) is now called Kucova.

    When referring to places in former Yugoslavia, I have used the traditional Albanian forms e.g. Kosova, not *Kosovo-Metohije*, as in Serbian usage.

Urban street names are in a state of flux, with many names being changed, but some from the communist period are still in use. Street maps have been updated as far as it has been possible to do so. Up to date information from official sources in Albania has often been difficult to obtain, particularly for provincial towns.

Abbreviations. In addition to generally accepted and self-explanatory abbreviations, the following occur in the guide:

Hx. = Hoxha (Muslim priest)
liq. = lake or river
m. = nautical miles
mal. = mountain
PLA = Albanian Party of Labour
Pr. = Prifti (Christian priest)
qu. = city
SOE = Special Operations Executive

Foreign words which appear in the text
Besa = Oath of Trust, given on cessation of a Blood Feud
Bey = Ottoman feudal lord
Çeta = originally, a bandit gang, later, a guerilla group
Gheg = Albanian who lives north of the Shkumbini river or in Kosova or FYROM
Hakmarrje = Blood feud
Han = Inn
Fis = Clan, or extended family grouping
Kanun = Traditional Clan practice used to regulate the blood feud in northern Albania and Kosova
Kaçak = Guerilla movement
Komitadjis = Guerilla fighters
Millet = Grouping of Ottoman subjects organised on a religous basis
Pashalik = Ottoman administrative area
Porte = the Constantinople central government, the Ottoman sultan
Sandjak = Ottoman administrative division, part of a Vilayet
Tosk = Albanian who lives south of the Shkumbini river
Vilayet = Ottoman province

Macedonia: nomenclature

With the end of the existing state of Yugoslavia in 1990 and 1991, the territory that was occupied by the Socialist Republic of Macedonia has attempted to gain international recognition as an independent state. Much controversy has been generated about the name of this territory, with Greece strongly resisting the attempts of the government in Skopje to obtain international recognition for their country under the name of 'Republic of Macedonia'.

In this Blue Guide I have from time to time used the name '**Macedonia**', and the abbreviation **FYROM** (Former Yugoslav Macedonia) to denote the territory that used to be occupied by the ex-Yugoslav republic, as it is frequently necessary to mention it, given the long land border with Albania, stretching from the Mal i Korabit mountains in the north to the Lake Prespa region in the south. The use of this, or any other name, for the territory concerned, does not imply any view on the vexed question of recognition, but only denotes a conventional verbal usage for the purposes of the Guide.

The question is complicated by the fact that most Albanians regard their neighbours as 'Macedonians', only if they are ethnic Slavs, and that the twenty per cent or so of the population of the ex-Yugoslav republic of 'Macedonia' who are ethnically Albanian are known as 'Macedonian Albanians'. They generally live in territories of FYROM adjoining Albania, in the western mountains. Slav-speakers in Albania, who amount to about 15,000 people, are generally known as 'Bulgarians' by Albanians, which is a linguistic rather than ethnic definition, based on a perception of the language the Slavophones use which is seen as a dialect of Bulgarian, although, historically, some of the Slavophones originally came from Serbia. Albanians call the capital of FYROM, **Skup**, rather than **Skopje**. Both forms are used in the text.

Statue of Bajram Curri (1862–1925) in the town named after him in north east Albania, see p. 272

ALBANIA IN ANTIQUITY

Professor Frank W. Walbank, CBE FBA

Prehistoric Albania

From palaeolithic times onward there was human habitation in the lands comprising modern Albania; and since 1945 Albanian archaeologists have been actively investigating settlements of neolithic (c 6000–c 2600 BC), Bronze Age (c 2600–c 1000 BC) and, from c 1000 BC, early Iron Age peoples living there. Among the most important Bronze Age sites are those at **Maliqi**, **Treni** and **Podgori** (near Korça), and **Gajtan** south-east of modern Shkodra. Mound-burials (*tumuli*) in many parts of the country belong to these Bronze Age cultures or to the Iron Age, when a growth in the number of fortified sites indicates an increasingly warlike society. Problems have arisen, however, in the interpretation of all this material. The point at issue is to decide which of the cultures revealed at the various sites are to be associated with the appearance of the Illyrians. Albanian archaeologists, for whom the Illyrians are their own ancestors, are of the opinion that the Illyrians were an autochthonous people who developed, within Albania, a common Illyrian language and culture during the Bronze Age. Other scholars consider that the Illyrians were among the invaders of Albania from 1250 BC onwards and that they played a part in the break-up of Mycenaean civilisation in Greece. Yet others put the arrival of Illyrians in Albania, in substantial numbers, as late as the 10C BC. In any case, it is certain that some Illyrian tribes were in place in the 11C and 10C BC and that by the 7C all the leading tribes were occupying the districts where they are later to be found (and, of course, on the Albanian hypothesis, much earlier).

The term 'Illyrian' was taken and extended by the Greeks from one particular tribe, the 'Illyrians properly so called' (Pliny, *Natural History* 3.144), who inhabited the area between Scodra (modern Shkodra) and Dyrrachium (modern Durres); and it is used as the linguistic and ethnic description of the numerous peoples who at one time occupied much of the Balkan peninsula as far north as the Danube. Their common language was Illyrian. Unfortunately knowledge of it is scanty, since it has left no inscriptions or written remains. Scholars therefore have only place-names and names of Illyrian men and women to work on and, in consequence, they are mostly hesitant in pronouncing on the characteristics of the language. It seems likely, however, that it was an Indo-European tongue and the ancestor of modern Albanian.

Illyrians and Greeks

How to characterise the tribes inhabiting the ancient Albanian lands ethnically and linguistically has also been a highly controversial issue. Albanian scholars argue vehemently and passionately for the view that all the tribes within Albania and even beyond its present southern frontier were Illyrian in origin. The 1C Greek geographer Strabo, however, reckons all the peoples lying south of the Acroceraunian Mountains as Epirote, that is to say Greek (7.7.5). As Illyrian (7.7.8) he lists the *Taulantii* (in the coastal plain around Tirana), the *Bylliones* (on the right bank of the Aous, modern Vjosa), the *Parthini* (in the Shkumbini valley) and the *Brygi* (north of the Taulantii). Some tribes, he reports (7.7.8), were said to be bilingual; and indeed the Bylliones, and perhaps others, were later strongly Hellenised. Strabo's view receives some support from the fact that in 200 BC the chief city of the Bylliones, Byllis, lay on the circuit of the sacred envoys sent out from the panhellenic shrine of Delphi in connection with the Pythian festival. This shows that Byllis was then regarded as Greek, since envoys only visited Greek cities. Strabo's division is also confirmed by the 2C AD Alexandrian historian, Appian (*Illyrica* 1), who, while assigning vast areas throughout the Balkan peninsula to the Illyrian peoples, defines the southern Illyrian frontier as the boundary with the Chaones, who inhabited the area from the Shushica to the middle Vjosa. In fact, as we shall see shortly, when cities sprang up south of this boundary in the 4C BC and after, they were in all essential respects Greek—in language, cults, administration, architectural style and city lay-out—though they clearly contained an Illyrian element in their populations. Probably Greeks and Illyrians were originally inter-spersed in this area rather as Greek and Albanian villages lie side by side in the valley of the southern Drinos today.

The rugged and mountainous districts of northern Albania, in contrast, were wholly Illyrian. It was from one Illyrian tribe, the *Albani*, who according to the geographer Claudius Ptolemaeus (2C AD) inhabited the hinterland of Durres, that the Albanians of today derive their name, which is first recorded in Norman-French as *Albanie* in the epic *Chanson de Roland* (composed around AD 1082–84). Their chief town, Albanopolis, was probably Zgërdheshi (see below).

Life among the tribes

Life in ancient Albania followed a similar pattern for both Illyrian-speaking and Greek-speaking tribes, since it was shaped overwhelmingly by the geographical features of the land. Albania has always been a harsh country with over two thirds of its area dominated by mountains. Especially in the far north, bordering on Montenegro and Kosovo, lofty and precipitous mountains enclose narrow valleys at a high altitude and communication between these is possible only by way of a few difficult passes. This is in fact one of the wildest areas in Europe. Further south the same pattern persists, though less harshly. There a series of large rivers—the Black and the White Drin, uniting at Kukesi to reach the sea near Shkodra, the Mati, the Shkumbini (ancient *Genusus*), the Seman (ancient *Apsus*) with its tributary the Osumi, and the Vjosa (ancient *Aous*)—thread their way through the mountains and, with their waters swollen by the winter rains, debouch onto the coastal plain where, prior to modern drainage schemes, they produced marshy flood areas in the autumn and in the spring. Such floods limited cultivation and offered serious obstacles to the traveller, who was in consequence obliged to follow a devious route skirting the hills. This is a land which has always split the popula-tion into small isolated communities and where isolation breeds suspicion and conflict.

Throughout most of antiquity down to the time of the Roman conquest the story is one of small kingdoms and constant warfare between hostile tribes. Largely because of the dominating physical features of the land, the pattern of life there has tended not to change greatly from one age to another, right down to compara-tively recent times. We can trace this pattern in the early centuries of the first millennium BC, when a semi-nomadic pastoralism was widely practised. Small groups of families led their flocks of sheep and goats up to the high pastures in spring and brought them down to the lower pastures in autumn, in a seasonal rhythm followed by Vlachs and other Balkan nomads down to the present day. These early pastoral groups produced a variety of goods, sometimes in excess of their needs—cheese, wool, hides, rugs, clothing and leather-goods. The size of such groups will have fluctuated to match the availability and quality of pasture. From time to time small groups will have coalesced for protection and the larger group-ings so formed would provide the basis for the major tribes, the names of about seventy of which are known. In due course the headman of a tribal confederacy would achieve the status of a king. Some Bronze Age and Iron Age *tumuli* may belong to villages not yet located, but many must represent the burial grounds of such transhumant, nomadic groups. If one may draw conclusions from the evidence of communal ownership which is provided by later records of slave-manumissions at Buthrotum (modern Butrint) and elsewhere, these early commu-nities probably treated their flocks and other possessions as the property of the whole group. It also appears that women here enjoyed a higher status than they did later in Greece.

Pastoralism was not the sole means of livelihood among the early tribes. On the rich and fertile plains around Lake Ochrid in the Korça basin and, to some extent, in the coastal area (though, as we have seen, cultivation was hampered here by spring flooding) farmers living in villages grew cereals (wheat, barley), fruit (apples, pears, cherries), vegetables (beans, peas) and vines; and the name of one tribe living near Lake Ochrid, the *Enchelei* ('Eel-people'), may suggest a concern with fishing. Pigs were also kept, timber was hewn and copper mined and worked. There were important deposits of copper and iron in the districts of Mati and Mirdita in the north. The many fortified hill-settlements with substantial walls, which date from this period, indicate, however, that for the farmers, craftsmen and herdsmen living within them life was dangerous and violent. There was a constant threat from less settled marauders coming from the north. But in addition there was probably a good deal of small-scale fighting between the various settlements, reminiscent of the feuding prevalent among the Albanian mountain communities in modern times.

Greek colonies: 7C–6C BC

From the mid-7C onwards the social and economic development of both shepherds and farmers, Greek-speakers and Illyrian-speakers alike, was strongly influenced by the founding of Greek colonies on the coast. This colonisation came after a period of social and commercial intercourse between the native peoples, here mainly Illyrian, and Greek traders who had become regular visitors to these shores. An important role was played by Corcyra (modern Corfu), a Greek colony founded c 703 BC from Corinth as a station on the route to southern Italy and Sicily. It was probably in 627 BC that the Illyrian Taulantii, harassed by Liburnian pirates from the northern Adriatic, invited the Corcyreans to found a colony at **Epidamnus**. The isthmus on which the colony stood was probably called **Dyrrachium** (an Illyrian name) and this became an alternative name for the colony; it survives today as Durres. From the outset both names were used, but Dyrrachium eventu-ally became the preferred form, partly perhaps under Illyrian influence but also because later, as Latin became familiar following the arrival of the Romans, Epidamnus was associated with the Latin word *damnum*, meaning 'loss', and was felt to be ill-omened. Epidamnus occupied an excellent site, its citadel standing on an extended hill above its two harbours. It gained its later strength from commerce and agriculture and probably also drew on the silver mines of Damastium in the interior.

No less important was a second colony, **Apollonia**, founded in 588 BC by a joint company of Corinthians and Corcyreans on a site already frequented by Corinthian traders and controlling the lower reaches of the Vjoses (which had its mouth further north than today). The Taulantii were also involved in this foundation and a strong Illyrian presence, revealed by a cemetery with mound-burials as well as by the names on some tombstones, persisted throughout Apollonia's long history. An inscription found at Olympia, and already seen there by the Greek travel-writer Pausanias in the 2C AD, celebrates the defeat and destruction by Apollonia of another nearby Greek city, **Thronium**, and the annexation of territory from the native **Abantes** (or Amantes), who lived between the rivers Vjosa and Shushica. Apollonia possessed a famous bitumen mine situated at the Nymphaeum (probably near Selenica, where bitumen is still extracted); the high-quality pitch which it provided was used especially for caulking ships. With its large and fertile hinterland, Apollonia rapidly developed into a strong trading city. In the 6C a Greek city was founded (perhaps by colonists from Corinth and Corcyra) at Buthrotum (modern Butrint), on an Illyrian site in the territory of the Chaones. Along with its high citadel it occupied a peninsula well placed between the sea and a freshwater lake useful for fishing. The foundation flourished and Buthrotum remained a prosperous city down to Roman times.

Urbanisation of the interior: 4C BC

The importance of these developments on life in the lands of what is today Albania should not be underestimated. The establishment of regular Greek cities, linked by trade, social intercourse and religious cult with the cities of Greece proper broke down the isolation of native communities and introduced the peoples of these coastal areas to the products and way of life of a more advanced culture. Moreover, besides their maritime trade the Greek colonies developed links with the interior, introducing foreign commodities and modifying traditional tribal ways there as well. As a result of these contacts, but also in response to the social evolution and increasing wealth of the inland communities, cities now began to develop where previously there had been only armed refuges.

This growth of urbanisation, more marked in the south, is a feature of the 4C and 3C BC. From around 330 BC the Molossians, who lived in the highlands of Epirus, built up a strong confederacy, which in due course came to control large parts of southern Albania. Several cities now appeared in this area. The administrative centre of the Chaones was at **Phoinike**, which occupies a fortified hill about 8km inland from Saranda. Subsequently **Onchesmus** was founded as its port on the site of Saranda. Further north lay **Amantia**, the chief city of the Amantes (see above), which Albanian archaeologists have located on the hill of Ploça, 35km from Vlora, between the Shushica and the Vjosa. Another settlement, slightly north-west of Ploça, at Mavrova, can be identified as ancient **Olympe**; it was probably subject to Amantia. Across the Vjosa at Gradishta, near Ballshi, lies **Byllis** (see above) and, south of it, at Klosi, yet another town, probably ancient **Nikaia**. In recent years inscribed material has enabled Albanian archaeologists to identify two cities, hitherto familiar only by name. Thanks to the discovery of voting-tablets bearing its name, **Antigonea** is now known to be the impressive settlement at Jerma, near Saraganishta, on the hills opposite Gjirokastra; and inscribed Hellenistic tile-stamps have shown **Dimale**, known from Polybius and Livy, to have been at Krotina near Berati. At **Selca**, high up among the hills west of Pogradeci, recently excavated shaft-tombs and rock-tombs, similar to some found in Macedonia, evidently belong to a city yet to be discovered. There are also unidentified urban sites at **Margellic** near Fier, at **Irmaj** opposite Gramshi and at **Garzeza**, north-west of Byllis. Berati was probably **Antipatrea**, founded in 314 BC by Cassander, later king of Macedonia, who named it after his father Antipater; and Antigonea was evidently a foundation of Pyrrhus of Epirus, named after his first wife Antigone.

The appearance of these cities brought a change in the pattern of life. Many turned from agriculture and (often transhumant) stock-rearing to a settled urban existence, which brought with it a diversification into skilled occupations—the making of superior local pottery, metal-working and other crafts, each requiring the use of specialised tools. Such cities were usually protected by defensive walls and stood on prominent heights, often controlling important routes. That they were already economically quite advanced is shown by the fact that they all used coinage in their everyday life, most of it minted in the Greek coastal cities; but Amantia, Byllis, Olympe and **Oricus** (which lay on the coast south of Vlora) coined their own bronze for local use. Inscriptions recording slave manumissions (see above) testify to the existence of slave-owning in Byllis, Nikaia and Buthrotum and presumably this was true elsewhere. These cities were modest in size, but they offered many amenities to their inhabitants. Theatres have been excavated at Byllis, Oricus, Buthrotum and Phoinike; and there were stadia for racing at Amantia and Byllis. Everywhere there were temples, dedicated to the Greek deities—Zeus, Heracles, Artemis, Aphrodite—whose names figure on inscriptions. Inscriptions also tell us something of local administration. Generals (*strategoi*) and magistrates called *prytaneis* are recorded from Nikaia and Byllis; and Nikaia possessed a *gymnasiarch*, responsible for the gymnasium, the athletic and cultural institution which formed a focal point in the life of a Hellenistic Greek city. Elsewhere we hear of organised military patrols (*periploi* and *symperipoloi*) and magistrates called *damiourgoi*. The graves at Selca contained delicate jewellery, some of it imported from as far away as Egypt. Such glimpses of civic life show that these cities were organised on similar lines to Greek cities elsewhere. The whole area was well-populated and prosperous.

In both the higher lands and the coastal plain north of the Shkumbini urbanisation came a little slower. Already in the 4C, however, Lissus (modern Lezha), with its imposing acropolis of Acrolissus (410m), acquired a ring of walls 2200m long. Its coinage and the presence of Rhodian and Apulian vases show it to have been no mere fortress, but a city with a flourishing commerce. Scodra, originally a fortress of the Labeatae, later achieved importance as the capital of Genthius, king of the Ardiaei (see below). Coins of Scodra depict a *lembus*, a small galley with a single bank of oars. This craft, which probably carried a fighting crew of 50, was much employed by pirates. As a symbol on Scodran coins it perhaps indicates one activity of the Ardiaeans who now occupied the city. Half an hour south-east of modern Kruja lie the impressive ruins of Zgerdeshi, a 4C city of about 10 hectares, which may be the **Albanopolis** mentioned by Claudius Ptolemaeus (see above).

The Ardiaean kingdom: 4C–2C BC

Already in the 7C BC the Illyrians figure as enemies of the kingdom of Macedonia, which lay to the east in what is now northern Greece. The Taulantii, for example, raided that kingdom under their leader Galaurus. But it is only from the 4C onward that the Illyrians begin to appear regularly in Greek sources. One Illyrian leader, Bardylis, built up a rich kingdom and twice killed or expelled the king of Macedonia, but in 358 Philip II, the father of Alexander the Great, inflicted a serious defeat upon him and forced him back to the north and west of Lake Ochrid. In 335 BC, before crossing into Asia at the outset of his remarkable career of conquest, Alexander himself defeated the Taulantii under their king Glaucias not far east of Korça; and after Alexander's death (323 BC) the same Glaucias appears as an ally of Apollonia and Epidamnus fighting against Cassander, the regent of Macedonia, and in 313 as master of Epidamnus. The early 3C saw the Taulantii controlled by Pyrrhus, the king of the Molossi and commander (*hegemon*) of the Epirote Alliance. But Apollonia and Epidamnus successfully resisted Pyrrhus' domination under an Illyrian ruler, Monunius. After the collapse of the Epirote monarchy in the late 230s BC the southern tribes joined a new federal body, the Epirote League, and there followed a period of prosperity for the whole area, including the coastal cities. The seals on *amphorai* (wine jars) from Rhodes, Corinth, Cnidos and Cos are evidence for their wide trading connections.

The disappearance of the Epirote monarchy coincided with the growth in power of an Illyrian confederacy centred on the Naretva valley in Dalmatia, the *Ardiaei*. This tribal grouping had already existed in the 4C BC, when it is said to have owned large numbers of slaves—perhaps acquired in piratical raids. In the mid 3C the Ardiaei took to raiding western Greece in their swift *lembi* (see above). These raids included the west coast of the Peloponnese—Elis and Messenia—and even reached Laconia. The Ardiaeans' capital was now at Scodra and in 233 BC the Macedonian king, Demetrius II, unwisely hired them to help his allies, the Acarnanians, who were being attacked by the Aetolians. The Illyrians used the opportunity to seize the Chaonian town of Phoinike by treachery and eventually retired north after securing both the Epirotes and the Acarnanians as allies.

About this time Agron, their king, died, leaving his widow Teuta guardian to his heir Pinnes. Complaints that Ardiaean freebooters were attacking Italian shipping in the Adriatic now led the powerful state of Rome (which by this time had come to control most of Italy) to send a naval force against Teuta (229 BC). Helped by an Illyrian renegade, Demetrius, ruler of the island of Pharos, the Romans were soon victorious and established a protectorate comprising Corcyra, Apollonia and Epidamnus, the Illyrian Atintani, who inhabited the highlands towards the Black Drin (Drini i Zi) the Parthini in the Shkumbini valley and the city of Dimale. Under the peace terms Teuta agreed not to sail south of Lissus (modern Lezha) with more than two *lembi* (and those unarmed). Shortly afterwards Demetrius, together with Scerdilaidas, the new ruler of the Ardiaei, broke the treaty by sailing south of Lissus, and in 219 BC the Romans again crossed the Adriatic and expelled Demetrius, who promptly attached himself to Philip V, the young king of Macedonia. Shortly afterwards Philip allied himself with the Carthaginian commander, Hannibal, who had invaded Italy over the Alps from Spain and southern France in order to attack the Romans on their home ground. Philip made repeated attempts to secure access to the Adriatic through central Albania and in 212 BC he seized Lissus. But the end of the war with Rome in 205 BC saw him expelled from all areas west of Pindus.

During the next two decades the coast of Albania was an important bridgehead for Roman armies operating in the Balkan peninsula, first against Philip V (200–197 BC) and then against Antiochus III of Syria (192–189 BC), who had invaded Greece, invited in by the Aetolians. Around 170 BC the Ardiaean king, Genthius, made an ill-judged alliance with Perseus, the king of Macedonia, against Rome, with whom Perseus was at war. In support of his ally, Genthius attacked a Roman army in the Pindus region, was defeated, trapped in Scodra and obliged to surrender. His defeat signalled the end of the independent Illyrian kingdom. Further south the war had split the Epirote tribes and many had backed Perseus. The result was devastating. In 167 BC the Roman commander, L. Aemilius Paullus, carried out a punitive strike throughout Epirus; seventy cities were simultaneously wiped out (after first handing over their portable valuables), and 150,000 people enslaved. It was a blow from which the whole area was slow to recover (Strabo, 7.7.9). Henceforth all present-day Albania was under Roman control.

Albania under the Romans

The arrival of Rome put an end to the independence of all the tribes within the area, Epirote and Illyrian alike, and from 146 BC onwards central Albania constituted part of the Roman province of Macedonia. Roman domination brought the *pax Romana*, the Roman peace, and this produced some prosperity. To take two examples: the Roman agricultural writer Varro informs us that the herds of cattle in Epirus were outstanding for both the size and milk output of the animals, and Strabo (7.7.8) comments on the prosperous fish-curing industry on Lake Lychnidus (Ochrid). The Roman protectorate remained nominally free, but the mainland peoples not included in it had to pay tax to Rome—except for those tribes that had taken the Roman side in the war, the Taulantii, the Pirustae (who formed part of Dassaretia between Lake Ochrid and the Osumit) and some tribes in Dalmatia. The Ardiaean kingdom was divided into three parts, one of which coincided roughly with Albania north of the river Matit, including Lissus and Scodra. Though technically free, the inhabitants of all three areas were debarred from intermarriage and the ownership of property beyond their frontiers. Soon after 146 BC the Romans built, on the line of an older way, what was to become one of their most famous roads, the **Via Egnatia**. Its two branches started from Apollonia and Dyrrachium (Epidamnus) and joined up a little west of Elbasan. The road then went on up the Shkumbini, rounded Lake Ochrid to the north and thence continued to Thessalonica and eventually Byzantium. The Via Egnatia developed into a vital link between east and west. Movement along it was accompanied by the growth of settlements along its route, thus bringing the fruits of trade to the interior of the Balkan peninsula and furthering Romanisation within Albanian lands.

From now on the whole area was relatively peaceful and prosperous—though in 48 BC it was drawn briefly into the Roman civil war, which was at that time being fought between Caesar and Pompey. In that year the coastal area and range of low hills south of Durres were the scene of a protracted military duel, in which Caesar tried, ultimately without success, to enclose Pompey's defences with an even longer line of circumvallation.

During the late republic and under the empire established by Augustus in 31 BC the coastal cities were increasingly exposed to Roman influence. In 65 BC Cicero's close friend, T. Pomponius Atticus, bought rich estates astride the river Thyamis, south of Buthrotum. He was only one of the many absentee landlords in Epirus referred to by Varro. Others emigrated to settle in the area. **Lissus**, for example, received a *conventus civium Romanorum* (lit. 'corporation of Roman citizens'), and already in the time of Julius Caesar (d. 44 BC.) was granted the status of a 'municipal town' (*municipium*).

Its walls were now rebuilt under the authority of the chief magistrates, the *duoviri quinquennales* (a Board of Two, with special duties and elected every fifth year). Little is known of Scodra. But in the cities further south a considerable Italian immigration is reflected in the names on inscriptions now preserved in various Albanian museums. Apollonia, which Cicero described as a 'famous and important city', possessed many Italian families, like the Villii, who were to play an important part in municipal life. It housed a rhetorical school comparable with those at Rhodes and Athens. The young Octavian—the future emperor Augustus—was studying there in 44 BC when he learnt of Julius Caesar's murder and, as his heir, hastened back to Italy to claim his inheritance. The 3C BC theatre was restored in the 2C AD and excavation has revealed other impressive public and private buildings. As time went on, the population contained an increasingly important Illyrian element. Dyrrachium also prospered. In the days of Caesar it enjoyed the status of a free city; and in 30 BC it received an influx of Italians, whom Octavian had expelled from their lands to make room for his veteran soldiers. From Augustus' time onward it enjoyed the formal status of a Roman colony—*colonia Iulia Augusta Dyrrhachinorum*—and inscriptions mention its chief magistracy, the *duoviri*. The huge 3C (AD) amphitheatre was used for gladiatorial games. Its 20,000 seats imply a total population from the immediate area of c 80,000 persons. There was also a Roman colony at Byllis, and a colony of veteran soldiers planned for Buthrotum by Caesar in 50 BC was eventually set up there by Augustus. The title *colonia Augusta Buthrotum* figures on the city's coinage. The Roman consul of 16 BC, L. Domitius Ahenobarbus, is celebrated on one inscription as the patron of the colony. Throughout the first three centuries of our era the whole coastal area and lower river valleys of what is today Albania enjoyed the fruits of the Roman peace and a flourishing urban life, though in the hills away from the coast and the Via Egnatia villages remained primitive and isolated, as they have always been.

Towards the close of the 3C AD the emperor Diocletian (AD 284–305) reorganised the Roman provincial system. Under this new scheme the part of Albania east of Korça came under **Macedonia Secunda**, the part north of the river Matit was assigned to **Praevalitana**, and the rest was divided between **Epirus Nova** and **Epirus Vetus**, with Oricus, the Acroceraunian range and everything south of the Vjoses included in the latter province. With the division of the Roman Empire under Arcadius and Honorius (AD 395) all the lands of modern Albania became part of the Byzantine Empire.

ALBANIA DURING THE OTTOMAN CONQUEST

HERZEGOVINA
Castelnuovo
SERBIA
Cattaro
Podgorica
CERNOJEVIC
Cettigne
Rijeka
Zabljak
Budua
Pulati
Gashi
Džakova
Krasnik
R. Drin
Prizren
(Vulpiani)
Drivasto
Antivari
Scutari
OJAN
Puka
ZACCARIA
Dagno
Sotti
Dulcigno
Zadrima
Alessio
R. Mati
Selishtë
Petrella
CASTRIOTA
Diba
Krvya
Petralha
Debar
Svetigrad
AKCAHISAR
V.
Durazzo
THOPIA
R. Arzen
Tirana
Ohri
Tumenisht
PAVLO KURTIK
V.
R. Shkumbi
Elbasan
CARTALOS V.
Mokrea
MUZAKIYE
N. MUZAKI
R. Semeni
Berat
R. Devoli
TOMORINCE V.
BELGRAD V.
ISKARAPAR V.
Korça
KANINA
Arta
R. Vijosë
R. Osum
Avlonya
Kanina
KLISURA
HIMARAN.
Argirokastron
LAHTOKASRI
N.
SOPOTO N.
VAIONTA
N.
Buthinto
Yanina
Saiada
Magaraki
Suboto
Parga
TOCCHI
Phanari
Paxos

0 — 50 kms	
. . . .	Ottoman Sancak of Arvanid in 1431
KLISURA V.	Sancak Divisions (V=Vilayet: N=Nahiye)
Venetian Lands in 1444	
League of Alessio in 1440	
MUZAKI	Principal Members of League

ASPECTS OF MEDIEVAL ALBANIA BEFORE THE TURKISH CONQUEST

Stephen Hill

Byzantium and Albania are concepts which change in a chameleon-like manner. The '*Byzantines*' for instance would have referred to themselves as Romans (Romaioi), and unless the '*Albanoi*' referred to the Ptolemy in the 2C AD as inhabiting the area which is now central Albania were the ancestors of the later Albanians, the term 'Albanian' itself would not necessarily have meant very much to anyone living in the area between the 4C and 11C. The Byzantines exercised considerable influence in the territory which we now call Albania, and for much of the time were in complete or partial control of it, although there was a long period from the 7C to the 9C when such control lapsed. The problem with the terms 'Albania' and 'Albanian', on the other hand, is more complex, since it was during the period of the Byzantine Empire that these terms appear to have come into being. To abuse the old cliché, however, Albania emerged 'not with a bang, but with a whimper'. Moreover, as we shall see, it is not possible to date precisely the first appearance of a concept of Albania which corresponds in any meaningful way to the manner in which the term is used today. The terms 'Albania' and 'Albanian' will therefore be used in their modern geographical sense, except in contexts where an alternative meaning is indicated.

The southern half of the Balkan region was effectively part of the eastern Roman Empire, and it appears that Illyria embraced Christianity relatively early, the first Illyrian bishoprics being founded in the 2C. By the 4C the Illyrian provinces contained around forty bishoprics, eleven of which were in the area of modern Albania. Yet Christianity was at first an urban phenomenon, associated particularly with the Greek-speaking cities of southern Illyria. For this reason the distribution of bishoprics by the 6C corresponded with those areas where the degree of Classical influence was highest; such bishoprics were either close to the Adriatic coast or sited along the Via Egnatia. On the other hand, many of the bishoprics in the northern and more mountainous parts of Albania were not founded until the restoration of Byzantine influence in the 9C.

It is clear, then, that the early Byzantine period saw the perpetuation of ethnological distinctions in Albania. These distinctions are manifest in the archaeological record, and emerge from a consideration of the early Christian buildings of Albania. The practice of laying mosaic floors, for instance, was very popular in the cities of southern Illyria in the Roman period, and this continued in the early Christian basilicas of Albania, some of which have been exposed to view. As in most areas of the Byzantine world, three-aisled basilicas, such as were built at Byllis and Buthrotum, dominated architectural thinking in early Byzantine Albania. There is, however, a range of early Byzantine churches in Albania which exhibit more unusual features. Particularly remarkable is the presence in the region of a series of churches with triconches incorporated in their plans. For instance, the basilica at Arapaj, near Durres, terminated at its east end with just such a triconch, a clover-leaf shaped triple apse rather than the usual single semicircular apse. The single-aisled chapel at Antigonea, which was perhaps designed for a funerary purpose, also terminated in a triconch. In its turn, the basilica at Lin exhibits a variation on the theme since it had a single apse at the east end, but conches were added to the outer walls of the north and south aisles of the basilica.

As well as the basilicas, there were some early churches in Albania, especially baptisteries, which were centralised in form, being based especially on square and circular plans. There is a large centralised church with three conches at Butrint, and another such church at Lin. Perhaps the most remarkable of the centralised buildings, which is as notable for its mosaics as for its architecture, is the baptistery at Butrint. This building contains two concentric rings of columns inside a square plan: at the centre of the building was set a sunken quatrefoil font.

The well-preserved basilica at Butrint exhibits another remarkable feature, since it contains a tripartite transept. The overall plan of this basilica is in fact cruciform, since the transept arms extend northwards and southwards beyond the outer walls of the aisles. This church, which is usually attributed to the 6C, owes its good state of preservation to the fact that it was restored in the medieval period, when the east end was strengthened by the insertion of a secondary inner apse, and the columns of the nave were replaced with piers.

In these respects the early Byzantine churches of Albania exhibit a series of features which demonstrate that they belong with the important group of architecturally related churches constructed in the coastlands and islands of the Aegean and southern Asia Minor. In these regions basilical thinking dominated the planning of early Byzantine churches with congregational functions, but there too the basilicas regularly contained significant sophistications such as triconchal apses. Similarly, the tripartite transept in the basilica at Butrint has parallels in the churches of Salonica and, more commonly, southern Asia Minor.

The architectural sculpture of these Albanian churches supports this view of their coastal associations. Thus a particularly interesting marble capital from Dyrrachium, which is now in the Tirana museum, derives from the so-called 'Theodosian' capital with its lower register of upright acanthus leaves above which, at the corners of the capital, are set four animal protomes in the form of sheep. The Dyrrachium capital is attributed to the 5C, and parallels for it can be found in Salonica, and, above all, in Cilicia in southern Asia Minor, where the form was particularly popular in the late 5C.

The preceeding paragraphs have contained numerous references to parallels between the early Byzantine monuments of Albania and those of southern Asia Minor, more especially those of Cilicia and neighbouring Isauria. The association reflects cultural realities in the early Byzantine world, where the sea was often a more useful means of communication than overland routes, but there was a still more precise connection. Cilicia and Isauria were the homeland of the group of itinerant architects and builders known as the 'Isaurian Builders', and it is worth noting that not only the plans, but also the sculptural decoration and the mosaics in the Albanian churches are highly redolent of Isaurian associations. We know that there was a considerable diaspora of the Isaurian Builders after the death of Zeno (474–91), and it would be entirely appropriate that they should have been active in the area of Dyrrachium at the time of Anastasius, especially since it is likely that the Isaurian Builders were active in Salonica and Ravenna at about this time.

The distinction between the more classicised southern parts of what we call Albania, and the more Illyrian interior and northern regions can be seen from the distribution of the sites of significant early Christian monuments enumerated above. All the sites with important churches and mosaics are in fact in the southern half of Albania and on or near the Adriatic coastline or the Via Egnatia.

Nevertheless all areas of what is modern Albania remained populated, albeit with some at a less opulent level, throughout the early Byzantine period, as can be detected from the fortifications of this period and from finds of early Byzantine cemeteries.

Whilst they may not be as precisely datable as the churches, the castles of Albania are of vital importance for illustrating some degree of continuity in terms of settlement. This could not be discerned simply from a study of the churches, which evidently declined in terms of wealth and magnitude around the middle of the 6C.

It has been suggested that the fortress at Scampi on the Via Egnatia, which resembles those at Vig and Paleokastra, may first have been erected in the late 4C to early 5C, perhaps after the Gothic invasions of Illyria in 378. The original fortification, which is a fine example of late Roman military planning, is of a type which is entirely appropriate to Scampi's position on the Via Egnatia. It consisted of a rectangular enceinte (c 348 by 308 metres), with walls three metres thick constructed in *opus mixtum* with regular brick courses. U-shaped towers projected from all four sides, and there were deeply projecting fan-shaped corner towers, the angles of which were themselves strengthened with solid brick construction. At some point in the early Byzantine period the walls of Scampi were repaired, and it appears that by the 5C or 6C the site was in use as a civilian settlement. The castle was again restored by the Turks in the 15C.

External and internal pressures led to many changes in the Illyrian provinces. One of these, early in the 4C, was the division of the Prefecture of Illyricum into eleven provinces, the four southernmost of which were Praevalis, Dardania, New Epirus, and Old Epirus. Modern Albania consists of New Epirus, which had its metropolis at Dyrrachium, much of Praevalis, and parts of the other two provinces. When, in 395, the empire was split into eastern and western sectors, southern Illyria went to the eastern empire and the eastern church, whilst northern Illyria went to the western empire, under the ecclesiastical authority of the Pope. Already in the 5C Albania had seen invasions of Visigoths, Huns, and Ostrogoths. The situation became more complicated with the onset of Slav invasions in the 6C. The uncertainty arising from these external pressures doubtless led to the increasing fortification of the Illyrian regions during the period. The early 6C saw the first fortress constructed at Tirana. More strikingly, according to the Suidas this period saw Anastasius fortifying his home town of Dyrrachium, which was presumably a particularly important undertaking, one befitting the metropolis of New Epirus.

The walls of Dyrrachium, are best preserved on the south and east sides of the city. They were originally constructed from solid brick, and have Turkish repairs and restorations in stonework. Some impression of the magnitude of these walls can be gained from Anna Comnena's lively account of Bohemond's siege of Dyrrachium in 1107–08.

> I must explain briefly the plan of the city of Dyrrachium. Its wall is interrupted by towers which all round the city rise to a height of eleven feet above it (the wall). A spiral staircase leads to the top of the towers and they are strengthened by battlements. So much for the city's defensive plan. The walls are of considerable thickness, so wide indeed that more than four horsemen can ride abreast in safety.

Anna's description was in fact designed to lay stress on the remarkable size of

Bohemond's siege engines which were so high 'that the city towers were over-topped by as much as five or six cubits. ...Like some giant among the clouds...'. Since it was the height and width that Anna was anxious to emphasise, she neglected to record that Dyrrachium was equipped with a triple circuit of walls extending to seven kilometres in circumference. The massive scale of Dyrrachium's defences ensured the continuing importance of the city throughout the period of Byzantine influence in Albania.

A major refortification of the Balkans, including Albania, is predictably reported by Procopius as taking place during the reign of Justinian, whom he describes as constructing a vast number of *castella* in the Balkans, including 167 which were built in the southern provinces of Illyria. Procopius's account probably reflects conditions in the century and a half before Justinian, but even if Justinian was responsible for all that Procopius attributes to him, his efforts merely served to halt temporarily the process of decline in the Illyrian provinces. During the second half of the 6C, the region was subject to endless revolts and invasions. Thus Justinian's army had to put down a revolt in Illyria in 551, and tried to turn away a series of barbarian incursions, one of which moved almost up to Dyrrachium. Some sense of the scale of the problem can be gained from Procopius's description in the *Secret History*:

> Illyria and the whole of Thrace, the country from the Ionian Gulf to the outskirts of Byzantium, including Greece and the Chersonese, was overrun almost every year by Huns, Antae, and Slavs, from the time when Justinian took control of the Roman empire. The invaders inflicted incurable damage on the inhabitants of these areas, for I think that more than 200,000 Romans were killed or enslaved in each invasion, so that the whole region came to look like the wilderness of Scythia.

The desperate state of affairs in the Balkans in the later 6C is also brilliantly described by Gibbon:

> The fortifications of Europe and Asia were multiplied by Justinian; but the repetition of those timid and fruitless precautions exposes to a philosophic eye the debility of the empire. From Belgrade to the Euxine, from the conflux of the Sava to the mouth of the Danube, a chain of above fourscore fortified places was extended along the banks of the great river. Single watch-towers were changed into spacious citadels; vacant walls, which the engineers contracted or enlarged according to the nature of the ground, were filled with colonies or garrisons; a strong fortress defended the ruins of Trajan's bridge, and several military stations affected to spread beyond the Danube the pride of the Roman name. But that name was divested of its terrors; the Barbarians, in their annual inroads, passed, and contemptuously repassed, before these useless bulwarks; and the inhabitants of the frontier, instead of reposing under the shadow of the general defence, were compelled to guard, with incessant vigilance, their separate habitations.

After the death of Justinian in 565, the problem deepened, since the barbarians began to settle in Illyria rather than moving away. Avars crossed the Danube in 568 and defeated the Byzantine army. There followed a series of Byzantine campaigns against the Avars in the period from 579 to 582, which ended in what must have been a very unsatisfactory peace, since Menander refers to the presence of 100,000 Avars in the Balkans by 580, and John of Ephesus writes of Avars settling in Illyria by 584.

Slav migrations into Illyria in the late 6C, which can be detected from the archaeological record, served to emphasise the already clear distinction between the cities of the plain and the settlements of the interior. By the beginning of the 7C the Byzantine hold on Illyria was virtually lost. During the reign of Phokas (602–10), Slavs reached the Adriatic coast. Heraclius (610–40) was too troubled by problems with the Persians to take on an active role in the Balkans, and it is reported in the *Miracula Sancti Demetrii* that the whole of Illyria was terribly ravaged by the Slavs who 'brought with them their families and everything they possessed'. It was these waves of Slav invasions at the end of the 6C and in the early 7C which finally caused the abandonment of many early Byzantine sites in Albania, and the withdrawal of the Byzantine army to Thrace. The text of the *Miracula Sancti Demetrii*, which may be dated to the early 7C, contains in fact the last reference to Illyrians. One further indicator of the weakening and ultimate disintegration of the Byzantine hold on the region was the migration of refugees from southern Illyria to Macedonia, the Peloponnese and perhaps to Constantinople itself.

In the period from the early 7C to the first half of the 9C Albania was outside the Byzantine sphere of influence and under increasing Slavic domination. The Slavic presence in the Illyrian region from the 7C onwards is well attested by the distribution of Slavic place-name forms, although it seems likely that the density of Slavic settlement may have been less great in southern Illyria. Given the lack of historical evidence, this period is capable of description as a 'Dark Age'. The archaeological record is similarly obscure, but artefacts from early medieval cemeteries in northern Albania have been used to demonstrate the existence of the so-called 'Komani-Kruja culture'. The artefacts from these cemeteries, often situated at the base of contemporary castles, are apparently of local manufacture and relate closely to earlier Illyrian forms, whilst at the same time showing considerable signs of contemporary Byzantine influence. But as well as the locally produced artefacts, the grave-goods found in the Komani-Kruja cemeteries include imported Byzantine objects, which may well have come in via Dyrrachium, and brooches which appear to be of Slavic origin. The finds from Komani-Kruja sites demonstrate not only that early medieval Albania was not in complete decline, but also that there was a shift in settlement from the low-lying sites of the Roman period to more defensible positions in the uplands.

The phenomenon of the Komani-Kruja people is of considerable significance, since it has been suggested that this culture may represent continuity from the Illyrian cultures which are otherwise lost to the historical and archaeological record. Some indeed have wanted to make the modern Albanians the successors of the ancient Illyrians and have therefore tried to find in the Komani-Kruja people a proto-Albanian society.

The 9C saw renewed Byzantine interest in the Balkans, and signs of renewed prosperity in Albania itself. An early sign of Byzantine authority reasserting itself was the creation during the reign of Nicephorus I (803–11) of the maritime Theme (naval command) of Cephalonia, which was intended to control the Adriatic. By around 850 most of what is presently Albania was incorporated in the Byzantine province (Theme) of Dyrrachium, which included the whole of New Epirus, and part of Praevalis, whilst Old Epirus was included in the adjacent Theme of Nicopolis. Although Albanian territory was to change hands repeatedly in the following centuries, not least because of the arrival of Bulgars and Latins, it is interesting to note that by the 9C there was in existence a geographical entity which resembled what we now think of as Albania.

Early in the 9C new bishoprics were set up at Kruja, Stefaniaka, Lezha, and Kunavia. The creation of these new bishoprics indicates that the old ethnological and religious divisions within Albania, which were still strong in the 7C, had broken down during the intermission in Byzantine control. Further new bishops were created in northern Albania during the 10C.

Byzantine control of Albania in the 9C was still troubled by Serbian migrations, and from the middle of the century the Bulgarians started to infiltrate the region. By the end of the 9C they had penetrated almost as far as Dyrrachium, although the city had not fallen. The Bulgarians remained in Albania until the death of their Tsar Simeon in 927. At the end of the 10C the Bulgarian kingdom was re-established under Tsar Samuel, and this time the Bulgarians succeeded in taking Dyrrachium. Consequently Albania was the scene of Byzantine campaigns in the early part of the 11C, when the emperor Basil II the Bulgar-slayer restored Byzantine control of Albania with his victory in 1018 at the battle of Beligrad (Pulcheropolis/Berati). By this time the Classical name of Pulcheropolis seems to have been replaced by the Slav form Beligrad.

In the 11C the Theme of Dyracchium was under the authority of a Duke, and divided into various provinces. The Duke had command of the Theme's army, which consisted of a mixture of mercenaries and peasant soldiers who were obliged to present themselves armed when summoned by the general. Despite the success at Beligrad, Basil did not succeed in re-establishing Byzantine control very securely, and the 11C was marked by a series of insurrections involving both the peasantry of Albania in 1040 and 1080, and the dukes of Dyrrachium themselves in the 1070s. In 1043 we hear of Albanians apparently involved in the revolt of George Maniaces, the Duke of Sicily, against Constantine IX Monomachus.

These revolts are the historical context for what appear to be the first Byzantine references to Albanians. Michael Attaliates reports that George Maniaces sailed from Italy to Dyracchium, from where he marched on Constantinople. Attaliates describes Maniaces's troops as consisting of a mixture of *Romaion kai Albanon*. There has been considerable debate about whether Attaliates's Albanians came from the Balkans or from Italy, and it has even been suggested that they might have been mercenaries from Scotland. Ducellier in contrast argued that Attaliates's Albanians must have come from Albania, in view of Attaliates's statement that, after the failure of the revolt, the Albanians, who had been equals with the Byzantines in church and state, became enemies of the Byzantine empire. This seems to indicate that the Albanians supported Maniaces as allies rather than as mercenaries.

The issue is further confused since Attaliates reports the involvement of a tribe called the Arbanitai in the revolt in 1078 led by Nicephorus Basilaces, Duke of Dyrrachium. In this case, at least, there can be no doubt that the Arbanitai came from Albania, and, more precisely, from northern Albania. By the end of the 12C there was actually a principality of Arbanon, based on Kruja in northern Albania.

In May 1081, the Normans, led by Bohemond, son of Robert Guiscard, landed in Albania. For the next three years the Byzantines had to campaign against the Normans, and in October 1081 the Byzantine emperor Alexius Comnenus personally led an expedition to Albania, which is vividly described by his daughter Anna Comnena in her epic history, the *Alexiad*. Alexius was defeated outside Dyrrachium and was forced to withdraw, leaving the acropolis in the control of the Venetians, and the command of the rest of the city in the hands of Komiskortes, a native of Arbanon. At a subsequent point in her narrative, Anna refers to Guiscard being shot at from all directions by people she calls Arbanitai.

Whether Attaliates's Albanians and Anna Comnena's Arbanians are the same people, or whether the latter are a distinct group within the former may never be resolved, but it appears that by the 11C the Byzantines were aware of a distinct ethnic group in part, at least, of what is now called Albania. The subsequent history of Byzantium and Albania is troubled. The 11C and 12C saw the continuation of Norman campaigns in the country, and in 1096 the first Crusade devastated Albania en route to the east. Byzantine authority became increasingly weak, especially after the death of Manuel Comnenus in 1180. From about 1190 to 1216 there was a semi-autonomous principality of Arbanon, which initially included most of the mountainous zones of Albania. After 1216 Arbanon was controlled successively by the Despotate of Epirus, by the Bulgarians, and from 1235 by the Byzantines in Nicaea. In 1269 Charles I of Anjou landed in Albania, and on 21 February 1272 he founded the Latin kingdom of Albania, which covered most of Albania from the Drin to Vlora. By the 14C Byzantine writers such as Gregoras and Cantacuzenus were using the terms 'Arbanite' and 'Albanian' to apply to all Albanians.

Cantacuzenus records the last Byzantine efforts in Albania with his account of the efforts of Andronicus III Palaeologus to quell a rebellion in the area of Berat. Andronicus, who was obliged to take Turkish mercenaries with him, defeated the Albanians in 1341, but the description of his campaign sounds more like large-scale brigandage in that he is said to have captured 300,000 head of cattle, 5000 horses, and 300,000 sheep. This was clearly the last gasp of Byzantine activity in Albania. Andronicus died in 1341, precisely at the point when the Serbian empire was established by Stefan Dushan. The Serbs invaded Albania in the 1340s and by 1347 Latins and Byzantines alike had been driven out of the country.

The last Byzantine campaigns sound more like border raids on pastoral mountaineers than proper war. Modern Albanians would doubtless find in these observations more indicators of continuity from the ancient Illyrians, who were, after all, mountaineers, brigands, and shepherds.

THE END OF OTTOMAN RULE AND ALBANIAN INDEPENDENCE

Miranda Vickers

The very nature of Ottoman rule delayed the rise of Albanian national consciousness, as all the Empire's subjects were divided into groups or *millets*, not according to their ethnic origin or language but according to their religion. Thus, because of their Muslim faith, most Albanians were classified as 'Turks'. However, the Albanian's privileged position within the Empire far outweighed any liabilities of membership. Although Turkish occupation resulted in total stagnation as regards economic development, many Albanians viewed the Ottoman administration as giving them a sense of security from their Slav and Greek neighbours.

Of all the Balkan subject people, the Albanians were the most inclined to convert to Islam. Historically, Albanians have often found it advantageous to change their religion according to momentary interests. Their saying '*ku është shpata është feja*', 'where the sword is there lies religion', refers to their past political experiences. The beginning of the 18C saw a decline in the previous Ottoman policy of relative religious tolerence, as Islamic pressure on the Empire's Christian population intensified. The threat posed by the Russo-Turkish wars of the 18C encouraged the Turks to pursue a policy of Islamisation in sensitive regions. Therefore, a capital tax was levied on all non-Muslim subjects. Those who converted to Islam received grants of land and had their taxes lowered. Uncertain of the loyalty of their Christian subjects, the Ottomans wished to create a substantial and compact group of Muslims in the Albanian inhabited regions of Shkodra, Monastir, Kosovo and Janina. These, it was hoped, would be ideologically, politically and socially committed to the basic interests of the Empire, whilst providing recruitment to maintain peace on its vulnerable frontiers.

The continuous weakening of Ottoman authority allowed the Albanian feudal lords, or *Beys*, to rely more on their own personal power than on central Ottoman rule. These *Beys* extended the limits of their pashaliks, thus increasing their revenues and influence. This eventually led to wars and rivalries between the smaller and larger *Beys* and plunged Albania into feudal anarchy.

The situation remained as such throughout several decades. By the third quarter of the 18C the mass of small feudal estates was merged into two huge *pashaliks*. The first in northern Albania with Shkodra as its capital, and ruled by the Bushatis. The second in southern Albania with Janina the capital, and ruled by Ali Pasha of Tepelena. In 1757, the feudal lord Mehmet Bey Bushati appointed himself overlord of the region of Shkodra. But it was under his son, Kara Mahmoud, that the *pashalik* of Shkodra achieved its distinction. Behaving more like an independent prince, Kara Mahmoud extended his rule to Kosova in the north, and as far south as Berat. By the time of his death in 1796, he was known as the Prince of Albania, having turned Shkodra into an important commercial centre, and his *pashalik* into an autonomous Albanian state.

The second great *pashalik* was governed by Ali Pasha of Tepelena, who, in return for services rendered to the Ottomans, was appointed governor of Janina by the Porte in 1788. Assisted by his sons, Ali extended his authority over all of southern Albania, and a large part of northern Greece. For 18 years he fought the Souliot League, and in 1803, at the height of his power, he finally captured Suli, its mountain stronghold. Ali Pasha won a reputation for ruthless persecution of his subjects; maintaining his *pashalik* by regular tribute and bribes to Constantinpole. When Ali formed ties with *Philiki Etaria*, a Greek revolutionary organisation, the Ottoman authorities became concerned about the possibility of mass Christian support being given to Ali. By 1821, some 5000–7000 Greek fighters had joined Ali. Thus, the Sultan decided to crush Ali Pasha. Following a long siege at his citadel in Janina, Ottoman agents finally assassinated Ali, and sent his head to Constantinople.

During the domination of Albania by Ali Pasha and the Bushatis, the influence of the *Beys* had sunk to a low point. However, after the disappearance of the Great Pashaliks, the old once-powerful Muslim families tried to regain influence. When the Russo-Turkish war of 1829 came to an end, Sultan Mahmoud II resolved to break the disobedience and semi-independence of the Albanian Beys. On 26 August 1830, the Ottoman Commander-in-Chief, Mehmet Reshid Pasha, invited all the southern *Beys* to Monastir on the pretext that they would be rewarded for their loyalty to the Porte; 500 of them were treacherously murdered. Finally, in

1865, in order to render any alignment of the Albanians impossible for the future, the country was divided up into the four *vilayets* (administrative regions) of Shkodra, Monastir, Janina and Kosova (added in 1878), each with its own Ottoman governor and garrison.

Whilst many Albanians profited under Ottoman rule, their cultural advancement was severely restricted. Nowhere was the Albanian language taught, nor had a standard alphabet been devised. Books in Albanian were virtually non-existent, and what few schools there were, taught in either Turkish or Greek.

The Prizren League 1878–1881

The first signs of a threat to the privileged position of Muslim Albanians within the Ottoman Empire came with the crisis which erupted in Bosnia-Hercegovina in 1875. Here, rebels backed by Russia, Serbia and Montenegro demanded autonomy from the Porte. In the hope of saving the Ottomans from inevitable defeat, the Great Powers hastily signed a protocol obliging the Porte to form an autonomous province in Bosnia-Hercegovina. the Ottomans ignored the protocol, giving Russia the excuse to declare war in April 1877, joined by Serbia and Montenegro. In January 1878, Serbian troops invaded the region of Kosova, and the Montenegrins advanced towards Shkodra. In February the Greeks also took advantage of the situation by invading the *vilayet* of Janina. The Serbs expelled those Albanians living in the region between Leskovac and Nis, which they then annexed to Serbia. The Albanian population was driven into the Kosova region where relations between Serbs and Albanians were already strained.

Following the defeat of Turkey in March 1878, Russia imposed the Treaty of San Stefano. This was designed to curb Austro-Hungarian influence in the Balkans, and strengthen Russia's position in the area. Substantial territories inhabited by Albanians were ceded to Serbia, Montenegro and a greatly enlarged Bulgaria. Serbia was alloted a large part of the Sandjak of Pristina, Montenegro received the regions surrounding and including the towns of Pec (Peja) and Podgorica. Bulgaria received vast areas including Korça and Debar (Diber). The Powers were alarmed at the prospect of Russian domination of the Straits and the enlarged Bulgaria. They therefore compelled Russia to submit to a new peace settlement at the Congress of Berlin in June 1878, presided over by Bismarck. The Congress drastically reduced the frontiers of Bulgaria, and the Albanian areas were returned to Ottoman control. Serbia's claims were curtailed and she remained with the areas she had occupied before the war. Montenegro was granted the Albanian inhabited areas of Plava, Podgorica and Ulcinj.

It was this decision which served to escalate the Albanian's resolve to defy any ruling designed to dismember their lands. The *vilayet* of Kosova was compelled to put up the most opposition to territorial amputation and therefore grew into the centre of strongest resistance. A few days before the Congress of Berlin, on 20 June 1878, a meeting of Albanian nationalist leaders was held in the Kosovar town of Prizren. It was attended by over 300 delegates, mostly from Kosova and western Macedonia, and became known as the Albanian League. Its primary purpose was to organise political and military opposition to the dismemberment of Albanian territory and to petition the Sultan to unite the four *vilayets* of Kosova, Monastir, Shkodra and Janina into one political and administrative unit.

One of the first acts of the League was to address a memorandum to Lord Beaconsfield, Great Britain's delegate to the Berlin Congress. It read, 'Just as we are not and do not want to be Turks, so we shall oppose with all our might anyone who would like to turn us into Slavs or Austrians or Greeks, we want to be Albanians.' At first the Porte supported the League in the hope that it might exert some pressure on the Great Powers to reconsider the entire 'Eastern Question' and the dangers resulting from further extension of the independent Balkan states, so propping up weakened Ottoman rule in the Balkans. Before long, however, the Albanians began substituting political protest with armed force. The League reacted to the territorial concessions to Montenegro by amassing an army of thousands of volunteers on the Montenegrin frontier. The Montenegrins began a general offensive only to find themselves quickly defeated by the Albanians.

The Montenegrin failure forced the Powers to reconsider the decisions made at Berlin. In January 1880, the Porte suggested to the Congress Commissioners that, instead of awarding to Montenegro areas inhabited by Muslim Albanians, the Catholic areas of Hoti and Gruda could be surrendered while still allowing the persistent Montenegrin claim to Ulcinj. When rumours of this suggestion spread, many Muslim and Catholic Albanians declared that, if this be the case they no longer considered themselves Ottoman subjects. They would henceforth defend their land themselves. At the end of April 1880, when the Ottoman army withdrew from the Albanian inhabited regions of Montenegro, the forces of the League took possession of them. The Powers began to understand that the League was not just a puppet organisation created for manipulation by the Ottomans. After much discussion, the Powers informed the Porte that the conduct of the Albanians was such that the Porte appeared to be in no position to suggest territorial concessions opposed by the Albanian League. They informed the Porte that if it did not compel its subjects to yield, then the Powers would occupy the Ottoman port of *Smyrna* (modern Izmir). This finally prompted the Porte to act, and reinforcements were sent to oversee Ulcinj's surrender. The Albanians refused, fierce fighting followed between Albanians and Ottoman troops, and at the end of November 1880, Ulcinj was handed over to Montenegro. Thus ended any co-operation between the League and the Ottomans.

As the northern branch of the League was resisting Montenegrin encroachments, the southern branch was occupied with petitioning the Powers against the loss of Albanian inhabited territory to Greece. What the Albanians called Chameria (or southern Albania), the Greeks called Northern Epirus. The whole region had a very blurred ethnicity. Although the southern, Tosk dialect of Albanian was used in conversation, Greek was also universally understood. Traveller's accounts of the period noted that it was difficult to say whether Epirus was Greek or north-western Greece was Albanian. The Province of Epirus then comprised the four *sandjaks* of Berat, Gjirokastra, Janina and Prevesa. The Albanians desired the unification of the southern *vilayets* with those of Shkodra, Uskub (Skopje) and Kosova. The Congress of Berlin had invited the Greeks, the Ottomans, and the Albanians to come to some agreement over the disputed territory. The negotiations dragged on until an agreement was eventually reached in 1881, by which Greece was to receive Thessaly, and Arta in Epirus, but not the Janina *vilayet*.

During the last decades of the 19C, the northern Albanians were in a state of armed conflict along the border with Montenegro, and also beginning armed resistance to the Porte. On 18 January 1881 the forces of the League took hold of Pristina, a month later they took control of Uskub and Diber. Having expelled the Ottoman administrators from Kosova, they prepared to march south. The growing Albanian movement directly challenged Ottoman rule and created conditions which invited foreign intervention. Therefore, the Sultan was advised to crush the League. On 22 April, 1881, the Ottoman army marched into Kosova, occupying Prizren after stiff resistance. The League's leaders were exiled to remote parts of the Empire.

The Young Turk Revolution 1908

The programme of the Albanian League exercised a powerful influence on Albanian political thought for several decades. The League became the first barrier against the expansionist policies of the neighbouring Balkan states, turning the nationalist movement into a unified entity, which demanded administrative and cultural autonomy within the framework of the Empire. The motivating force behind this early expression of Albanian nationalism was self-preservation, not a desire to disturb the status quo. The Ottomans tried to destroy the League, but they could not destroy the spirit of national awareness it had created, nor hinder its growth. The Ottomans began to fear the ability of the League to speak for the first time, with a single voice, on behalf of the majority of Albanians.

Although, at the Berlin Congress, Bismarck had declared impatiently that there was no Albanian nationality, the Powers could no longer dismiss the 'Albanian question'. Following their stand against both Montenegro and the Porte, the Albanians had become an international problem. The period following the official dissolution of the League saw a series of local revolts sparked off by Ottoman administrator's attempts to collect old taxes and impose new ones. The years leading up to 1908 were filled with various Albanian revolts and uprisings, as the Porte underwent a deep economical, social and political crisis. The Empire was decaying and near to collapse. The League therefore took the initial step of effecting a common unity between northern and southern Albanians, enabling them to channel and focus their aims towards the eventual unification of all the Albanian inhabited *vilayets*. The spirit of the League lived on through various cultural activities. Some 30 Albanian language newspapers and journals were established throughout the Empire and abroad, also a number of Albanian language schools were opened.

Albanians, especially Kosovars, took a prominent role in the Young Turk Revolution of 1908, which overthrew Sultan Abdul Hamid. The Young Turks promised to relieve the Albanians of their heavy taxes, to award them full constitutional rights together with their traditional privileges, and allow Albanian language schools. In 1908 elections were held, followed by a constitution which ended the absolutist regime. Over 20 Albanians became deputies in the new Young Turk parliament, and for a brief time Albanians enjoyed Ottoman benevolence.

It was not long, however, before deep divisions appeared in relations between the Albanians and the Young Turks. Albanians were discontented with Ottoman centralisation. They advocated decentralisation of the Empire and autonomy for the various national regions. A clash was inevitable, as the Young Turks believed in the enforced Ottomanisation of all subjects to keep the Empire strong and intact. However, the Young Turks were unaware of the extent to which Albanian national sentiment had grown since the formation of the Prizren League. Many Albanians now saw themselves not just as Muslim members of the Empire, but also as members of the Albanian nation. The main cause of the deteriorating relationship was the conflict that arose over the Albanian alphabet. The Young Turks insisted on the use of traditional Arabic script, but there were huge popular gatherings in favour of the much simpler Latin alphabet. As demand for Albanian national development grew, the adoption of the Latin alphabet was seen as a way of uniting both Christian and Muslim Albanians, making them more conscious of their common heritage. In 1908 a Congress of Albanian nationalists formally adopted the Latin alphabet. The Young Turks responded by closing down all Albanian newspapers, national clubs and schools in a determined effort to suppress Albanian nationalism.

Albanian relations with the Young Turks continued to deteriorate. In March 1910, a revolt broke out in Pristina after people refused to pay new taxes levied from Istanbul on goods imported into Kosova. The revolt quickly spread to the whole *vilayet*. The Porte replied by sending 20,000 troops to Kosova. In June 1911, after their military operations had failed, and urged on by the Great Powers, Sultan Mehmet V paid a visit to Kosova in the hope of appeasing the Albanians. Austria-Hungary, in particular, feared the weakening of the Kosovars would strengthen Pan-Slavism. Kosova stood as a buffer to Serbian expansion. Therefore, Austria continued to argue for the maintenance of the status quo. The Sultan granted a general amnesty to the rebels, which few took heed of.

On 11 September Italy declared war on the Ottoman Empire, in the hope of capturing Tripoli; the Porte was easily defeated in North Africa. The other Balkan states saw in the Porte's weakness a chance to take advantage of the situation, and put into effect their claims on Ottoman territory. Desperately in need of support, the Porte once again tried to appease the Albanians by promising financial support for Albanian cultural activities. But by now the repressive measures of the Young Turks, and the breaking of their promises, had only increased Albanian nationalist and separatist ideas. In December 1911, the Albanians decided to begin a general insurrection, starting once again in Kosova, later expanding southwards. Arms and money had been arriving from Albanian colonies in Egypt, America and Italy. The Kosovars had been amongst the earliest supporters of the Young Turk Revolution, now they were compelled to defend their national integrity against it.

With the diplomatic support of Austria-Hungary, the General Insurgent Committee of Kosova called on Albanians to rebel. By July 1912 almost all Albanian inhabited areas were under the control of the rebels. In the autumn of 1912 the Balkan states had formed an alliance agreeing to divide up the Porte's European possessions between them. On 8 October 1912, Montenegro opened hostilities, followed by Serbia, Bulgaria and Greece declaring war on the Porte. The Albanians hoped to follow a course of neutrality, but this became impossible as the Balkan allies pushed further into Albanian territory. Following the old dogma, better the devil you know, the Albanians fought alongside the Porte against the allies. As the Porte desperately sought the mediation of the Great Powers, the Albanians decided to make a bid for independence before the Balkan allies overran their lands.

Only the creation of an independent Albania could now secure Austria-Hungary's interests in south-eastern Europe. Therefore, with Austrian support, delegates from all the Albanian regions met at the Congress of Vlora on 28 November, 1912. Here, under very uncertain circumstances, the independent state of Albania was proclaimed.

In July 1913, the London Conference of Ambassadors declared Albania to be an independent sovereign state under international guarantee. Although the Conference formally recognised the new state, a major part of northern and western Albania was given to Serbia and Montenegro. Greece received the large southern region of Chameria, leaving the Albanian state reduced to the town of

Shkodra and its surrounding territory. More than half the Albanian population was left outside the borders of the new Albanian state. In the peace treaty made with the victorious Balkan allies in May 1913, Turkey renounced all rights in Albania. In June, after 500 years of occupation, the last Ottoman troops left Albanian soil.

Ismail Kemal headed Albania's provisional government, and in November 1913, the Powers selected a German, Prince William of Wied, as their candidate for the throne of the new principality. However, the Prince lacked any administrative experience, and the difficulties in governing Albania proved insurmountable. The Italian government openly intrigued against him, and found ready collaborators among ambitious Albanians who aspired to the throne themselves. Six months after his arrival, Prince William left Albania never to return.

The First World War

The outbreak of war in 1914 gave Albania's neighbouring countries the opportunity to seize what land they could amidst the confusion of rapidly mobilising armies throughout the Balkans. In October Greece occupied southern Albania; at the same time the Italians took control of the port of Vlora. To encourage Italy to enter the war on the side of the Entente, a secret treaty, made in London in April 1915, agreed to partition Albania between Greece and Italy, leaving a small autonomous state in the central regions. When Serbia fell in 1915, Austria-Hungary took over most of central and northern Albania, while the southern sections remained in Italian and French hands. Albania was thus in an extremely vulnerable position at the end of the war.

At the Paris Peace Conference, the Serbs, Italians and Greeks put forward territorial claims at the expense of Albania, but these were strenuously resisted by the Albanian delegation. Albanian emigrants living in Europe and America sent representatives to Paris to argue for the restoration of their nation. In June 1920, around 3000 Albanians, mainly peasants, fought a battle with Italian soldiers, which led to the eventual withdrawal of all Italian troops. The same year Albania was admitted to the League of Nations, and in November 1921 the Conference of Ambassadors in Paris recognised Albania as an independent sovereign state.

Albania's political situation remained disturbed as the country essentially reverted back to its pre-war state. Brigandage and lawlessness were rampant, and Albanian society continued to suffer from the vendetta obligations of her still heavily clan-based social structure. Albania's first election was held in 1921, from then until 1924, the country underwent frequent changes of government. In June 1924, Mgr. Fan Noli, Orthodox Bishop of Durres, became Prime Minister. He had been educated at Harvard and was imbued with democratic ideas. But his hastiness in inaugurating a scheme for the rapid modernisation of the country was wrecked by the opposition of the powerful landed *Beys*, who objected, in particular, to the Bishop's plans for agrarian reform. When, in December 1924, Ahmed Zogu, son of a Muslim chief of the Mati district in central Albania, returned from political exile in Yugoslavia at the head of an armed force, Fan Noli was overthrown. He left Albania and returned to the United States where he resumed his ecclesiastical and literary career.

Meanwhile, the victorious Zogu, who had already held various public appointments including Minister of the Interior, set about liquidating or exiling his most dangerous foes. In January 1925, a Constituent Assembly proclaimed Zogu

President. As he conspired incessantly to remain in power, Zogu inadvertantly helped to give Albania some measure of stability and unity. In 1926, a British officer was installed as Inspector General of the Gendarmerie. Despite the chronic bribery, he was able to instill a basic respect for law and order. Brigandage diminished to the point where traffic could pass freely along the few roads and, as a result, trade improved. Plans were drawn up for the systematic drainage of swamps in order to combat the endemic malaria and produce more agricultural land. In 1928, Zogu crowned himself Zog I, King of the Albanians. He argued that a monarchy was necessary to create the notion of continuity and stability for the young country. However, Zog badly needed financial assistance from abroad in order to continue with his development plans.

Italian socio-economic penetration of Albania

Zog's overt political ties with Italy had begun in earnest in November 1926, when the two states signed a pact pledging friendship and mutual support. The pact effectively guaranteed the Italian government's right to maintain the political and territorial status quo in Albania, together with the maintenance of Zog's own personal regime. This was paralleled by increased Italian economic penetration and the settling of Italian colonists on the southern lowland plains. Much Italian investment for the building of bridges, roads and harbour development projects, was for Italian military and strategic purposes. Nevertheless, Italy did finance a few small commercial enterprises such as cigarette and soap factories, a cement mill, tanneries and public buildings, thus capitalising on her exclusive patronage over Albania. Italian architects also transformed Tirana from a sleepy old Ottoman town into something resembling a capital city. Streets were widened and paved, and much of the central area was completely rebuilt around an enormous square named the Piazza Skanderbeg.

Tirana's new ministry buildings housed the large number of Italian advisers who worked on public projects and 'supervised' the Ministries. Italian advisers also worked to influence the school curricula to conform more closely to that of Italy. They favoured Catholic schools and sought to introduce Italian as Albania's second language, a feat not realised until 1933. Although the Italians did contribute to economic development, they also caused severe inflation and discrimination against Albanians in the labour market. Italian immigration led to a rise in property and land prices, together with higher food prices in the major towns. At the same time, Italy had gradually begun to exert political pressure on Zog by exploiting his financial weakness. In the mid 1920s Italy had granted a large loan to Albania. Like Fan Noli before him, Zog had been unsuccessful in gaining financial support from the League of Nations. The international community had accepted his humiliating dependence upon Italy. In 1931 Zog obtained another Italian loan of 100 million gold francs to be repaid at 10 million a year on very easy terms, but the price extracted by Italy for their generosity was greater involvement in Albania's affairs. This included more economic privileges and the admission of more Italian colonists to settle on land reclaimed from the newly-drained malarial swamps.

Throughout the 1930s, Zog increasingly relied on Italian economic assistance as Italian politicians constantly took advantage of Albania's economic and diplomatic weakness. Direct Italian subsidies had allowed the Albanian government to balance its budgets, but at the cost of the country becoming a virtual Italian protectorate. As Italy began tightening the economic screws on Albania, Zog began to fear for his country's independence. He therefore hurriedly instigated several anti-Italian gestures. Italy's proposal for a customs union was rejected and various Italian advisers were dismissed. In April 1933, all private schools were put under Albanian control, a move primarily intended to target Italian schools. Before long, however, Zog was forced to dilute his nationalistic stance and face the harsh realities of his tiny country's vulnerable economic and political situation. He thus felt obliged to adopt a few tactical reverses regarding his foreign policy. In November, Zog seized the opportunity to display evidence of Albania's cooperative attitude by voting against a League of Nation's resolution to impose sanctions upon Italy for its invasion of Ethiopia, whereupon a new Treaty of Accord was signed between Italy and Albania in March 1936. Italian credit again flowed, Catholic schools were permitted to reopen and Italian educators began to return. Italians reappeared as advisers in the civilian administration as well as the military. The Italians were allowed to deepen the port of Durres so that it could harbour their ocean going ships. This was in return for yet another huge and almost interest-free loan.

Meanwhile, in June 1936, Count Galeazzo Ciano, Mussolini's son-in-law, had become Italian Foreign Minister. After visiting Tirana for the first time in April 1937.Ciano argued for the total annexation of Albania, which he said could provide homes for up to two million Italians. By the summer of 1938, the Italians controlled every essential sector of the Albanian state. Up to 170,000 Italian men were working in Albania on tree planting, irrigation schemes and road construction. This was the core of Albania's present-day road system. The dependence on the Italian economy had increased to the extent that by 1939 Italy accounted for 92.1 per cent (as compared to 68.4 per cent in the preceding year) of Albanian exports, and 82.5 per cent (36.3 per cent in 1938) of imports. Whilst Ciano busied himself with colonisation plans, Mussolini agonised over whether to invade Albania. An attack on Albania had been discussed months previously, and Easter week of 1939 had been set as a possible date as early as the beginning of February. On 25 March 25, Mussolini delivered an ultimatum demanding a formal Italian protectorate over Albania and the right to maintain Italian military garrisons in the country. This meant the virtual capitulation of Albanian sovereignty.

THE FASCIST INVASION AND THE COMMUNISATION OF ALBANIA

Sir Reginald Hibbert, GCMG

Having come to power with Yugoslav help, Zog switched from 1925 onwards to reliance on help from Italy. He started with an economic and financial agreement and a national bank seated in Rome. A security pact followed in 1926, and a 20-year defence treaty a year later. Zog had himself made king in 1928: his rule became increasingly personal and he lacked the means to resist Italy's pressures. When Hitler began to alter the map of Europe in 1939, Mussolini quickly followed suit by invading Albania. Zog fled into exile and Albania became a province of the Italian Crown. In October 1940 it became the springboard for Italy's invasion of Greece.

By the end of the year, Greece had thrown the Italian army back into Albania and occupied the southern part of the country. This was not a liberation for Albania, as Greece regarded the regions of Korça (*Koritsa*) and Gjirokastra (*Argyrokastro*) as Greek lands. In April 1941 Germany invaded and destroyed Yugoslavia and then invaded and occupied Greece. Albania was now engulfed by the European war.

At this time Britain was standing alone against Germany and Italy. France had been knocked out in 1940. The Soviet Union was not invaded until June 1941. The United States was not to be drawn in until the end of 1941. In its concern to support Greece and Yugoslavia, Britain had become interested in the possibility of fomenting resistance to the Italians in Albania. Responsibility for this devolved on the Special Operations Executive (SOE), which was set up in London in late 1940. Its efforts, working out of Belgrade and Athens, were swept away by Germany's crushing of Yugoslavia and Greece. But SOE continued to keep a watch on Albania from Istanbul and Cairo, using the services of a few British officers who had trained Zog's gendarmerie and had been the only bulwark against Italy's pre-war takeover of everything Albanian.

When Germany destroyed Yugoslavia she allowed Italy to annex to Albania the province of Kosova and the Dibra area of Macedonia, thereby realising Albania's national dream in baneful circumstances. Later, after Italy was knocked out of the war in the autumn of 1943, Germany restored the Zogist constitution in Albania, but with a Council of Regency in place of the monarch. Greater Albania, the ideal to which all Albanians had long subscribed, thereby assumed the doomed shape of a puppet state ruled by Quislings.

At the end of 1941, after the German invasion of the Soviet Union had made the war against Germany respectable in communist eyes ('anti-fascist' instead of 'imperialist'), a communist party had been formed in Albania under the tutelage of emissaries from the Communist Party of Yugoslavia. Its principal figure from the start was Enver Hoxha. It was puny in size and unsteady in ideology, but it rapidly assumed the role of organising anti-fascist resistance to the Italian and German occupiers. Within a year it took the lead in setting up a country-wide National Liberation Movement.

At first a few prominent non-communists made common cause with the communists; but for most leaders and chieftains and their followers communism was synonymous with Slavdom and was more to be feared than Germany. The war aim of these 'nationalists' was to wait for Germany to be defeated by the western allied powers and then to get the latter to accept Greater Albania as the post-war successor to the pre-war Little Albania.

In the second half of 1943, as Britain and the United States began to bring the war back to the northern shores of the Mediterranean, the British Special Operations Executive, working from Cairo, infiltrated a number of British officers into Albania to liaise with and foment resistance to the Italians and Germans . They soon found Enver Hoxha and his communist colleagues and the National Liberation Movement which they controlled. At this time the Movement was being rapidly expanded into a National Liberation Army with battalions, brigades and eventually, in 1944, divisions. The British officers also found a rival, but looser, organisation, the *Balli Kombëtar* (National Union), whose main aim was to frustrate the communists. The British were prepared to arm and equip anyone who would fight the Germans. The National Liberation Army (the Partisans) qualified. The attitude of the *Balli Kombëtar* and 'nationalist' elements in general was more equiv-ocal: they wanted supply before resistance, while the British wanted to see resis-tance before supply.

The collapse of Italy in September 1943, far from easing Albania's predicament, made it worse by bringing in the Germans in force. As the winter came on, the Germans set about destroying the Partisans. In this task they received the passive and often active help of the *Balli Kombëtar*. Enver Hoxha and his movement were driven out of the centre and north of the country and came very near to being destroyed in the first weeks of 1944. By a narrow margin they survived in the mountains of the south. As the spring approached, the devastation spread by the Germans had the effect of boosting recruitment by the Partisans. The *Balli Kombëtar* were discredited and the National Liberation Movement became the dominant force throughout south Albania outside the German-held towns. In May 1944 Enver Hoxha and his colleagues proclaimed themselves to constitute a provisional government of Albania.

At this time the north of the country was beyond their grasp. The mountain regions were still under the sway of local chieftains. In mid-1944 Enver Hoxha despatched the 1st Partisan Division northwards to assert the power of the National Liberation Movement against both the Germans and the chieftains. The most prominent among the latter was Abas Kupi, who stood for the restoration of King Zog but who had in 1942 and 1943 cooperated with Enver Hoxha. During the winter, when the National Liberation Movement (Partisans) appeared to have been eclipsed, the British officers in north Albania had tried to stimulate the 'nationalist' chieftains to resist the Germans. A particular effort was made with Kupi. The chieftains temporised, being more concerned about the advance of communism (the Partisans) than about the presence of the Germans. The drive of the 1st Partisan Division into the north in mid-1944 put an end to any hope of a 'nationalist' resistance. The Partisan forces soon seized Kupi's strongholds and steadily reduced the other chieftains one after another. At the same time they engaged the Germans at Dibra and Peshkopa. By the end of August the Germans were driven from Dibra; and the Partisan forces, by now undergoing a phenomenal expansion through popular recruitment, turned their attention to the final target, Tirana, and to the subjugation of the mountainous north and Kosova. Tirana fell to them in November. In the same month Enver Hoxha had his provisional government of Albania made permanent. Albania passed under communist rule.

The only material supplies which Enver Hoxha and the Partisans received came from Britain via the SOE. In 1944 most of it was delivered by parachute by Dakota aircraft of the US Army Air Force operating from Italy. In 1943, the Royal Air Force had performed this task in longer-range Halifax aircraft, operating from North Africa. The American OSS (Office of Strategic Services) had an officer at Enver Hoxha's headquarters from the spring of 1944 onwards. The Soviet Union sent a liaison officer to Enver Hoxha in August 1944. One or two emissaries from Tito were always at Enver Hoxha's elbow.

The weapons, ammunition and clothing supplied by Britain played an important part in equipping the first few brigades which formed the spearhead of the Partisan army. But even these brigades, and certainly the rest of the army, were clothed and armed in a motley, haphazard way, largely with booty taken from the Italians. It was a peasant army, leavened in the summer of 1944 by young men from the towns. The core of the army survived in the depth of the 1943/44 winter by its fortitude and endurance in very harsh conditions. The speed with which it multiplied in numbers by the spring of 1944 took everyone by surprise. For the young people who flocked to join the army in 1944, it was quite simply the army of national liberation. For Enver Hoxha and his small core of leading communists, it was the instrument for imposing communist dictatorship.

The Partisan war was fought in the mountains, far from modern tourist routes. In the north it was in the Drin and Mati valleys and the Albanian alps beyond the Drin. In the centre it was in the Cermenika massif north of the Shkumbi and in the hills near Tirana. In the south it was in the mountains between the highways running up from Greece.

The British officers with the Partisans shared the Partisans' austere mode of life, quartered in the mountain villages of a devastated countryside. But the Partisans, being militarily organised, were able to hold ground and receive supplies dropped at night by parachute. The officers in the centre and north depended more on the traditional hospitality of the Albanian mountain villagers. They were able to receive fewer supplies from the air, as effective resistance to the occupiers failed to materialise and the people feared German reprisals. The officers were divided into liaison 'missions', each with its wireless set and a wireless operator and sometimes with a non-commissioned officer trained for para-military activities. Each mission had a broad area of operation. The whole country was covered. The missions had a chequered existence pushed to and fro by Italian and German offensives and by local opinion blowing hot or cold, depending on shifts in the balance of fighting both inside and outside Albania. They moved about on foot and horse- or mule-back, often at night and always over mountain tracks in every sort of weather, very severe in winter, beautiful in summer.

Village life was ruled by the customary law of the mountains, overseen at various levels by local chieftains of different degrees of importance, and enforced occasionally by the harsh practice of the blood-feud. It was a simple existence in the mountains. The houses were scattered and built of stone for defence. The guest-room upstairs was reserved for men: the women and children lived below, often next to the stable. The host would sit cross-legged facing the fireplace, and the rest of the men would arrange themselves in rough order of seniority on both sides. Ritual greetings and hand-rolled cigarettes would be exchanged. The host would brew coffee Turkish-style and distribute it in little cups, which had to be drunk noisily to show appreciation. A raki-drinking session would usually follow, with increasing conviviality in the firelight, enhanced by pine-flares or oil lamps or candles. After a long delay (enough, for example, to kill and skin and boil a sheep or goat or bake bread) a meal would be served. A low round table would be rolled in and the senior men would sit cross-legged round it, turned with their right arms to the table. Hunks of bread would be cut or broken from a disc-shaped loaf, of maize in ordinary houses, or of rye or even wheat in rich ones. All would dip into the common dish—sheep or goat or chicken on rice on high days, soup with beans and a little meat in it on low days, cheese in whey on poor days, and now and then some peppers or other vegetable. In summer there was fruit of all sorts. And everywhere there was plenty of excellent water from the local spring. After supper, all would turn in, still fully dressed, to sleep in a row on each side of the room, rarely on mattresses, most often on carpets, with blankets or quilts as coverings. The obligation to be hospitable to strangers was taken very seriously; but it was subject to much strain by the circumstances of the time. The fact that the officers carried gold coins with which to pay their way tended to have an unavoidably corrosive effect.

The Kosova question played a big part in the politics of the time. Thanks to the Germans, Kosova had been taken from Serbia and joined to Albania. Most Albanians wanted it to stay that way after the war; but the Allies could not promise this. Communism tended to be regarded as Slav or Serbian and therefore un-Albanian. It made little headway in Kosova, where the popular aim was to be free of Serbian rule. It tried to make much of pre-war declarations by the Yugoslav

Communist Party in favour of self-determination, implying that this meant that Kosova could choose to be Albanian after the war. But, from the end of 1943 onwards, as Tito became increasingly the prospective ruler of Yugoslavia, he became more concerned to cultivate Serb feelings and made it clear that Kosova was going to stay with Yugoslavia. This led to a growing tension with Enver Hoxha, who tried steadily to give his communism a nationalist colouring.

When the war ended for Albania in late 1944, Enver Hoxha moved quickly from a national liberation mode to a communist revolution mode. A harsh dictatorship was clamped down on the Albanian people and they were subjected to a process of collectivisation in every sphere of life. This was to be screwed tighter for four decades, ending in the deprivation from which post-communist Albania has the greatest difficulty in escaping.

Britain and the United States severed their relations with Albania in 1946, by when it had become clear that Enver Hoxha intended to remain implacably hostile

World War II resistance hero, Saranda, 1994

to them and to the freedoms for which they stood. The Corfu Channel incident in October 1946, when two British warships were severely damaged by mines laid off the Albanian coast, and Albania's subsequent refusal to accept a ruling by the International Court, put paid to any thought that the war-time relationship might be turned to peacetime benefit.

In the immediate post-war period, communist Albania was a client of Yugoslavia. The Soviet Union seemed content that it should be so. Enver Hoxha's policy of carrying out rapid revolution isolated Albania and played into Yugoslavia's hands, although Hoxha was aware that he himself was not much

trusted by Tito and the other Yugoslav leaders, partly because of his streak of nationalism. By 1948 it was clear that Tito was moving to eliminate Hoxha and put a more compliant leader in his place, probably with the aim of bringing Albania into the Yugoslav Federation. But when Tito defied Stalin in 1948 and was anathematised by Moscow, Hoxha was able to carry out a coup against the Yugoslav tendency in the party and so ensure his own survival.

ALBANIAN COMMUNISM AND DEMOCRATIC TRANSITION

James Pettifer

The history of Albania since the end of the Second World War has in essence been that of isolation from the mainstream of international events. In the earlier period, in the 1950s, Albania was at least a member of the international communist movement and played a full part in its assemblies and deliberations, but for much of the time since the break with the Soviet Union in 1960 and then, subsequently, the People's Republic of China, in 1976, there was only increasing and sometimes almost hermetic international isolation.

The history of the immediate post-war period is in many respects still obscure. It will remain so until all archives in Moscow, Belgrade and Tirana are open to historians. The immediate priority of the communist leaders was to consolidate their hold upon power and to prevent the return of any vestige of the pre-war political leadership. Civil war still raged in Greece, and when the Greek left wing was defeated with the help of the United States many believed that a similar fate would befall communist Albania. It was also widely believed that the Tito-Stalin split in the international communist movement would mean the end of communism. But the outcome was to lead to the consolidation of Enver Hoxha and the Party of Labour in power, in fact it assisted him insofar as his hold on the party was not complete until the liquidation of his enemies who supported Tito, like Koçi Xoxe, in 1948.

At the end of the war Albania was in an economically devastated state, as a result of the Axis occupation, the antiquated nature of the pre-war infrastructure and industrial equipment, and the havoc wreaked by several years of occupation, resistance activity, sabotage and guerilla operations. There were very few personnel indeed with any scientific or technical qualifications, and almost no indigenous capital at all. It was natural for the small, impoverished country to seek a larger and richer partner, and in the context of the communist movement at the time, this meant the Soviet Union and its allies. The first priority was to develop the extensive mineral resources of the country, to provide a reliable source of foreign revenue, to modernise and collectivise agriculture, and to begin a programme of industrial development. A central feature of the latter was electrification, through the construction of large dams to use the hydro-electric potential of the Drin and other river valleys. A concomitant benefit was to complete the drainage of the coastal marshlands, something that had begun before the war under King Zog, and so reduce the incidence of malaria. In terms of social policy, a central objective was the eradication of illiteracy, which was very widespread, and to begin the provision of basic health and education services.

In December 1944 state control over most of the means of production was established, and the mines and the property of political exiles was nationalised. In January 1945 all Italian and German owned assets were confiscated, and the National Bank and the 111 joint stock companies in existence were also brought under state control. By the end of 1947, private sector economic activity had been practically eliminated. In August 1945 the main land reform was promulgated, where land was given to previously landless peasants. About 8000 landowners were dispossessed, without compensation, and land owned by 480 religious institutions was also seized. About 10,000 other landowners who owned land in excess of the limits laid down by the new law were partly dispossessed. Collectivisation proceeded relatively slowly until 1955; prior to that peasants were grouped in co-operatives. In the mountains collectivisation was not seriously attempted until 1966; before that about 46,000 independent peasant holdings remained.

The first state plans for the economy were put forward in 1947, on an annual basis. The first Five Year Plan, on Soviet lines, was carried out between 1951 and 1955. At this stage emphasis was put on hydro-electricity development, the engineering and timber industries, and basic education. The next plan, running from 1955–60, concentrated on oil, nickel, chrome, and coal, in the extractive sector, and the agricultural reforms. During these years, the economy maintained relatively high growth rates, and the Albanian people undoubtedly saw some limited economic benefits from the socialist system, although at a high price in terms of loss of personal liberty and the near-militarisation of labour. These levels of growth were never matched in the following years, after the withdrawal of Soviet technical and material aid after the split in the international communist movement in 1960. Enver Hoxha blamed the problems on the 'savage imperialist-revisionist blockade of the country'. Although economic development programmes were drawn up with the People's Republic of China, which became the main customer for Albanian chrome ore, the levels of investment never matched the Soviet period, and what was done was increasingly concentrated on grandiose and wasteful examples of Stalinist industrial philosophy such as the ferro-chrome concentration plant at Elbasan.

During all these years, until his death in 1985, Enver Hoxha retained overwhelming personal dominance of the Party of Labour, the Communist Party, by a mixture of guile, terror and the intelligent use of placemen and southern Tosk ex-partisan loyalists from the wartime period. A cult of personality began to develop around Hoxha quite early on, and by the mid-1960s had assumed overwhelming proportions, unparalled in any communist country except Maoist China or North Korea under Kim Il Sung. The basically ultra-centralist and authoritarian pattern of decision making remained in force until the mid-1980s when, after Hoxha's death in 1985, a programme of very cautious 'liberalisation' was embarked on by his chosen successor, Ramiz Alia. But the basic structure of the one-party state remained, and it was not until the great changes in eastern Europe in 1989, and in particular the bloody end of the Ceausescu regime in nearby Romania that serious attempts at reform were made. The press was freed, with opposition newspapers being permitted for the first time, the previous restrictions on contact with foreigners were removed, and the formation of opposition political parties began. But during 1990, the popular appetite for change far outpaced the cautious relaxation of control of the communist authorities and rioting and attempts at mass emigration became common. Thousands of refugees had fled to Greece in January 1990, and this was followed by the seizure of most western embassies in Tirana by crowds of young people in July 1990. In September 1990 a legal reform abolished the death penalty for most anti-state offences. In the winter of 1990–91 most of the remaining symbols of the one-party state were physically demolished, including the colossal gilded statue of Enver Hoxha in central Tirana.

The first democratic elections were held in March 1991, and the partially reformed Party of Labour was able to hang on to power, largely thanks to the votes of peasants, still about two-thirds of the population, who were fearful of change. But serious political problems soon overtook the new government, with a general strike in May 1991 forcing its resignation and replacement by a national unity coalition, including non-communists. Chronic instability continued during the summer of 1991, culminating in a remarkable mass emigration movement in August 1991, when over 25,000 people seized ships moored in Durres harbour and forced them to sail to Italy. Food rioting was also recurrent. In response to the chaotic situation, a major programme of European Community food aid was started, 'Operation Pelican', administered by the Italian army which moved into large old military bases near Durres and other lowland cities. Intermittent unrest continued throughout the rest of the year, and in the early months of 1992, with serious rioting involving loss of life at the southern town of Pogradec. There were widespread calls for new elections, which were eventually held in March 1992 and resulted in the victory of the opposition Democratic Party, led by leading cardiologist Dr Sali Berisha. The new government has embarked on a programme of privatisation and the construction of a free market economy.

The proximity of Albania to the war in ex-Yugoslavia has so far limited economic and political progress, but considerable steps forward have been taken in some spheres, such as in the restoration of public order after the 'Years of Anarchy' between 1990 and 1992, in the establishment of a modern commercial culture in Tirana and the larger lowland cities, and a marked increase in agricultural production since the privatisation of land. Cereal production remains a problem.

The next tasks for the government include the provision of infrastructure improvements, such as reliable water and electricity supplies, the construction of sewage systems, and the reduction of very high unemployment.

It has not yet proved possible to develop a constitution which has popular consent. Some Albanians consider undue power has accrued to the President, and concern over human rights problems and threats to press freedom has been expressed by Amnesty International and other organisations. The television remains state controlled. Relations with Albania's Balkan neighbours are often difficult with the intractable Kosova problem always likely to lead to serious conflict with Serbia. Negotiations are in progress with Greece to try to establish a visa system to control Albanian labour migration to Greece, and to improve educational provision for the Greek minority within Albania.

It remains to be seen whether international aid and foreign investment will be forthcoming on a suffucent scale to achieve the economic and social objectives of the government. Parliamentary elections are due to be held in spring 1996.

Zogist rally in Tirana, 1937

PRACTICAL INFORMATION

Passports

Passports are necessary for British and American travellers entering Albania. Visas can be obtained at the border crossings, Rinas airport, or at Albanian embassies abroad.

The current price for UK citizens for a visa lasting one calendar month is 5 dollars. If you are buying a visa at a port of entry, visitors will avoid delay if they have the correct number of dollars available. They should be brand new, or in mint condition (see below). Charges for citizens of other countries vary, the maximum being about 40 dollars at time of writing. Some countries, such as the United States, are currently exempt from visa requirements.

If you are likely to be a frequent visitor, particularly for business purposes, it is possible to apply for a multiple entry visa. These are issued for three, six or twelve month periods. They are not available at embassies or places of entry and personal application must be made to the Ministry of the Interior in Tirana. A multiple entry visa is not normally granted unless more than one single entry visa has already been purchased.

Customs

Luggage is examined by Albanian officials at ports and places of entry. Visitors are free to bring in whatever goods they require, subject to normal restrictions on items such as firearms, ammunition, and narcotics. Customs duties are sometimes charged if expensive items of electronic equipment and similar goods are imported. There is no limit to the amount of foreign currency that may be imported or exported for personal use, although if large amounts of money are involved, receipts for transactions and full business records should be kept.

Embassies and Consulates

The **British Ambassador** is Mr Andrew Tesoriere. His office is in Rruga Vaso Pasha, No 7/1, Tirana (tel. and fax from UK 00 355 42 34973/4/5), though it likely that he will be moving offices in 1996 and these numbers may change. Contact the FCO after June 1996. Albania desk officers in the FCO in London are available on tel.0171-270 1414; fax 0171-270 1415.

Albanian representation in London is by His Excellency Pavli Qesku, Embassy of the Republic of Albania, 4th Floor, 38 Grosvenor Gardens, London SW1 OEB, tel. 0171-730 5709, fax 0171-730 5747.

The **US Embassy in Tirana** is in 103 Rruga e Elbesanit, Tirana, tel. 32875, fax 32222. The current Ambassador is His Excellency Joseph Lake. The United States diplomats reoccupied the building in 1993, after being dispossessed since August 1939. A new headquarters and embassy for the European Union in Tirana is being built near the British Embassy. The European Bank for Reconstruction and Development office is in Room 311, Hotel Tirana International, tel. 42-32898, fx 42-32898, representative resident is Mr Antonio Faneli. The offices of major inter-national organisations such as UNICEF and the World Bank are all generally to found in this area of the city.

Albanian Embassies abroad include:

Belgium: 35 Rue Capouillet, 1060 Brussels, tel. 322 534 8754.

France: 131 Rue de la Pompe, 75016 Paris, tel. 33 1 45 53 51 32.

Germany: Durenstrasse 35, 53173 Bonn, tel. 49 228 351044, fax 49 228 351048.

Italy: Via Asmara 9, 00199 Rome, tel. 396 8621 8214, fax 396 8621 6000.

USA: 1511 'K' Street, NW, Suite 1010, Washington DC, tel. 1 202 223 4942, fax 1 202 623 7342.

The Albanian mission to the **United Nations** is located at 320 East 79th Street, New York, NY 10021, tel. 1 212 249 2059.

Information on tourism and related matters is available from the Ministry of Tourism, Marketing Department, Bul. Deshmoret e Kombit 8, Tirana (tel. 26459/27931, fax 27931).

Currency regulations

There are now no currency regulations in force restricting the amount of hard currency the visitor may take into Albania, or the amount of Albanian lek which may be exported. Records of large sums should be kept.

Money and exchange. The monetary unit is the lek, which used to be divided into 100 quindarkas. With inflation, the latter have disappeared from circulation. Lek notes are issued in one, three, five, ten, fifty, one hundred, two hundred, five hundred and one thousand lek denominations. The lek is not yet an officially convertible currency, in European banking terms, but in practice it is easy to exchange lek with US dollars in most centres, and back, although sometimes at an adverse exchange rate. The US dollar is the foreign currency that is used as a bench mark for all transactions, and the visitor should bring dollars for their own personal spending purposes.

N.B. It is strongly recommended to bring small denomination, brand new notes, to avoid disputes over possible forgeries (see below). Otherwise notes must be in mint condition, even a small tear or other minor imperfection will often result in rejection.

Hundred dollar or other large denomination bills may be rejected, even if they are brand new, by some people. Most British banks now operate a quality standard for used dollar bills to qualify for use in the ex-Soviet Union, the traveller to the Balkans should insist on this quality. If they do not, new German marks or Swiss francs are the most acceptable substitutes. Greek drachma are also in wide circulation in southern Albania. But if visitors intend to use currencies other than dollars, they should familiarise themselves closely with the relevant mark–dollar–Swiss franc–lek exchange rates. Most Albanians have a reasonable idea of what the dollar is worth in relation to the lek at any particular time, but frequently know little of the value of other currencies. British visitors should avoid the use of sterling, which is largely unknown, particularly in rural Albania.

At the moment money changing in the streets with black market traders is permitted, and the visitor can usually obtain a 5 to 10 per cent advantage with hard currency over the official bank rate, that is, at the time of writing, about 90 lek to the dollar. But these transactions should only be attempted with caution. While most black market operators are honourable people, some are not, and the visitor who has disclosed, by participation in the black market, a substantial amount of hard currency, may find himself followed and robbed.

N.B. As elsewhere in eastern Europe and the Balkans there are growing quantities of counterfeit dollars in circulation. Anyone planning business in Albania should purchase one of the patent machines available to detect forgeries. Tourists should familiarise themselves with the informal checks that can be made on dollar bills, i.e. the rough edge at the top

centre over the watermark. **Pre-1991 bills with the 'thin' white top edge should not be taken, as even if in good condition they are unlikely to be accepted in many places. In business transactions all currency should be checked before acceptance. This is now conventional and offence is not caused.**

By and large credit is not common in Albania, and cash is the norm for all transactions. Some establishments in Tirana will take American Express and Visa cards, but Access and most other credit cards have yet to establish themselves, except Eurocard and Diners Club in a few places. Visitors should take whatever money they are likely to need in cash, or perhaps partly in US dollar denominated travellers' cheques, if visiting Tirana, Shkodra or a large urban centre.

It is possible to cash travellers' cheques and Eurocheques at the **National Bank of Albania** in Skanderbeg Square, Tirana, and at a number of private banks and money changing offices here and in other large cities. The **Arab Albanian Islamic Bank** has an efficient service, at 8 Rr. Deshmoret e Kombit, Tirana (tel. and fax 28460). The **National Commercial Bank of Albania**, Rr. 'Zhan D' Ark', Tirana (tel.33338, fax 33208) is the most important commercial banking institution. Other private banks include the **Savings Bank of Albania** (Rr. Deshmoret e 4 Shkurtit 6, Tirana, tel. 23587) and **Dardania Bank** ('Veve' Centre, Tirana, tel. 28759, fax 42566). There are at the moment few facilities in smaller towns, although there are signs that this may change in the near future, with the establishment of more privately owned banks. The National Bank is open from 08.30 until 13.30. It is a crowded, difficult institution, with long delays, and most regular travellers to Tirana regard its use as a last resort. The large hotels in Tirana will usually cash travellers cheques for residents.

Medical advice

Visitors to Albania, whether alone or on an organised tour, should bear in mind that they are travelling in the poorest country in Europe, that, until the last war, had very serious public health problems. Although there have been dramatic steps forward taken since then, with the eradication of the main scourges, malaria, in the lowlands, and TB and syphilis, in the highlands, many serious problems remain. In the aftermath of communism, the public medical facilities are in a debilitated, not to say derelict state. Although Albanian doctors are well trained and competent, the conditions in which they work are frequently very poor. The dramatic rise in casualties caused by the burgeoning number of private cars is a particular problem.

All visitors to Albania, on whatever basis, should have the fullest possible medical insurance. Insurance policies should be carefully checked for war exclusions as some companies regard Albania as falling within the war exclusion zone of ex-Yugoslavia. People with conditions that may require urgent attention should bear in mind that transport within Albania to hospital is often slow, and that flights from Tirana, for emergency repatriation purposes, are infrequent by comparison with most European capitals. If moving outside Tirana, travellers should carry with them all medical equipment and drugs they are likely to need. It should not be assumed that even the commonest preparations such as plasters or aspirin are available, even for those with hard currency. If a preparation is really vital, a spare supply should also be carried. Medical goods are a frequent target for thieves and their security within luggage arrangements should be carefully considered.

A number of doctors are listed in the guide who practice in different Albanian cities. Most of them speak English, or another foreign language. If consulted, a small fee, in dollars, should be negotiated beforehand. A useful clinic specialising in treating foreigners in Tirana is the ABC Health Clinic, Rr Ludovik Shllaku 14, tel. 26820, fax 34708 or 42002 (Dr C.J. Burnett).

Although Albania, to date, does not appear to have very widespread HIV and AIDS problems, visitors are advised to carry a comprehensive first aid kit including disposable plastic syringes. It is also wise to carry a supply of antibiotics and a preparation usable against gastro-enteritis and intestinal problems. Water purification tablets are useful if a stay in some of the more primitive lowland cities is planned. Condoms and other contraceptive devices are often unavailable and should be carried by the visitor if required.

Visitors should ensure before leaving that their tetanus and other routine inoculations are up to date, and an anti-hepatitis vaccination is an absolutely essential precaution, particularly in the hot summer months. There was a small cholera outbreak in the Berat region in the autumn of 1994 and this vaccination can be also be taken although it is not of universal efficacy. Carrying a supply of anti-louse shampoo is advised if work involves contact with the poorest sections of urban society.

Specialised medical preparations, foods, and nappies for babies and small children, are not always available but supplies in the main urban centres are improving.

Swimming in lowland rivers is not recommended as, however inviting, they are polluted by sewage discharges. The rivers of the mountains offer good bathing. Local enquiries are advised before sea bathing, particularly in the coasts adjacent to cities such as Vlora which are near major river estuaries. Port and harbour beaches are not recommended.

Security

General

Any visitor to Albania needs to consider personal security issues carefully, as in all Balkan countries in current circumstances. Since the end of communism, the Albanian people have entered a world of freedom, but with considerable material deprivation. It is not surprising, therefore, if the Western visitor is a tempting target for thieves, as in many other countries with a comparable standard of living. It was, however, an unfortunate fact in Albania that with the end of the one-party state, the actual institutions of the state itself became discredited and, in some areas, the police used to have considerable difficulty in enforcing the law, particularly between 1990 and spring 1992. The position in most large towns has improved considerably since then, but problems in some areas remain.

Border security

Security for independent travellers in some border areas remains at best very uncertain and around parts of the Greek-Albanian border has deteriorated in the last three years. The border with Kosova is very dangerous, with shootings by Serbian border guards a regular occurence. The main problem for the security forces on the Montenegro border is diesel and petrol smuggling and associated Mafia activity (see below). Care is needed with the FYROM border as incidents involving encounters between the FYROM border guards and smugglers are not unusual.

If travellers must go to border regions it is sensible to seek advice beforehand on local conditions, which vary widely. The office of the European Union Border Monitoring Mission in Villa 6 in Tirana usually has up to date information.

Organised crime
Visitors, especially business visitors, should be aware of the growth of organised crime in Albania, as everywhere else in the Balkans and eastern Europe. In general the Albanian situation, although deteriorating in the coastal cities such as Vlora and Durres, which have many links with southern Italy, and in Tirana itself, is not yet as bad as in some neighbouring countries. Independent security advice for the foreign investor is essential. If local security staff or bodyguards are employed for any purpose whatsoever it is essential for their references and background to be checked by experts.

Advice on the security aspects on setting up a business in Tirana is available from consultants in the UK, Switzerland and USA. In the UK Control Risks Ltd, 83 Victoria Street, London SW1, tel. 0171 222 1552 are specialists in this field. In the USA and Switzerland, Kroll Associates are well known.

Visitors should refuse all requests to carry goods through borders for third parties as drug trafficing is increasing in Albania, particularly in the lowland ports and on the border with FYROM.

Personal security
Generally speaking, the visitor should behave in Albania with tact and show respect for local customs, especially those concerning religion and family life. In some places there is a revival of Islamic traditions and a greater conservatism, particularly concerning women's dress. On the other hand, the lowland cities are becoming fully Westernised. Ostentatious jewellery, clothes, watches, cameras and video recorders should be avoided. Some experienced travellers in Albania carry a separate 'dummy' wallet containing a modest amount of cash to hand over to thieves, as a device to protect the main resources. It is also wise to carry an emergency supply of money hidden, for example, in the sole of a shoe.

But as well as commonsense personal precautions, the visitor needs to bear in mind the extremely primitive state of much of the social infrastructure, the very poor condition and concomitant dangers on most main and all secondary roads, the lack of a reliable telephone system if difficulties are encountered and the limited number of garages, breakdown services, and spare parts for vehicles.

Visitors of either sex should avoid wandering around Albanian cities late at night, particularly in some of the poorer and more rundown provincial centres, and in downtown Tirana itself. The shanty towns of displaced ex-rural people that are beginning to grow up around Tirana and other lowland towns are dangerous. **Avoid**. Thieves are often armed and if encountered, should not be resisted. Markets often harbour pickpockets.

The condition of urban roads and pavements is often very poor, and the pedestrian needs to be on the lookout for open culverts, missing manhole covers, and so on. Many Albanian city streets outside central Tirana are not clearly named, and the visitor should ensure before setting out that he or she is clear about the destination and how to get there. Many streets have been renamed everywhere for political reasons, but many Albanians still use the old names. If lost, stay in the main streets in open areas and ask for assistance and avoid entering tenement blocks. Although most Albanian people are very kind and helpful, be cautious about accepting offers of assistance. Traffic conditions are chaotic, and many accidents occur every day as a result of random encounters between vehicles, farm livestock and the general population.

The serious crime rate appears to worsen in the winter months, and improve considerably in the summer. The officially reported murder and serious crime rate has fallen somewhat recently. The visitor can enjoy genuine freedom and reasonable security between April and September. In the winter conditions deteriorate. Many parts of Albanian cities are affected by power cuts, and can be plunged into total darkness without warning. Rota power cuts are very common, where a particular sector of a town will be cut off for a number of hours each day. A small pocket torch is essential, and a supply of candles for the hotel room. Spare batteries should be carried as they may be difficult to obtain locally.

In the countryside savage dogs belonging to shepherds are common hazards, particularly in mountain areas. They are generally bred from mastiffs and protect the herds from wolves. They should not be approached. Wolves themselves are becoming more common in the high mountains in southern Albania, but rarely venture near human settlements except in the severest winters.

For the independent traveller, the key to security in Albania is good planning, particularly in matters such as transport and accommodation. Particular care should be taken with the choice of transport drivers. Unofficial taxis, especially at border crossings, should be avoided unless the contact is made on the basis of a personal recommendation.

Traditional patterns of Balkan banditry have revived in some areas, particularly in the south east, in Shkodra and in the border areas adjoining Montenegro, based there on petrol smuggling Mafias. When social tension is high in some more difficult towns, such as Shkodra on occasions during the 1994–95 winter, the police discourage people from using the streets after dark and enforce a *de facto* curfew.

Business conduct

Since the end of communism there have been many changes in the atmosphere of Albanian economic and political life. In many ministries staff have been compulsorily retired for political reasons. Visitors on business should not expect high standards of efficiency, particularly the exchange of written communications. This is often not the fault of those concerned. Many organisations still lack what in the West would be regarded as the most basic business equipment, particularly in the sphere of electronic communications. There is a chronic shortage of telephone lines that affects everybody in business.

But most Albanians are helpful and anxious to assist the foreigner discharge his or her business. It is important to be very specific, particularly on paper, about what is required, and how a particular project can in practice come to fruition. The law in some areas remains unclear, and concepts such as tort and contract are unfamiliar to most Albanians. There is no tradition of commercial law, and few qualified personnel in this field, although the position is improving. The banking system is cumbersome and slow and adequate time should be allowed for the transfer of funds in any transaction to take place. Corruption in public life is growing, particularly in matters such as planning applications.

Despite these problems, a flourishing small business culture has developed in the last two years, especially in Tirana, and the legal situation for many activities has become clearer. As yet, there is very little investment in Albania by international or large foreign companies, but this may change if the political situation in the Balkans stabilises.

The foreign businessman should exercise great caution in any transactions that involve land purchase, as disputes over local ownership are very

common. **All legal documentation provided in land tenure matters should be independently verified. Document forgery is a common problem.**

Women travelling in Albania

Women have begun to travel independently in Albania in the last three years and reports received of experiences vary enormously. Some female correspondents have described excellent trouble-free holidays, others nightmares that involve serious embarrassment. In the past women, however experienced on the road, did not usually go on holiday or business on their own in Albania, unless they were working in a formal organised framework at a conference in Tirana, for example. In Tirana and most other large towns that is no longer necessary, providing common-sense precautions are taken. Elsewhere, less has changed. It is very arguable how far women travelling alone in many parts of the countryside can be secure, certainly on a first visit, and participation in an organised tour is recommended. Women are particularly vulnerable to the vagaries of Albanian transport arrangements. Rape and sexual harrassment have reappeared, although on no worse a scale than in most places in Europe and much less than the urban USA.

Security in the cheaper hotels is poor and they should be avoided except in an emergency. Visitors should bring all necessary personal and sanitary requisites, which are not always obtainable outside the main cities. Conditions in maternity hospitals are not generally very good, and a visit by a pregnant woman should not be considered if there is any likelihood of confinement.

Visiting the Albanian communities in Kosova, FYROM and Montenegro

About two million ethnic Albanians live in ex-Yugoslavia, most of them in western FYROM and in what used to be the autonomous region of Kosova, in south-west Serbia. In the last two years, with developments in the Albanian national movement, and the war in ex-Yugoslavia, these communities have become much more important and more people have been attempting to travel to them. It is possible to reach these communities from Albania, via the Quaf e Thanës pass, near Lake Ochrid, then to Albanian towns in FYROM such as Tetovo. It is not difficult to reach Kosova from there, by bus, or from Skup (Skopje) itself. The local train that sometimes used to run from FYROM to Kosova does not usually do so now.

N.B. Travellers should bear in mind that while social conditions in FYROM are reasonably tranquil at the moment, there were riots in February 1995 in Tetovo, and that Kosova is legally part of Serbia which is a country that is at war. Inter-ethnic relations in FYROM are tense, and local contacts are recommended if independent travel in the Albanian areas of western FYROM is planned. Travel insurance is generally invalid in Serbia. The US State Department and the British Foreign Office do not recommend visits.

There are, however, no restrictions on anyone travelling where they wish at the moment, and many people do use these routes. The Foreign Office in London very strongly advises visitors to inform the British Embassy in Belgrade of their whereabouts. The British Chargé d'Affaires in Belgrade is Mr Ivor Roberts, CMG. His embassy telephone number is 381 11 645 055, or fax 381 11 659 651. An emergency number is available: 381 11 645 087. If these numbers are unavailable due to telecommunications' difficulties, emergency advice is available from the East

Adriatic Unit desk of the FCO in London (tel. 0171 270 1414). Travellers should be aware that it is often very difficult to make telephone calls from within Kosova and in rural areas in FYROM.

Both the Albanian majority and the Serb minority welcome foreign contacts. Travellers should bear in mind that food, alcohol and cigarettes are in good supply but there are many shortages of other goods as a result of UN sanctions.

N.B. The Serbian police and paramilitary presence is very heavy in many places, particularly the Albanian dominated towns in western Kosova such as Pec and Gjakova. Local Albanians may be unwilling to associate openly with foreign visitors in public places for security reasons. Travellers should carry their personal documents at all times and expect to be stopped and questioned on occasion by the security forces.

Camera use is not recommended, and under no circumstances whatso-ever should visitors attempt to photograph the Serbian security forces, or their military or police buildings. Pedestrians are not allowed within designated areas surrounding military and other government buildings, particularly the provincial military control buildings in Pristina.

Generally speaking, the Serbian police and paramilitary units are well trained, in the formal sense, and behave correctly towards foreigners but this cannot always be relied upon in current circumstances.

The German mark is the currency of choice in south Serbia, US dollars are definately not recommended. It is strongly recommended on security grounds for visitors to Pristina to stay in the Grand Hotel, in the main street, or the Kosova Polje Hotel. Albanian families are legally unable to accommodate visitors in their houses and should not be requested to do so.

Visas are required for Serbia and Montenegro, including Kosova. They cannot be obtained at the border but must be applied for and purchased at Yugoslav embassies in the country where the traveller normally resides. A letter of invitation from a Yugoslav citizen is required and should accompany the application. A charge of £15 per visa is currently made at the Yugoslav Embassy, 5 Lexham Gardens, London W8 (tel. 0171 370 6105) for a visa lasting one month. Visitors contemplating business contacts in Kosova should bear in mind the United Nations' sanctions regulations, information on which is available from the Department of Trade in London. The same applies to Montenegro, but there are no current visa requirements or trade restrictions for FYROM. Applicants should allow at least a month for the application to be processed by the embassy.

Kosova is under a state of emergency and martial law and anyone going there should only do so after careful planning and with local contacts in Kosova itself. Visitors with archaeological interests are recommended to contact Dr Edi Shukriu, at the Kosova Democratic League offices in Pristina. There are many **Illyrian** and **Classical sites** and **Ottoman buildings** of great interest in Kosova. The outstanding **Serbian religious monuments** such as **Gracanica church**, near Pristina, and the **Patriarchate** at Peç should not be neglected on ideological grounds. In antiquity Prizren was known as *Vulpiani*, and was founded in the 2C BC. The small but economically influential Greek community in Pristina welcomes contacts. Visitors can most easily make contacts by patronising one of the Greek-owned bars in Pristina, such as *El Greco*.

About 15 per cent of the population of Montenegro is ethnically Albanian, with settlement concentrated in the south adjoining Albania. Ulcinje (*Dulcingo*) is the most Albanian town in Montenegro. Of the 24,000 inhabitants, about 17,500 are ethnic Albanians. The name ' Ulcinje' is probably derived from the ancient Illyrian word for 'wolf', *Ukas*. Montenegro is effectively Serbia's junior partner in the as yet unrecognised Federal Republic of Yugoslavia (FRY), and has been seriously affected by the ex-Yugoslav crisis. Only those with experience of Balkan wartime conditions should contemplate travel there. The British Embassy in Belgrade should be informed of plans as for Kosova. The border crossing point is known as *Tozi*, in Montenegran (see p. 50).

Getting to Albania

Tourist information
Tourist information is best obtained from the specialist travel operators (see below) who organise tours to Albania. The old Albanian state tourist organisation, Albturist, is in the process of reorganisation under privatisation, and in any case does not have representative offices in foreign cities. It does, however, have a central office in Tirana, where the guides are helpful. Several other private travel agencies in Albania have been established. Visitors to Albania will find a surprising number of Albanians speak at least one foreign language, and are often very well informed about their country, particularly its history.

Tour operators
Specialist tour operators in the **UK** include Regent Holidays, 15 John Street, Bristol BS1 2HR (tel. 01179 211711, fax 01179 254866). In the **USA**, refer to: Lindi's Travel Agency Inc, 1030 E. Montauk Highway, Copiauge, NY 11726; Nationwide Travel Saver Inc, 37234 Dequindre, Sterling Heights, MI 48310; Arberia Airlines, 275 Madison Avenue, Suite 1018, New York, NY 10016, tel. 212 338 9717.

Shkreli Travel specialises in trips to Albania, tel. 1 718 931 1000.

The Albanian-American newspaper *Illyria*, 2321 Hughes Avenue, Bronx, NY 10458 tel. 1 718 220 9614, fax 1 718 220 9618 is a useful source of information in the USA about planned charter tours.

In the United Kingdom, Bradford University South East European Studies Unit organise tours from time to time (Ms Antonia Young, tel. 01274 383834).

Cycling holidays. Bicycles are a very common means of transport in Albanian cities. Visitors can usually find someone to hire a heavy, usually Chinese-made 'roadster' bicycle. Enquiries can be made at local cycle shops. Great care should be taken with the increasing number of motor vehicles competing for road space, and other hazards.

Cycling in the Albanian countryside is arduous and should only be considered by those who feel they can cope with the rugged terrain. Spare parts for Western-made cycles are not generally obtainable and visitors should bring all spares that they may need.

Special interest holidays. The Albturist organisation and Regent Holidays are happy to organise holidays for special interest groups. In the last two years this has been a successful and expanding area of Albanian tourist industry development. Groups from Britain have included birdwatchers, coleopterists, cave explorers and mountaineers.

Air services

The most practical method of reaching Albania reliably is by air. European air services are dominated by **Swissair**, which provides an excellent service by direct flight from Zurich, to Rinas airport, about 30km outside Tirana. Buses and taxis run from Rinas to Tirana. Planes leave Zurich in the morning, and return the same day. The early morning Swissair flight from Heathrow links directly with it, so London can be left at about 08.00, to reach Tirana by 16.00. Swissair also runs an efficient and reliable air cargo service, which has adequate security for goods at Rinas airport. **Austrian Airways** and **Adria** both fly from London and run reliable and efficent schedules, although most travellers feel without the consistent quality of the Swissair service. Visitors interested in a holiday in Slovenia can break the journey there on an **Adria** flight if they wish to do so. **Lufthansa** has just started a service from Heathrow three times a week, via Frankfurt.

There are also flights from Athens, with **Olympic Airways**, and from Rome, with **Alitalia**. The Alitalia flights from Rome have a poor reputation for reliability, particularly in the winter months. Some correspondents have reported very serious difficulties with the Alitalia administration in Tirana, with irresponsible over-booking.

Olympic flights from Athens are reliable but are sometimes prone to cancellation in winter, because of adverse weather conditions. The flight on Tuesdays generally stops at Ioannina, in northern Greece, to pick up passengers, and can be boarded there.

There is a very good value **British Airways** Heathrow–Thessalonika daily service. The air fare is at least £100 cheaper than any of the direct flights. This is well worth considering, particularly for travellers going to southern Albania or Tirana, now that there is a good quality express coach service from Thessalonika–Tirana (see below). The coach travels via Korça and Elbasan and can be boarded or left en route. It is a beautiful and scenic journey.

If the traveller has a little more time, it is very pleasant to take the local Greek bus from Thessalonika to Kastoria or Florina, spend the night there, and travel by taxi to Albania at the Kapshtica border post. Cheap taxis to Korça can easily be found at this recommended crossing. Bear in mind northern Greece can be very cold in winter, especially January and February. **Olympic** also have a weekly direct flight from Thessalonika to Tirana, on Thursday mornings, returning later the same day, which goes on to Athens.

Swissair has an office in Tirana in Skanderbeg Square which can provide current flight information. It should be borne in mind, though, that it is not always possible to run a direct computer link for ticket sales with Zurich, and the more arrangements that can be firmly made before entering Albania, the better. In the UK **Regent Holidays** (tel. 01179 211711) has negotiated cheap ticket prices with Adria and Swissair.

Reliable and good value ticketing on the BA London–Thessalonika route and on Olympic flights is available from **Griffin Travel**, 21 Angel Gate, City Road, London EC1 V 2PY, tel. 0171 814 9977, fax 0171 814 9978 (Mr T. Sirianos), or direct from **British Airways**, tel. 0171 897 4000.

There are also flights from Bari in Italy, Zagreb in Croatia, and Albanair from Vienna and various German and Swiss cities. A new airline, **Arberia Airlines**, has been started in the United States, to serve Albania, but careful enquiries should be made before committing to any of these flights. Some are more in the nature of charters than anything else, where the exact flight departure may be delayed until the majority of tickets have been sold. For the time being at least, the traveller would probably be well advised to make arrangements with one of the mainstream international carriers, other than **Alitalia**. The travel companies who specialise in Albania will make their own charter arrangements.

Tirana is now linked with nearby Balkan capitals such as Sofia and Budapest by air. **Hemus** and **Balkan** run a reliable regular service to the Bulgarian capital. Air traffic control in FYROM has not yet been modernised and travellers are not recommended to use Skup (Skopje) or Ochrid airports at the moment, particularly in winter.

Ferry services
Ferries from Italy
Ferry services run from Trieste and Bari in southern Italy to Durres and Vlora. They are, however, primarily cargo boats and do not always leave at regular intervals. As a rule of thumb, a boat leaves Trieste for Albania about twice a week. It will take vehicles, providing space is available. Facilities for passengers are poor, and anyone contemplating using this route should take an adequate supply of their own food, drink and tobacco with them. There are also ferries from Ancona to Durres (once a week); Ortona to Durres (once a week); Brindisi to Durres (once a week); Brindisi to Vlora (four times a week), and from Otranto to Vlora (three times a week). Local enquiries in the Italian ports are essential, and the reliability of services cannot be taken for granted. A catamaran service *Lavikinga* runs from Bari to Durres, but only in good weather.

Ferries from Italy to Montenegro
With the partial lifting of the United Nations' economic sanctions on Serbia and Montenegro, a ferry service has been started between Bari, and Bar, in Montenegro, which could be useful for visitors to northern Albania if they have the appropriate documentation to enter Montenegro and then Albania. Visa regulations for Montenegro are stringent, and the same as for Serbia (see below, and p. 51). There are serious security problems in Montenegro at the moment and this route is not recommended. If it is used with a vehicle it is important to fill up with fuel in Italy before departure, as supplies in Montenegro can be very unreliable.

Ferries from Greece
A regular daily boat service runs between Saranda in southern Albania, and Corfu, for foot passengers only. There are very cheap charter flights to Corfu April-October and this is the cheapest way to approach Albania. The boats leave Corfu at about 10.00 and returns from Saranda at 16.00. The journey takes about an hour. In the summer, two boats a day run, cost about 5000 Greek drachma.

In the times of intermittent political tension between Greece and Albania in the last 18 months, the boat has often not operated at all, and at least one tourist organisation mentioned above has stopped using the Corfu route completely for entry purposes. On other occasions it has been taken over by the Corfu police for repatriating illegal immigrants. Although in practice it may well be possible to find someone in Corfu to take you to the Albanian coast, and vice versa, this is no longer a reliable method of getting to Albania, and can be very expensive. It is technically illegal in Greece to use a charter flight to enter a 'third' country, such as Albania, although the law is not in practice enforced.

If the traveller has arrived in Corfu but finds the boat is not running, the most economic solution is to take the coach to Ioannina, then the local bus from

Ioannina to the border point at Kakavia, then the bus or a taxi to Tirana. The Greek coach services are efficient, and it is a beautiful and interesting journey. Buses leave the central bus station in Ioannina about every hour or so for the Kakavia border crossing. The weather is often difficult in autumn and winter, and all-weather clothing and boots are essential.

Rail services

There are currently no direct foreign rail connections with the Albanian network, with the closure of the Shkodra–Podgorica link under UN sanctions regulations, although reopening for frieght is planned. The railways suffered very badly from the social turmoil of the transition years, and many passenger services in the country were not operational because the rolling stock had been burnt out during riots.

Since 1993 internal services have been restored on most routes and provide a very cheap and interesting way to travel between some of the main cities. The Tirana–Korca route is particularly pleasant. The trains are slow and do not have very good facilities and travellers should take whatever food, drink, toilet tissue and cigarettes they will need. Crime on the trains is minimal as armed members of the public order police patrol them.

The freight network continues to operate, mainly as a means of transporting mineral ores to Durres for export.

By road

As stated elsewhere, travellers are advised not to bring their own vehicles into Albania because of the very difficult problems of physical security of the vehicle, and the problems with insurance cover, but there is no legal obstacle to doing so at the approved border crossings. Caravans are not recommended. The car driver should be able to produce proof of ownership and a current driving licence. Involvement in a road accident in Albania is considered to be a potentially serious offence, and a driver should expect to be detained for a short period while the circumstances of the accident are investigated. A very full spares kit should be carried, and reserve supplies of oil and petrol. Petrol and diesel shortages are still evident in some areas. Petrol costs about 90 lek a litre. Diesel costs about 50 lek a litre. Unleaded petrol is becoming available. In an emergency it is usually possible to find the odd gallon of petrol for sale in urban markets, if at a high price.

Heavy duty tyres should be fitted, and a steel plate undershield to protect the sump is advisable. A temporary windscreen should be carried, and wire headlamp covers, if possible. Travel after dark in many districts is inadvisable. If it is winter, or the weather is wet, great caution should be exercised in the selection of routes, as many secondary roads that are usable dirt tracks in the dry become impassable in the wet, and some are subject to rockfalls and landslides, particularly in the northern mountains. Waterfalls that are safely confined in the dry months can turn roads into raging torrents. Many routes in the mountains are blocked by snowfall in the winter. Snow chains for tyres are needed. In summer clouds of dust can obscure visibility.

Secure parking is important. It is advisable for vehicles to be locked up in a compound at night. The current charge in most towns is about $5 a night. Many drivers remove windscreen wipers, and other removable items while their cars are parked.

Fiat, Mercedes Benz, BMW and Land Rover are the companies with the most reliable supplies of spare parts in Albania. Japanese and American four-wheel drive vehicles are becoming more commonly available for hire. The garage run by the Red Cross in central Tirana has a good reputation for repairs.

If car purchase is planned a **Mercedes Benz** or strong, heavy car that is capable of dealing with Albanian roads is essential. There is a large second-hand car market on the southern outskirts of Durres. A full engineer's report on a vehicle should be obtained before purchase. Dealers in car spares are found on the outskirts of Tirana on the Durres road.

Border crossing points and road transport
The situation with the different crossings is complex and unpredictable, and it is worth trying to make a spot check on local conditions before taking a vehicle through.

The most popular crossing used to be from Montenegro, in the north at **Hani i Hoti**, but the war in ex-Yugoslavia has diminished legal traffic. **Avoid**. See below and page 264. An additional crossing, on the road south of Lake Shkodra, is proposed, although it is not known when it will begin to operate. The crossing at **Kakavia**, with Greece, is very busy, sometimes chaotic, particularly now there is a regular bus service linking it with Ioannina and Athens. **Recommended for pedestrians, but not for vehicles until the new Greek border post currently under construction is built.** The other Greek border crossing, at **Kapshtica**, near Korça, is less used, although there is an improved road on the Greek side linking the border crossing with Kastoria. **Recommended, with or without a vehicle**. A taxi to Kastoria in Greece costs about £15 sterling from the border post. Security measures against illegal immigration are heavy on the Greek side, documents should be carried at all times.

It is possible to cross from Albania into FYROM at **Quaf e Thanës**, near Lake Ochrid, although this route was often very congested with commercial vehicles when the Greek border blocade of FYROM began in Febuary 1994 and has not improved much since. **Avoid if you are crossing with a vehicle**. The more northern border crossings with FYROM are usually quiet. **Recommended**. A new crossing south of Ochrid has opened at **Tushmishti**, about 5km east of Pogradec. **Recommended for vehicle drivers, but not for pedestrians** as transport is lacking on the FYROM side. The crossing to FYROM on the Debar/Peshkopia road is **recommended for vehicles and pedestrians**, although the weather can be difficult in winter. There are many places of interest nearby, on both sides of the border line, such as the Roman sulphur baths at Baniste, in FYROM.

The border crossing point at **Qafa e Morines** 26km east of Kukes, with Serbia, is formally open, and it is possible, *in extremis*, to cross here, but travellers are ill-advised to do so, with recurrent problems of arbitrary border closures, lengthy delays, harassment by the border police, and theft and confiscation of travellers' goods and personal effects. **AVOID**

At all border crossings the traveller should exercise commonsense and caution, particularly at quiet times, where the unscrupulous may be tempted to prey on the unwary or badly organised traveller. Transport and pick-up arrangements should be planned, or it is possible to find yourself paying very large sums of money to be taken to Tirana or wherever with highly unreliable transport.

Buses and coaches
There has been a considerable improvement in coach transport to Albania and within the country in the last three years. Coach travel is best undertaken early in

the day. Some services start as early as 05:30. Many routes do not operate after midday. A coach service linking **Athens** and **Tirana** has been started and leaves most weekdays early in the morning from the central long-distance bus station in Athens. The journey should take about 14 hours. There is a daily service linking **Thessalonika** and **Tirana**, via **Korca**. The fare from Thessalonika to Korca is about 5000dr. (£13) at the time of writing.

There are a growing number of private coach services linking urban centres within Albania. Fares are very low i.e. about £2 sterling to go from Tirana to Shkodra. **Minibus services** are developing, and are often much quicker than coaches. **N.B. Avoid overloaded vehicles.** In many towns there are 'teacher buses' *autobusët e mësueseue*, which take teachers out to the surrounding villages for the day. They can be a useful source of lifts.

Long distance coach services linking **Tirana** with cities like **Pristina** and **Prizren** in Kosova have started, travelling via Elbasan and the mountain pass at Quaf e Thanës, passing through FYROM en route. Tickets are sold from a kiosk at the side of the *Hotel Tirana International* in Skanderbeg Square. Buses also run from here to **Istanbul**, via Thessaloniki.

It is possible to reach **Bulgaria** and **FYROM** from **Tirana** by changing coaches in Skup (Skopje). On occasion through coaches also run. The bus from **Skup** to **Sofia** leaves at 08.30 from the car park next to the Old Railway Station, near the Hotel Bristol. That journey can take anything from five to twelve hours, depending on the level of congestion on the FYROM/Bulgarian border. This has worsened considerably since the Greek border blocade of FYROM started in Febuary 1994 and travellers should take adequate supplies with them, and very warm clothing if making the journey in winter. Some buses have been held up by local Mafia gangs en route, and valuables should not be taken on your journey. Electronic goods such as laptop computers are a particular target for thieves.

Northern Albanian kulla, Dragobi, see p. 274

GENERAL INFORMATION

Hotels

Until recently, Albania was a country without a tradition of **hotels**, except for the ubiquitous Ottoman *hans*, whose primitive conditions have been described graphically by many pioneer travellers in ex-Ottoman countries. Hospitality to the stranger was a domestic, family matter in Albania, a serious obligation, gladly undertaken.

The great majority of the hotels a contemporary visitor to Albania is likely to use have been built during the communist period. They were, until recently, almost all run along similar lines by the Albturist organisation. It is proposed that they will in due course be privatised and there has been some limited progress in that direction. In the main they are modern functional establishments, built to a common design, without much character or distinction although some of them benefit from the spectacular surroundings in which they are situated. It is an unfortunate survival of communist-era practice that foreign visitors are often charged several times as much for a hotel room as Albanians.

Tirana has several new hotels, in addition to the *Dajti Hotel* and the *Hotel Tirana International*. The *Dajti* has been in existence for a considerable time, but was refurbished under the guidance of Soviet hotel experts in the early 1960s (see p. 97). The *Hotel Tirana International* is a modern concrete block, the upper floors having fine views across Skanderbeg Square. It has recently been taken over and refurbished by southern Italian entrepreneurs, with financial assistance from the European Bank for Reconstruction and Development. A single room costs about $70 a night, a double about $125 equivalent. There are money exchange facilities in both hotels. Each hotel also has duty free shops, open to non-residents, with a variety of Albanian handicraft goods, and foreign cigarettes, wine and spirits. Generally speaking, prices are reasonable and the quality of goods is high. Particularly good buys are pipes (Albania is the leading world producer of quality briar), rugs, copperware, filigree silver, jewellery and embroidery. This hotel embodies the ethos of the Italian business community in Albania.

The *Hotel Europark* is an impressive new building on the opposite side of the road from the President's residence. It was built by the Austrian Rogner organisation for the international business market, and is much the most luxurious and expensive hotel in Tirana. A double room with a shower is US $170 a night, $140 for a single room. Suites and apartments are also available, from between US $200–250 a night. There is a swimming pool (guests only), garages and a pleasant restaurant serving international and Middle European cuisine. The design of the restaurant is modelled on the Ardenica Monastery. There are 137 rooms in total, and facilities for business conferences. (General Manager, Mr Reinhard Schmit, Assistant Manager Mr Valentin Prifti). The hotel opened in August 1995. Although it is expensive, and the atmosphere is rather Teutonic in some respects, the staff are cheerful and helpful, and rooms are very well equipped and comfortable. There are some interesting prints of Albania in the public rooms. **Recommended**.

From time to time, pressure on hotel space is considerable, when there are parliamentary elections for example, and many foreign visitors need accommodation. Reservations should be made in advance by fax (*Tirana International Hotel*, telex 2113; *Dajti Hotel*, telex 2148; *Europark* 42459 (tel), 42458 (fax)).

A Kuwait company, MAK, is building a new luxury hotel near the University. It is planned to open in 1997.

If these hotels are full, the *Arberia Hotel*, in the main street behind the *Hotel Tirana International* is an alternative, and there are a number of newly refurbished small guesthouses and hotels beginning to open, as well as the possibility of renting rooms in private houses. Estate agencies are developing in Tirana and the larger cities and can assist with flat rentals for longer term visitors. This is something worth exploring as with many families working abroad in Greece and elsewhere, this is a useful possibility for many vistors.

There is generally a single large hotel in each major provincial centre that was used for foreign visitors on organised tours.In practice, it is often still the only hotel. The standard of these hotels varies from the decent to the squalid. The better among them, such as the hotel overlooking the lake at Kukes used to be, would perhaps rate as about two stars under AA classification in Britain. In all cases these hotels have a coffee bar and restaurant. In many of them there are problems with water supply and the condition of fittings and equipment, and standards of cleanliness are not always high. It is possible, but difficult, to make reservations in advance at provincial hotels. The independent traveller should seek assistance from the Tirana Travel Agency, or other travel agents in Albania, before leaving the capital city. In practice, it is usually possible to obtain accommodation on the spot, when required, as a result of the modest number of tourists visiting Albania in recent years.

It is also now legal for foreign visitors to Albania to stay in rooms let by families. There is as yet no formal mechanism for finding one, and local enquiries are necessary. Conditions are frequently crowded, but charges for a room are modest and if the visitor is serious in his or her interest in the country and preferably has some familiarity with language and customs, a stay can be a rewarding experience.

There are no separate facilities for student or young persons travel in Albania.

Camping
There are at the moment no officially organised camp sites in Albania. Camping developments along the coast south of Durres are being planned.

Food and drink

There has been a dramatic and very welcome improvement in the standard and variety of food available in restaurants and cafés in Tirana and the main towns in the last three years, although problems can still be encountered in more remote and smaller places. In hotels breakfast is a plain small meal, an omelette is often the main hot food on offer, and bread and jam. Lunch and dinner follow fairly traditional Balkan patterns, with a meat dish being served with a 'Greek salad', including a type of feta cheese. Visitors with a knowledge of Turkish cuisine will notice that influence on many dishes. Beer and wine are drunk with meals. Good bottled mineral water is widely available. Maize is eaten in the countryside. Pasta dishes such as macaroni are also common; olives in the south; peppers, tomatoes and other vegetables such as carrots are often made into compotes. Okra is a popular vegetable. Albanian yoghurt, called *kos*, is generally excellent.

A new culture of private restaurants is establishing itself, with pizza bars and cheap Italian-style restaurants being particularly popular, but Chinese, Turkish and French establishments have also been started in Tirana. The new private markets are a good source of fresh salad stuffs and fruit. Grapes, melons and watermelons in Albania are particularly good, and can often be bought for a few lek by the roadside. Albanians are keen vegetable growers and supplies of the common Mediterranean products are improving rapidly in the aftermath of land privatisation. In Ottoman times Albanians were famous for their gardening skills.

An increasing number of imported food products are beginning to make their presence felt in the Albanian market, and kiosks sell good quality wine, brandy and a variety of other goods which can be very useful for picnics.

Wines and spirits

Both the quality and quantity of wine and spirit production have increased considerably in the last two years. Although there is further work to be done before Albanian wines can compete effectively on international markets, reliable quality standards are being achieved and great steps forward made compared to the products available four or five years ago.

Raki is the national drink, a colourless spirit made from grapes, in the lowlands, or plums, in the mountains. It can be very good indeed. Famous areas for raki production are Permet and Skrapar but it is made everywhere in Albania. It is usually very strong, and should be treated with respect. At its best it has a delicate, fragrant bouquet. The Albanian toast is '*Gëzuar!*'. Unlike the Slavonic countries to the north, it is not essential from the etiquette point of view to drain the glass at one go.

Albanian **wines** can also be quite good, although quality varies, with most people preferring the red wines to the white. The Merlot grape is the most common. This is a sector of Albanian agriculture which is already beginning to benefit quickly from privatisation, and there is every reason to expect a steady improvement in quality and consistency as new vinification equipment is installed. *Kallmet* from Shkodra is a quality red wine, while *Shesh i Zi*, and white Reislings, from near Durres, are good drinks for daily quaffing.

The best Albanian brandy is the *Skanderbeu* variety, similar in character to lighter Greek brandies. A type of ouzo is produced in some places in the south, but as in Crete, is not really regarded as a suitable drink for a man who is confident of his masculinity.

Maps

There are very few maps of Albania available, other than sections of atlases which show either the general relief of the country, or only the main roads. Within Albania, the maps of the country that had originally been made under Italian occupation in the late 1930s and subsequently improved upon during the early post-war years were closely controlled by the government until 1990, and the end of the one-party state, to the extent that it was a specific criminal offence for anyone employed by the central cartographic institute to disclose their contents to a foreigner. In the main cities, most main streets were not openly named, in the Hoxha period, in order, in the view of the regime, to make the task of foreign invaders more difficult. Many streets have been renamed in the last two years, for political reasons, although the old names are often still used in speech, especially by older people and supporters of the Socialist party.

The only good maps available within Albania that show the names of the majority of towns and villages and the majority of roads are those printed under the auspices of the Ministry of Transport—*Harta e rrjetit rrugor te republikes se Shqiperise*—which are clear and comprehensive maps to the scale 1:200,000, but they are not on open sale yet and difficult to obtain without assistance from government officials. There are also maps printed in the United States, generally based on the Albanian Transport Ministry models, by the Central Intelligence Agency, and available from their publications offices in Langley, Virginia, USA.

Two good general road maps have appeared on the UK market, the Euromap Albania, published by Geocentre at £5.99, and Bartholomew's Albania, available from Stanfords,14 Long Acre, Covent Garden, London WC2E 9CP, tel. 0171 836 1321.

Visitors with specialised interests in the mining industry should try to obtain the geological maps published by the Ministry of Industry and Minerals, *Harta Gjeologjike e RPS te Shqiperise*, Scale 1:200,000.

Visitors should exercise considerable caution in respect of road quality. Generally speaking, only the main roads in the lowlands can be expected to have asphalt surfaces, and all other roads are very poor indeed. If the Transport Ministry maps can be obtained, the roads marked red can be expected to have metalled surfaces, although often in a very poor state of repair; the yellow marked roads are dirt tracks, although sometimes of a reasonable kind; and the white marked roads should only be attempted by four-wheel drive vehicles during the drier part of the year, or on foot, or by mule or donkey.

A useful map of the Albanian administrative areas is available from the Albanian Mapping Centre, Tirana, on 1:400,000 scale.

A map of the Albanian railway system is published in the UK by Quail Map Company.

Albanian topographical names

Albanian names for geographical features and places are generally composed of the relevant Albanian word, followed by a name, thus Qafa Peje means Peje Pass, Mali i Gramozit are the Grammoz Mountains. The following words may be useful in understanding geographical features, and to help find where places are.

Albanian Indefinite	Definite	Meaning in English
bjeshkë	bjeshka	alpine pasture
breg	bregu	bank or shore
buzë	buza	water's edge
çukë	cuka	peak
fushë	fusha	plain, meadow, clearing
gjî or gjin	gjiu or gjîni	bay
grykë	gryka	gorge
gur	guri	stone or rock
han	hani	inn
hurdhë	hurdha	pool, pond
kolibe	kolibja	hut
katund	katundi	village
kënete	këneta	marsh, lagoon
kodër	kodra	hill
krua	kroji	spring
lak	laku	dale
liqen	liqeni	lake
lum	lumi	river
majë	maja	summit
mal	mali	mountain

pellq	pellgu	marsh, pool
qafë	qafa	pass
shé	sheu	torrent
shkëmb	shkëmbi	cliff
urë	ura	bridge
va	vau	ford
varr	varri	tomb
zall	zalli	shingle

Village names

Albanian village names are often formed from plant and tree names, from saints names and from personal names.

Indefinite	Definite	Meaning	Example
arnê	arnêni	larch	Arrn
bli	blini	lime tree	Blinishti
bre	breu	fir	Bregas
dardhë	dardha	pear	Dardhe
kallam	kallami	reed	Kallmi i Kaliquit
kullumri	kullumrija	sloe	Kulumbria
lajthi	lajthija	hazel	Lejthizë
mollë	molla	apple	Molla e Lurës
qarr	qarri	oak	Qarr
shkozë	shkoza	hornbeam	Shkozanj
shtog	shtogu	elder	Fusha e Shtogut
thanë	thana	dogwood	Quaf e Thanës

In Albanian the ending *-ishte* added to tree names indicates a grove or wood, thus *rrapishte*, a wood of plane trees, *ullishte*, an olive grove. Place names formed from **saints' names** are:

Shëngjin	St John
Shëngjergj	St George
Shënkollë	St Nicholas
Shënmri	St Mary
Shënpal	St Paul
Shtëpenz	St Stephen
Shtoderr	St Theodore

Place names formed from personal names

Christian	Muslim
Lekaj	Ahmet Beu
Markdedaj	Halilaj
Nikaj	Hajdaraj
Vuksanaj	Hoxhaj

Useful words and phrases

Yes	Po
No	Jo
Hello	Tungjatjeta
Goodbye	Mirupafshim
Please	Ju lutem
Good morning	Mirëmëngjes
Thank you	Faleminderit
Good afternoon	Mirëdita
Good evening	Mirëmbrëma
Goodnight	Natën e mirë
Ferry	Traget
What time is it?	Sa është ora?
Where is...?	Ku është...?
taki rank	agjensia e taksive
bus station	stacioni i autobusit
hospital	spitali
doctor	doktori
police station	rajoni i policisë
Which way is the...?	Nga është rruga për në...?
castle	kala
mosque	xhami
church	kishë
museum	muzeum
archaeological site	quendra arkeologjike
Do you speak English?	A flisni anglisht?
Do you understand French/German?	kuptoni frëngjisht/gjermanisht?
I do not understand Albanian.	Unë nuk kuptoj shqip.
How much does it cost?	Sa kushton?
Where is the restaurant?	Ku është restoranti?
What do you have to drink?	Çfarë ka për të pirë?
I would like to drink...	Do të doja të pi...
wine	verë
beer	birrë
raki	raki
water	ujë
What do you have to eat?	Çfarë ka për të ngrënë?
I want some bread, please.	Dua pak bukë, ju lutem.
I want meat	Dua mish
soup	supë
cheese	djathë
salad	sallatë
vegetables	zarzavate
potatoes	patate
eggs	vezë
pasta	makarona
fruit	fruta
apples	mollë
oranges	portokaj
pears	dardha

grapes	rrush
figs	fiq
apricots	kajsi
coffee	kafe
tea	çaj
sugar	sheqer
milk	qumësht
hot chocolate	kakao
white coffee	kafe me qumësht
I don't eat meat/fish	Nuk ha mish/peshk
I need a telephone	Dua të marr në telefon
Which way is the hotel/the restaurant?	Nga është rruga për në hotel/ restorant?
I want to change dollars to lek.	Dua të këmbej dollarë me lek.
How many leks will you give me for one dollar?	Me sa lek e këmben një dollar?
Where is the bank?	Ku është banka?
town	qytet
village	fshat
house	shtëpi
flat	apartament
theatre	teatër
cinema	kinema
opera house	opera
shop	dyqan
today	sot
yesterday	dje
tomorrow	nesër
tonight	sonte
on the left	në të majtë
on the right	në të djathtë
here	këtu
there	atje
I am	Unë jam
You are	Ti je
He/she is	Ai/ ajo është
We are	Ne jemi
You are	Ju jeni
They are	Ata/ato janë
I have	Unë kam
You have	Ti ke
He/she/it has	Ai/ajo ka
We have	Ne kemi
You have	Ju keni
They have	Ata/ato kanë
I want	Unë dua
You want	Ti do
He/she/it wants	Ai/ajo do
We want	Ne duam
You want	Ju doni
They want	Ata/ato duan

What is your telephone number?	Sa e ke numrin e telefonit?
What is your address?	Cila është adresa juaj?
My address in England is...	Adresa ime në Angli është...

Postal and telephone services

Post offices in Albanian cities are open from 08.00 until 20.00, in the larger centres, with earlier closing hours in smaller towns. Postal counters often close about 19.30. Poste restante service is available. The main post office in Tirana is at the side of Skanderbeg Square, in a large unmarked concrete building on the left-hand side of the street opposite the National Bank. The street is not named; if in difficulty, go to the front of the National Bank and ask to be directed to 'Posta'.

The Albanian postal service is slow but reliable within Albania, but difficulties are often encountered with the receipt of foreign mail. It is unwise to post goods or money to Albania from abroad. To post an airmail letter from Albania, ask for 'Recommandé' service. Generally, letters from Albania to the UK take about ten days, although this can vary considerably either way.

Public telephones available in Albania are in the post offices, and in mobile phone wagons in the larger cities. Although it often takes time to make a connection, international calls can be made. It is usually easier to get a line late at night. Calls to Russia, FYROM, Greece and Bulgaria seem to cause most problems. Fax transmission is often unreliable, although there are machines available in some centres; the problems with lines in Albania and Greece may 'scramble' the text. The European Bank for Reconstruction and Development is financing a major expansion of the international network, which should bring a dramatic improvement in service in due course.

The code used for telephoning Albania from the UK is 00 355, Albania to the UK is 00 44.

Newspapers and publications

Foreign newspapers and magazines are beginning to become obtainable in Tirana, on a regular basis, in the *Hotel Dajti* and *Hotel Tirana International*, although they may also be seen occasionally on street stalls and in kiosks. The Albanian press is diverse, with the main newspapers being *Koha Jone* (independent) *Rilindja Demokratike*, supporting the Democratic Party, and *Zeri i Popullit*, supporting the Socialist Party. There are many other newspapers for particular parties and interest groups, including an Islamic newspaper, and newspapers published in the Greek language, by the Greek minority. Some Albanian newspapers are quite widely distributed now in the larger Greek towns and cities.

Privately owned publishing houses are becoming established and a wide variety of books are becoming available. A very few of the old state bookshops still exist but by and large confine themselves to selling non-political publications of a technical and educational character. Albanian television remains closely supervised by the government. The *Albanian Observer* and *Albanian Daily News* are very useful for business visitors.

Albanian language phrase books and dictionaries are widely available in kiosks. The BBC Albanian Service on the radio is seen by most Albanians as a prime source of news and commentary. The Voice of America is also popular.

Night life and relationships

Cinemas, theatres and concert halls have reopened after the very difficult period between 1990 and 1992, when many were closed. Tirana and the larger lowland cities have developed a new cafe society, similar in atmosphere to that of southern Italy, and cafés stay open late, especially in the summer.

In urban areas there has been a considerable relaxation in the moral code since the end of communism, with its ultra-conservative and puritanical ethos. A gay rights group has been formed, and homosexuality is no longer illegal. Popular prejudice against homosexuals is widespread, and discretion is essential. The public parks in Tirana are traditional meeting places.

Young women in Tirana and the lowland cities are much freer than they used to be, although this is not yet the case in many rural areas, particularly in the north and north east. Nonetheless anyone contemplating a close friendship or relationship with an Albanian woman should perhaps bear in mind that her family is likely to take a close interest in developments, and remember that marriage prospects for Albanian girls are still very closely linked to virginity. Women who form close links with Albanian men should be aware of the highly patriarchal nature of many Albanian families.

Time zone

Albanian time is the same as ex-Yugoslavia, one hour ahead of Greenwich Mean Time (GMT).

Public holidays and working hours

The pattern of public holidays is changing at the moment, with the end of the limited number of days off allowed under communism to celebrate particular political anniversaries, and the growing observance of traditional European religious holidays.

Generally speaking, Albanians work a six day week, with government offices opening early in the morning and closing at about 15.00. Saturday is now a working day, having been the weekly day off in the communist period. Sunday was then a working day, as part of the regime's pro-atheism stance.

Christmas and Easter are celebrated, particularly in the relevant areas of the country such as the Catholic region around Shkodra. Ramadan is observed but has little effect on shops or working arrangements.

Shops open from about 09.00 until 21.00, although in midsummer they close in the afternoon for the siesta period, from perhaps 15.00 until 17.30, re-opening until 20.00 or 21.00.

It is customary in Albanian cities to take a *volta* (in Albanian, a *xhiro*) about 18.00, when the streets suddenly fill with people who walk and converse after the end of the siesta period.

Generally speaking, it is best to undertake business in Albania fairly early in the morning, particularly if government officials or ministries are involved.

Festivals

Under the communist regime, the main national cultural festival was the Gjirokastra Folk Festival which took place in September. This was a large event that was held in the citadel in the southern provincial city, which was attended by many international visitors. After a period of transition in its organisation, it took place again very successfully in Berat in 1995. It will be held in the citadel there regularly in the future. An encouraging sign is the new Shkodra folk music festival, which has been mainly organised by Kosovar refugees. Kosova is a vigorous centre of traditional Albanian music at the moment.

Hunting and fishing

Albania has very large areas of forest and mountain land, and a rich variety of wild animals, including deer, wolves, bears, jackals, foxes, wild boar and lynx. In the past, hunting them was essentially the preserve of the politburo and senior communist party leadership, to the extent that quite large areas of forest, such as at Drenova, in Korca province, were set aside for their exclusive use. Large scale breeding of game such as pheasant also took place there. The possession of shotguns or hunting rifles was prohibited for the general population. The government is now attempting to formulate a policy for hunting. In practice shotguns are becoming much more common, and hunting takes place unofficially in many regions. The government lays on bear hunting expeditions for some foreign heads of government.

The visitor is not at the moment allowed to import weapons into Albania, and until the legal position is clearer visitors should not attempt to do so. Albania abounds with mountain streams which offer very good trout fishing. There are also many lakes, particularly in the north, which are well stocked with coarse fish. Fishing equipment is generally not available and visitors should be careful to bring whatever they may require with them. Permits are not required.

Visiting archaeological sites

Over the last four years there have been many changes in the organisation of the Albanian Archaeological Service. As a result it is difficult to generalise about the opening hours and visiting arrangements for archaeological sites. As a rule, Albanian sites fall into four categories. The first is those major sites, like Apollonia, or the citadel at Shkodra, which are open, continuously attended, and where it is only necessary to pay a small fee to visit during normal daytime hours, but where the museum may be wholly or partly closed, either for reasons of security or because of personnel problems. The second is 'open' sites such as the amphitheatre at Durres, where the site may be visited free at any time, but where a particular section, in that case the important early Christian wall decorations, are not generally open. The third group comprises mainly churches and mosques. Under communism, if they were of sufficient cultural importance to survive the anti-religious campaigns unscathed, they were locked up all the time and only open to visitors on organised tours. They are now open, in principle, and may either have been returned to the local community for religious use, as is the case, for instance, some of the early Orthodox churches around Korça, while some of the larger monuments continue as national heritage sites. With the latter, opening arrangements are often uncertain, in a formal sense, but with most of them it is generally possible for the determined visitor to find someone locally who either has the key or knows how to obtain access. The fourth group are the wholly 'open' sites, such as the Illyrian gateway and associated buildings at Lezha, which may be visited freely at any time, without charge.

Illegal excavation is a widespread problem in Albania, particularly at some of the larger Classical sites, such as Apollonia, which have only been partly excavated. The visitor should expect to be offered coins and small artefacts surreptitiously, often by children. Some serious thefts from sites took place in the last four years, such as the Classical bust from Apollonia, and twelve other artefacts, and three heads from Butrint. Happily, both hordes have been recovered, the former in Germany, the latter in Corfu, and in Parga.

There are generally few guidebooks on sale at archaeological sites. The visitor should be aware of the absence of signs, particularly anything indicating the frequent steep drops and other hazards for the unwary. Particular care needs to be taken with large citadels in this respect, such as the castle at Berat, or Rozafat citadel at Shkodra.

A compass and binoculars are useful in many places.

Conservation of historic buildings

In the communist period many historic buildings were lost or damaged. The worst problems were with religous buildings, such as Shkodra cathedral, and the wholesale and indiscriminate destruction of hundreds of smaller churches, *tekkés*, and mosques, but there were also important losses of secular structures, such as large parts of the historic Ottoman buildings in Korca market. Efforts are being made to restore buildings in many places, although often hampered by shortages of resources. A major aid programme from international cultural bodies is urgently needed.

Fauna and flora

With its many remote and unspoilt landscapes, Albania has a remarkable variety of plants and also some of the last refuges of rare mammals and birds that have disappeared from other regions of the Balkans. In both cases, distribution is largely affected by the division of the country into the lowland and highland regions, with climatic conditions that are dominated by Mediterranean and continental influences, in each case.

But as elsewhere, there are many threats to wildlife and the natural environment. In Albania most of these come from two interrelated problems: the drying out of the marsh and coastal swampland that dominated large areas of the country up until the end of the Second World War, and environmentally unsound industrialisation under communism. Although the coastal marshes were very unhealthy from the human point of view, they supported a rich wildlife, some of which has been threatened by land drainage, and where some species, such as the Dalmatian pelican, are virtually extinct. Industrial projects have produced very serious pollution in some places, such as Elbasan, and a variety of less serious environmental problems in others. Although wildlife protection laws were introduced under communism, they were difficult to enforce in remote areas, particularly in many of the mountain districts, where there was little support for the dictates of the regime, and where carrying guns and hunting was a respected tradition.

But the remoteness and underpopulation of many areas, and the large surviving areas of forest, have provided refuges for many birds, plants and animals. The richness and beauty of the countryside and forest has often provided both visitor and inhabitant with some happy distractions from the frequent difficulties of Albanian life. The extensive oak, conifer and beech forests provide a home for the wolf, the fox, the jackal and the ferret, while the higher pine forest contains the brown bear, wolf, the pine marten, two kinds of wild cat, the lynx and the weasel. Those interested in **Albanian mammals** should contact Dr. Ferdinand Bego, Faculty of Natural Science, Tirana University. He estimates there are approximately 400 **wolves** in Albania today. Wolf conservation and study programmes in the Balkans are organised by the Wolf Society of Great Britain, Prospect House, Charlton, Kilmerdon, BA3 5TN.

Roe deer, chamois and wild boar are common in some areas. Albania has no fewer than 14 species of bat, and about 350 native birds. They include migratory and non-migratory species. Residents include crows, sparrows, indigenous duck such as the shoveller duck, two varieties of partridge, pheasants and herons. The most common migratory birds include the nightingale, the stork, swallows, cuckoos, larks, thrushes, geese, pigeons and woodcock. Two rare species of grouse inhabit the dense pine forests on the high mountains. Birds of prey are common in many localities, including eagles, falcons, buzzard, sparrow hawk, and several varieties of owl, including the bearded owl, the horned owl and the little owl.

Albanian reptiles include the water snake, the house snake, the fourline snake, the Montpellier snake and the very poisonous Balkan adder. There are many varieties of toads, frogs, salamanders and lizards, some unique to Albania, as well as two species of tortoise, the common and the Mediterranean, the latter only being found in the south of the country. Scorpions are found in southern Albania. They are not poisonous, but can give a painful bite.

About 260 varieties of **fish** inhabit Albanian waters, with most common varieties of Mediterranean fish being found along the coastline, and trout dominating the mountain streams. Lakes are inhabited by carp, eels and other coarse fish and otters live on the banks in some places. The unique fish of Lake Ochrid are referred to in the text of the Guide.

As a result of the great variety of its relief, soils and climate, Albania is one of the richest areas for **plant life** in the Mediterranean. 3221 different types of plant grow in Albania, divided into two clear groups, those that grow either side of a line running north-south from Shkodra to Leskovik. To the west there is typical Mediterranean flora, making up about 35 per cent of the total of the plant life; to the east there are the plants that grow in the mountainous part of the country. In the country as a whole, there are 489 plants which are characteristic of the Balkan peninsula, about 40 of which are unique to Albania. Most of these are found in the high mountainous zones, and some of them are relics from the glacial and preglacial periods, including the asphodel, *Narthecium scardicum kosan*, the Balkan dioscorea, *Dioscorea balkanica kos*, the wild driada, *Dryas octopetale* and the reticulate willow, *Salix reticulata*.

Oak **forest** makes up about 20 per cent of the forested area of the whole country. In other areas, Mediterranean scrub is dominant, up to altitudes of 800m, with the most characteristic plants the myrtle, tree strawberry, heather and mastic tree, with the warmest south-west coast areas supporting the prickly pear, the laurel, fig, black-bark hornbeam and eucalyptus. Much of the remaining forest is of pine and beech, depending largely on altitude, with the treeline in northern Albania at about 1600m, 1800m in central Albania, and reaching up to 2300m in the most sheltered places in the south, where the Balkan white pine marks the upper limit of growth. Apart from the beech, other common trees in the deciduous parts of the forests include the mountain maple and the white birch. The Macedonian fir is common in the south, while sub-arctic conifers like the black pine are found on the exposed slopes of the northern highlands.

National parks

Since the Second World War, six national parks have been established in Albania, as well as the Botanical Gardens in Tirana. They total about 18,000 hectares of land, in most cases in remote forest areas.

The **Divjaka National Park** lies on the shores of the Adriatic between the mouths of the Shkumbini and Seman rivers, with an area of 1194 hectares. It is primarily a coniferous forest, with the Umbrella Pine (*P. pinea*) and Wild Pine (*P. halepensis Mill*) dominant, although ash, elm, poplar and a dense undergrowth of Mediterranean shrubs also flourish.

The **National Park of Theth** is in the Dinaric Alps at an altitude varying between 610–2750m above sea level, and an area of 2700 hectares. It is mostly beech forest with some conifers, and broad-leaved trees such as ash and hornbeam.

The **Lura National Park** of 1300 hectares is in the Lura Mountains, and consists of black pine, fir and beech. It is notable for its glacial lakes and their rare waterlilies (see Route 14).

The **Dajti National Park**, on the outskirts of Tirana, is particularly interesting for its wild flowers and different climatic zones (see Route 11).

The **Drenova National Park** covers about 1350 hectares of fir and pine forest near Korça, on the slopes of the Morava mountains (see Route 8).

The **Llogara National Park** has an area of 1040 hectares and lies at an altitude of 1000m above sea level, along the top of the cliffs between Vlora and Himara (see Route 6). It consists mainly of black pine with some fir trees.

Etiquette

Albania has its own distinctive traditions of etiquette, and enormous goodwill will be created if the foreign visitor is aware of them. In general they are intimately linked with the concept of hospitality, **Mikpritësi**, the notion of the guest approaching that of the sacred visitor that readers of Homer and Classical literature will be familiar with, but where the guest also has certain clear obligations to the host. While informal patterns of behaviour are gaining ground, particularly in the lowland cities, the old traditions are widely respected in most places, even among the Westernised young.

After fifty years, when it was against the law to invite a foreigner into your own house, Albanians are anxious to meet strangers and to recapture these traditions of hospitality. When entering a traditional house, particularly a Muslim household, it is customary to remove one's shoes, and to slip on one of the numerous pairs of plastic sandals or slippers inside the outer door. The guest will be shown into the main room, and it is customary to wait to be shown where to sit, which will usually be in the corner of the room on the long sofa. In more modern houses, or flats, the guest chair will still usually be in the corner of the room. Cushions will often be provided, and a small mat or rug may be put under the feet. The guest will be offered coffee, a glass of cold water and small dishes of jam or preserved fruit. The coffee should be drunk first, and it is a male tradition that to make a noise in doing so shows appreciation. The water may then be sipped and the jam eaten at leisure.

Tobacco plays an important part in Albanian life. The *Llulla*, or to use the Turkish word, the *Chibuk*, was a very long pipe, often a metre or more long, with its base on small wooden wheels that was passed round after dinner in Ottoman Albania. Albanians nowadays are often heavy smokers and the guest will be offered cigarettes, and unless the guest is a confirmed non-smoker, he or she should accept. **Albanian tobacco** is very good, light, mild and aromatic, and some interesting old Turkish varieties are grown, of exceptional fragrance, such as *Tarabosh*, near Lake Shkodra. It is polite to carry cigarettes to offer to the people you will meet. Western cigarettes are welcome presents, *Camel* being as popular in Albania as *Kent* is in Romania. It is now possible to buy packets of tobacco from street kiosks, usually *Tarabosh*, for those who roll their own cigarettes.

After a few minutes, **raki** is served, in very small glasses. As stated elsewhere, it is not customary to swig it down in one gulp, but to sip it slowly. Now that the guest is relaxed, the family will be introduced, which in Albania may well mean the extended family, the *fis*, or clan, and may comprise a considerable number of people. In traditional households the men will be introduced first, starting with the eldest brothers. If the head of the household's mother is alive, the *gjyshe*, or granny, corresponding to the *yeya* in Greece, will follow in a privileged position, and will sit and watch as the succession of males are brought into the room, ending up with the youngest boys. She may comment to the guest on their particular qualities, activities, or role within the *fis*. The brothers in the family will stay with the guest, but the other males will make temporary appearances only. The women will then follow, in order of age. In Muslim households only the *gjyshe* will stay with the guest, the younger women will withdraw after introduction. The younger girls may not be introduced to the guest at all.

If a meal is involved with the visit, a quite long period of time may elapse while raki is drunk with the hosts. The *gjyshe* will leave the room when this begins. It is customary to toast the health of the host's family. *Jete te Gjate!*—May you have a long life!—is a useful phrase to learn for these circumstances. The meal will be served on numerous small dishes, with cheese, yoghurt and various meats served togther. There will almost certainly be far more food placed before the guest than could possibly be eaten, and nobody expects the guest to try to eat it all. The display is a sign of the host's goodwill and generosity. In response, the guest should make sure that each dish is sampled and appreciation expressed. The men will often eat on their own, the women in another room, and the guest will be seated at the head of the table. He will often be given the only knife, usually a sheath or hunting knife of considerable size, a traditional sign of hospitality, trust, and the absence of violent conflict between the company. It is polite to pass the knife around for everybody's use. The guest should expect very direct enquiries about their religion, finances and political views, and should not be afraid to reciprocate.

If accommodation is offered the guest should accept whatever room is involved, without question, even if it is the host's own bed. Under no circumstances should money be offered to the host unless a simple commercial arrangement for accommodation has been agreed beforehand. It is necessary, though, to show appreciation for hospitality, through gifts. Scotch whisky is coveted throughout Albania, after many years when it was totally unobtainable at any price, and the traveller in Albania should carry a supply for these occasions. Johnny Walker Red Label and Bells are particularly appreciated. Albanian women find considerable difficulty in obtaining good quality soap and cosmetics, and these make very welcome presents for a hostess. Tea and coffee are also much appreciated.

Gestures are important in Albanian social life. As well as the usual handshake, it is normal for men who are friends to greet each other with a light touch, although not a kiss, on either cheek. The famous confusion, where an Albanian shakes his or her head if 'yes' is meant is common. To place the flat of the hand on the chest is to say 'thank you'. To stroke the shoulder lightly means 'good luck'. When walking down the street, it is common for walkers of either sex to link arms.

Dress in Albania is informal, but the traditional love of colour and fine ceremonial clothes is beginning to reassert itself, particularly in more culturally conservative communities, and in the north. Traditional costume is worn for weddings. In Tirana and the lowland cities fashionable Italian clothes are very popular among the successful young business people.

Visitors should bear in mind that most Albanian men always cover their legs, and shorts are not often worn. Albanian women dress modestly and very revealing clothes are not usual. Dress on the beach is the same as in most of Western Europe, with bikinis quite acceptable, but topless and nudist bathing and sunbathing are definitely not practised. That said, there are many remote places in the country where those who wish to enjoy themselves in this respect without causing local offence may do so.

The wearing of the white fez is becoming increasingly common in some areas, particularly by older men, religious Muslims, Kosovars, and strong supporters of Albanian nationalism.

Symbols and the national flag

The Albanian national flag with the black double headed eagle on a dark red background is one of the most ancient flags in Europe. It used to be Skanderbeg's flag, under whose leadership Albania fought heroically against the Turks in the 15C. The symbolism of the bicephalated eagle is that of the religiously divided Albanians, when the Albanians were divided into Christians of the Western Catholic tradition and the Orthodox East. The National Assembly of Vlora which proclaimed Albanian independence on 28 November 1912 approved the flag as a symbol of the Albanian nation. The horizontal open-winged eagle symbolises the lack of submission of the highland Albanians to foreign conquest. The communist regime added a yellow five-pointed star to the flag, which has now been removed. Flags of this period have become collectors' items.

Folk culture

Albania has a very rich folk culture. It was first studied in the 19C, initially mostly by foreign scholars who were interested in linguistics. The ballad of *Doruntina* was the object of a pioneering study by the German poet Burger. In general, there is a marked difference between the northern Gheg and the southern Tosk traditions. In the north songs are usually sung by a single individual, and the dominant pattern is of heroic narrative, on historical themes, usually the struggle against the Turks. In the south music and song are more communal, with songs and poems for several performers, often with a choral element. There are also many different folk dances for each region. In the south dances are often accompanied by polyphonic songs, of great antiquity. Some scholars contend that these Epirote survivals are the nearest linear descendants of the chanted choruses of ancient Greek tragedy. In the commoner dances the performers move in a straight line, although there are other forms of dances in which the performers move in a rectilinear pattern, and with pirouettes.

Albanian music uses a variety of traditional instruments, some of which are unique to the country. The flute is the most common instrument, along with the bagpipes, the drum and the *lahuta*. The *lahuta* is a stringed instrument resembling the medieval and Renaissance lutes of northern Europe and is one of the most ancient instruments still in use in Europe. It was used by the ancient oral poets to call the attention of the audience to their recitations. In the north the *ciftelia* is widely played, a small mandolin with a very long thin neck and two strings.

The Institute of Popular Culture in Tirana has been collecting traditional songs, dances and poetry since the war, and has over a million verses, 40,000 proverbs, and about 10,000 musical recordings. A useful volume for those who do not read Albanian is *Chansonnier Epique Albanais* (Tirana, 1983), which includes many well known popular verses.

By far the most popular organised sport in Albania is football. A league existed before the war, centred on Shkodra, but a marked expansion took place under communism, when two leagues were formed. Every town of any size has a team. The standard is quite high for a small country, and many Albanian players now play abroad in leading teams in Greece and Italy. Basketball and volleyball also have large followings and Albania frequently does well in international competitions. Weightlifting is also popular, cycling and gymnastics. Many sports where Albania has a potentially talented team suffer from lack of training facilities, such as swimming, where the only heated pool of any size in the country is in the far north, at Shkodra.

Backgammon is widely played, and a number of card games. A popular form of street gambling is a type of roulette, where the players bet on which number a small wooden arrow will rest on when it is spun over a paper covered board.

The Albanian language and literature

The Albanian language is one of the least known European languages, with a reputation for difficulty, and obscurity in its process of word formation and grammatical structure. Native speakers call their language *Shqip*, a substitution for the medieval term of *Arbërisht* although this word is still used to describe the Albanian dialect spoken in southern Italy. It is the only survivor of the ancient Indo-European linguistic group usually known as Phrygo-Thracian, or Illyrian. Scholars differ in their views on the exact degree of respective influence from Thracian and Illyrian. A very few words of the ancient language survive in the works of ancient Greek writers, and in early place names and personal names, but there are no written literary remains in any meaningful sense of the word until the second half of the 15C.

The first substantial book in the language that has survived is the *Meshari*, the Litany of Don Gjon Buzuk, that was published in 1555. The only extant copy of this work, preserved in the Vatican library, is written in an archaic form of Gheg Albanian, the northern dialect. It seems that Buzuk was a Catholic priest working in Albania as a missionary, probably in or near *Scutari* (modern Shkodra), and he compiled the work based on an alphabet he invented himself. This was necessary because of the unique consonant sounds of Albanian, not found in other languages. The Albanian alphabet in its modern form was only obtained in 1908, at the Congress of Monastir (Bitola), following a period known in Albanian literary history as the Battle of the Alphabets; until then, Catholic Albanians had tended to use a version of the Latin alphabet, while Orthodox and Muslims usually used Greek letters, with modifications, but many other alphabets were also in use, some with as many as 50 characters. There were also many Albanian works written in the Arabic language.

The 17C saw the publication of Bardhi's Albanian and Latin Dictionary, in 1635, and a number of other works on didactic religious themes. But little in the way of substantial literature emerged from Albania until the beginning of the 19C. The Ottoman occupiers made ruthless attempts to suppress Albanian, with a particular fear of anti-Turkish propaganda developing in Albanian schools, which were forcibly closed, and the teaching of Albanian was made a punishable offence.

There were few centres of printing and publication, given the extreme backwardness of most of the country. The great richness of oral Albanian was not reflected in indigenous literature at all, and only a little more so in the diaspora centres such as Cairo, Belgrade and Constanza. But in the 19C Albanian literature began to develop, with the works of Spiro Dine (1845–1922), whose work *Waves of the Sea*, a mixture of folklore and original narrative, was published in Sofia in 1876. He was followed by Thimi Mitko of Korça, who published a collection of proverbs and folk tales called *The Albanian Bee* in Alexandria in 1878.

The literary movement linked with the wider growth of Albanian national consciousness in the work of Naim H. Frasheri. Born in 1846, he learnt Turkish, Persian and Arabic from a local teacher, and later became censor at the Ottoman Ministry of Education at Istanbul but he continued to write mostly in Albanian and became a champion of Albanian popular education. He was so well thought of in Istanbul that he was allowed to publish a periodical called *Drita* (Light), and to open an Albanian school at Korça. Among Frasheri's works are a long epic poem about Skanderbeg, pastoral poetry, a Universal History and a book about the Bektashi movement.

In the 20C, prominent figures have been Ndre Mjeda (1866–1937), a lyric poet, and Anton Cajupi (1866–1930), who dedicated his best poems to the unity of the Albanians. Fan. S. Noli (1882–1965), as well as being a statesman and publicist, was also a poet of distinction and a translator of Shakespeare. Although a large number of minor figures wrote interesting works in the mid-century, it was not until the work of Ismail Kadare that the voice of the Albanian people found a world audience. His novels such as *The General of the Dead* Army (1964), *Doruntine* (1968) and *Broken April* (1974) explore the dilemmas facing the Albanian people in the aftermath of national liberation and the struggle for a democratic society. Although successful under the communist regime, Kadare became a leading dissident, fleeing the country in December 1990 to live in exile in Paris.

Under communism, after 1952, an administrative decision was made in Tirana that the national literary language would be based on the southern Tosk dialect. This was made on political grounds, linked to the leading role of many Tosks in the communist movement, and was bitterly opposed by some leading literary figures both within the country, and academic Albanologists outside it, such as Professor Max Lambertz of Leipzig University. Gheg continued to be written, but after 1972 no new literary texts were printed in it. At the moment, in pluralist Albania, there are signs of a revival of interest in writing in Gheg, but until the means of publication are restored, in terms of an adequate supply of paper and printing machinery, it is difficult to say how far it will make a comeback as an independent literary dialect. Outside Albania, the language continues to be spoken and written in many centres of the diaspora.

Since 1993, there has been a marked expansion of publication, and a large variety of books are avaialble in Tirana and the other main Albanian cities. A good Tirana bookshop with some books in foreign languages is to be found at the corner of the central park near the rear entrance of the Ministry of Defence.

Publication in the Arberesh-Albanian dialect in Italy has resumed at Potenza, Parigi and in the main Arberesh centre of Consenza.

Religion in Albania

Broadly speaking, Albania has been seen by northern Europeans and Americans as a Muslim country, with about 65 per cent of the population said to follow the Islamic faith, about 10 per cent Catholic, mainly in the north-west around Shkodra, and 20 per cent or so Orthodox, in the autocephalous Albanian Orthodox Church. Some leading figures in the Orthodox church are of Greek origin and have been the subject of controversy, such as Archbishop Anastasios Yanulatos of Tirana.

But these formal divisions conceal many complexities of belief and adherence, and do not reflect either the diversity of faith in the country, or the effect of the persecution of believers and attacks on religous buildings under communism.

During the years of the pro-atheism campaigns, from 1967 to 1976, in particular, attacks on religous institutions and individual believers were conducted with a fanatacism and brutality unequalled in any other country in the communist world, and the results will be with Albanians for many years. Beginning in Durres in 1967, the campaign imitated important aspects of the contemporary Chinese Cultural Revolution, where school children imitating the 'Red Guards' were encouraged to vandalise and damage church and mosque buildings, while the state decreed that all minarets and many churches were to be demolished and the mosques and churches were turned into industrial, agricultural or commercial buildings. Burnings of religious books were common, and destroyed many important libraries and historic texts and manuscripts. Many priests and imams were imprisoned or put to death.

Within the old communities, Albania had its own particular traditions of belief. In particular, the large Bektashi community, formally Muslim but in practice quite independent of the Sunni or Shi'ite communities, was highly influential. It is also difficult to evaluate how far traditional allegiances have survived the 50 years of communist oppression of religion, ten years involving very intense persecution. Some informed observers think that Muslim adherence has dropped substantially, and that the number of active believers is hardly greater than the number of active Christians. In 1967, when the worst persecution started, the country had about 1500 mosques, 200 *masjids* of the Bektashi sect, and about 400 Catholic and Orthodox churches. At present about several hundred mosques are functioning, and rather fewer churches, although numbers are increasing all the time. Some Bektashi *masjids* have reopened.

There was a great increase in **Islamic building** activity in 1993–94 and by the middle of 1995 the mosque has resumed its place as a dominant feature in many parts of the Albanian visual and cultural landscape. Some mosques which were only subject to minor damage under communism have reopened and their minarets have been rebuilt. These are often the smaller mosques in less important towns and villages, which the Hoxhaites did not consider worth total demolition. In some places, such as Koplik and Shkodra, major new mosques have been built by Islamic powers such as Saudi Arabia. Kuwait, Qatar, Abu Dhabi and Egypt have also been active in mosque construction and the revival of Isiam. Turkey has restored a number of historic mosques from the Ottoman period. Islamic missionary groups of a radical, although not always mainstream Shi'ite nature are active in Albania in a few places, mostly from Iran and Egypt. Albanians are studying Islamic theology abroad in many centres, such as Kuwait, Saudi Arabia, Turkey, the Lebanon and Syria, and will in due course return as Imams which should speed the revival of Islam a good deal. In some cases it is likely they will be of a radical persuasion, although historically there has been very little direct Shi'ite influence in Albania.

Although not taking place on the physical scale of the Islamic revival, there have been, and are, a number of important **Christian building** projects in progress such as the restoration of the Roman Catholic Cathedral at Shkoder, the largest in the Balkans, the construction of a very large new Orthodox church at Sarande, and the development of a large number of smaller restoration and construction projects. An Orthodox theological college has been established at Durres.

Much religious literature is printed outside Albania at the moment, although local publication houses are beginning to develop, mostly sponsored by foreign missionaries, as in the past. Hundreds of thousands of copies of the Koran have been donated to Albania by Libya and Saudi Arabia.

The visitor should bear in mind Albanian history when considering Albanian religion, and visiting churches or mosques. Historically, the Albanians have seen religion as a practical matter, on the whole, and have often changed belief as a result of the pressures arising from the turbulent history of the region and various foreign occupations. One of the few remarks of Enver Hoxha, the communist dictator, still in popular parlance is his phrase that 'the true religion of the Albanian is being an Albanian', itself a phrase taken from the 19C nationalist Pashko Vasa.

In antiquity, Christianity spread in Albania along the route of the Egnatian Way, and from the old Roman provinces of Dalmatia and Illyria, and replaced the pantheistic religion of the Illyrian and Epirote tribes. Later the Eastern Christian Church, based on Constantinople, established itself in the south. After the conquest of the Ottoman Turks, many lowland tribes accepted Islam, often after pressure from local *beys* and forced conversions were common, although the mountains tended to stay Christian, particularly in the north.

The **Catholic Church** has maintained a continual presence in Shkodra since the Middle Ages, benefiting from geographical links across the Adriatic, and the proximity of Venetian and Austro-Hungarian cultural influences. But the scope for expansion of the Church has always been limited by the extreme poverty and back-wardness of the northern highland hinterland, and few monasteries or seminaries have ever been established. As a result clerical training before the First World War was a preserve of Habsburg seminaries, and the *malissori*, the highland tribal priests, were actively hostile to the Allies between 1914 and 1918 and were widely accused, with some justification, of encouraging collaboration with the Fascist occupiers after the Italian invasion in 1939. As a result, the Catholic Church was singled out for particularly vigorous persecution under communism, with the cathedral in Shkodra being turned into a volleyball court and many priests were imprisoned or executed. At the moment the Roman Church is attempting to re-establish itself, with the restoration of its buildings a priority. Priests are in very short supply. A notable event in 1991 was the establishment of a branch of Mother Theresa's Sisters of Charity in Tirana. Mother Theresa is an ethnic Albanian from FYROM and has made a strong personal commitment to help the Church revive in Albania. The Pope visited Albania in April 1993.

Orthodox Christians in Albania often come from the south and are Tosks who have been under the influence of aspects of Greek language and culture for a very long time. The recent history of Orthodoxy in Albania is complex, and highly polit-ically controversial, with the Church only becoming fully autocephalous in 1937. Under Ottoman rule, the Patriarch in Constantinople was recognised by the Sultan as political leader of the whole *millet* of Christians following the Greek rite. As the

Balkan countries gained their national liberation from the Ottoman empire, each national church generally received from the Patriarch the *tomos*, a charter of independence. The Albanian church, though, was a minority in a mostly Muslim country, with poor relations between the Catholic and Orthodox believers. The Patriarch was confronted in the mid-1920s by the Albanian leader Fan Noli, who wished to see the Albanian church fully independent. Becoming premier in 1924, he tried to persuade the Patriarch to consecrate Albanians as bishops but failed to do so. As a result, he turned to the Serbian Metropolitan at Pec, in Kosova, who did agree to his wishes. When King Zog assumed power, as a Muslim, he recognised Vissarion, the newly consecrated Bishop of Tirana, as head of the Albanian church. The Patriarch declared the intervention of the Serbian Metropolitan to be null and void, and the issue remained unresolved until 1935 when negotiations reopened with the Patriarch. In 1937 a *tomos* was issued and a Synod elected an Albanian, Kristofor Kissi, as the first primate of an autocephalous church. The primate and many bishops and priests were forced to leave the country after the Italian occupation began in 1939.

Under communism the Orthodox church carried on a clandestine existence, with intermittent persecution in the 1950s and '60s before the full scale onslaught on the church in the early 1970s. Many remarkable buildings were destroyed or damaged in this period, although some icons were hidden successfully and have survived. Old controversies have re-emerged recently, with the Patriarch attempting to appoint ethnic Greeks to be bishops in the summer of 1992, causing a storm of protest in Albania. Many Albanian believers saw the exercise as a Greek attempt to exert control over their reviving church. In some places, as at Ardenica Monastery near Fier, it has been difficult for the Church to recover icons that have been seized by the state under communism.

Central Albania, particularly the lowland areas, is the terrain of the **Muslims**. Most here are formally orthodox **Sunnis**, and the community originates from the days of mass conversions by the Turkish occupiers. Northwards, conversion was on an irregular tribal basis, with an approximate boundary along the Accursed mountains in the north-east, between Gusinje and Shala, as the limit of Muslim influence. The Mirdita tribes remained Christian. In the central lowlands, the Ottoman *beys* broke up the tribal structure and reduced the tribesmen to serfdom. Here mosques are found, in most towns, but in the remoter areas of the countryside they are virtually non-existent.

In southern Albania, and in Tirana, an important strain of Islam is **Bektashi**. This little known sect was founded by a Persian, Haji Bektash Veli, who died in 1338. Its doctrines have something in common with Buddhism and Zoroastrianism, with a substantial philosophical content. The central emphasis is on progressive initiation into closely guarded mysteries, and most conventional Islamic rules are ignored, such as abstention from alcohol, the veiling of women, and the need to turn towards Mecca in prayer. There is a kind of Communion service, with bread, wine, and cheese. Bektashis hold that God is the Divine Spirit of Goodness, the life and soul of everything, which is manifested at different times through different beings, so Christ is revered by Bektashis as a carrier of the Divine Spirit. Bektashis have also taken over elements of paganism, finding God on mountain tops, in streams and in caves. The Teaching of the *Baba*, the Bektashi *hoxha*, takes place in a *tekké*, emphasising tolerance, humility, simplicity and practical kindness, and rejecting conventional Muslim fanaticism.

Bektashism was introduced into Albania from Corfu by *dervish* Sari Sallteku in the late 13C. He founded seven *tekkes*, including one on the mountains above

Kruja, where he was said to have slain a dragon. The sect grew steadily throughout the country, except in the Catholic areas, but at the beginning of the 19C the Sultan attempted to suppress them, particularly as Ali Pasha, the great independent ruler of Epirus, had become secretly converted to the sect. He saw their potential for creating Albanian self-awareness and sponsored the spread of the Bektashi religion in central and northern Albania. Many early leaders of Albanian nationalism were Bektashis. In 1922, an assembly of delegates from the tekkes resolved to break away from the authority of the Supreme Bektash of Ankara (himself an Albanian) and Tirana became the headquarters of the sect. In 1929 it was recognised as being autonomous within the Muslim community, with new statutes being drawn up in Korça. There was substantial Bektashi influence on the government of King Zog, before the Second World War.

Under communism the sect was persecuted and most *Babas* were forced to become agricultural labourers, or fled into exile. *Tekkés* were vandalised. There is a large community of Albanian Bektashis in Detroit, in the United States, which is helping with the restoration of the *tekké* buildings, which is proceeding apace.

With the restoration of freedom of religion in 1990, a large number of **foreign evangelical groups** are active in Albania. Some of them are mainstream Christian evangelists, others hold a variety of highly unconventional views and beliefs. It is too early to tell whether their efforts are bearing any fruit although the historical precedents for this kind of missionary activity are not very promising. It is said that in 1994 there were about 4000 evangelical Protestants in Albanian congregations.

A kiosk specialising in Islamic publications is to be found near the Ottoman Clocktower, in Tirana.

Ethnic minorities in Albania

By far the largest ethnic minority in Albania is **Greek**, with large numbers of **Roma** (Gypsies) and **Vlachs** and '**Macedonians**', and a very small community of **Armenians**. There are also a number of individuals of direct **Turkish** descent. The 400-strong **Jewish** community emigrated en bloc to Israel from Tirana in 1991. The small groups of **Serbs** and **Montenegrans** in the north of the country generally left Albania in the aftermath of communism but many have returned as a result of resettlement difficulties in wartime ex-Yugoslavia and have become much more culturally assertive in 1994-95. The 2000 strong community generally live in and around the village of Vraka, north of Shkodra. An association to defend the interests of this group was formed in May 1995. At various times since the war there have been large numbers of Russians, Chinese and Koreans in Albania, their numbers dependent on the political vagaries of the regime, but there is no evidence to suggest any have stayed on in Albania now.

The **Greek** minority have been in Albania for a very long time, with Greek nationalists claiming direct lineage from antiquity, while Albanians believe the minority are descended from indentured labourers brought in by the Ottoman *beys*. Their number is a highly controversial question, with the Albanian government admitting about 40,000 people, the Greek government claiming at least 100,000, while some irredentist Greek organisations representing *Vorio Epirote* (Northern Epirus) interests claim as many as 200,000.

In contemporary Albania, Greek settlement is concentrated in the region adjoining the Greek border centring on the cities of Saranda and Gjirokastra, in the valley of the Drinos river, with a long chain of Greek villages strung out along the river between the border and Gjirokastra, and the coast of the Albanian Riveria as far north as Vlora. The traditional Greek community in Korça (*Koritsa*) seems to be in decline, although there is a Greek presence in many villages around the city. There are also a substantial number of Greeks in Tirana and other large cities, some of whom held important posts under the communist regime. The last communist defence minister, for instance, Mr Simon Stefani, was of partly Greek origin. Greeks are prominent in the legal and medical professions in Tirana. Some of these people were from communist families who had gone into exile in Albania after the defeat of the Left in the Greek civil war. Some changed their names from Greek into Albanian forms, in order to comply with the political imperatives of the Hoxha regime. The Greek community in the south, as Orthodox believers, suffered greatly under the anti-religious campaigns of the Hoxha regime, particularly in the 1970s. There were also sustained attacks on educational provision in the Greek language and restrictions on Greek language books and publications. It should be noted that these policies were not a communist innovation. Greek language education had been terminated by the mid-1930s under an edict of King Zog.

The Greek community now has been rebuilding its institutions under democracy, and seeking closer cultural and economic links with Greece. The Greek political movement, OMONIA, has members of parliament in Tirana in the Human Rights party. This process has also begun to extend to political links, with demands from some of the leaders of the Greek community for independence from Tirana rule and *enosis*, unity with Greece. The organisations within Greece in the *Vorio Epirot* movement have claimed a large area of Albanian territory for Greece. They are campaigning for the integration into Greece of all land as far north as the Shkumbini river, based on the implementation of the 1914 Protocols of Corfu. These secret agreements between the Powers were revoked by the Ambassadors Conference in 1921 when it was decided to set up a central Albanian state with its capital in Tirana. The Albanian government has made it clear that these Epirote movement demands are tantamount to border revision and would, if acceded to in Athens, mean a war. Some Albanian nationalists in the south have begun campaigning for the return to Albania of what they call *Cameria*, identified as the region of Greek Epirus inhabitated by Muslim Albanians before the Second World War. The visitor to the Greek minority areas of the south should bear in mind the great political sensitivity of these complex matters, although in both Albanian and Greek villages he or she will undoubtedly be welcomed with traditional warmth and hospitality, irrespective of nationality or political views.

There are estimated to be between 50,000 and 100,000 **Vlachs** in Albania, with the largest area of concentration being in the south-eastern mountains in Korça region. The Vlachs speak a language based on Latin, akin to modern Romanian, and most scholars accept their ultimate descent from remnants of the Roman garrisons in the region. They are the pastoralists of the Balkans par excellence, expert at running very large herds of sheep and goats. Their villages are generally found at the heads of valleys, by a good water source. Generally speaking, the Vlachs suffered less from cultural repression under communism than the Greeks, and many elements of their traditional language and culture survive in their mountain fastnesses. An Albanian Vlach association has been formed; Vlachs are beginning to go to Bucharest again to complete their higher education in subjects such as medicine; cultural contacts with Greek Vlachs have resumed; and there are some grounds for optimism about the future. The secretary of the national Vlach Association is Mr Thermistocles Cule, Rruga Conferenza Pezes,

Pallati 225 apt 15, Tirana. Those seeking expert guidance on Vlach matters should contact Dr Tom Winnifrith at Warwick University in the UK, who has been conducting academic research on the Albanian Vlachs for some years.

The number of **Roma** (Gypsies) in Albania is unknown, although most cities have a traditional Gypsy quarter: in Tirana it is near the railway station; in Gjirokastra near the Old Bazaar. The total may amount to as many as 100,000 people, although some estimates are as low as 60,000. In Ottoman times particular trades were the preserve of the Gypsies, certain types of metalwork in particular. Albanian Gypsies fall into two main groups: dark skinned people who appear to be fairly recent immigrants to the country, probably from the large communities in Macedonia, and people of much lighter skin colour, known in Albanian as the *Yevgjet* people, who are more sophisticated culturally, and must have lived in Albanian cities since early Ottoman times, if not before. In their own mythology, they believe they emigrated to Albania from Egypt. Some scholars believe they are descended from Ottoman levies raised in Egypt in Muhammed Ali's time. The Gypsies call the Albanian people the *Gaxhie*. Under communism, although Gypsy cultural traditions were not openly repressed, they suffered various serious forms of discrimination, and there is much to be done, in Albania, as elsewhere, before the Gypsies have a respected place in society.

There are estimated to be about 10,000–15,000 Slav-speaking **'Macedonians'** in Albania, most of them concentrated in villages near Peshkopia, or in the region near Lake Ochrid. The latter is on one of the great ethnic crossroads of the Balkans. The southern group near Ochrid speak a language that is closely related to Bulgarian, and are thought to be descended from immigrants from the east who moved into the area when it was under Bulgarian rule. The Peshkopia villagers speak a language with more Serbian elements, apart from the area near Shishtaveci, where Bulgarian elements predominate. These people are known as the *Gorani*. Some of the early leaders of communism in Albania, such as the disgraced and executed Koci Xoxe, were from this group. They are campaigning for more educational provision in their mother tongue and for more local control over their affairs.

The few hundred **Armenians** in Albania, mostly in Tirana and Vlora, form a fascinating little group. Some are descended from Ottoman administrators, others arrived as refugees after the Turkish genocide in Anatolia during the First World War. They are nearly all professional people, with a preponderance of doctors and dentists, and many were active in the Partisan resistance against the Axis occupation. As a result, although not many were actually communists, they were not treated as badly as some small groups under Hoxha, being partly exempted from the governments 'Albanianisation' campaigns, for instance. In the last two years, teaching of the Armenian language has resumed and cultural resources are being built up again, with particular assistance from the Armenian community in Thessalonika. A cultural association, 'The Armens of Albania', has been formed. The secretary is Mr Harutiun Jahanexhian, Rr M Gjollesha, Pallati 7, Shk.3, Apt 19, Tirana.

The Albanian diaspora

Albanians have always migrated from their mountainous and poor country in search of better prospects abroad. Such information as is available about population movements in antiquity suggests that the Balkan adage that 'the mountains lose their men' was as true then as it has been since.

In more recent historical times, by far the largest settlements of Albanians abroad were in Sicily and southern Italy, and in Greece and Turkey. Large movements of people took place between 1444 and 1468 and, under Ottoman pressure, were added to in the next three centuries. The people concerned were of southern Tosk speaking descent, and have succeeded in maintaining themselves in Italy to this day, although the use of the language appears to be declining in the present generation. In 1910 there were still seven Albanian communes in Sicily, about 50,000 people, and 72 in Italy itself, with a population of 154,000. In 1921, of these, about 80,000 used Albanian as their first language. The writer Norman Douglas gives the best available picture in English of the life and culture of these communities in his book *Old Calabria*.

These settlements had been preceded in the 13C and 14C in Greece, with large groups settling in Attica and the Morea after 1358, and on islands such as Hydra, Spetse and Andros. In the present day villages in Attica such as Fili and Aspropirgos, to the west of Athens, have a strong Albanian presence although the use of the language is dying out. There are also one or two Albanian villages near Florina, in the north, bordering former Yugoslavia. Christian Albanians have fled from Ottoman Albania, and lately from communism, at various times and established themselves in Greece. Albanian sea captains from Hydra played a key role in the Greek War of Independence in the 1820s and many distinguished Greeks since have had Albanian blood in their veins. The English traveller and antiquary Colonel Leake estimated in 1840 that there we re about 200,000 Albanians in Greece. These numbers are likely to have been maintained until the Second World War, although with a declining cultural identity, until a large group, the Muslim *Cams*, of Epirus and the adjacent region stretching south to Arta, were expelled from Greece back to Albania. Albanian villages in the Grammos mountains were destroyed in the Greek civil war and most of their inhabitants never returned after 1949.

During the **Ottoman period**, particularly in the 19C, Albanians rose to many high positions in the Empire, supplying several Grand Viziers to the Sublime Porte. Mehemet Ali, the founder of Egyptian nationalism, was an ethnic Albanian, born in 1769 at Kavalla where his father was an *aga*. He volunteered for service against Napoleon in 1798, and raised an Albanian corps in Egypt, subsequently being elected pasha in 1803 by the sheiks of Cairo. After defeating a British attack in 1807, he massacred the Mamluk corps. He then reduced the Wahabi fanatics of Mecca and Medina in 1816, and founded Khartoum in 1823. In 1831 he invaded Syria and Anatolia and defeated the Turks at Konya. A second attack on the Ottomans followed in 1838. In 1849 he was murdered by his son but his dynasty continued until 1956 and the Nasser revolution.

Perhaps the most famous Albanian of all in Ottoman times was Ali Pasha of Tepelena. The 'Lion of Ioannina' was born in 1741. His father and two brothers were burnt alive by the Turks and his whole life and career were his revenge. After service under the pashas of Berat, Scutari (modern Shkodra) and Ioannina, he took Ioannina by surprise in 1800 and made it his capital. He established a vast realm stretching from Berat in the north, to Arta in Greece in the south, with his own army of 16,000 men. He was recognised as ruler of an independent state by the Powers, such as Britain and France, and established a famous court at Ioannina, visited by Byron, with a vast personal retinue, a harem of hundreds of women and an atmosphere of arbitrary despotism. In 1819 the Sultan attacked him, and in 1821 he surrendered and was assassinated.

Albanians were numerous as provincial governors, and were particularly pre-eminent in the Ottoman army itself, bearing out the famous proverb dating from early Imperial times, 'To the Armenian, the Pen, to the Albanian, the Sword'. The Albanian regiments were famous for their fierce, uncompromising attitude in warfare and the soldiers' ability to put up with extreme physical hardships. Albanian communities were established in many centres of the Ottoman world, in cities such as Cairo, Aleppo and Damascus, and in many cases survive as identifiable communities to the present day. The founder of modern Turkey, Mustafa Kemal, known to the world as Ataturk, was from a Macedonian-based family reputed to have Albanian stock. His mother grew up in southern Albania.

In more recent times, the largest **diaspora** has been in the United States of America. This developed in two quite distinct waves, the first starting in the second half of the 19C, as refugees from the turmoil of declining Ottoman rule, or simply as poor labourers looking for work, which continued on and off until 1939. Numbers then were estimated to be in the region of 60,000, with the major centres in New York, Boston and Detroit. Some important developments in modern Albanian history have been connected with this element of the diaspora, such as the founding of the autocephalous Albanian Orthodox Church by Fan Noli in New York. Many of the early immigrants were Orthodox, and from the Korca region. After the establishment of communism in 1944, many anti-communists went into exile in the United States, swelling Albanian numbers, now estimated to be in the region of 250,000 people. The community has prospered, now being the largest owners of catering establishments in New York City and New Jersey, with Albanian language newspapers and with a growing and influential lobby in Washington. Some émigrés have returned to Albania with the end of the one-party state and have set up joint venture companies with native Albanian interests. There are also substantial numbers of Albanians living in exile in Canada, with many in Toronto, and in Australia, with Melbourne, Sydney and Perth the main centres. Melbourne is also a centre of the Macedonian Albanian diaspora.

Ethnic Albanians from **Kosova** in former Yugoslavia migrated abroad in large numbers as *Gastarbeiters* to Germany and Switzerland in the 1950s, 1960s and 1970s, and there are large and well organised communities in Zurich, Geneva, the Ruhr, Hamburg, Munich and Stuttgart. Albanian mosques are being built in some German cities, such as Hamburg. The Swiss Kosovar community is very numerous, well organised and influental, centred on Basle, Berne and Zurich. A substantial number of Albanians also left Yugoslavia for Turkey after the repression of Kosova political struggles in 1945, adding to the existing communities there. There is a growing and vigorous Kosovar community in London, currently estimated at about 6000 people. Information is available from the Kosova Information Centre, 136 Buckingham Palace Road, London SW1, tel. 0171 730 1050, fax 0171 730 8973 who publish a useful news broadsheet. Kosovar restaurants and clubs are opening.

A **new diaspora** of Albanians has begun in the last four years, with the mass emigration attempts involving the storming of borders and ship highjackings, with about 20,000 people estimated to have reached Italy by these means, and a very large number of migrant workers starting to go to Greece, Italy and elsewhere.

Numbers going to Greece are difficult to estimate, as the Greek police arrest those without visas and return them, and some workers only stay a few months of the summer for seasonal work, but at least 400,000 Albanians are likely to have worked in Greece at some time since December 1990 and the breach of the Greek border with Albania. As many as 50,000 may be resident in Greece at any one time.

It is the policy of the current Albanian government to seek the right for Albanians to work in the prosperous countries of northern Europe as *Gastarbeiters*. It remains to be seen whether this will materialise, given rising unemployment in most Western countries, a reduction in the amount of unskilled work available as a result of technological change, and growing nationalist prejudice against immigrant workers and economic migrants. In 1995 negotiations started with Greece to attempt to regularise the flow of illegal immigration from Albania.

The Kanun of Lek Dukagjini and the Code of Revenge

Albania is known throughout the world as the pre-eminent country of **revenge**, with the **blood feud** a factor in the social life of the many remote mountain communities. The Albanian character is seen as a product of this world, with immense emphasis being put on personal loyalty and bravery, but with a common disregard for the requirements of the state legal system. An awareness of the mechanisms of the blood feud is an important aid to understanding some aspects of Albanian society.

The communists spent a good deal of time and energy in trying to stamp out revenge killings, *Hakmarrje-Akmaria*, as they are known in Albanian. In this, they were following in the footsteps of King Zog pre-war, in his drive to integrate the northern tribes into the modern state. The communists consistently claimed that they had succeeded where King Zog had failed, although much of the evidence does not support these claims, insofar as many revenge issues were concealed under political rhetoric, even in the internal battles within the communist party itself. Perhaps the most well known in the West was the liquidation by Enver Hoxha of his old number two and comrade in arms from the Partisan war, Mehmet Shehu, during a Central Committee meeting in 1981. It should be borne in mind how important the *fis*, or clan, is in Albanian society. In 1962, for instance, of the 52 members of the Albanian Party of Labour central committee, no fewer than 28 were related, and eight were married to each other. It can also be argued that many of the feuds between the different resistance groups during the war, and the subsequent reprisals by the PLA after it took power, had substantial tribal origins. Some aspects of the Partisan's successful guerilla warfare campaign may be connected with the fact that some Partisan leaders, like Myslim Peza, had 'outlaw' backgrounds, and were accustomed to hiding out in the mountains long before the Axis occupation.

A principal target of communist propaganda among the peasants, particularly in the northern highlands, was the **Kanun of Lek Dukagjini**. *Kanun* is a word of Turkish origin, meaning legal code, and many *Kanun* existed in Ottoman times in different regions of the Empire. The *Kanun of Lek Dukagjini*, in popular parlance the **Law of Lek**, is a voluminous compendium of tribal and clan customs passed down largely unchanged since ancient times, and used by the tribal elders to try to regulate the intermittent anarchy of the mountains, and to control the operations of the blood feud. Thus the *Kanun* lays down the circumstances under which it is permissible to kill an enemy, and those where it is not. Many northern villages have an expert in *Kanun* interpretation who can advise the village elders, an assembly of the oldest men akin to the ancient Spartan *gerousia*, on the correct way to interpret ancient customs in contemporary Albanian society.

Little is known of the exact origin of the *Kanun of Lek*. The Dukagjin were leading tribal chiefs in northern Albania, referred to in Vatican documents as early as 1216. The Lek of the *Kanun* is probably Lek Dukagjin the Second, '*Lord of Dagno and Zadrima*', who fought against the Turks. When the invaders took Scutari in 1472, he fled to Italy. He was excommunicated by Pope Paul II in 1464 for his 'unChristian code'. Later Dukagjin chiefs became Muslims. The *Kanun* so promulgated places great emphasis on the need to preserve personal honour and the honour of the *fis*. The only way this could be done was by shedding the blood of the enemy, and in turn that bloodshed had to be avenged. In this way endless cycles of murder developed, with the need to kill being placed on the shoulders of the young males as soon as they came of age, and minor disputes that in other societies might be settled by a fine or period of imprisonment leading to many deaths. The world of the Albanian mountains this century differed little from the world the ancient Greek tragedians depicted, where the rule of law had a tenuous hold, and where blood revenge was the dominant ethos.

Clearly society would soon completely destroy itself if these **revenge cycles** continued without control or interruption, especially in remote communities with small populations, so a key concept derived from the *Kanun* is that of the *Besa*, or sworn truce. A *Besa* can be arranged on any pretext but most commonly arose from a request from the killer, the *Gjaksor*, to the avenging 'Lord of Blood', the *Zot i Gjakut*. If the *Besa* is agreed by the elders of the *fis*, all local quarrels are postponed, and the obligation on the killer to flee to a safe place outside the tribe, and on every house to give him hospitality, is lifted. When a *Besa* is intended to be permanent, it may be reinforced by a blood brotherhood ritual or marriage alliance.

The above procedure applies only to the most serious outbreaks of revenge within the *fis* itself, and where the killing of males is involved. Blood may be taken for killing a woman but the price is small. The only privilege the *Kanun* offers women is freedom of movement while men who are 'in blood' dare not venture out. The only way women can achieve equality with men under the code is to become sworn virgins and adopt male costume and habits. In the same way killing is not punishable under the *Kanun* for revenge for rape or adultery, or where the killer is able to murder his victim on the same day as the offence was committed. Crimes outside the *fis* are treated quite differently, and in many cases offences which are considered to be crimes in Western society, like theft from other tribes, are not really considered to be crimes at all under *Kanun* traditions.

With the end of communism there has been a marked revival of interest in the *Kanun*, particularly in the north. Written editions of the text are widely available in Tirana kiosks. *Fis* experts on *Kanun* interpretation are beginning to re-emerge after years of clandestine existence, and patterns of revenge killings have begun to reappear. A common cause has been conflict over the **privatisation of the land**, where the pre-1944 owners have taken their land back and evicted 'newcomers' to the village who came during the years of the communists' collectivisation campaigns. A much publicised instance occurred in Tirana in February 1992, where a man was beheaded with an axe in a hotel lobby in revenge for a killing his father had committed in a northern village over 40 years before.

A blood feud reconciliation agency has been established in Shkodra in 1994. Academic anthropologists have estimated that there are currently about 2000 blood feuds in progress in Albania, involving as many as 60,000 people. Those with particular interests in this field should contact Ms Antonia Young, of Bradford University South-East Europe Research Unit, in the UK.

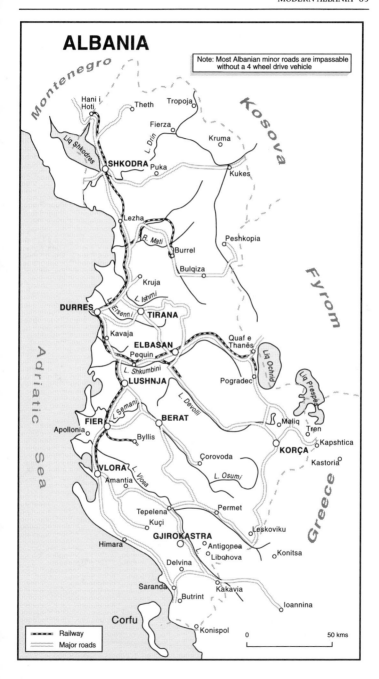

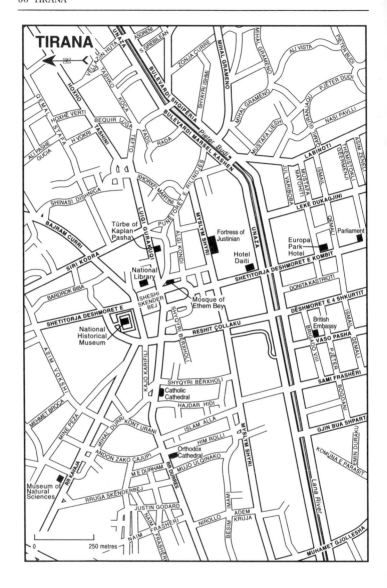

TIRANA

Key labels on map:

UN AZA · VEL · GJIN HUTA · ASDRENI · S GREBILEAN · ZONJA CURRE · MIHAL GRAMENO · MIHAL GRAMENO · ALI VISTA · PJETER BUDI

TASHKO · KOCA · SHAYRI ISHMI · BULEVARDI SHQIPERIA · MUSTAFA LIESHI · PJETER DUDI · GURNAJAQU · NASI PAVLLI

HOXHO · HOXHE VERTI · BEQUIR LIGA · FADIL · BULEVARDI MARSEL KASHEN · Pjeter Budi · LABINOTI · THEMISTOKLI · ASIM ZENELI

O EMAL · STAFA · H VOKRI · TASHINI · TEFTO · RADA · XHORXHI MARTINI · PUNETORET E RILINDJES · MUSTAFA · MATOHITI · JUL VARIBOBA · GEERMENJI

ALI PASHE · GUCIA · SHINASI DISHNICA · MYSLYM SHYRI · ALGI KONDI · UN AZA · LEKE DUKAGJINI · QEMALI · ISMALI

BAJRAM CURRI · LUIGI GURAKUQI · Türbe of Kaplan Pasha · Fortress of Justinian · Europa Park Hotel · Parliament

SIRI KODRA · National Library · Hotel Daiti · SHETITORJA DESHMORET E KOMBIT

BARDOK BIBA · SHESHI SKENDER BEJ · Mosque of Ethem Bey · DONITA KASTRIOTI · DESHMORET E 4 SHKURTIT

SHETITORJA DESHMORET E · SHYQYRI BERXHOLI · RESHIT ÇOLLAKU · British Embassy · ISMALI · VASO PASHA · QEMALI

ASIM VOKSHI · National Historical Museum · KAJO KARIFILI · SAMI FRASHERI · BRIGADO VIII · PJETER · BOGDANI

MEHMET BROCA · SHYQYRI BERXHOLI · Catholic Cathedral · HAJDAR HIDI · GJIN BUA SHPART

MINE PEZA · KONT URANI · ISLAM ALLA · HIM ROLLI · MYSLYM SHYRI · KOMUNA E PARASIT

MIHAL DURRI · ANDON ZAKO ÇAJUPI · Orthodox Cathedral · PAEMIN DURAKU

RR KAVAJA · M E DURHAM · MUJO ULQINAKO · IMAMI · Lana River

Museum of Natural Sciences · RRUGA SKENDERBEJ · JUSTIN GODARD · NAIM FRASHERI · NIROLLO · BESIMI · ADEM KRUJA · MUHAMET GJOLLESHA

0 250 metres

I TIRANA AND ENVIRONS

1 · Central Tirana

From Rinas airport, about 20km, depending on route taken.

Tirana is the capital city of Albania and the centre of a fertile lowland region, with well watered marl and alluvial soil (pop. 206,100 in 1984, now increased by perhaps 200,000 people). It occupies an attractive situation at the foot of the Dajti mountains, at an altitude of 200m above sea level, and is the centre of the cultural and political life of the country. Although the city can be chaotic, not to say turbulent, and life in it is never easy or uncomplicated, either for the inhabitant or the visitor, it has a real charm, often mixed with an engaging eccentricity that soon engenders feelings of great loyalty and affection in most regular visitors. That said, a first encounter with life in Tirana can be something of an ordeal for many Western visitors, who may find the poverty and social deprivation they see in some areas disturbing. In the last three years the city centre has been transformed in atmosphere by motor vehicles and the new commercial culture post-privatisation. Less has changed in the outer areas, where insanitary shanty towns resembling those surrounding Turkish cities are developing.

Tirana has some notable individual buildings in the centre of the city, but has suffered from the vagaries of its history, and does not have the architectural coherence of some of the historic Albanian towns. It was a small place with a population of only about 12,000 people when it became the capital after the First World War, and still has some of the atmosphere of a minor Ottoman provincial city. It was described by Joseph Swire, in the late 1920s, as 'a jumble of crazy mud brick houses, threaded by cobbled alleyways'. Parts of it remain so today.

The orange trees growing in the streets will remind visitors that they are not very far from the Adriatic. Tirana lies at the head of the open lowland basin of the Ishmti river which issues from gorges in Mount Dajti 8km east of the city, and the fertile land has grown wheat, maize, olives and vines since ancient times. In the Turkish period it was a place of many gardens and woods, but most of these disappeared as a result of the Italianate redevelopment of the town during the Zogist period. A substantial Turkish bazaar area had survived, but some of this was destroyed by Zogist redevelopment, and during the battle for Tirana in 1944. The remainder was demolished in redevelopment of the city centre during the communist period.

The city has seen many historic events during the struggle for democracy in recent years, of which perhaps the most dramatic was the demolition of the colossal gilded statue of Enver Hoxha in Skanderbeg Square in 1991. Even in times of political tranquillity, which in the Balkans nowadays are inevitably rather rare, the visitor should expect to find an atmosphere of intense political discussion among many of the people they are likely to meet, irrespective of occupation or background, recalling Swire's observation, 'that when in the Balkans a man talks, he talks politics.'

The new commercial culture of small shops and kiosks has brought many benefits to Tirana, but also some serious difficulties. Traffic conditions are very bad, accidents involving pedestrians are frequent, and the urban environment is beginning

Tirana looking towards Mount Dajti

to suffer serious stress, with a marked increase in air pollution and damage to the parks caused by small commercial developments. Water, sewage and electricity supply problems remain serious, although a new electricity network is under construction and should bring improvements shortly.

The weather in Tirana is generally very pleasant in the spring and autumn, but like other Albanian lowland cities, it can be a torrid and exhausting place in the heat of the summer and a tourist visit is not particularly recommended in late July or August, with the city enduring intense heat, clouds of malevolent insects and frequent water shortages. In spring or autumn it can be very wet, with exceptionally heavy thunderstorms.

■ **Post office**. In a small street adjoining the National Bank at the corner of Skanderbeg Square.

■ **Bank**. The National Bank of Albania in Skanderbeg Square. Various private banks and moneychangers are opening all the time.

■ **Railway station**. The railway station is at the north end of Boulevard Deshmoret e Kombit.

■ **Taxi**. In taxi ranks outside the main hotels.

■ **Long distance coaches**. On the south side of Skanderbeg Square, adjoining the market in second-hand cars. Information and tickets available from a small kiosk by the side of the *Hotel Tirana International*, and from the coach station by the *Dynamo* football ground. Buses to the north and Durres run from the Sports Palace, *Asllan Rusi*.

■ **Restaurants**. There are new restaurants opening all the time in Tirana.

Standards vary widely, and it is best to seek personal recommendations. Establishments which are usually reliable include *Chez Laurent*, Rr. Konferenca e Pezës, *Kinez*, Rr. Konferenca e Pezës 17, *Hotel Dajti, Hotel Europark, Hotel Tirana International, Hotel Diplomat* in Rr. Vasil Shanto, *Kalaja*, Rr. Muslim Shyri, *La Perla*, Rr. K. Kristoforidhi, *Made in Italy*, Rr. Qamil Guranjaku, *Shatri*, Rr. Jeanne d'Arc, *Bushi*, Rr. Budin 6, *Taverna Lasku*, Rr. Qemal Stafa 182, *Arilta*, Rr. Bajram Curri 178, *Shqiponia e Zeze*, Rr. Vildan Luarasi 24, *Petrela*, Rr. Hasset Shijaku 26, *Bemano*, Rr. Emin Duraku 8, *Château de Bois*, Rr. Sami Frasheri, *L'Aigle Noir*, Rr. Sidi Kodra.

■ **Local buses** from park by the railway station and the *Dynamo* football ground.

■ **Car hire**. *Hertz*, 41 Bulevardi Deshmoret e Kombit, tel. 571987, 572005, fax 572088, telex 39509, 39537 or *Twaik Est*, Rr. Durresit, 144, tel & fx 23781. If a vehicle is only needed for a short time, it is much easier and less stressful to hire a taxi and driver. Prices are not especially cheap, but are generally fair and drivers' local knowledge can be indispensible, even for the regular visitor. The rank outside the *Hotel Dajti* has experienced and helpful drivers, on the whole, some of whom speak a little English or German. A price for a days' work can be negotiated. A journey to a border crossing point such as Kakavia will cost about $90 at the moment. **Avoid unofficial taxis**.

■ **Police**. Police Headquarters, tel. (042) 233 22. Police stations, tel. (042) 244 55, (042) 248 17, (042) 245 29, (042) 254 73.

■ **Interpreters**. Interpreters can be found by informal contacts through the offices of the main foreign aid organisations and embassies. The current rate is about $10 a day.

■ **Medical care**. Central Policlinics (out-patients dept.), tel. (042) 222 35; University Medical Centre (operator), tel. (042) 321 21 or 326 31, emergency service, tel. (042) 326 20; Dr Perit-Shroci (internist-cardiologist), tel. (042) 258 10 (home); Dr Vangjel Todi (surgeon), tel. (042) 321 68 (home); Dr Samedin Gjini (oral surgeon), tel. (042) 337 93 (home). The main hospitals of Tirana are located in a large complex adjacent to the military academy in and around Rruga Bajram Curri, on the north-east outskirts of the city.

History

Tirana has been inhabited by tribal people since prehistoric times, as neolithic remains found in the vicinity of the city indicate. The site does not seem to have had any particular importance in Illyrian or Classical times. Although the emperor Justinian built a Byzantine fortress in Tirana in AD 520, restored by Ahmed Pasha Toptani in the 18C, a town to all intents and purposes only came into existence in 1614 when it was founded by a local feudal lord, Süleiman Pasha Mulleti. Before then, the place had only been mentioned as a small village on the plain by the Venetian chronicler Marin Barletius, in 1418, under the name *Plenum Tyrenae*.

In the Middle Ages the region was dominated by nearby Petrela Castle, and there were settlements at Preza, Ndroq and Lalmi, in the vicinity. The name, Tirana, has the same etymological origin as the capital of Iran. The original fortress of Justinian may have been the building referred to by Procopius of

Caesarea called *Tirkan* in the 6C AD. The town founded by Pasha Mulleti was a small Ottoman provincial centre, with a mosque, public baths and a commercial area. It grew fairly rapidly to be an important centre on caravan routes, particularly in the 18C when the Mosque of Ethem Bey was built. Tiranan prospects were adversely affected by the death of Kaplan Pasha in 1816, after which the city fell under the rule of the Toptani family, the period of rule of the mentally deranged megalomaniac Esat Toptani being particularly harmful.

Throughout the 19C it continued as a town of modest size, with little or no industrial development, until it was chosen as the new capital of the country by the Congress of Lushnja in 1920. The first school had been opened in 1901, and a branch of the patriotic organisation *Bashkimi* in 1908. Many important political events took place in Tirana in the inter-war period, such as the assassination, on 20 April 1924, allegedly on King Zog's orders, of the student radical who murdered Esad Pasha Toptani in Paris in 1920. The Tirana Pact was signed in November 1926 between Italy and Albania, ostensibly a treaty of friendship and mutual assistance but in reality an important step leading to the ultimate annexation of the country by Mussolini. On 1 September 1928 King Zog crowned himself King of All Albanians, in Tirana. The city was occupied by the Italian puppet government from 1939–42. After the liberation on 17 October 1944, following the Battle of Tirana between the retreating Axis troops and the Partisans, Enver Hoxha set up the communist dominated Provisional Government on 28 November 1944.

The city grew considerably in size in the communist period, and has become an important industrial centre. Industries established include a brickworks, a meat processing plant, foodstuffs combines and motor vehicle and tractor spare parts factories. In recent years it has become a magnet for displaced country dwellers affected by land privatisation, and emigrants from northern Albania, and the population is currently rising rapidly.

Travellers arriving in Tirana will normally find themselves in or near Skanderbeg Square, the centre of the capital city and the administrative life of the country. Tirana is an easy city to find your way around if itineraries are started from the Square, but often difficult otherwise.

If arriving by air, **Rinas airport** (see also p. 222) is about half an hour's journey by car from the centre of the city. It was established originally as an airstrip in the interwar period, and extended by the Italian occupiers. The first air transport service to Albania had been established by a German company in 1922. On a clear day there are fine views from the aeroplane windows north to Lezha, with its citadel, and across to Kruja, where Skanderbeg's castle can be seen on the mountainside. Below are small fields with the newly privatised plots. The airport at Rinas is small and not used to handling large numbers of passengers, and although the staff are friendly and try to be helpful, conditions can be chaotic. Overbooking on outward flights with some airlines can be a serious problem, and all flights should be confirmed in good time. See section Getting to Albania p. 52. Delays can be prolonged in bad weather. There is usually a small airport bus which takes people into Tirana, and a variety of taxis and private cars are available, although care should be taken in the choice of drivers.

The road leaves the airport, and crosses flat farmland used mainly for fruit growing and arable farming for 3km direct, then turn left by a small war memorial, then joins a minor road running south from Kruja, via Kamza, 6km towards Tirana (16km).

13km ftom Kamza, up a dirt track leading to the east, is the village of **Priska**. Near here, before the war, was the country house of the powerful Toptani bey family, and it was an important centre for the nationalist resistance during the negotiations between the Zogist and Ballist leaders in autumn 1943. Ihsan Toptani, the clan head, kept close relations with the British military missions and left Albania with Abas Kupi at the end of the war.

The **Krrabe mountains** (see p. 111) can be seen on the left, and a plain to the right. On the hillside above the road junction is a ruined late **Byzantine castle**, near the village of Preza. It has associations with Skanderbeg's campaigns against the Ottoman Turks. In winter the snow-covered Krrabe peaks are both dramatic and forbidding, and give the newly arrived visitor an immediate sense of the grandeur and remoteness of much of Albania. On the outskirts of the city are rows of apartment blocks by the side of the road, old factory buildings and agro-complexes. Cars are usually stopped at a routine police check point. On entering Tirana, past factories and apartment blocks, follow the main road through to the centre of the city and Skanderbeg Square.

A. Skanderbeg Square and vicinity

Skanderbeg Square in its present form is entirely a creation of the communist period. It was laid out on the basis of town plans developed between 1952 and 1956. During the Battle of Tirana in the Second World War (1944) between the Partisans and retreating Axis forces, which lasted three weeks, the area in and around the square was particularly hard hit, with losses of historic buildings of major importance, particularly the Mosque of Süleiman Pasha. Before the post-

Central Tirana in 1936, showing the Zogist ministerial buildings

war redevelopment, much of the west side of the square was occupied by the Turkish bazaar quarter. Until 1991 a huge gold-leaf covered statue of Enver Hoxha stood here, something that many people who saw it felt belonged in spirit to the world of the later Roman emperors, when the 'divine' nature of the imperial office-holder was forcibly imposed upon the minds of millions.

Up until 1990, the square was almost free of motor traffic, but this has changed. Traffic is often dangerous in the day, although the quiet of the old days, when the communist regime did not allow private car ownership, can be easily recaptured at night. It is, however, basically a great pedestrian precinct and a place to walk and meet friends, and to assemble for political demonstrations. The days when it was dominated in the early morning by the hissing sound of thousands of bicycle tyres on the paving are over.

On the east side is what used to be called the **Palace of Culture**, which was completed in 1956 to Soviet designs, although the building programme suffered from the break with the Soviet Union and the withdrawal of Soviet technical experts. It is a solid, rather unattractive concrete structure, now in a poor state of repair. It houses a concert hall, at the moment the home of the National Opera, which seats 1100 people, a cinema and other cultural facilities. Tickets are available from a box office open in the mornings on the side of the building nearest the *Hotel Tirana International*. Albania has a fine operatic tradition, with many good, well-trained singers, and you should not be put off a visit by the unattractive exterior of the building. Even in the communist period, Albanian tenors were much in demand in Italian opera houses for their vocal skill, power and range, and were among the first Albanians to be allowed to travel abroad to work.

In the rear part of the building is the **National Library**. This has several hundred thousand books, and offers facilities for members of the public and students to become readers. There is a membership fee of 100 leks. To borrow books, foreigners must pay a deposit of 1000 leks. It was founded with the assistance of the British philanthropist and friend of Albania, Lady Carnarvon, in the 1920s. It was then known as the Herbert Library, after her son (see p. 124), the late Hon. Aubrey Herbert MP. The British Foreign Office made a donation of books in 1934. The entrance is on the side of the building opposite the Mosque of Ethem Bey. Substantial sections of the bookstock are being replaced or reorganised, with the large Marxist–Leninist section having been removed entirely, and sections on disciplines such as economics and history are awaiting similar changes. Donations of books are very welcome. Ask for the Librarian, Ms L. Bubsi.

Further down this street, and to the left, is a small street market, within which is the ****Mosque of Mahmud Dashi**. It is entered by a short tunnel between two one-storey market buildings. On the right is the entrance to a new Islamic school. The mosque is about 100 years old, but has an older atmosphere. The minaret was demolished in 1968, and is due for restoration, the 30-foot-high stump remains by the side of the building.

It is a very attractive mosque, evocative of old Ottoman Tirana and its bazaar, with a three arched portico made of wood, side windows in a poor state of repair, with the very beautiful dark interior in need of restoration, the floor laid with thick carpets. A wooden staircase leads to a fine but rickety women's gallery upstairs. There is a very well proportioned dome, painted pale blue. It was used as a tobacco store under communism. If well restored this could become an outstanding building. It is known as one of the more radical mosques in Tirana with some Egyptian influence evident. A restoration plan is being discussed with the Turkish government. The imam is Mr Hafiz Shaban Saliaj.

There is a bronze bust of the national hero Avni Rustemi (1895–1924) on the roundabout near the market. The impressive late Ottoman house on the far side of the roundabout was the Tirana Gestapo HQ during the Axis occuption, then a communist administrative building. It now houses the city's Islamic organisations.

Next to the Palace of Culture, on the north side of the square, is the **Tirana Hotel International**. It was Albania's first high-rise concrete building, with 324 rooms. It was opened in 1979, and was very much in the atmosphere and arrangements of many East European hotels of the period. It was hitherto something of the 'poor relation', in Tiranan terms, of the *Hotel Dajti*, but offers modern air-conditioned accommodation, restaurants, a bar, a coffee shop and duty-free shops. It was refurbished in 1993/94 by southern Italian entrepreneurs and is now a centre of their new business culture in the city. As elsewhere in Tirana, water shortages and power cuts are sometimes a problem. There are very good views of the city from rooms on the higher floors. The atmosphere is rather impersonal, but the restaurant serves good quality Italian cuisine at a reasonable price.

It is open to non-residents and is a useful place to meet people. It is possible to make international telephone calls and send faxes or telexes from the communications booth in the hotel, behind the central reception. There is an exchange desk in the front hall. The numerous money changers who hang around the entrance will usually offer a few per cent better rate. Taxis can be hired from the parking area opposite the hotel entrance. Also opposite the hotel are a number of newly-established small shops, including one selling particularly well-made traditional musical instruments. In the winter it is possible to go cross country skiing on Mount Dajti from here, ask the desk to telephone Mr Ilir Mati for equipment hire.

Walking 300m to the left of the hotel, you will notice an enormous hole in the ground on the opposite side of the road. This is known in Tiranan slang as *Hadjim's Hole* after the prominent Kosova investor, now in custody in Switzerland, who attempted to build a new hotel here before his arrest. It was intended to be the first Sheraton Hotel in Albania. On the *Hotel Tirana* side is a small side street, Rruga Bardhok Biba. Emigré silversmiths from Kosova are beginning to establish themselves in this area. In the second shop to the left down this street, now a photographic shop, there used to be the pre-war tobacconists where Enver Hoxha worked when he was a clandestine communist organiser in the city. It became a second-hand bookshop, the *Flora*, under communism, but was destroyed during rioting in 1991. About 500m along the next street, on the left, is a large **Ottoman house**, with fine exterior woodwork, that was made into a museum (interior currently closed).

The main street, **Rruga Bajram Curri**, leads north east out of the city. It is worth a short walk along it to see the several large **Ottoman Bey mansions**, town houses of landowners, some in poor condition, but all charming, battered survivors from a bygone era in Albanian life and society. Just before the right turn to Rruga Kater Deshmoreve is a statue of Vojo Kushi (1918–42), a Partisan hero in the Second World War. After 500m, the **Old Medresé** building is situated where the road forks. It may now be returned to Islamic educational use, after being taken over by the state as a hospital administrative building under communism. Opposite it is an attractive part of **old Ottoman Tirana**, with a jumble of alleyways, rickety old buildings, red tiled roofs and trailing vines and fig trees.

NATIONAL HISTORICAL MUSEUM

Returning to the Square, cross the road by the Hotel Tirana to the **National Historical Museum. This museum contains works of art of great importance and should not be missed. It is also exceptionally well laid out and informative, and perusal of the displays will give the uninitiated visitor a sense of the many complexities of Albanian life and history from the earliest times to the present day. At the moment it is undergoing reorganisation, for ideological reasons, and all sections after the year 1924 are closed.

The impressive large mosaic on the façade shows ancient Illyrians, Albanian nationalists, and anti-Axis guerillas fighting for Albanian freedom.

Enter the large hall and turn left. (Admission at the time of writing was 300 lek.)

Turn left across the entrance hall, towards the Ancient History Halls.

Ancient History Halls

This section of the museum includes the earliest cultures which flourished in the territory inhabited by the ancient Illyrians. These cultures mark the beginnings of the history of the Albanian people. Exhibits include flint tools used for hunting and defence during the **Palaeolithic period**, with finds collected from Xare and Shen Maria of Saranda, Dajti, and from the Tren cave (3rd millennium BC) in the Korça district.

The **Neolithic Age** is represented by stone tools, bone, animal horns, terracotta vessels, seals, jewellery, cult objects, and rock paintings.

Among objects from the **Bronze Age** are a two-handled vessel known as the **Illyrian vessel** which dates from the end of the Bronze Age and the birth of the indigenous Illyrian culture. Among the most important finds of the Bronze Age are the 'Adriatic' type of swords with the two main types known as the Dalmatian Albanian and Shkodra swords. The Mycenaean vessels, the Celtic swords and Aegean daggers testify to the exchanges with neighbouring tribes.

At the beginning of the last millennium BC iron tools appeared. A considerable number of Illyrian tombs belonging to the **Iron Age** have been unearthed in the country. At that time the Illyrians inhabited a broad area which stretched as far as the rivers Drava and Sava in the north, Ambakia Bay in the south, the Vardar in the east and the Adriatic and Ionian seas in the west. This period was marked by economic development, which in turn led to increased economic and social differentiation, revealed in extant tomb inventories.

The 6C and 5C BC saw the beginning of the urbanisation process and the emergence of the **Illyrian town** as an economic and commercial centre. While the Illyrian towns were developing as administrative units, the Greek colonies along the south coast of the Adriatic were playing an important role in the relations between the Illyrian world and the Mediterranean world. At that time Illyrians were well-known for their successful agricultural economy. From the period 4C to 1C BC survive models of animals and fruit, and of the God of Abundance, in bronze and stone. Towns which are represented here include Lissus, Shkodra, Dyrrachium, and Apollonia. It was from these towns in the 4C–5C BC that the Illyrian states emerged.

The period after the **Roman invasions** is represented mainly by tomb reliefs and terracotta pots and a rich collection of finds from the excavations of medieval graves.

The Medieval Halls

The Medieval Halls on the second floor include objects from the 13C up to 1830. The section opens with a map displaying the economic and cultural development of the Arberi lands up to the time of the Ottoman invasion. The development of relations between the Arberi, the people of medieval Albania, with other nations, especially the Venetians, are indicated on this map. During this period of economic consolidation, the Arberi nation became firmly established. Exhibited here are trading documents written in Latin.

The rooms also contain material from the castles of Durres, Prizren and Berat. Among paintings on display are the icons 'Three Jerarks' (14C) and 'St George' (15C) as well as the 'Epitaph of Glavenica' (1373) found in Berat. The room also contains stone inscriptions from the 13C kingdom of the Arberesh Progron.

In the next room a map shows the Ottoman invasions up to the end of the 15C. The Albanian uprisings and the Battle of Kosova Plain (1389) are presented in two more maps and are shown as an alliance of the Balkan princes against the Ottomans. The campaign of resistance led by George Kastrioti Skanderbeg occupies the rest of this room, with maps and engravings of the Lezha Summit (1461) which marked the unification of the Albanian people in their struggle against the Turks and the map of the three unsuccessful sieges at Kruja by sultans, Murat II and his heir Mehmet II. Copies of the sword and helmet of Skanderbeg are also on display; the originals are in the arms and armour collection of the Kunsthistorisches Museum in Vienna. Skanderbeg died in 1468. His 28 battles are marked on a map; he was victorious in 25 of them.

At the centre of the hall is a wall-painting by Fatmir Haxhia showing Skanderbeg and his warriors before a battle. Some 1000 works in 21 different languages detailing his foreign relations efforts with other countries can be seen.

The second medieval hall covers the beginning of the 16C up to the beginning of the 19C. After Skanderbeg's death, there was a mass exodus by the Albanian people to the mountains and in emigration to southern Italy and Greece. In the hall is a wall-painting representing the efforts of Albanians to continue their resistance after Skanderbeg's death. Another room is decorated in typical northern Albanian style with many original clothes, utensils and weapons.

In the next room are items from the later Ottoman period (17C–18C). Art and architecture flourished with the building of churches and mosques, and here are the icons of Onufri (16C) and David Selenica (18C), and a collection of silver weapons. The end of the 18C and the beginning of the 19C was marked by the emergence of two *pashliks* in Albania, the Karamehmet Pasha in the north and that of Ali Pasha Tepelena in the south.

Renaissance Hall (1831–1912)

The third floor hall begins with the period of national unification and includes a sculpture of Agim Lokaj, from Prishtina in Kosova. The crafts began to flourish during this period, for example in Prizren at this time there was an annual output of 10,000 weapons. Internal and external trade developed as well. Albanian tradesmen travelled as widely as Egypt, Marseille, London, Madrid and Odessa. Exhibits include photographs, drawings, maps and various crafts. In the right-hand corner of the room, there is a collection of costumes from all regions of Albania. This period also saw a general reawakening of the struggle against the Ottoman Empire, with the founding of the Prizren League of 1878.

During this period the Albanian alphabet was created. Many societies were set up abroad to promote the Albanian language, in Romania, Bulgaria, Istanbul and

Thessaloniki. In a corner of the room is an interesting display devoted to the brothers Frasheri—Abdyl, Sami and Naim—who struggled for the freedom of Albania. There is also a special display for the independence victory of November 1912, with a sculpture of Ismail Qemal, by Odise Paskali.

Independence Hall (1913–24)

This period starts with a display representing the activity of the Vlora government after 28 November 1912.

A section shows photographs, arms and objects belonging to patriots involved in the struggle of the Vlora people against the Italian invasion of 1914, and the Congress of Lushnja.

The efforts of Albanian patriots for the democratisation of the country in 1920–24 are shown in various displays, with photographs of Avni Rustemi, Jani Minga and Luigj Gurakuqi. These efforts were crowned in the revolution of June 1924 led by Fan Noli. However, his government was shortlived. It was crushed by conservative forces under the leadership of Ahmet Zog, who was to rule Albania until 1939, when the country was invaded by fascist Italy.

Contemporary Hall (1925–)

This section was closed for reorganisation at the time of writing. A working party made up of academic experts and members of the different political parties is due to report to the government on new exhibition arrangements.

On the south side of the square is an impressive bronze **equestrian monument of Skanderbeg**, the Albanian national hero who led the resistance against the Turks in the 15C. It was erected in 1968 on the 500th anniversary of Skanderbeg's death, and was designed and made by the sculptors Odhise Paskali, Andrea Mano and Janaq Paco. It stands in a small garden, to the south of which is the group of Italianate **government ministries** built in the 1930s by King Zog after a general plan designed by the Italian architect Armando Brasini. The statue is supported by very large masonry blocks, in imitation of ancient Illyrian walls. The widest selection of Albanian newspapers and magazines is available from street sellers operating on the low walls flanking the garden. The government ministries are charming ochre-painted buildings, and are the best surviving example of the Zogist redevelopment plan for the city. They look particularly attractive in the evening sun, as crowds of Tirana residents take their evening *volta* below and past them.The fascist decorative elements on the façades were removed in 1993.

To the west side of the Skanderbeg statue is the National Bank, an ugly squat modern brick building. The black market money changers congregate in this area. Behind this area is the Teatri i Kukullave, an attractive rambling old inter-war building with two low wings on either side. Plays for young people are performed here. Tickets can be bought in the entrance hall.

The pre-war Parliament building was situated near here. To the east is the *****MOSQUE OF ETHEM BEY**, on the south east corner of the square. This beautiful and elegant building, with its exquisitely proportioned minaret and nearby clocktower, embodies for many visitors the essence of Tirana. It is perhaps the finest example of later Islamic architecture in Albania, best seen across the square early on a bright winter morning with grey lignite smoke surrounding the white tower of the minaret. The latter is very thin and comes to a particularly sharp point. The portico is sheltered by a red tile roof, the dome with black lead. The scene can bring to mind Byron's famous lines about Albania from *Childe Harold's Pilgrimage*:

Land of Albania! Let me bend mine eyes
On thee, thou rugged nurse of savage men!
The cross descends, thy minarets arise,
And the pale crescent sparkles in the glen,
Through many a cypress grove within each city's ken.

The exterior wall paintings of the mosque are of outstanding artistic quality and historic interest, and can be seen from the raised floor of the external portico. They show a fanciful dream world, of ideal cities floating on clear lakes, surrounded by forests of exotic trees and delicate flowers, that has something in common with the imaginative world of the poetry of Coleridge.

The building was constructed between 1794 and 1821, and the art is a product of the self-confidence of the Romantic era of Ali Pasha in Albanian life. The dome was completed by 1807. The construction of the minaret is of architectural interest, being an unusual polygonal shape on a square base. The interior is a compact carpeted prayer room, with a warm and welcoming atmosphere. It was finished by 1820 and renovated in the 1870s. The tombstone of Ethem Bey of Balkis used to stand outside the front entrance. It was removed under communism, and should be replaced shortly. The mosque is very much in use as a place of worship, and to see it on a Friday when large numbers of characterful elderly men wearing white fezes are at prayer is to witness a renewal of the dominant religious traditions of the Ottoman world in Albania.

Behind the Skanderbeg statue is the **Boulevard Shetitorja Deshmoret e Kombit**, one of the main avenues in Tirana, a broad tree-lined street designed, in part, for mass demonstrations. It was originally built by the Italian occupiers for fascist parades in the 1930s when it was known as the *Viale Savoia*. It leads past public buildings to the university at the far end, a large building from the same period but not obtrusive from this distance. It has a lower floor entered through three neo-Romanesque arches, and an oblong façade, above which the hills fringing Tirana can be seen.

Keeping to the left side of the road, you pass part of the **Ministry of the Interior**, behind which was the **Headquarters of the Secret Police**, the *Sigurimi*. The organisation is now known as SHIK, the National Information Service. On the opposite side of the road is the **Ministry of Defence** headquarters. Crossing Rruga Myslym Shyri, a modern building on the left behind an empty statue plinth is the **Museum of Modern Albanian Art**. This houses exhibitions of contemporary paintings, some of which are for sale. Although opening hours are irregular, it is always worth a visit and is a good place to purchase pictures by contemporary artists. It was opened in 1976. The permanent collection is undergoing reorganisation, with the ejection of many socialist realist artists whose work was included on primarily political grounds.

The empty plinth was occupied until the summer of 1991 by a monumental bronze statue of Lenin made by a Russian sculptor called Tomsky. On the opposite side of the street a similar empty plinth used to be seen. This was occupied by a bronze statue of Stalin, made by an Albanian sculptress, Kristina Koljak. It was removed by the authorities earlier in 1991, a year of tumultuous changes in Albania. It was noteworthy as being the last statue of Stalin standing in a public place in Europe, and probably the only one outside his Georgian birthplace, China or North Korea.

Next to the Gallery is the **Hotel Dajti**, a handsome old building and a venerable Tirana institution, attractively situated behind a group of large pine trees. This used to be the best hotel in Tirana, before the renovation of the *Hotel Tirana International*, and the opening of the *Hotel Europark*. It has been host to many famous visitors. It was built by the Italians and was a centre of collaborationist intrigue during the Second World War. Under the one-party state it was generally reserved for foreigners' use, and was notorious for the degree of *Sigurimi* surveillance of visiting politicians, diplomats and journalists. Originally built in the 1930s, it was refurbished under the direction of Soviet hotel experts under communism, and has a large entrance hall, coffee shop, bar, duty-free shop and jewellery shop. It is possible to make international telephone calls and send fax and telex messages from the communications centre at the far end of the entrance hall on the left. At the far right-hand end is a large, attractive dining room with high vaulted windows, a place to reflect on the fact that, if walls could speak, virtually everyone of importance in post-war Albanian history had passed through the room.

In the summer there is a pleasant open terrace where it is possible to dine outside. The rear rooms have good views of the Dajti range. A variety of dealers in old jewellery, books and pictures haunt the entrance hall, and it is a good place for collectors to make contacts, although care is needed and visitors should avoid invitations to view goods or conduct transactions in private houses, especially if that means carrying large quantities of cash.

In general, most visitors to Tirana find the *Dajti* to be an indispensable institution, an oasis of peace and quiet, with old-fashioned courtesy and formality from the staff. It is much cheaper than the *Hotel Tirana International*. The bar of the *Dajti* used to have a truly Balkan atmosphere, where a motley variety of Albanians and foreign visitors met and discussed politics and business in clouds of tobacco smoke and drank tiny glasses of raki, but much of this attractive world has gone with the advent of so many new cafés.

Opposite the *Dajti* is a main **public park**, an attractive green lung in the middle of the city. It is being overtaken by numerous cafés and kiosks, some with poor sanitary arrangements and the park is deteriorating, with many trees and shrubs in poor condition. Planning control of new development is urgently required. It was suspected of being the site of one of the hidden cemeteries of British soldiers who died in Albania in the last war, and excavations were made here in the summer of 1992, although the results were inconclusive.

N.B. The park should be avoided at night.

Walking down the street, you cross the canalised river Lana that rises on Mount Dajti. It is heavily polluted, avoid contact with the water. On the left is a dramatic modern structure, the old **Enver Hoxha Memorial**. It was opened in 1988, on the 80th anniversary of Enver Hoxha's birth, and was designed by his architect daughter, Pranvera. It has been compared to a concrete flying saucer that has landed in the middle of Tirana, and is a striking example of Albanian modernist architecture. Before February 1991, it contained more or less everything that Hoxha ever touched or used, and in the centre was a sitting marble statue of Hoxha by Kristaq Rama. In some respects, it resembled an embryo, hidden within a strange concrete womb. An illuminated star was mounted on the top of the exterior, from which light rays were projected down the side of the building. It was, in its way, one of the weirdest museums in the world. All the Hoxha exhibits have now been removed and the building has been turned into a no doubt more useful but also rather mundane international trade and conference centre. It is to be hoped that there will be a selective reassessment of the future of some of the old exhibits, as many of them cast interesting light on the recent history of Albania, and on the anti-Axis during the war. Part of the ground floor has been taken over by the Soros Foundation as a computer training centre. There is a good café in the lower ground floor—through the north entrance, then down steps to the lower ground floor.

Opposite the memorial, if you follow the riverside walk for about a kilometre, you come to the old 'Albania Today' exhibition hall, which for a time in 1991-93 housed the Museum of Popular Culture. It has now been taken over by commercial interests, and is the **Albanian Centre for Foreign Investment Promotion**. There is a very large open street market in the park nearby.

Returning to the main street, beyond the *Hotel Europark*, you come to the **Parliament Building**, an attractive modern building where the legislature meets. The pre-war Parliament occupied a site near the National Bank building. In the public park on the south side, there is a memorial to the first Tirana mosque, Al-Fozan, constructed there in 1414. It has Arabic and Albanian inscriptions, and was unveiled in 1993. Cross the road here to the other side of Boulevard Shetitorja Deshmoret a Kombit, and behind high railings is the **Presidential Palace**, a three-storey building of nondescript appearance. The side road by the palace leads to the '**Block**' area, that until 1991 was a closed, heavily guarded residential area for party leaders and members of the Politburo. It is worth a short detour to see the protected, rather suburban circumstances in which the communist leaders lived. About 150m down the road on the right was **Enver Hoxha's house**, a square modern three-storey building with a pleasant garden. Almost exactly opposite, on the left-hand side, was **Mehmet Shehu's house**. Both have now been taken over for public service use.

Enver Hoxha

Enver Hoxha was born in Gjirokastra on 16 October 1908 to a Muslim family living in fairly comfortable circumstances. He was educated at French lycées in the city and in Korça between 1924 and 1930. In the early 1930s he studied biology at the University of Montpellier in France, and then moved to Paris, where he joined the French Communist Party in 1935. He returned to Albania the following year and took up a teaching post at Korça lycée, and in 1937 took part in the foundation of an underground communist organisation there. During the war he played a prominent part in the foundation of the partisan resistance movement, and entered as head of the National Liberation Front in Tirana in the autumn of 1944. In 1945 Hoxha married his girlfriend, Nexhmije Xhangolli, also an active partisan, who came from a Muslim family in Diber. They had three children, Ilir, born in 1948, Sokol, born in 1951 and Pranvera, born in 1954.

He did not win undisputed leadership of the Albanian Party of Labour, as the communist party was known, until the culmination of the Tito–Stalin split in 1948–49, when he organised the liquidation of rival Koci Xoxe, but afterwards never lost authority until his death in 1985, although in later years he suffered from a crippling illness. He was buried in the Martyrs' Cemetery in Tirana until 1992 when his body was removed and reburied in Tirana cemetery. In Tirana slang nowadays he is known as *Dulla*, the Ugly One, while his wife is called *Sorra*, the Crow. She was sentenced to a period of imprisonment in 1993 on corruption charges.

Mehmet Shehu

Mehmet Shehu (1913–81) was the commandant of the Partisan resistance in the national liberation war. He was the son of a Muslim sheik (priest), from Mallakaster, and attended military schools in Italy before becoming a communist and fighting with distinction in the Garibaldi batallion of the International Brigade in the Spanish Civil War. In the Second World War he became commander of the First Partisan Brigade, based at Vithkuq. After the war he was army chief of staff, secretary of the party central committee and, after 1954, Prime Minister. He played an important part in the split with the Soviet Union, warning pro-Soviet elements at the Fourth Party Congress in February 1961 that 'those who attempt to disrupt unity will receive, if necessary, a bullet in the head'. He died in mysterious circumstances in 1981, with serious claims being made that he was shot by Enver Hoxha himself during a politburo meeting. He was at first buried in the Martyrs' Cemetery, but his body was quickly removed and its present whereabouts is unknown. He is generally regarded as a man of very high military abilities, many of whose achievements were appropriated by Enver Hoxha as part of the cult of personality.

Return to the boulevard by the same route, then walk back up towards the square. In a small garden to the left are **bronze statues of the Frasheri brothers** (see p. 197), founders of Albanian nationalism. The next large building, on the corner of Rruga Ismail Quemali, used to be the Party of Labour Central committee building but has now been taken over by the Finance Ministry. Then there are more gardens, and the Ministry of Defence. Return to Skanderbeg Square past the statue of Skanderbeg.

B. South Tirana

This part of the city contains an attractive large park, the University, the National Archaeological Museum, the old Palace of the Brigades, the Martyrs' Cemetery and the Residence of the President. Exploration of it can be done on foot, by taking a short taxi ride from central Tirana to the Martyrs' Cemetery, and then walking back into the city; but this walk is more secure if a companion is present, and in daytime.

The taxi will follow Rruga Labinoti out of the city, in the general direction of Elbasan. On the left you pass the grandiose Italian Renaissance-style building in large gardens that used to be the **Italian Embassy** but has now become the **American Embassy**. About 300m further down the road on the left, a new **Italian Embassy** has been built, an attractive white neo-classical structure, with Ionic columns. Down a small road to the right is the **Romanian Embassy**. After passing the university on the left, the road goes up a hill through woods, and the Martyrs' Cemetery is reached by a left turn into parkland. On the right-hand side of the road is the **Residence of the President**, a large building originally built for King Zog although extended under communism (not open to the public). Behind it, at the edge of farmland, are various military and police buildings.

The **Martyrs' Cemetery** is worth a visit, as it shows the high cost of the war for Albania, with hundreds of graves of partisan heroes stretching down the hillside; and there is a very good view of Tirana to the north, where its central position on the fertile plain below Mount Dajti can be appreciated. The communist leaders' remains have now been removed from honoured positions, in the central section. The cemetery is dominated by the enormous standing figure of '**Mother Albania**', holding an uplifted Torch of Freedom, in the socialist realist style, although not a bad example of the genre.

Walking down the hill from the cemetery, you go through pleasant woodland; on the left is the **Palace of the Brigades**, with the headquarters of the senior military command. You then turn left through the wood into a very large **public park**, planted with shrubs and deciduous trees. Pre-war, important embassies were here, such as those of Greece and Germany. In the centre of the park is the newly-erected monument to the 43 British soldiers who died in Albania during the Second World War, the tomb of the Frasheri brothers, memorials commemorating partisan battles in the war and a number of sculptures of varying quality. The great Albanian nationalist Faik Konica was recently reinterred here. The atmosphere is pleasant and usually free of the air pollution that can sometimes be a problem in central Tirana. Elderly men playing cards often sit on the wooden benches and tables. On the south side of the park is **Tirana Lake**, with pleasant views across to the wooded hillside on the far bank. On the far side of the lake, down a slope towards Rruga Frong Bardhi, is **Tirana Zoo**, a modest little institution that was more or less empty at the time of writing, apart from a wolf, a fox and an eagle. To the west is a military barracks occupied by part of the Tirana garrison.

Follow the slope of the park to the east and you come down to the main road opposite the **university**. Until 1957, Albania was the only country in Europe without a university. When it was established, eight faculties were set up, teaching 68 different disciplines. There are about 8000 students at the moment, drawn from all over the country and from Kosova. Students from the university played a prominent role in the demolition of the one-party state and its institutions, particularly in the winter of 1990–91. Next to the university is the National Archaeological Museum, beyond which is the **Qemal Stafa Stadium**. It was built in the 1950s and enlarged in 1971, and can accommodate over 20,000 spectators. It is mostly used for athletics and soccer matches. Qemal Stafa (1920–42) was a resistance hero and communist leader.

NATIONAL ARCHAEOLOGICAL MUSEUM

The **National Archaeological Museum, has a collection of about 1800 objects excavated from different sites in Albania. The visitor with only a general interest in prehistory and the ancient world may find the excellent exhibits from these periods in the National Historical Museum in Skanderbeg Square sufficient for their needs, particularly as that museum contains what are generally accepted to be the finest ancient works of art discovered in Albania, such as the 'Goddess of Butrint'. But there is much of interest here, and it is well worth a visit (opening times 10.00-16.00 daily). The museum is mainly notable for the richness of its Illyrian collection, which is the largest in the world. Much of it has been unearthed in excavations organised since the war at sites such as Zgërdhesh, Hollm, Rrips and Gajtan.

The layout and lighting of this museum has much improved recently. Enter through a glass door in the main entrance hall, to Room I, past a bookstall and souvenir shop on the left. Publication of *Illyria*, and other journals has now resumed. On the right are a number of examples of Byzantine stone carvings on columns, and a 2C AD **statue of lion**, from Apollonia.

Room I contains material from the New Stone Age in Albania, flints, ceramics bone needles and other items from Cakran and Dunavec. Other cases display material from the New Stone Age from Kamnik and Maliq, including the first human images found in Albania, small carved female deities, and carved deer antlers.

Room II is devoted to the Bronze Age, **case I**, ceramics and weapons from Cinemak and Pazhok, **case II**, the Iron Age with material, mainly swords, daggers, a tripod, spear heads and other weapons, from Kuçi i Zi, Barc, Rapcke.

Turn left to cross **Room III,** with material from Amantia, showing growing Greek influences, with ceramics, small cult objects, silver coins and jewellery, and terracotta figures. From Byllis and Apollonia there is similar material, but with a higher standard of workmanship and technology.

Return to the main corridor and proceed to the **Main Display Hall**, with works from the Classical period from Butrint, Antigonea, Selca and Zgërdhesh. There are stone carvings, ceramics, weapons, a very large **3C *pithos** from Apollonia, Hellenistic sculpture from Apollonia, a ***bust of the Emperor Hadrian** and of the Emperor Marcus Aurelius, and of Emperor Caracalla, all from Apollonia. There is a very fine case of Hellenistic material from Amantia, small marbles, glass and weapons, sickles, a colossal foot and toes. On the east wall are four marble statues from Apollonia, a **statue of a young man**, 2C from Apollonia, tombstones with Greek inscriptions, and amphorae.

Returning towards the entrance there are four cases of medieval exhibits, from the Arberesh, Koman and Byzantine periods, with good examples of jewellery from Pishkove, Berat, Rehove, Symize, Pogradec and Kanina.

Return to Skanderbeg Square along the main boulevard from the university central administration building.

C. North Tirana

In general, the area north of Skanderbeg Square does not have very much to interest the foreign visitor. From the square, walking north along what used to be called *Boulevard Stalin*, in Italian times *Corso Vittorio Emanuele III*, on the left is an open area behind the National Historical Museum that has become the main second-hand car market in the city, a business that is dominated by refugees from Kosova with Swiss connections. Second-hand cars are obtained in Switzerland, imported and then resold in Tirana. On the far side are two newly-opened souvenir shops and galleries of art and craft works, which give a welcome opportunity to purchase local artefacts, and are well worth a visit. The central Swissair office has recently moved to this street. The kiosk selling long distance bus tickets is passed on the right, near the *Hotel Tirana International*. Before the war a large Orthodox church used to stand here. West of it was part of the Turkish bazaar. About 200m along on the right is the Journalists Club, then some distance further the head-quarters of the Republican Party and after another 500m, the Maternity Hospital. On the opposite side is the offices of *Zeri i Popullit* newspaper, then the *Arberia Hotel*, the best of the second-class hotels in the city, with a pleasant café on the ground floor, then various scientific institutes and university laboratories.

The road ends with the entrance to the main station. The street to the left, facing the station, is called Rruga Mine Peza and leads towards the prison, down a side street to the right, the headquarters of the Social Democratic Party, the building housing the **National Archive** (director Mr Luan Maltesi), the Gypsy Quarter and the Partizani sports stadium, then joins the main road to Durres out of the city. The first French restaurant in Tirana, *L'Aigle Noir*, is situated near Siri Kodra Street, by the prison.

To the right, facing the station, is Rruga Reshit Petrela, which leads towards an industrial area, and the hospital complexes, about 2km further on in Rruga Bajram Curri, and the Military Academy. Joining Rruga Alexander Moissi, named after an internationally famous 19C Albanian actor, it leaves Tirana to Mount Dajti (see p. 109).

N.B. Security in this part of the city is not very good and care is needed. Journeys at night are not particularly recommended.

D. West Tirana

This part of the city contains some attractive Ottoman streets and individual build-ings, the Diplomatic Quarter, and the Orthodox and Catholic cathedrals. There are also an increasing number of small shops selling useful goods, fresh fruit and vegetables in particular. Some airlines operating from Rinas airport have offices in this district.

Leaving Skanderbeg Square, on the right-hand corner of the square and the Rruga Conferenca e Pezes is a small shop on the corner selling interesting textiles and traditional musical instruments. Pre-war this street was known as *Via Mussolini*. About another 50m along are the offices of Adria Air, then Malev, the Hungarian airline. A small shop selling interesting ceramics is opposite the Malev office. An American Express office is under construction on the opposite side of the road, beyond which is the office of Balkan, the Bulgarian airline. Continue down the street, past some impressive Ottoman houses. A very fine tall ochre-painted *Italianate building of the Zogist period can be seen behind the low houses to the right, with an interesting double-doored entrance and fine balconies. Next on the left, by the junction with Rruga Mujo Ulqinaku, is the **Catholic Cathedral**. It was originally dedicated to St Cuore, and was a Jesuit foundation. In the interwar period Jesuit influence was dominant over Albanian Catholicism for a time. This is a large, unattractive inter-war building that suffered considerable damage during the anti-religious campaigns in the communist period, when it was turned into a cinema. It is beginning to be restored but there is much to be done. It was reconsecrated by the Pope in April 1993. Opposite the cathedral is a small **mosque**; it was built in 1932–34, with a pleasant light and airy interior. It is one of the Tirana mosques that has fallen under the influence of more radical Muslims. In the small side street by it, the Rruga Kont Urani, is the **Residence of the British Ambassador**. The interesting old building near the end of the street with neo-classical balconies used to be the headquarters of Tirana radio.

About another 150m along the street, down a small alley on the left, is the **Orthodox Cathedral of the Holy Evangelist**, a large fairly modern church that was restorated in 1992/94. It was only completed in 1964 to be closed down in February 1967 in the period of persecution of religion. It replaced the old Orthodox Cathedral that used to stand behind the *Tirana Hotel*, which was totally destroyed in the war. It has a pleasant, airy whitewashed interior and a very welcoming atmosphere. There are two fine icons by the altar, of the Virgin and St Nicholas. The Orthodox Archbishop is his Holiness Anastasios Yannulatos (tel. 34117). His residence is in the lower diplomatic quarter.

About a 400m further down the street on the right, is the **Museum of Natural Sciences** (open Mon, Wed and Fri between 09.00–14.00; admission free). It was established in 1948, and since 1957 has been a scientific institute within the University of Tirana. It is divided into three sections, covering botany, zoology and geology, the latter with particular reference to the Albanian mining industry. At the time of writing the botany section is awaiting reorganisation.

In the **botany hall** there are 12 exhibition cases showing segments of dried plants from the main Albanian regions. The most interesting section from the point of view of the foreign visitor is that devoted to medicinal plants of which Albania has an outstanding range and number—over 300—and has led to the country becoming the largest exporter of medicinal plants outside the tropical countries. The flora exhibits show examples of the 3200 species indigenous to Albania, and the 32 unique species, such as *Wulfenica baldacci, Forsythia europea, Aster albanica* and *Discorea albanica*.

The **zoology section** is divided between seven rooms, the first two showing invertebrates, the remainder vertebrates. **Room I** displays aquatic invertebrates, including sponges, parasitic worms and molluscs, including an exhibit showing the 26 varieties found in Lake Ochrid, gastropods, snails, oysters, cockles, cuttle fish and octopus.

Room II shows crabs, insects, spiders, grasshoppers, cockroaches, dragon flies, crickets, earwigs, plant fleas, aphids and vine lice, beetles, bees, butterflies, flies, and echinodermes. **Room III** is devoted to fish, **Room IV** to amphibians and reptiles, including the unique varieties of toad found in Albania. **Rooms V and VI** are occupied by birds. The most interesting part is on Albanian birds of prey. **Room VII** displays stuffed examples of mammals found in Albania, such as the mole, bat, fox, otter, wild goat, deer, wild cat, **wolf**, wild boar.

In each zoology room there is a map showing the distribution of particular species in Albania.

The **geology section** displays examples of the many minerals found in Albania, and exhibits illustrating the development of the mining and extractive industries.

Further down the street to the right is the Mehmet Akif College, a Turkish educational institution.

Crossing back to the left-hand side, there is a small shop that sells folk costumes, then, at the junction with Rruga Skenderbeu, the **Diplomatic Quarter**. It used to be necessary to have a foreign passport to be admitted to this street by the police control at either end, following the rioting in July 1991 when a number of embassies were seized by thousands of Albanians wishing to leave the country. The German Embassy, in particular, was ransacked and had to be rebuilt afterwards. Walking down the street on the right-hand side, the **Greek Embassy** is on the left, followed by the **Egyptian** and **German Embassies**. On the right is an apartment block used by embassy staff, then the **Czech Embassy**, **Bulgarian Embassy** and the **French Embassy**. It used to be known as the *Via Frasheri*.

The far end of this street meets the Rruga Kongressi i Permetit. On the opposite side about 100m to the right is the *Yugoslav Embassy, one of the finest late-Ottoman public buildings in Tirana, with rows of arches of different sizes and a pattern of extravagant decoration on the ochre-painted walls. Turn right here and follow the street back towards Skanderbeg Square. On the right, after about 400m, are the Law Courts and the Public Prosecutor's Office, then the **Vatican Embassy**, a late Ottoman house with a remarkable, theatrical frontage.

E. East Tirana

This area contains some notable monuments and historic buildings, most of which can easily be reached on foot from Skanderbeg Square, and also the main open air food market. Walking past the Mosque of Ethem Bey, on the right, and the entrance to the National Library on the left, on the immediate right is the *Clock tower, an attractive Turkish building. It was built in 1830 and is a landmark in the city. It was restored in 1993. About a 100m further on, in the middle of the pavement, is the *Türbe of Kaplan Pasha, an early 19C Ottoman tomb, circular, with its roofless structure supported by elegant columns. It is badly in need of restoration and protection from traffic. Under the empire, much of the town of Tirana spread in this direction, away from the mosque and the Old Bazaar area. On the right is a small park and children's playground that was a well-known gathering point for dissidents to meet foreigners under the one-party state. To the rear of the park are various government buildings. Much of the land in the vicinity was owned by the Toptani family.

Facing you at the road junction is a large bronze statue, the 'Partisan' monument which commemorates the 127 partisans who died in the struggle to liberate the capital in autumn 1944.

The Battle of Tirana

The Battle of Tirana was fought between 15 September 1944, when the First Partisan Brigade received the order to march on the capital, and 17 November of that year, when the last phase of the battle was concluded. In the preparatory phase, between 25 September and 29 October, the 3rd, 4th and 5th Brigades left bases in Dibra, Krrabe and elsewhere and began systematic attacks on enemy communications and supply lines. On 10 October formations from the 1st and 4th Brigades moved into the capital and attacked the German headquarters in the Medrese building, killing a number of officers and also setting fire to various installations elsewhere in the city. At this time the partisans faced a German garrison of about 2500 troops in the city, based in King Zog's Palace, the central Post Office, the National Bank and the Tomorri cinema. The 1st and 4th Brigades were then reinforced by the newly-formed 23rd Brigade, in the capital.

The main phase of the battle began on 29 October and lasted 19 days. In bitter house-to-house fighting the Axis troops were gradually cleared from Tirana, after an initial assault from the 1st Brigade coming from the direction of the Elbasan road. Local people constructed barricades to protect the soldiers, and suffered very heavy casualties, substantially higher than the partisan troops themselves. Particularly bitter fighting took place in the Old Bazaar area, which was more or less destroyed.

In the second phase of the battle German aircraft bombed the city on 7 November and partisan reinforcements engaged German troops in a wider area, including areas on the periphery of Tirana and outside it. German forces were reinforced by troops evacuated from Greece in the later stages of the battle. The city was liberated in the morning of 17 November. A victory parade was held on 29 November 1944. An account of the battle is to be found in *La Bataille pour le liberation de Tirana* by the commander of the 1st Brigade, Mehmet Shehu.

Turning right here, follow the street down with the public gardens on the right-hand side and shops on the left. The Mosque of Süleiman Pasha, constructed in 1614 and totally destroyed in the last war, stood near here. It was also known as the Old Mosque. It was notable for its fine colonnaded portico and interior wall paintings. After about 600m is a shop that specialises in foreign language books, although stock is often limited. At the end of the street are some attractive Ottoman-period buildings on the left-hand corner that belong to the Toptani family, opposite a grand Italianate house that was part of the royal residencies until 1939. In the last war, it was used as Nazi headquarters. It now houses a scientific institute.

Turn left here around the corner to find the **Tanners Bridge**, *Ura e Tabakëve*, a charming small Ottoman structure built over the tiny river Lana. It was built in the 18C. Turning left up this street, Rruga Xhoxhi Martini, and walking about five minutes, passing the offices of the Albanian Telegraphic Agency on the left, you reach the **Foreign Ministry**, a large oblong modern concrete building. Visitors should report to the small window on the left-hand side of the building, up a set of steps.

Beyond the Foreign Ministry, turn left down one of the alleyways running into the main street, and go back towards Skanderbeg Square through what remains of the old Ottoman part of the city, with an interesting, often charming mixture of small whitewashed one-storey houses, larger buildings dating in some cases from the Zogist period and occasional modern shops. On the far side of the alleyways is a **street market**. This is a good place to shop for food, particularly fruit and vegetables, brought into the city by peasants from outlying districts.

N.B. This area is not recommended at night.

Bearing right from the street market, follow the narrow alley into Rruga Luigj Gurakuqi, which runs east from Skanderbeg Square to meet Rruga Qemal Stafa and then goes to Mount Dajti.

Turning left here, on the right is a small street, Rruga Kristoforidhu. Follow this street until the end, about 500m, then turn left. On the left a short distance along the street is the ***Fortress of Justinian**, of which only impressive high Ottoman walls can be seen. Before 1939 it housed the national museum.

The fortress was originally built by the Emperor Justinian in the 6C, and mosaics from that period have been found in the interior. But it must have soon fallen into complete ruin after the Slav invasions and all of what can be seen nowadays was built in the 18C by the Toptani family, in a large-scale construction of a Turkish military command post and garrison. There has also been various later rebuilding in the interior, so that it is difficult both to gain access and also to understand very much of the original internal layout. At the moment much of the interior buildings are occupied by scientific and university institutes and foreign aid agencies. There are some fine Ottoman paved roads, and the walls' strength and size indicate the military importance of the garrison to the Ottoman governors.

A well-preserved late 19C ***Ottoman domestic house** can be seen from the entrance arch. This building houses a geographical and cartographic institute. It is a very fine example of a late 19C Tirana *bey's* house, and if open the interior is well worth seeing. Approach by a gate in the wall, 100m up an Ottoman cobbled road, with a high modern wall on the right. There are the remains of early 19C wall paintings under the eaves, with two main wings and recessed central steps. On the left is a square Ottoman house of the same period. The most outstanding interior feature is the octagonal wooden ceiling up the steps from the central entrance hall, with a very finely carved central wooden ceiling boss.

Continue along this street to the side of the Museum of Modern Art, then turn right back into Skanderbeg Square.

2 · Environs of Tirana

There are a number of interesting places to visit which are close to Tirana and which may give the business traveller with limited spare time or those passing through the city, an opportunity to see something of the Albanian countryside and its monuments without a major expedition being necessary. They can be reached by taxi from central Tirana at a modest cost.

This castle is one of the finest ruined citadels in Albania, built in the Byzantine period around an ancient central tower on an outcrop of limestone rock above the river Erzeni. It is well worth a visit, which can be made from Tirana in a round trip of about 2½ hours. Follow the main road from Skanderbeg Square in the Elbasan direction, passing the new Italian Embassy, and the grandiose 30s' architecture of the American Embassy. Leave Tirana past the presidential palace, originally built for King Zog, continuing in the direction of Elbasan. To the right is an attractive small new mosque on the hilltop, funded by a Kuwaiti Islamic foundation and opened in 1993. To the left, a large new **Orthopaedic Hospital** is under construction, a gift from Saudi Arabia. The road passes through pleasant, fairly prosperous lowland countryside, with grapes and fruit cultivation being widespread. The villages here of **Sauk** and **Farka** produce pottery. After 5km the road begins to climb, with a fine view of Mount Priskës (1353m) in the Krrabe mountains on the left. The road crosses the Erzeni at the village of **Stermasi** (10km), before which **Petrela Castle** can be seen, with high ruined walls built on top of very steep wooded slopes, in a natural defensive position giving the occupants control of the river valley. On the right-hand side of the river bridge is an old Ottoman military post and a pillbox. Cross the river by this bridge and continue another 2km where a right turn is found, in the village of Mulleti, with a sign to the castle.

Mulleti was founded in the 18C by Süleiman Pasha Mulleti, founder of Tirana itself. In the village there is a monument to the important battle here between the Partisans and the Axis forces in 1944. The modern village depends on the nearby lignite mine. Turn right here, a poor-quality road but with an asphalt surface. Follow the 3km to the top, where the modern village is found, a small cluster of houses and tourist cafés below the castle walls. The larger of the cafés is a pleasant place, and serves good homemade raki. The village, of about 1000 inhabitants, is a favourite haunt of courting couples from Tirana, and for wedding celebrations. It is surrounded by olive trees of great antiquity, some said to date from early Byzantine times.

PETRELA CASTLE

The site of the ****CASTLE** was occupied from very early times. The name appears to be of mixed Greek and Latin origin, from *Petra Alba*, the White Rock. In the centre of the existing ruins is a **tower** dating from about AD 500, around which much later Byzantine fortifications dating from the 11C to 14C have been built. Access is by a small iron gate, halfway down the rock, on the east side. If locked, it is possible to scramble to the top by a steep path on the south side.

In general, construction followed a rough triangular plan, around the contour of the top of the hill, with round towers at the corners and double walls. During the

Ottoman invasion, the castle was said to be the residence of Skanderbeg's sister, and played a part in the resistance to the Turks. After Ottoman power in Albania was securely established, the castle was garrisoned by janissaries for a time but soon fell into disuse and ruin. There are very fine **views** of the surrounding countryside and mountains in all directions. Visitors should be aware of the precipitous drop into the river valley on the north side of the fortifications.

From the iron gate a narrow road about 4m wide winds round the hill towards the central entrance gate of the castle. The road appears to be of late Byzantine origin, with a pebble base. There are very fine wild flowers along the road side in spring. 80m up from the empty gatehouse on the left of the road and recessed into the hill are the **foundations of a small mosque**. It is surrounded by Byzantine brickwork on the edge of the hill, and the mosque may have been constructed from an earlier Byzantine building. It was built for the first Turkish garrison of janisseries, probably soon after the Ottoman conquest. A little further up the road on the same side are the foundations of a larger mosque, probably built a little later when the garrison was reinforced.

After 200m the road turns sharp left, to a series of limestone steps leading to the **inner tower**. There is a central gate in the outer walls, on either side large defensive corner towers, the west tower is well preserved, the east tower less so and covered with vegetation.

Inside this outer wall is the inner tower, with a bell suspended from an iron frame at its highest point. This was placed on the site of one of Skanderbeg's original series of signal beacons, stretching from Kruja to Berat. A huge bonfire was lit on the platform to warn the next beacon point of Turkish military movements. Above the gatehouse was the site of the tomb of Mamica, Skanderbeg's sister. To the south is a storeroom and water cistern, and a magazine 6m deep. The arch above the cistern is made of early Byzantine brickwork.

THE BEKTASHI TEKKÉ OF TIRANA

This is a very interesting excursion, which only takes an hour or two, and offers the visitor a chance to see something of the religious life of this little-known sect which has played such an important part in Albania, particularly the 19C nationalist movement. The *tekké* is situated near a complex of apartment blocks in Rruga Ali Demi, on the extreme eastern outskirts of Tirana. It is difficult to find and as it is situated in a very deprived area, unaccompanied visits are not recommended.

The *tekké* is a large, not particularly attractive 1920s' building, in a state of some dilapidation, although restoration work is in progress. After the assault on the building by pro-atheism campaigners in 1967/68, it was used as an old people's home. The library was burnt in 1967. It is necessary to ask for the *Baba*, the Bektashi priest, to be admitted. This is currently Baba Reshat Bardhi. Baba Reshat is a well-known figure in Tirana and a mine of information on the sect, its doctrines, history and place in Albanian society; if you have time, there is much to be learned from a discussion with him. The main hall is a large circular room, in which there are portraits of prominent Bektashis, to the right of which is a small meeting room. In this room there are photographs and other documents illustrating the connection of this *tekké* with the Bektashi *tekké* in Detroit, members of which are assisting the restoration of this building. To the left there is a large assembly room. In here there are some very interesting paintings on Bektashi themes. The main prayer room is at the rear of the building, a simply-furnished, not to say austere room, with an embroidered cloth hung in the east end showing the foundation of the sect by the Persian Haji Bektash Veli.

The *tekké* reopened in March 1990, and in 1991 resumed contacts with foreign Bektashi organisations.

On the south side of the *tekké*, the bodies of two leading Tirana Babas, Salih Dede (1876–1941) and Ammet Ahmataj (1916–80) have been disinterred and reburied in an impressive new **tomb** building, with a green and white fluted roof. Sheep reared for sacrificial purposes graze around the buildings.

Assembly of the Bektasi babas, Tirana, 1935

MOUNT DAJTI

This is another worthwhile excursion from Tirana, although between the end of November and March the Dajti range is often snow-covered and it may not be possible to reach the top. The hills give very good views over the Tirana basin and across the lowlands in the direction of the Adriatic coast. The northern part of the range has been designated as a national park, with fine deciduous forests and many rare plants and flowers. The complete journey involves travelling 27km from the centre of the city, on a good asphalt road to the top of the mountain, but it is not necessary to go the whole way, if time is short or weather conditions are difficult, in order to appreciate the views.

Mount Dajti has been inhabited from the earliest times, with much evidence of prehistoric settlements. The current name of the mountain appears to be linked with the worship of the ancient Greek goddess *Diktynna*, a mother goddess who was especially venerated on Crete, although cult centres have been found as far afield as Marseilles and Athens. The name may be related to other Mount Diktes found in the ancient world, or, in the view of Strabo, the ancient Greek word *diktyon*, the fisherman's net which is supposed to have saved the goddess when she leapt into the sea to escape the unwelcome attentions of King Minos. The woods on the mountains would certainly provide confirmation of this theory, insofar as *Diktynna* was a goddess of hunting, of woods and of mountains and wild places, with many of the same attributes as Artemis.

Follow the main road out of central Tirana, as if going to Rinas airport. Then turn right for Mount Dajti. The road leaves Tirana past a military base and begins to climb through olive groves, fruit plantations and past a quarry on the left. Follow on to the top, often via series of hairpin bends, into the woods that grow on most of the mountain slopes. The road narrows and care is needed in many places with unprotected road edges and debris on the asphalt, particularly after heavy rain. There is no access to the highest point (1612m) which is occupied by the Albanian television relay station and military communications posts. The road ends, for practical purposes, near a rest home and a hotel which has been purchased by a branch of the Scientology movement. The Kuwaiti 'MAK' hotel group has opened the *Chateau Linza Motel* here, which is rather expensive but has dramatic views. Return by the same route to Tirana.

PEZA

Another worthwhile excursion is the road to **Durres**, via Peza village. Leave Skanderbeg Square in the Durres direction; the city ends with fine avenues of poplar trees that were planted in the Zogist period in the French style. Unfortunately many of them have been cut down to make up for fuel shortages in the city in recent years. The road enters good farming country, with wide open fields growing a variety of arable crops. Good quality fruit and vegetables can be bought from peasants along this road at most times of the year. On the right is the village of Yzberish (3km). Continue along the road until Vaqar, where the Erzen river is crossed, with the wide gravel bed of the river on the right-hand side of the road. Flow is generally limited outside the times of the winter spates. The river bed is mined for gravel. After another 5km, make a left turn to Peza, easily recognised by the large concrete monument in the socialist realist style at the side of the road. Follow this road 6km to Peza village.

Peza is a typical lowland village and is worth a visit from Tirana, to see how lowland country dwellers live. About 800 people lived here in the 1950s, but the population was increased by about a third after an influx of newcomers from the highlands in the aftermath of the collectivisation of agriculture. Three *fis* dominate the village, with about 200 people in each clan related to each other. Most of the newcomers have now left after privatisation has restored the land to the original owners. The visitor will notice the common grazing land on the slopes of the hillsides, the small plots where each family grows vegetables, and the greenhouses which used to belong to a state farm enterprise.

Apart from its pleasant rural aspect, the village has been witness to events of great importance in modern Albanian history. Peza was host to the conference in 1942 that had a marked influence on post-war Albanian history. This meeting is commemorated by a small museum (currently closed) and a statue, on the right-hand side of the road on entering the village. On 16 September 1942, the National Liberation Conference was held here, bringing together communists and non-communists, with the aim of uniting the Albanian people against the Axis invaders. The Conference elected the National Liberation General Council to organise the resistance campaign. Although many non-communist nationalists attended the gathering, it was an early triumph for Enver Hoxha and the communists, insofar as their superior organisation and determination enabled them to dictate the political direction of the local National Liberation Councils that evolved from it afterwards. In military terms, the Peza gathering was a great success, in that the number of Partisan *çetas* increased very rapidly in the next twelve months, and they began to inflict significant damage on the Italian occupiers. In response, the Italian high command organised widespread reprisals in the Peza area, among others, burning down hundreds of peasants' homes and massacring local people suspected of helping the resistance.

Near Peza is the village of **Shesh**, which produces a good wine, *Shesh i Zi.*

Return to the main Tirana–Durres road by the same route, or continue to Durres (24km) through good farming land and low hills.

KRRABE PASS AND THE MONASTERY OF SHENGJIN VLADIMIR

Another interesting excursion in good weather is to the **Krrabe Pass**. This is the main direct route to Elbasan (48km).

Leave Tirana by the main road to the south east, as for Petrela Castle (see above). Instead of turning towards the castle, follow the main road through rolling countryside, mostly given over to vineyards and fruit plantations, passing through Berzhita village. The road then begins to climb steeply after the small coal-mining town of Koliti. A narrow road to the left leads into the valley of Pellumbas. There are interesting exposed basalt rock formations to the left as the road climbs via a series of hairpin bends into the mountains, through attractive deciduous forest and scrub. The road here is frequently congested and large lorries sometimes have difficulty negotiating the hairpin bends. As the Pass is approached, the road climbs very steeply indeed, with outstanding **views** over a dozens of small conical wooded hills towards Kavaja. In the far distance is great peak of **Mount Tomorri**, above Berat. The road narrows towards the top of the Pass (1932m), and great care is needed. At the highest point on the left are the ruins of the *Kulla of Graceni*. As the descent begins, there are spectacular views over the central Albanian mountains, with jagged limestone crags sticking out above deep valleys and thick forests. The Pass used to be notorious as a haunt of **wolves**. Writing in the 1930s, the English traveller Bernard Newman noted:

> The shepherds have to keep a careful watch on their flocks on the mountain pastures, and I noted that their rifles were always ready for business. In the winter, when the flocks are withdrawn to sheepfolds in the villages, the wolves sometimes become desperate with hunger. They form themselves into packs, and raid a valley, devouring everything they can find. Several people lose their lives every winter in Albania when the wolves come down from the mountains. Sometimes there is a real pitch battle between a village and a pack of wolves. One village actually borrowed the services of soldiers with machine guns, and actually killed over 200 wolves on a single day.

About 2km before you reach Elbasan, there is a small track to the left of the main road by a hairpin bend that leads to the ****Monastery of Shengjin Vladimir**. This is a building of great historic and religious interest, but it is within a military camp, and access has been impossible until recently. Follow the track for about 1km, and you will be met by the camp guards. If you ask for the monastery, they will tell you to park near the camp entrance and the buildings can be approached on foot a little further along the track on the right, above the Kush river valley, a tributary of the Shkumbini.

History

This monastery was the only monastery in Albania dedicated to the Serbian saint and prince, John Vladimir of Dioclea. An ally and probably a vassal of the Byzantine Emperor Basil II, John Vladimir was forced to surrender his lands to Tsar Samuel of Bulgaria, and he was imprisoned. His confinement was cut short by romance. Tsar Samuel's daughter, Kosara, fell in love with him, and the Dioclean prince was restored to his throne. But in 1016, two years after Samuel's death, he was treacherously lured to the city of Prespa by the Bulgarian Tsar John Vladislav, and murdered. He was venerated after his death throughout the Balkans as a Christ-like figure, and his relics were said to be kept in the Elbasan monastery. In Serbia itself, his cult was soon forgotten, for probably internal political reasons. In the 16C, Karl Topia, the powerful Albanian feudal lord, was buried in the nave of his monastery church.

The monastery is reached through a small iron gate set in a high wall, which leads into an attractive garden with fig and fruit trees. Follow the high wall on the right side of the garden to the end, and then turn right. Walk about 75m, to where there is a small Romanesque arch set in the wall. Inside is the **Church of Shengjin**, a very sad, roofless early-medieval building bearing the marks of the violence and destruction here both during and after World War II, and in the anti-religious campaigns under Enver Hoxha. It was reconstructed in its present form in 1380, by a member of the Topia family, then feudal lords of Durres and Elbasan. In 1967, the

Church of Shengjin Vladimir, near Elbasan

church roof was removed and burnt. The nave measures 15m x 13m, with two carved Byzantine columns remaining near the altar. A number of 18C and 19C tombstones are set in the outer south wall. Most are inscribed in Greek, indicating that this was then the church of the now defunct Greek minority community in Elbasan. All interior fittings have been destroyed, and the remaining frescoes in a small alcove in the north wall, and in a large recess in the east wall, are in a very poor condition and in need of emergency restoration if they are to be saved.

There is a primitive wooden cross set in the north east corner of the church, which is where local people believe the saint was buried. A feast day in honour of the saint is celebrated on 4 June. The locals have been taught he was Bulgarian, and if asking directions ask for the '*Kishë Bulgareci*', the Bulgarian church.

On the south side there are some dilapidated houses that used to be used as dormitories for monks, and pieces of Byzantine masonry are to be found almost everywhere in the vicinity. Beyond these houses is an impressive 19C house with a very fine, if overgrown, garden where the Bishop of Elbasan is said to have lived in earlier days.

The monastery is a remarkable, atmospheric monument, which has survived terrible times; it will be a great pity if insufficient resources are available to save the remaining fabric of the building, and to make it more accessible to the interested visitor.

The road descends towards Elbasan, leaving the forest and entering old olive groves, then comes into the town past an electricity transformer station and the metallurgical complex. On the outskirts of the city is a concrete monument to the battle of 11 November 1944 between the 15th Partisan brigade and the retreating Axis forces (see Route 3).

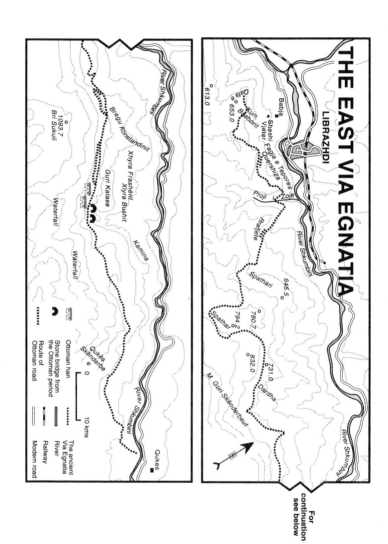

THE EAST VIA EGNATIA

LIBRAZHDI

River Shkumbini

613.0

Dafa e 653.0

Babja

Kurr.
Bashorit

Shesh çagja e Teporesë
Vjeter Quershtra

Proji i Zoje

Rrafele

River Shkumbin

Rrafele

Spathari

645.5

Spathari

794.2

780.1

832.0

731.0

Dardha

M. Guri Skenderbeut

River Shkumbin

For continuation see below

River Shkumbini

Bregu Konstandinit

Xhyra Frashërit

Xiyra Bushit

1093.7
Bri Sukulli

Guri Kalase

Waterfall

Kamina

Waterfall

Oukes
Skenderbe

0   10 Kms

River Shkumbin

Oukes

Ottoman han	The ancient Via Egnatia
Stone bridge from the Ottoman period	River
Route of Ottoman road	Railway
	Modern road

II THE VIA EGNATIA, DURRES TO LAKE OCHRID

3 · The Via Egnatia, Durres to Elbasan and Quaf e Thanës

From Durres to Quaf e Thanës pass, on the border with FYROM, about 168km, via Kavaja and Elbasan. Follow the main road as described in the itinerary. The road is generally good, but with some poorer stretches, particularly between Elbasan and Librazhd. New road construction is in progress in some places.

The **Via Egnatia** was one of the most important roads in the Roman Empire, running from ancient *Dyrrachium*, modern Durres, on the Adriatic coast, across Albania to Lake Ochrid, and then from Macedonia to Constantinople. This ancient trade and military route followed the Shkumbini river valley through central Albania, and although only a modest amount of the Roman surface remains, some paving can be seen from time to time. The modern road is a good-quality asphalt route linking Durres with the important industrial centre of Elbasan, then running through some of the most beautiful and dramatic mountain scenery in the centre of the country. Following it enables the visitor to discover important remains of Roman and Byzantine Albania, in the same way that exploration of *Vorio Epirus* reveals the parts of the country most under ancient Greek cultural influence.

DURRES

Durres (pop. 124,900) is an interesting historic city with some of the most important Roman remains on the coast of the Adriatic, including the largest known Roman amphitheatre in the Balkans, an important museum, mosques, the summer palace of King Zog, a modern seaport and long stretches of sandy beach. The bay, one of the best anchorages in the Adriatic, and the strong defensive position of the city, based on the ridge that rises sharply from the centre of the medieval town, has ensured it a place in almost every important historical event in Albania. It has been said that since the year 1000, it has changed hands 33 times. As the modern and medieval towns occupy the same site as the ancient city, archaeological excavations are very incomplete, although there is much for the visitor to see despite the many practical difficulties investigators have faced.

- **Medical care**. Central Policlinics (outpatient dept.), tel. (052) 222 22; District Hospital (emergency service), tel. (052) 233 24; Dr Miri Hoti (surgeon), tel. (052) 222 06 (home); Dr Hurma Cerma (cardiologist), tel. (052) 235 24 (home).

- **Hotels and restaurants**. The *Adriatic*, tel (052) 23612, fx (052) 23051; *Durres* or *Apollonia* (see below). Private rooms are also available. The *Hotel Illyria* near the museum is cheap and just about habitable. There is a good private fish restaurant, the *Grilli de Mare*, to the left of the Hotel Adriatic.

■ **Police**. Police Headquarters (operator), tel. (052) 222 51. Police Station, tel. (052) 225 44.

■ **Railways and coaches**. A rail service to Tirana has now been restored. An hourly coach service to Tirana operates from the square outside the railway station. Taxis are also found here.

History

Durres was known to the ancient Greeks as *Epidamnus*. The name may be an adaptation of a previous name given by local Illyrian tribes. According to Thucydides, it was founded in 627 BC by colonists from Corfu. Corfu at this time was under the control of Corinth. In 435 BC conflict between the settlers and their Corinthian masters led Athens to support the cause of Corfu, and so Epidamnus was peripherally involved in the causes of the Peloponnesian War (432–404 BC). Thucydides describes the political instability in the city in this period, 'As time went on, Epidamnus became both powerful and populous; but there followed years of political unrest, caused, they say, by a war with foreign inhabitants of the country. As a result of this, Epidamnus declined and lost her power. Finally, just before the war between Athens and Sparta, the democratic party drove out the aristocratic party, who then went over to the foreign enemies of the city and joined them in making piratical attacks upon it by sea and land'. In 313 BC the city was seized by an Illyrian chieftain, Glaucias, and in 229, under its Illyrian name, *Dyrrachhium*, entered into an alliance with Rome. It was used by the Romans as a bulwark against the Kings of Macedon, and became the terminus for the Via Egnatia, and also of the link road running southwards to Greece via Apollonia and Butrint.

When the civil wars in Rome broke out at the end of the republican period, Pompey evacuated his forces from Italy in 49 BC and established himself at Dyrrachium. On 28 November of that year Caesar sailed from Brindisi and landed at Spila. His army was attacked there by Pompey's naval commander, Bibulus, sailing from Corfu. Pompey's troops advanced from Lake Ochrid and reached the line of the Shkumbi river. Shortly afterwards, Mark Antony landed near the modern town of Shëngjin with 7000 infantry and 800 cavalry, and attacked the fortress at Lezha, taking it on 3 February 48 BC. Pompey moved north to intercept him on the Mal i Kercokes but failed to do so; Caesar made a detour through the Krrabe Pass and placed his forces between Pompey's position and Dyrrachium. On 5 May he was attacked by Pompey's forces but the battle proved indecisive, and all the troops involved moved south into Greece where eventually Pompey was utterly defeated at the battle of Pharsalia.

Subsequently Dyrrachium became a prosperous trading and administrative centre; Cicero stayed there for a time in AD 58. In a letter he commented that the city had the advantages of being a *civitas libera*, a free city, and that it was an '*admirabilis urbs*' but that it was very crowded. The aqueduct was built between 117 and 138 AD by Emperor Hadrian, and repaired by Alexander Severus in AD 222. It was an early focus of the development of Christianity. As early as AD 58 Durres was said to have 70 Christian families. It was seriously damaged by an earthquake in 345, and became part of the Eastern Empire in 395. In 449 it became an archbishopric but was sacked by Theodoric and the Ostrogoths in 478. The Emperor Anastasius I (491–518), a citizen of the city, built a complex series of defensive walls, remains of which can still be seen. In 518 another earthquake seriously damaged the city. They were successful in defending the town against frequent attacks from the Bulgars in the following centuries. They were perhaps the final glory of the ancient city. In the 6C Procopius wrote of Durres: 'It is a town jutting from the land into the sea. It enjoys all the benefits the sea and land can give it. When you sail in from the Ionian Sea, a magnificent sight meets your eye'. In the 7C the acropolis was reconstructed. In the early 9C the city was a centre of Byzantine power in the Adriatic.

The Norman lord, Robert Guiscard, attacked the Byzantine city from Apulia in 1081 and defeated the Emperor Alexius Comnenus, taking it in February 1082, but the Byzantines recovered it soon afterwards. In 1081 the castle was reconstructed by Georgios Paleologus, when it is mentioned in chronicles as Praetorium. In 1185 it was taken by William of Sicily, but he lost it to Crusaders who gave it to the suzerainty of Venice in 1203. At that time it was called a '*metropolis*' by the chronicler Bryennios, an indication of its prosperity. In that century the *Theme* of Durres had nine towns under its jurisdiction, *Scampa, Byllis, Amanthia, Aulon, Listron, Alipis, Sceuptron, Pulcheropolis* and *Apollonia*. In 1153 Durres was mentioned by the Arab geographer, Ali Idris, as a flourishing merchant town. Durres was retaken by the Emperor Theodorus in 1205, after which it passed to Manfred of Sicily and to Charles of Anjou. In 1273 the city was destroyed by an earthquake, after which it was reoccupied by John of Anjou and Philip of Taranto. After being annexed to the Frankish Kingdom of the Morea (the modern Peloponnese), it was taken by the Serbs in 1336 and held by the Topia family as vassals of the Ballashas. This dynasty, Serbian but Catholic and nationalist, held the city during the period of feudal anarchy that culminated in the great southward migration from the northern highlands of 1368.

In 1392 the city returned to Venetian rule. Important developments were made to the harbour and city walls in this period, remains of which can still be seen. It was besieged by Mehmet the Conqueror and his Turkish army in 1466 but was not taken by them until 1501. As early as 1436, the Italian chronicler Ciriaco d'Ancona wrote that the walls were in ruins. A German knight, visiting in 1496, called it 'a great but ruined city'. The city did not prosper under its new conquerors, and declined in importance throughout the Ottoman period: the Turkish traveller Evlia Çelebia described the fortress as abandoned in 1670. In 1880 its population was only about 5000 people. It was then known by the Turkish name of **Dratsch**, or Montenegran **Draç**, and was a large village with a jumble of muddy streets around a bazaar. In the middle of the 19C the population had been only about 1000 people, living in 200 households.

But its strategic position soon brought Durres into prominence in the period of the Balkan Wars, when it was occupied by the Serbs in 1912–13. In the same year, Esad Pasha Toptani led a separatist movement opposing the Vlora government's authority and set up the Senate of Albania which was intended to replace it. Durres then briefly became the capital of the country under Prince Wilhelm of Wied. Esad Pasha was surrounded in the city in December 1914, but was relieved by the Serbs in June 1915. Italian cultural influence was growing in this period in Durres, with the language widely spoken and several Italian schools being established. On 15 December of that year Italian troops arrived to cover the Serbian retreat from Belgrade, in 1916 it was made a submarine base by the Austrians and in October 1918 it was bombarded and taken by the Allies. Many Austro-Hungarian ships were sunk in the harbour.

The Provisional government of Albania was established in Durres between 1918 and March 1920. It ceased to be the capital after the Congress of Lushnja when Tirana was chosen as the new capital and the government of Prince Wilhelm of Wied moved there. In the inter-war period the city was a favourite residence for King Zog and benefited economically from the period of Italian annexation. In 1927 Vuk Djurashkovitch was arrested as a Yugoslav spy in the city, as part of the anti-Yugoslav agitation organised by Zog following the Pact of Tirana. At the time of the Italian annexation the population was about 6500 people, almost all Muslims. In the Second World War it was an important port and military centre for the Axis forces. The first modern harbour, built in 1927, was destroyed by the Germans in 1944. Durres and the region was liberated on 14 November 1944. In 1947, the construction of the Durres–Peqin railway line was begun, the first railway in Albania. The Durres–Tirana line was built in 1948.

In the communist period, Durres grew as an industrial centre, concentrating on food processing, light engineering and cigarette production, and the development of the port as the main terminal for Albanian trade. Tourist hotels were built along the beaches to the south of the city. The region has also grown considerably more important for agriculture after the draining of surrounding marshland, notorious for malarial mosquitos pre-war. Rice, vegetables and cereals are the most important crops.

In 1990 and 1991 the city was the focus of mass emigration attempts, with ships being hijacked in the harbour. In August 1991 some 20,000 people crossed the Straits of Otranto by this means, to Bari. Subsequently the port was placed under Italian military control. It was then the centre of 'Operation Pelican', the European Community food aid operation in Albania. The city has undergone some loss of population in the last two years. An Orthodox seminary has opened in Durres recently, and an Islamic *medresé*.

Most of the city that is of interest to the visitor is to be found on and near the promontory above the modern port. Walk up from the port gates towards the impressive remains of the **Byzantine walls**. The round tower on the south-west point was rebuilt by the Turks in the 15C.

A statue near the base, surrounded by three bronze Venetian cannons, commemorates the abortive attempt to defend the city from the Italian invaders led by Abas Kupi and a small group of followers in 1939, one of whose names, Mujo Ulqinaku, appears on it, but not that of Kupi, or many of the other participants. This is also the case with another plaque on the base of the Ottoman tower itself and is a good example of the care with which historical inscriptions should be read in Albania. Kupi was execrated by the communist regime because of his activities in the nationalist, non-communist resistance, mainly in central and northern Albania, in 1943–44. Along with British Liaison Officers from SOE, he came from the Mati river estuary to the United Kingdom at the end of his campaign. An account of these events is to be found in *Sons of the Eagle* by Lord Julian Amery.

The scale of the defensive system indicates the importance of the city as a medieval military stronghold. Follow the line of the walls, keeping them on your left, uphill through the narrow streets before entering a wide boulevard that leads to the ****Roman amphitheatre**. It is the largest building of its kind in the Balkans, and

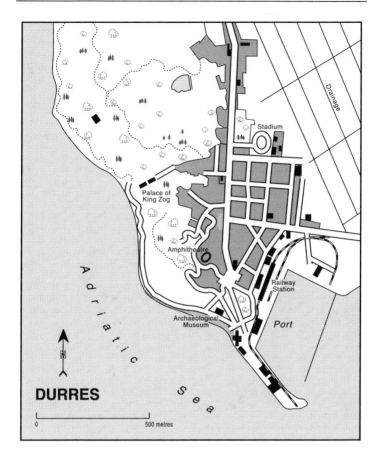

was begun in the 2C AD, during the reign of the Emperor Hadrian, on the side of a rocky hill. It was designed primarily for gladiatorial combat, and shows wild animals, and is a characteristically Roman structure, showing little trace of Greek influence. About 15,000 spectators could be seated, with entrances for the gladiators and wild animals on the north and south sides of the large arena, over 60m wide. The amphitheatre is only partly excavated, and Ottoman and modern buildings remain on the east and west sides of the arena, the centre of which is filled with earth and rubbish left from previous excavations. It nevertheless remains an imposing edifice, showing the importance of the city as a Roman army base when the colonisation of the southern Balkans was a priority for the Emperors, and when large numbers of landless Roman soldiers were being settled in the region.

A covered area on the west side of the amphitheatre contains an important **early Christian chapel**, under the ranks of seats. The amphitheatre as a whole may be visited at any time, but it is a matter of luck whether the attendant is present to unlock the entrance gate to the chapel. Walk down steep steps into the galleries underneath the arena, where the chapel is found, an early Christian building dating from the 6C. On the south wall is a mosaic showing St Stephen, the first Christian martyr, the Virgin Mary, and the Archangels Michael and Gabriel. On the west wall, a much less well-preserved mosaic shows St Sophia with angels. An inscription on the south wall indicates the chapel was at some point dedicated to one Alexander, probably an unknown private citizen who was martyred in the arena, although some have speculated that it may be the Emperor Alexander (912–913). The style of mosaic work indicates a date in the region of AD 750. To the south of the chapel is a small recess with a grave and marble headstone that may be that of an early Christian martydom in the arena. The chapel captures very strongly the atmosphere of the early Christian centuries, where the new religion was living quite literally within the ambience of the pagan world.

Elsewhere in the vicinity of the amphitheatre, excavation has revealed baths, other mosaics and the foundations of private houses dating from Emperor Hadrian's reign, but there has been little systematic work recently and there is not much for the visitor to see other than artefacts discovered which are displayed in the museum. Large quantities of pottery fragments and small artefacts are regularly dug up in people's gardens and the visitor should expect to be pestered to buy them by local children. Two late Roman columns stand on the south side of the road 300m below the amphitheatre. The enclosed area in which they stand was part of the Roman forum, with the base of a central fountain visible.

Walk a further 200m south to the town central square, laid out by the Italians in 1939, to the *__Great Mosque of Durres__, or the __Mosque of Fatih__. This impressive Islamic building is on a very small hill on the north side of the square. It was originally constructed between 1414 and 1494, and is now fully restored after building works funded by the Turkish government between 1992 and 1994. A squat white building with an elegant thin minaret and a very fine interior, it is one of the most pleasing Islamic buildings in Albania, with a single whitewashed dome, a square prayer room about 60 by 80 feet, and a high women's gallery. It was probably built on the foundations of an existing Orthodox church and dominates this part of the city. The three first-floor windows are flanked by impressive red granite columns which look as though they may have been taken from a previous Byzantine or Roman building. It gives a very light, clear, airy impression, a historic Islamic monument facing Christian Europe across the Adriatic. From the opposite side of the town square the oblong lower structure has a perfect balance with the shallow dome that seems to float above it in the summer heat. In the 1970s the interior was vandalised and it was turned into a youth centre, then a Museum of Atheism. The mosque is an active centre of Islamic education, with a small **medresé** in an attractive 19C *bey's* house to the right of the portico.

On the south-west side of the amphitheatre is the best preserved section of the **ancient walls** of the city, where Turkish and Venetian brickwork and stonework can be seen resting on Byzantine foundations.

800m to the west of the amphitheatre is a small museum in a domestic house dedicated to the memory of the great Albanian actor Alexander Moissi.

Alexander Moissi

Alexander Moissi was born in Trieste in 1879, into an exiled Albanian family. In 1883, they returned to live in Durres. In his youth he studied the theatre in Vienna and Prague, but became famous as the leading actor in the 1930s in Max Reinhardt's company in Berlin. He was particularly noted for his Shakespearian work, and for his Faust. He died in Vienna in 1935.

Walk south towards the sea and the tree-lined promenade for the **Archaeological Museum**, north of the port complex. This attractive building is set in a garden on the seafront which used to display Greek and Roman statuary and other objects found locally. After a major theft in 1991, some of the remaining garden objects have been removed for safekeeping. The most important garden exhibits used to be a large Corinthian capital from the 5C BC, and a Greek sarcophagus. The museum itself is divided into an east and west wing. Entrance to the museum costs 100 lek. It is open from 09.00 to 13.00 Wednesday to Saturday.

The east wing displays objects from the prehistoric and Greek settlements; the west room is given to the Roman and Byzantine period. In the **east wing** is the grave relief of a young man, marble, 5C BC; head of a woman, terracotta, 6C BC; fragmentary grave relief of a seated woman from the 4C BC, various Illyrian grave-stones, in typical stone cylinder forms; and Greek burial urns and vases. In the **west wing** Roman pottery is displayed; glass dating from the 1C and 2C AD; examples of Byzantine and Venetian pottery; part of a Greek sarcophagus with the head of a young man, from the 3C AD; a head of Hermes, 4C BC, and head of a young man, early 1C AD.

Objects that used to be displayed in the gallery outside, under the Ottoman colonnade, have been removed for security reasons at the moment, and are locked up in Tirana, although it is intended to restore them to the museum when conditions allow. They included a variety of minor statuary, some fragmentary, from the Roman and Hellenistic periods, predominantly grave reliefs and funerary monuments.

200m west of the museum, on the seafront, is a very large bronze monument of a Partisan hero, in the socialist realist style. In the sea, ruins of the pre-war harbour can be seen.

At the top of the promontory hill, the **Palace of King Zog** can be seen, a grandiose, operatic building in the Italianate style that was built in the early 1930s,

Palace of King Zog

which is approached up a winding road through pine woods. If transport is not available, a good view of it can be had from the side of the Skanderbeg Infant School below the hill. But if possible, the ascent should be made as from the top there is an outstanding view of Durres and the surrounding coast and seascape, a *magnifico panorama,* and the palace itself evokes the atmosphere of the period when Mussolini was taking over the country. It is not possible to see the palace interior, as it is used as a regional military and police headquarters, and photography of the exterior is not particularly encouraged. **Roman paving** has been found behind the palace but at the moment access to it is not possible. The palace stands on, or near, the site of an ancient castle, said to have been built during the reign of Emperor Athanasius I (491–518). It was later used by the Venetians.

In a small street below the palace is the Naim Frasheri secondary school. In February 1967 pupils of this school began the anti-religious campaign of the Party of Labour that culminated with the government declaration, later that year, that Albania had become the world's first atheist state. In imitation of Chinese 'Red Guard' campaigns, pupils were sent all over Durres and nailed up the doors of mosques and churches in a campaign the party called 'a small spark that lit a big fire that did away with the centres of religious obscurantism'.

Most of the bazaar area of Durres was either destroyed in the war or demolished in post-war redevelopment, but the central square of the city offers some pleasant small cafés and ice cream shops. Private restaurants are also beginning to be established. Smokers will enjoy the fragrant tobacco of Durres cigarettes which can be bought cheaply from street vendors.

The **beaches** of Durres stretch some 11km from the south of the city, and offer firm, fine sand and slope gently into the sea, making them very suitable for children. The *Adriatic Hotel* has a reasonable restaurant, and is an acceptable place to stay, though expensive. It was built in the 1930s by an Italian company, and has interesting dark red marble interiors, redolent of the Fascist period, and an attractive terrace overlooking the beach. The hotel requires modernisation, and has serious problems with its water supply. If the *Adriatic* is full, the *Durres* and *Apollonia Hotels* are habitable. Traditional Albanian musical instruments are often sold by local people on the hotel steps, and make attractive and interesting presents. Broken glass can be a hazard on some parts of the beach, and plastic shoes are useful.

To the east of the city is a large expanse of flat farmland that until the late 1920s was a malarial swamp. It was drained by the construction of canals, 10km long, by prison labour under Italian direction, and was one of the first public works projects under the Zogist regime. Much of the new land was given to Italian colonists from the Veneto and Puglia.

Other important Roman and Byzantine remains are on the outskirts of the city, at **Porto Romano**, 7km north, on the road to Bishti i Pallës, where a stretch of brick walls flanked by towers can be seen, probably built in the 6C AD as part of the outer defences of the city. According to Strabo, this first stretch of the Via Egnatia, from the old Roman harbour, was known as the **Candavian Way**. A lighthouse existed here in ancient times. A good stretch of the Via Egnatia, 300m long, where the paving has not been disturbed, can be seen at the foot of the white cliff of **Petra**, near modern Shkam, south of the hotels along the beach. It was here that Pompey's troops established their camp in 48 BC during the civil wars of the Roman Republic. In the Second World War, the Axis occupiers established a concentration camp at Porto Romano, where many members of the Resistance died.

At the village of **Arapaj**, 5km south-east of Durres where the Peza road to Tirana meets the Durres–Kavaja road, foundations of an important early Christian basilica were discovered in 1980. The building would have been one of the largest early Christian churches known. It may be the church of St Michael which was burned down by the Norman invaders in 1081. Mosaics have been found inside the cemetery room here. It is thought to date from the beginning of the 6C BC, with an unusual triple apse.

The modern road leaves Durres following the ancient route and passes through Kavaja, a medium-sized industrial town, then follows the river valley directly east to Elbasan, after which it goes through the Polisit mountains to the south east and approaches the border with FYROM. The latter stage is through the increasingly narrow gorge of the Shkumbini, with the peaks of the Jabllanica mountains to the north east forming a precipitous mountain wall that has protected Albania from outsiders throughout the ages. The important Illyrian site of Selca can be visited here en route (see p. 130). The road then climbs from the mining town of Perranjasi to the high border crossing at Quaf e Thanës, near the northern end of Lake Ochrid.

Follow the coast road south-east from Durres, with pleasant pine woods and sand dunes on the right, and a main railway line on the left. The railway is one of the most important economic arteries in Albania, carrying large quantities of mineral ore along the Shkumbini branch line that accompanies the road to Lake Ochrid, then branches south to the large lead-nickel mine at Pogradec. The southern branch running to Fier and the Patos oilfield is used for petroleum products. The beaches on the southern side of the pine woods are clean, sandy and uncrowded.

10km to the east is the small town of **Shijaku**. This is largely populated by descendants of Bosnian Muslims who fled Bosnia in the 19C.

After 13km the road reaches **Kavaja**, a run-down industrial town of about 20,000 inhabitants. It was established as an urban settlement in the 16C by the Ottomans. A clocktower and an 18C mosque are the only remnants from that time, among otherwise undistinguished modern buildings. The mosque has been well restored in the last two years, with an attractive, well-proportioned portico, with seven arches. It is built on the site of an earlier mosque constructed in 1414. The colonnade of the mosque, which reused ancient masonry from Apollonia, is now in the Durres museum. About 100m in front of the mosque is a small monument to the anti-communist demonstration held in the town on 26 March 1990 that was a landmark in the Albanian struggle for democracy.

Kavaja was an important place in the disintegration of the retreating Serbian army in 1916. The English nurse Flora Sandes witnessed the appalling conditions then, where 'mud flowed between the houses like a slimy river into which men plunged knee deep'. The town played a leading role in the struggle for democracy in 1990, with one of the first assemblies of a pluralist character being held in December of that year in the city. Industries include the manufacture of nails, screws, bolts and glassware.

The road follows through the town past derelict industrial buildings, an example of the way towns such as Kavaja grew around State-established factories in the communist period.

5km from Kavaja, up a dirt road leading east into the Mali i Robit hills, is the village of **Helmasi**. It used, before the last war, to be called *Herberti*, and was the scene of activity by the British–Albanian relief committee in the 1920s. It was named after Hon. Colonel Aubrey Herbert MP. A school was opened in the village in October 1927, with Emin Abazi in charge of educational arrangements, and at one time it had 210 pupils. Herbert's mother, Lady Carnarvon, was active in fund raising for it, and saw it as a memorial for her deceased son. British relief activity in Albania arose from an appeal made in 1923 by Robert Parr, then Secretary to the British legation in Tirana, for funds to help the starving and destitute Kosovar refugees in Albania, who had fled from the belligerent forces in the First World War and had only blackened ruins to return to, even assuming the Yugoslav authorities would allow them to cross the border. The British Government, under the then Prime Minister, Ramsay McDonald, made a contribution to the appeal.

> **Hon. Colonel Aubrey Herbert MP** (1880–1923), thought by many to be the model for John Buchan's hero *'Greenmantle'*, was a leading protagonist in the Albanian cause in the late 19C and early 20C in Britain. He travelled widely in the Ottoman Empire, and became a strong supporter of the Young Turk revolution in 1908. As a Conservative MP he upheld the Albanian cause in an often hostile and ignorant House of Commons in the Edwardian period. A close associate of Edith Durham, he was a founder member of the Anglo-Albanian Association in London. His record of his journeys *Ben Kendim: a Record of Eastern Travel*, published in London in 1924, is a very valuable memoir of Albania during the Second Balkan War in 1912.

9km south west of Kavaja is the small village of Bedeni, established as a forced labour camp in 1949. It was inhabited by ex-political prisoners from the gaols of Shkodra, Vlora, Berat and Gjirokastra. Hundreds of people died in conditions of extreme privation while working on marsh drainage works. Most were nationalist supporters of the Balli Kombetar movement.

The ancient Via Egnatia was met here by a small Roman road running from the coast near Kepi i Lagjit (11km). 3km south of Kavaja, the Via crossed a small river called the Darci, where two masonry bridge pylons dating from late antiquity can still be seen under the modern road. The modern road follows the route of the Via for a further 6km here, until the village of Gosa where the ancient road turned left and climbed the ridge behind the village to avoid the marshland of the Shkumbini river bed. Parts of the Via can be seen along the ridge, in a good state of preservation, until it joins the southern branch of the road running from Apollonia, near modern **Rrogozhina**. This is a small industrial town, which may have been the site of ancient *Asparagium*, where Julius Caesar established a military camp.

A modern road runs south west to the small seaside resort of **Divjaka** (14km) through swampland reclaimed during the first Five Year Plan (1951–55). Before the war the area was known as the Karavasta Marsh, formed in the 17C by alluvium carried down from the Seman and Shkumbi rivers, and was one of the last refuges of the Dalmatian pelican.

The road continues 8km to **Peqin**, in Roman times a minor urban centre. Ancient *Clodiana* was at Matmutaga, 4km east of Peqin. The foundations of a small bath dating from late Roman times can be seen, within more modern masonry dating from when it was made into a Turkish *hammam*, behind shops in the main street. Follow the road running alongside the wide river bed through the modern town. For most of the year the flow is limited, over the gravel and through the scrub and matted plants, but in early spring is subject to raging torrents and floods. The gorge of the Shkumbini narrows here, the road clinging to the hillsides. In winter minor landslides are common. 19km on is the junction leading to the oil refinery town of Cerriku, then the river is crossed. Above Cerriku is an important hydro-electric dam on Lake Banja. This road leads towards Korça (not recommended). At the far end of Lake Banja is the important military centre of **Gramsh** (46km from Elbasan). Follow on the main road towards the plain of Elbasan, the chimneys of the metallurgical complex being visible.

ELBASAN

Elbasan (pop. 101,100) was, until the beginning of the last war, one of the most pleasant and unspoilt Ottoman cities in Albania, with a mixture of eastern and medieval buildings, narrow cobbled streets and a large bazaar where Turkish could still be heard. There was a clearly defined Christian settlement within the castle walls, a Vlach district on the outskirts of the city and several fine mosques and Islamic buildings. At that time the population was about 15,000 people.

The distinguished English journalist J.D. Bourchier, then the Balkan correspondent of *The Times*, records that on a visit in 1911 he saw:

> the population celebrating *Bairam* in central space; wonderful primitive merry-go-round with gypsy minstrels (flute and drum), pushed round by men with poles; also a cartwheel poised on a tree top; *pekhilvans* (clowns) wrestling, mostly refugees from Dibra, thus gaining a precarious livelihood.

The city was also noted for its good public buildings, advanced education provision, public gardens and timber-built shops. But there was much wartime damage and an intensive programme of industrial development in the communist period that boosted the city to around 75,000 inhabitants, and the erection of many ugly modern structures. The culmination of this process was the construction of the huge 'Steel of the Party' metallurgical complex outside the city, in the valley of the Shkumbini, built with Chinese assistance in the 1960s and 1970s. It was called 'the second national liberation of Albania' by Enver Hoxha, and was designed to refine ferro-chrome, nickel and other ores so that they could be sold abroad in a concentrated form, rather than exported in their natural state. The complex also included steel production facilities. With its chimneys, the tallest in the Balkans, always belching smoke and emitting a stream of dangerous pollutants, the city became a byword for the problems of Hoxhaist industrial development, and soon meant that much of the hitherto prosperous agricultural area in the river valley was useless for all crops. The complex has now been largely shut down but it will take many years for the prosperity of Elbasan to be restored. Nevertheless, some outstanding Elbasan buildings from the Ottoman past have survived unscathed, and are well worth visiting, along with one of the best small museums in the country. The city is also an important administrative centre for the surrounding mountainous region.

■ **Hotel**. The *Hotel Skampa*, on the right as you enter the city from the west, is of a reasonable standard. The best hotel in the town is currently the *Hotel Akelida*, reached by a sharp left turn from the Tirana side of the town, with a pleasant quiet bar and good restaurant.

■ **Medical care**. Central Policlinics (out-patients dept.), tel. (0545) 35 00; District Hospital (emergency service), tel. (0545) 26 66; Dr Naim Demitri (surgeon, Otorino-laryngologist), tel. (0545) 20 84 (home); Dr Nimet Gjika (internist-cardiologist), tel. (0545) 30 75 (home).

■ **Police station**. Police Headquarters, tel. (0545) 23 00, 21 92, 26 00.

History

Elbasan came into prominence in the Roman period when it was known as *Mansio Scampa*. The word *Scampa* means rocks or peaks in the ancient Illyrian language. The Romans built a substantial fortress here, about 300m square, protected by U-shaped towers. In the 3C and 4C it became known as *Hiskampis*. It had developed as an important trade and transport centre near the junction of the two branches of the Via Egnatia coming from Apollonia and Dyrrachium. Ptolemy wrote that it was the town of the Eordaei tribe, who later migrated to Macedonia. It took part in the spread of Christianity along the Via, and had a bishop, cathedral and basilicas as early as the 5C. But as a town in a wide river valley, it was vulnerable to barbarian attacks once the legions were withdrawn, and despite the efforts of the Emperor Justinian to improve the fortifications. Hiskampis was destroyed by the Bulgars and Ostrogoths during the Slav invasions of the Balkans. Although some semblance of urban and military life must have continued for a time, as it is mentioned in the work of Procopius of Caesarea in the 6C, it was totally destroyed by the Bulgars in intermittent attacks over the next 200 years.

The site seems to have been abandoned until the Ottoman invaders built a military camp here, followed by urban reconstruction under Sultan Mehmet II in 1467, who constructed a massive four-sided castle with a deep moat and three gates. He named it *Ilibasan*, meaning 'strong place' in Turkish. It became a centre of Ottoman urban civilisation over the next 400 years. By the end of the 17C it had 2000 inhabitants, but over 900 shops, a sign of its regional commercial importance. The fortress was dismantled by Reshid Pasha in 1832. There was also particular emphasis on religion, and education, Elbasan having the first teachers' training college in Albania. In 1906 the American traveller John Foster Fraser noted the violence in the town, with regular murders of the Ottoman government functionaries.

In 1909, after the Young Turk revolution, an Albanian National Congress was held here to study educational and cultural questions. The delegates, all from central and southern Albania, endorsed the decision of the Congress of Monastir (modern Bitola, FYROM) to use the Latin alphabet rather than the Arabic script in written Albanian. The Muslim majority opposed Prince William of Wied in 1914. It was occupied successively by the Serbs, the Bulgars, the Austrians and the Italians between 1915 and 1918. Industrial development began in the Zogist period when tobacco and alcoholic drinks' factories were established. It was an early target for liberation by the strong Partisan brigades based in the surrounding mountains, and was taken from the retreating Axis troops on their way north in 1944.

Follow the main road towards Elbasan past the metallurgical complex, then into the centre of the modern town, and park outside the *Hotel Skampa*, a modern concrete building. It has a restaurant and souvenir shop. At the side of the hotel is one of the oldest buildings in the city, a ***Turkish hammam**, which was described by the Turkish traveller Evliya Çelebi when he visited Elbasan in 1672. It marks the boundary of the original Ottoman town, being built in the far corner of the bazaar. The roof is made of a series of small conical domes, covered in tiles. Beyond the wooden entrance door is a later structure that was built onto the original bath as an additional dressing room and social centre. The original building lies furthest from the road, a square structure containing hot, warm and cold rooms, and a latrine. It was reconstructed in 1874. There are eight upper level windows.

With privatisation, a quite disastrously inappropriate modern café has been opened inside the atrium, complete with video machines by the central hexagonal fountain, although the older parts of the bath to the south are much as they always have been, except for the intrusion of snooker tables. Although this does mean that it is possible to see the interior easily, which was not the case before, the whole development is a disaster from the point of view of the preservation of the ethos of one of the most important and attractive historic buildings in Elbasan.

Cross the road and walk about a kilometre to the right, where a tower on the corner of the Turkish fortifications can be seen. Inside the walls, on the far side, there is a clocktower and the King's Mosque, among later buildings, mostly small dwelling houses built in the 19C when the military importance of Elbasan had declined and parts of the fortress had been taken for urban use. On the opposite corner of the junction to the tower is another mosque, and the Kristoforidhi Museum.

The remains of the ****citadel** indicate the military importance of Elbasan to the early Ottoman conquerors, with the relatively complete south wall showing the scale and strength of the fortifications. Parts of the Roman and Byzantine masonry used in the rebuilding under Mehmet II can be seen, most clearly in the south-west tower foundations. There were 26 towers placed equidistant along the rectangular walls of the original building, each about 40m apart and 9m high. The ancient Via ran through the middle of the fortress. The interior of the citadel is quite interesting and worth a visit.

After the Ottoman peace had been established, a programme of public building began, of which the **King's Mosque** is the best surviving example. It is one of the oldest mosques in Albania, with construction beginning in 1492. It is of particular significance to visitors with interests in building construction, being one of the few structures remaining in Albania that shows Byzantine period methods. It was spared vandalism during the Hoxha period, being a sufficently important historic monument, but the structure was neglected and it is scheduled for restoration. The prayer hall is divided by wooden columns.

Returning towards the road junction, the **Nazireshte Mosque** is on the opposite side of the road, a square structure with a fine dome, but without a minaret. Along the roadside wall are the remains of a Turkish *hammam* and a large 18C prison.

On the far side of the complex of buildings within the original Turkish town is the **Church of Shen Maria** (St Mary), a long oblong basilica, with a richly carved and decorated wooden interior, built in the 19C between 1833 and 1868. It is difficult to find; ask for Rruga Albert Kavaja, and follow this street to the end of the inner town, then turn right through narrow alleyways. Note the red brick bell tower. The large size indicates the substantial Christian minority in Elbasan prior to

Albanian independence. In the communist period the church was turned into a 'Museum of Christian Art of the Turkish Period'. At the moment it is closed and its future is uncertain. On the opposite side of the small enclosed square in which it stands was a school, recently demolished during rioting in 1991.

The **Kristoforodhi Museum**, in a narrow street behind the Nazireshte Mosque, is dedicated to Kostandin Kristoforidhi, one of the Albanian translators of the Bible, and shows Albanian middle-class intellectual life at the time of the renaissance in the 19C. It is rarely open at the time of writing.

The other museums of Elbasan are currently difficult to gain access to, and in some cases their future is uncertain. These include the birthplace of the Partisan hero Qemal Stafa and the Museum of Popular Culture. The Museum of Education, in an attractive Turkish building in the Old Town, is generally open on weekday mornings. It is housed where the National Congress of 1909 met. The exhibits are of specialist interest.

Happily the ****Ethnographic Museum of Elbasan** has been reopened, in a double-fronted Turkish house on the far side of the public park, on the east side of the *Hotel Scampa*. This is one of the most beautiful and interesting small museums in the country, and is well worth a visit on any journey. It is open from 08.00 until midday. (In 1995 it was closed for a time pending the settlement of a property restitution dispute, hopefully it will be reopened soon.) The building in which it is housed is one of the few remaining large middle-class Ottoman period houses in the city, and stands on the edge of a jumble of one-storey Ottoman period buildings, mostly in a ramshackle condition. It was the first school building in the city, opening in August 1908.

You enter through a stone arch into small garden, past a brass monument on the left-hand side of the main gate commemorating early pioneers in education in Elbasan. The **lower floor** contains exhibitions of traditional tools and rural crafts, showing wool and goat skin weaving work, regional agricultural implements, copper and wooden tools, with a very fine traditional loom used for weaving goat's wool in the left-hand room. The most interesting exhibits are on the **upper floors**, particularly the finely arched *çardak*, the open balcony and internal area with very good carving on the wooden ceiling. Interesting traditional musical instruments are exhibited in glass cases here.

On the left is a room arranged for a traditional wedding night, with an Albanian bride's clothes set out. It shows very fine metal and silk work on the trousseau, and on the wall hangings. To the rear left is an equally traditional men's room, with sofa-lined walls, very fine wood panels, rugs and sheepskins. In the centre is a copper *mangall* to hold the fire, and an ornate plaster chimney.

The room to the rear left is a textile sewing room, where the women of the house would have spent much of their time. From the age of puberty, much of an Albanian girl's time was taken up with making her bridal clothes. The front room to the right is the women's room, with the same general pattern of furnishings as the men's room. It has a remarkable wooden cradle displayed, one of the oldest in Albania. Note the two dragons carved on the ends, to protect the child from the evil eye. The carved wooden ceiling is paricularly fine. There is a small recess for bathing in one corner.

Elbasan was the home between the wars of the English Albanologists, F.W. and Peggy Hasluck. F.W. Hasluck was the doyen of Bektasi studies, and his wife wrote seminal works on the ethnography of the northern highlands and the Albanian clans. During the Second World War, Peggy Hasluck, by then a widow, was the Special Operations Executive expert on Albania and was responsible, in Cairo, for briefing the British liaison offices parachuted in by SOE to assist the Albanian resistance.

She had an eventful personal life, and may well have been the first Englishwoman to have a romantic liaison with an Albanian clan leader. It was something that Paddy Leigh Fermour, a contemporary visitor in Elbasan, regarded as 'needing reckless courage on both sides'.

Her old house, at No 6 Rr Universitatit, is now next to the British run 'Home of Hope' children's home, which welcomes visitors. The Directors are Mike and Judy Smith. Her house is an interesting, modest little building, painted yellow.

South of Elbasan, on the road to Gramsh, are a number of attractive mountain villages, in increasingly remote countryside. The large **Lake Banja** with its important hydro-electric dam is also worth a visit if time is available, although the road quality is poor. **Llixhat** (12km) is a small spa. The Italian occupiers developed it, in the 1930s, for treating rheumatism and skin diseases.

1km along the main road east towards Libyazhdi is the **Elbasan Bektashi tekké**, about 0.5km down a track running left from the main road across vegetable fields, near the village of **Mengel**. It is an attractive small building at the base of the hillside, which appears to date from the late 18C or 19C, with a single domed central hexagonal chamber, and two side chambers. It is currently being restored. Elbasan was an early Bektashi centre in Albania, under the leadership of Shah Kalenderi, one of the first preachers of the Sufi religion to reach Albania.

5km south west from the centre of Elbasan important Roman remains have been discovered near the village of **Bradasheshi**. They are to be found near the metallurgical combine, beyond a crossroads on the outskirts of Bradesheshi village and a small road leading to the village of Fikasi. It appears that they are ancient *Mansio ad Quintum* on the Via. Extensive remains of Roman baths can be seen, with analysis of building techniques indicating construction in the 2C or 3C AD. A nymphaeum has also been excavated, and nine bathing rooms and large quantities of Roman ceramics.

At **Shelcan**, 14km south-east of Elbasan on the dirt track leading towards the Polisit mountains, is the medieval church of St Nicholas, with some interesting fresco paintings by Onuphre dating from the 16C.

The road leaves Elbasan following the river valley past large areas of derelict greenhouses that were once heated from the metallurgical complex. The modern road follows the left bank of the river, whereas the ancient Via was on the right-hand side. After 3km, Teqin Madhe, site of ancient *Scampi* is reached.

After 7km you come to **Labinoti-Fushë**. This small place was an important centre for the Partisan and communist movement during the Second World War. In 1943, a group of British liaison officers under the command of Brigadier Davies was parachuted in from SOE HQ in Cairo to join the Partisan HQ, in the mountain village of **Labinoti-Mal** (4km up a dirt track, left from the main road). Resistance operations in this area are described by Brigadier 'Trotsky' Davies in his memoir *Illyrian Venture* and in *Albanian Assignment* by David Smiley. The famous Ottoman bridge of Aga Bekiavi was destroyed here during World War I.

6km from Labinoti-Mal the road reaches Miraka, ancient *Mutatio Traiecto*. After 10km, there is a very fine**late Ottoman bridge** across the river, near Kamara.

17km further along the river valley is **Librazhd**, a small town, in very beautiful countryside, with the **Polisi mountains** to the right above the gorge. Librazhd grew up on the junctions of mountain paths to the Polisi to the south and the remote regions of Dibra, to the north. It is a centre of wine and raki production.

Both modern and ancient roads turn south east here for the final section in Albania. The Via climbed to its highest point over the river, following the upper Shkumbini to the peak of Darza, about 945m above sea level. Modern **Dardhë**, ancient *Grandvia*, is an attractive hamlet on a steep slope on the right bank of the river, 9km from Librazhd. The *Antonine Itinerary*, a Roman itinerary for the Via, notes the existence of three inns along this section. 9km from Dardha the Via reached the modern village of **Qukës**, ancient *In Tabernas*, after which the modern road turns east towards **Përrenjas**, 610m above sea level, leaving the Shkumbini valley and joining that of the river Raitsa. Ancient *Mansio Claudianum* was 9km east of Qukës, near Orake, on the road approaching Quaf e Thanës.

SELCA

The important Illyrian site of *Selca is reached by a road 3km on from modern **Kukes** village, 7km up the Shkumbini valley, then bear right at the road junction 2km towards Vërri, then a left turn up a narrow dirt track to a modern village known as Selca e Poshtme. The hill has been inhabited since prehistoric times, and was the site of an Illyrian town since the 4C BC.

History

Selca was an Illyrian fortified town, inhabited by the Dassaretai tribe, also known as the *Sasaretae*. They appear to have driven out the Encheleae tribe who dominated the coast of Lake Ochrid near modern Pogradec by the end of the 3C BC. Their territory was bounded on the north by the Dardanians, to the east by the Pelagonians in the Plakanka mountains and the Parauaei tribe in the Leskoviku region to the west.

Selca was founded in the 6C BC. It rose to power in the 4C and 3C BC, when walls enclosing an area of about three hectares were constructed. A number of impressive graves dating from this period have been found, and were excavated between 1969 and 1972, having been discovered in 1948. Selca flourished most between 300 and 100 BC, when the settlement stretched down the terraced hillsides below the hilltop over 7–8 acres of terraces. Prosperity was based on trade with the coastal regions along the Shkumbi valley, with agriculture dominated by stock breeding and viniculture. Until the Via Egnatia was constructed, Selca lay beside the main road linking the upper Devoli valley with the Greek colonial settlements on the coast. It became much less important and prosperous after the Via Egnetia was built and changes in trade patterns after the Roman colonisation of the Balkans.

Some of the excavation results have yet to be published, and the history of the site has been the subject of academic controversy, with some archaeologists claiming that it is ancient *Pelion*, and a connection with Alexander the Great has been postulated. The site is at an altitude of 1040m above sea level and archaeologists have proposed five main stages of occupation, starting in about 2700 BC, in the Neolithic period, then with two Bronze Age civilisations ending in about 1200 BC. After this an Iron Age settlement lasted until about 600 BC when a town was built.

In the spring of 335 BC Alexander the Great fought important battles against the Illyrian tribes in this area. Evidence of later fortifications have been found, and impressive works of Illyrian art in the graves, such as decorated clasps, a beaten gold badge, filigree work and other jewellery. The quality of ceramics found from the early period is particularly impressive. Coins from the Greek colonial settlements at Apollonia, Dyracchium and from Macedonian mints predominate. The Roman consul Publius Sulpicius Galba brought his army to Selca in 199 BC.

After a period of semi-abandonment, urban life in Selca appears to have resumed on a modest scale on the hilltop in the 2C AD. A wall to defend the south and east sides of the town was built of poor quality masonry in about AD 300. Settlement appears to have continued until about AD 570 when the town was finally destroyed in barbarian invasions, probably Slav tribesmen coming from the Via Egnetia, as Procopius describes. The last evidence of urban prosperity dates from the time of Emperor Valentian I, when the walls were refortified against Gothic tribesmen. The site was refortified a third time by Justinian. From the earliest times it appears to have been linked with the Illyrian settlements at Maliq and elsewhere on the plain of Korça. The same type of grey clay ceramics seem to have been made here as on the plain.

The beautiful and evocative **tomb entrances** are well worth the walk up the hill-side, as are the views of the surrounding countryside. Walk up the marked track on the side of Gradishta hill. The higher level tombs have colonnades in the Ionic style and show Greek influence. All were robbed in antiquity after being constructed between the end of the 4C BC and the beginning of the 3C BC. Five tombs have been discovered, with four cut by tunnels into the rock and one is lined with quadrangular stone blocks. The interior of the tombs reveals an antechamber and a burial chamber, with a stone bed for the corpse and shelves for burial effects. Above the tombs is an orchestra which was probably used for ritual ceremonies. The rock cut tombs are very rare in the Balkans and have been linked with similar tombs found at Canosa in southern Italy. In general the style of the tomb construction shows the strong Hellenistic influence on the new ruling elite of the Illyrian towns, with the use of the arch being probably adopted from Hellenistic monuments in southern Macedonia.

Return by the same route to the main road.

The modern road descends steeply down to the **Domosdova plateau**, site of Skanderbeg's first major victory over the Turks in 1444. Until the war much of it was marshy, but it is now good quality agricultural land. On the left of the modern road is the large ferro-nickel mine at **Pishkash**. It was developed as the source of feedstock for the Elbasan metallurgical complex in the late 1960s and early 1970s. The unusually shaped eroded mountain top above the mine is known as 'Skanderbeg's Seat'. After **Perrenjasi**, a nondescript industrial settlement, the road climbs in a long series of dangerous hairpin bends towards the border post with FYROM at Quaf e Thanës, 98km from Elbasan. An impressive new **mosque** is under construction in Perrenjasi, financed by the Abu Dhabi government. The views in all directions over the bare limestone hillsides are dramatically beautiful, particularly of Lake Ochrid. Great care should be taken on this road, as large trucks are frequently encountered on the way from FYROM via Quaf e Thanës (see Route 12).

III NORTHERN EPIRUS AND THE SOUTHERN MOUNTAINS

4 · Kakavia to Gjirokastra

The road is good of quality on the whole, standard width with asphalt, 31km to Gjirokastra from **Kakavia***. The border post with Greece at Kakavia is approached from* **Ioannina***, 57km, either by bus (every hour and a half, approximately) from the central bus station in Ioannina, journey time one hour, or by taxi. The latter costs between £10 and £15 for the journey, the bus about £2.*

The road towards Kakavia winds through attractive, empty deciduous woods, passing **Kalpaki** (34km) site of fierce battles between the Greek army and invading Italian forces in November 1940. There is an interesting small museum illustrating many aspects of the war in Epirus and southern Albania in 1940–41 at the junction of the byroad that runs towards the monastery at Vella. (See *Blue Guide Greece.*) To the east is the small village of **Mavropoulo**, scene of the famous broadcast Orthodox Easter services held for the Greek minority in Albania under communism by the late Metropolitan Sevastianos of Konitsa.

Motor vehicles will be stopped by Greek para-military police on entering the border zone, about 3km from Kakavia, and may be searched. Vehicles not entering Albania must be parked in the official car park 1km from the border. All travellers must report to the Greek police post on the right of the main border control gates for passport and customs control, then proceed to another passport inspection at the Greek border gate itself. It is then necessary to walk about 400m along a narrow road usually crowded with people, goods and vehicles to the gates marking the Albanian border, for the first Albanian passport inspection, then through the steel gates towards a three-storey concrete building housing the main Albanian border control. Passports and visas are inspected again here in the small office on the left; customs inspection is in the building opposite. Visitors with vehicles should allow at least 2 to 3 hours for these often slow and cumbersome procedures, pedestrians up to 1 hour. If drivers encounter a queue of trucks awaiting customs clearance, much longer delays should be expected. Luggage security can be a problem here.

For those awaiting clearance, the Greek army operates a small café in the upper part of the Greek passport control building, with a fine view to the north up the Drinos valley. An Albturist shop used to exist above the Albanian customs control office but is currently closed. If transport has not been arranged, it is usually possible to find taxis in the car park on the far side of the border gates on the Albanian side. If you are taking your own vehicle into Albania you are sure to be approached by people wanting transport, but lifts should not be offered.

Entering Albania and the wide flat expanse of the Drinos Valley, you will immediately notice the extensive border defence works, consisting mainly of lines of small concrete pillboxes—*Bunkere*—built on either side of the road and sunk into the hillside, and the remnants of the military installations and electrified fence that used to surround the country until 1990. The network of hundreds of thousands of pill-boxes over the whole country was built by Enver Hoxha in the aftermath of the Soviet invasion of Czechoslovakia in 1968 when he thought that Albania was also likely to be invaded by Warsaw Pact forces. They are now often used as public conveniences or shelters for livestock, or are being removed from the ground altogther, although this is often a cumbersome and difficult operation.

3km from Kakavia, the road crosses a wide, usually dry section of the Drinos river bed and turns north. The minor road to the south leads towards the village of **Vriseraja** (2km), and continues in that direction to meet the Greek border near **Koshovica** (18km). It soon becomes a poor dirt track and is not recommended. But this route was important in the fascist invasion of Greece in World War Two and about 500m south of Vriseraja is an interesting section of the paved road built by Italian engineers in the 1930s that later facilitated the movements of their motorised vehicles south into Greece. **N.B. This border area is insecure. Avoid**.

The main road runs north towards **Jergucati** (10km), a village at the junction of the road towards Saranda (40km). It then follows the Drinos valley north west, with the wide, often partly dry gravel bed of the river on the right, with a fine view over a wide flat expanse of fields and the towering range of the Buret mountains. Birds of prey can often be seen above the valley, reminding you of the etymology of the name of Albania, *Shqiperia*, Land of the Eagles, from the Albanian, *Shqiponja*, an eagle. Vehicles must stop at the mobile Albanian police posts on this road if waved down, and passports and vehicle documents may be inspected. It is some-times necessary to bribe the police here to be able to travel north towards Gjirokastra, or back south towards the border.

Settlement is concentrated on the west side of the road, in the series of villages of stone block houses built about 500m up the hillside. Most of the villagers are ethnic Greeks, and the Greek language is used throughout the district for many purposes, although Albanian is universally understood and has to be used for some official business. The Drinos valley villages have an attractive, coherent culture and have benefited considerably from the end of communism in economic terms. Although there have been many problems with the reorganisation of agriculture after privatisation, the area has not sufferred the same degree of depopulation as the ethnic Greek villages near Himara. Nevertheless, substantial areas of land remain uncultivated in many places.

After 7km, there is a left turn up a bad road leading to the village of **Zervati** (2km). Here is the church of Shen Maria (St Mary), an impressive building dating from the 10C with 16C additions. **Grapshi** is another typical example of these Vorio Epirote Greek settlements, the first village after the road junction at Jergucati. 1km after this junction is a small track leading from the main road east towards the village of **Peshkepi** (5km). On a low hill on the south side of the village is the church of Shen Maria (St Mary). It is disproportionately large for the settlement, and is thought to have been the site of the medieval bishopric of *Dryinopolis*, a title still claimed by the Greek bishopric of Konitsa, on the other side of the border. It was built in the early part of the 10C and is the earliest example of a cross-shaped church of the mid-Byzantine period in the Balkans.

6km further on is a right turn leading to **Libohova**, at the foot of the Buret range. This village was the home of Shanishane, sister of Ali Pasha and of the inter-war politician Avni Rustemi. The ruins of a citadel of this period can be seen in the village. It is in poor condition and used as a livestock pen. A large six storey mansion in the village was severely damaged in World War II but the walls remain. 22km along a very bad dirt track running east is the village of **Polican**, with the interesting **church of Shen Thanasi** (St Athanasios), dating from the early 16C.

11km from Libohova down a dirt track to the south-west is the mineral spring of **Glina**, source of an excellent naturally-carbonated mineral water that is bottled and distributed nationally. It is believed to be particularly beneficial for the urinary tract, the stomach and the kidneys.

> The original Glina village was virtually destroyed in the Second World War in bitter fighting between Balli Kombetar and ethnic Greek resistance groups from the 'Northern Epirus Liberation Front'. There was also fighting throughout the Gjere (Kairi) mountains between the same forces, that led to widespread depopulation and refugee problems, with the inhabitants of many Greek villages fleeing over the border to Greece. Enver Hoxha's Partisans were the main beneficiary. The history of these events is highly controversial.

The hilltops on both sides of the valley have yielded much evidence of Illyrian settlement, at sites such as **Karroqi**, **Mallcani** and **Vergoi**, but there is little to see to reward the visitor after the arduous and difficult climb to the hilltops other than fragments of Illyrian walls and magnificent views.

The most interesting village in the valley, and the largest, is **Dervicani**, 1km left from the main road, 12km to the north of the Jergucati junction. Follow a dirt track into the village. The church, an oblong 18C building, is in the process of restoration after many years of use as an agricultural machinery store under communism. The remains of the frescoes and screen vandalised during the 1970s can be seen. The size of the church is an indication of the general fertility of the valley and the much larger population it once supported. There is a good *kafenion* in the village near the church, under a large plane tree.

There is another interesting Orthodox Greek church, dating from about 1600, in the village of **Goranaxi**, 2km from Dervicani, along a very rough track, really only suitable for walkers or four-wheel drive vehicles. Park in the centre of the village; the church is near the junction of two streams. It has very beautiful rich internal paintings, and follows the architectural pattern known as the Athos Style in its construction. A mountain path above the village leads to the site of the old Ravenja monastery.

Every building in these and adjacent villages is constructed from small stone blocks using traditional dry-stone walling techniques; the paths are made of interlocked limestone blocks and piles of scree are seen everywhere. The austere but beautiful general environment brings to mind the epithet coined by the novelist Ismail Kadare for Albania, the 'Land of Stone'. The valley has a particularly rich musical tradition, with singing techniques that have preserved ancient and medieval polyphonic modes, and an opportunity to hear local performers should not be missed. In practice the best prospect for doing so is at a wedding, which tend to be held in the mid-summer months. Above the villages are the low peaks of the **Gjere** mountains (Kairi, in Greek), 1583m at their highest point.

Return to the main road and follow 8km north to Gjirokastra. On the right 3km from the city there is a fine Ottoman period arched bridge over the **Drin**. 2km from the town is a left turn leading to **Lazarati**. There is a beautiful Bektashi **tekké** in the upper village, dating from the 18C. The name of Lazarati suggests that it was originally the Gjirokastra leper colony. The *tekké* contains the grave of Baba Zemelirr, a Turkish *baba* of the 18C. The village is entirely ethnic Albanian and highly traditional, with interesting local crafts and costumes. Many inhabitants are strong supporters of the Balli Kombetar and Legaliteti movements. **In periods of**

tension with the Greek minority, intercommunal relations here are often difficult and unaccompanied visits are not recommended then. Continue until the left turn for Gjirokastra is reached (8km).

5 · Gjirokastra to Saranda and Butrint

Gjirokastra to Saranda, 61km, via Delvina (21km from Saranda). Follow the main road from Gjirokastra back towards Kakavia, turn towards Delvina and Saranda at Jerucati (18km), then take steep mountain road over the Gjere mountains. Butrint is 16km south of Saranda, by the coast road.

GJIROKASTRA

Gjirokastra (pop. 56,000) is an evocative and remarkable town, famous for its architecture, and for its dramatic views of the Drinos valley and the forbidding limestone peaks of the **Buret** and **Lunxherise** ranges. As a mountain stronghold, with a rugged grandeur and turbulent history, it seems in its atmosphere to represent to many visitors the very essence of Albania; severe, beautiful, and uncompromising in spirit.

It is a UNESCO World Heritage city, with a unique pattern of Ottoman-period buildings, particularly the citadel, mosques and the 19C merchants' houses, set on a rugged, sloping site. The low hills, on two almost parallel ridges, divide the city into different quarters, with severe, block-like architecture. All is dominated by the famous citadel, a magnificent medieval and Ottoman fortress that dominates the Drinos valley and has caught the imagination of travellers since the days of Byron, Hobhouse and Edward Lear.

Gjirokastra has been the setting for many important events in Albanian history, set as it is in a particularly sensitive and militarily strategic area of the country close to the Greek border; it was the birthplace of several prominent contemporary Albanians, including the communist dictator Enver Hoxha (1908–85), and the novelist Ismail Kadare. It was declared a 'Museum City' in 1961, and on the whole the conservation schemes adopted have been successful in preserving the unique character of the buildings.

In 1973 additional government rules were laid down for the protection of the city and it was divided into different zones: basically, the historic centre and the free zone. The historic centre was subdivided into the museum zone and the protected zone. Although in the last two or three years social and political upheaval and shortages of traditional building materials have caused some difficulties, on the whole the city has survived the changes and the blocks of modern flats in the free zone are not unduly intrusive. It is to be hoped that privatisation will not lead to a relaxation of essential planning controls, and the problems of advertising signs and commercial detritus.

The population is a mixture of Greeks, Albanians and Vlachs, with minorities of Yevgjet people, and some Roma (Gypsies). It is a centre of Greek language secondary education in the region, and was chosen to be the first place visited by the Eparch of Athens when he came to Albania in August 1991. As well as Albanian, some Greek is understood and spoken by most inhabitants, irrespective of ethnicity.

Not far from Gjirokastra is Saranda (see p. 145), a pleasant seaside resort with fine views across the Corfu Straits. It has some interesting Roman remains, and it is a good base to visit the outstanding Illyrian and Classical site of Butrint (see p. 147). Butrint is one of the most important archaeological sites in Albania, set by the beautiful Lake Butrint.

■ **Hotels.** Accommodation in Gjirokastra can be a problem. The *Gjirokastra Hotel* is decrepit and filthy. **Avoid**. The only hotel that can be recommended at all at the moment is the *Haxhi Kotoni Bed and Breakfast Hotel*, in Rr Bashkim Kokona. Some people are beginning to let private rooms which are strongly preferable, although there is often little privacy. A hotel owned by the ADI organisation has opened 2km north of the town on the Tepelena road. It appears to be efficient and well managed, with a restaurant and small, if rather expensive, supermarket. A single room is US $40, a double $60 (tel. 0726 3096).

■ **Bank**. Branch of National Bank as described in itinerary (see p. 141).

■ **Taxis and coaches** from the square opposite the *Gjirokastra Hotel*. Some buses stop on the main road in the lower town.

■ **Police**. Tel. (0726) 36 82

■ **Medical care**. Policlinics (Emergency room), tel. (0726) 22 22; District Hospital (Emergency service), tel. (0726) 23 10; Dr Aristotol Gushi (surgeon), tel. (0726) 22 94 (home); Dr Robert Asqeri (internist), tel. (0726) 37 26 (home).

History

Although originally an Illyrian settlement, with a connection with the Argyroi tribe, Gjirokastra also has a legendary origin, it being said that it was founded by a Greek princess called Argyros. In early antiquity the city site was almost certainly inhabited, but the area was dominated by the Illyrian city of Antigonea, on the opposite hillside of Jerma, near the modern village of Saraquinishta. Later Roman artefacts have been found in the vicinity. But then for many centuries Gjirokastra was wreathed in mystery and the city is not mentioned in written documents until 1336, when it was described by the Byzantine chronicler Kantakuzenos as a stronghold of the Zenebish family. Stone from nearby *Hadrianopolis* was probably incorporated in some of the early buildings, particularly the lower levels of the citadel which were rebuilt in that century by Gjin Bua Spata.

In 1417 it was seized by the Turks and remained an important centre of Ottoman power and administration for hundreds of years, becoming the centre of the *Sandjak* of south Albania. Fiscal registers for the years 1431–32 show that it then had about 160 dwelling houses. It grew in size considerably in the 16C, spreading outside the city walls. In 1812 it fell into the hands of Ali Pasha of Tepelena who held it for some time. After he was displaced by the forces of the Sublime Porte, the city became a centre of administration rather than of trade until the end of the 19C. During a rising in 1847 the peasants of the Drinos valley occupied the town but were unable to take the citadel and were defeated by the Ottoman troops.

From July 1880 Gjirokastra became a centre of Albanian nationalist activity, with the foundation of the Albanian League taking place here, and the Assembly of Gjirokastra discussed the question of independence from Ottoman rule. The strong Bektashi *tekké* in the city was a prominent influence in these movements. The dominant proposal at that time was of an Albanian state having autonomy in its internal affairs but relying on the Porte in the sphere of foreign relations. After Albanian independence in 1913, following the Second Balkan War, the status of the city and surrounding region was highly unstable and many years of political turmoil followed. The area around the city was ravaged by bitter fighting between Greeks and Albanians described by the French war correspondent René Puaux in his classic account *The Sorrows of Epirus*. Thousands of houses were reduced to fire-blackened ruins in vicious inter-communal conflict.

In February 1914 a Pan-Epirote Federation was founded in what had by then been renamed *Argyrokastro* by the Greek inhabitants, and the autonomy of northern (Vorio) Epirus was proclaimed under Georgios Zographos and Metropolitan Germanos of Koritsa. Large numbers of Greeks joined the 'Sacred Army of Koritsa' formed by Zographos, and succeeded in murdering so many ethnic Albanians, or driving them out of their homes in the region, that the Powers, on 17 May 1914, signed the Protocol of Corfu, recognising northern Epirus as Greek.

In the First World War the Greek army occupied the area from October 1914 until October 1915, when it withdrew before an Italian Expeditionary Force. On 3 June 1917, the Italian government representative, General Giacinto Ferrero, proclaimed in Gjirokastra 'the unity and independence of the whole of Albania under the shield and protection of the Italian Kingdom'. It was the first stage in a long, tragic relationship that was to lead to the annexation of the country by Mussolini. Italian influence at the Ambassadors' Conference in 1921 returned the region to Albania, although a state of anarchy prevailed for some time afterwards. The 'Provisional government of Autonomous Epirus' was established here in 1922, but did not last long.

At last a degree of stability was established under King Zog, with the development of some commercial enterprises, including a snuff factory. Under the Italian annexation the town was renamed *Gjinokaster*. In the Second World War the city was a centre of Axis administration, and was liberated by Greek troops and Albanian partisans in December 1943. Ismail Kadare has described the wartime period in the city in his book *Kronikë në Gur* (Chronicle in Stone). In 1946 Greece attempted, unsuccessfully, at the Paris Peace Conference to reincorporate northern Epirus into its territory.

Under communism, the human rights of the Greek minority were frequently violated, particularly in matters of religion and education. In May 1960 the problems of the minority were taken up by Nikita Kruschev on behalf of the Greek leader Sophocles Venizelos, and were a factor in the USSR/Albania split. An account of the religious persecution centring on Gjirokastra is to be found in *Northern Epirus Crucified* by Metropolitan Sevastianos of Dryinoupolis, published in Athens in 1984. In 1990 an association for the protection of Greek rights, OMONIA, was formed, with its headquarters in the city, which has obtained parliamentary representation in Tirana. Citizens of Gjirokastra were prominent in the struggle for democracy in Albania. An important event was the demolition of the monumental standing statue of Enver Hoxha on 8 August 1991 by rioting crowds. (A detailed description is to be found in my report for *The Independent* newspaper, London, 10 August.) Hoxha himself gives a description of his youth in the city in his *Vitet e Vegjëlisë, Kujtime për Gjirokastren* (Years of Childhood: Memories of Gjirokastra).

Among many of the ethnic Greek inhabitants a renewed campaign to rein-corporate northern Epirus into Greece is in progress, while some militant Albanian groups based in the city are attempting to reclaim areas of southern Epirus inside Greece, known as *Cameria*, where it is claimed ethnic Albanians were driven from their homes during the Greek civil war.

The city is approached up a steep hill from the main road, winding in a series of hairpin bends to arrive in Cerciz Topulli Square outside a modern hotel. (A monument to the liberation of the city on 24 December 1943 is passed by a bridge 1km up from the main road.) The hotel used to be called the 'A.Z. Cajupi Hotel' after a Gjirokastra partisan hero. It is now called the **Gjirokastra Hotel**, and urgently requires renovation and competent management, it is not really an acceptable place to stay, having been in decline for five years, but there are magnificent views from the balconies of the upper rooms. In winter, the city and the hotel are often very cold, and a sleeping bag, thermal underwear and warm clothes are essential.

The best way to explore is on foot. Two days are really needed to cover the most interesting streets and buildings, as climbing the steep slopes is arduous. Most of the important buildings lie on the slopes below the citadel. Turning left as you leave the hotel entrance, follow the narrow paved street up past the small shops, all of similar architectural design and originally constructed in the beginning of the 17C, on the site of a previous bazaar. Note the statue outside the hotel itself, commemorating women killed there by the Axis occupiers for their Partisan activities during the Second World War. This quarter is known as the **Old Bazaar quarter** and, as in other historical Albanian cities, was entirely separate from the residential quarters. Most of what can be seen now dates from the latter half of the 19C, when the bazaar was reconstructed after a devastating fire in 1872. The standard of craftsmanship in the stonework and wood carving is very high. Note how the design of the street and of the buildings emphasises the need of security against brigands from the surrounding region.

After about 500m, there is a crossroads. The windows and balcony of the corner house on the south side illustrate particularly well how the inhabitants could use them to see who was coming or to shoot at them without having to venture outside. Take a left turn here and proceed up the slope towards the citadel.

The ****CITADEL** is a magnificently situated large fortress, commanding the whole of the Drinos valley between Albania and Greece. Inside, it contains the National Museum of Arms, an exhibition of military equipment, the buildings of a prison and an execution yard. At least two hours should be allowed for a comprehensive visit, preferably longer.

Although the site was certainly occupied in ancient times, as part of the complex of settlement around *Antigonea*, all that can be seen now dates from two main periods of construction, the first beginning in the second half of the 13C, the second by Ali Pasha of Tepelena in 1811–12. The citadel has a combination of brutal scale and strength, coupled with a design using the terraces of the hill that give it a dramatic elegance and impressive atmosphere, the great dark granite blocks evoking in the mind the conflict and bloodshed that has so often affected the region in the past. The citadel and museum are entered from a small gate reached by walking up the fine Ottoman roadway running from the city to the citadel walls. There is a small charge for entrance—at the time of writing 100 lek. You walk

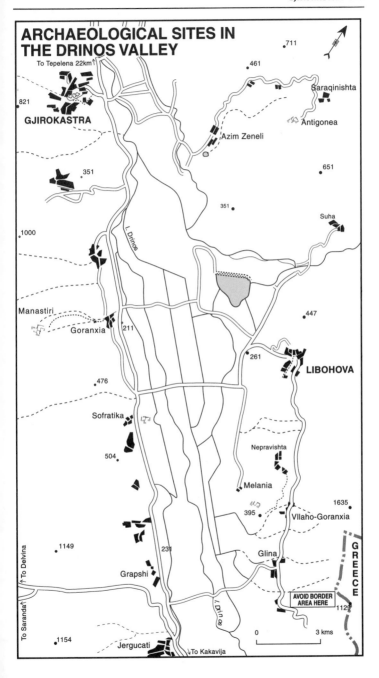

ARCHAEOLOGICAL SITES IN THE DRINOS VALLEY

- 711
- 461
To Tepelena 22km
- 821
GJIROKASTRA
Saraqinishta
Antigonea
Azim Zeneli
- 351
- 651
- 351
- 1000
Suha
I. Drinos
Manastiri
Goranxia
- 211
- 447
- 261
LIBOHOVA
- 476
Sofratika
Nepravishta
- 504
Melania
- 1635
- 395
Vllaho-Goranxia
- 1149
- 231
Glina
Grapshi
GREECE
AVOID BORDER AREA HERE
- 1129
To Delvina
To Saranda
I. Drinos
- 1154
Jergucati
To Kakavija
0   3 kms

Citadel of Gjirokastra

through a dark tunnel entrance into a long floodlit vault which houses most of the exhibits in the **National Museum of Arms**.

This exhibition has been situated here since 1971, and illustrates the development of weapons in Albania from the earliest times to the present. The large number of guns and other military equipment from the First and Second World Wars are of interest mainly to specialists, with an unusual example of a very early Italian tank at the far end. There are also some characteristic weapons from the late Ottoman period. Of greater general interest are the very good and well-displayed exhibits in the small inner museum near the exit, which houses a variety of hand weapons from the 18C, 19C and early 20C, including daggers, yataghans and pistols, some very richly decorated with silver filigree work. The exhibition of weapons from the period of Skanderbeg is also very interesting. A colossal statue in the socialist realist style near the exit commemorates the Gjirokastra Partisans' heroism in the war. Pass through the arch onto an open terrace with spectacular views of the Drinos valley northwards. At the far end is an old American Lockheed fighter, which the communist regime claimed was forced down in a spying mission in the 1950s. On the right are the entrances to cells dating from the use of this part of the citadel as a **prison** in Ottoman and Zogist times.

Follow the path through the walls beyond the aircraft, into the central area of the citadel, a very large flat enclosure which contains the ruins of what were mostly Ottoman civilian buildings. Keep on the left and follow the walls to the south-west tower. It appears that this side of the castle was not originally fortified and what the visitor sees now dates from Ali Pasha's time at the beginning of the 19C. Given the impregnable situation and sheer drop into the gorge, the decision of the early military architects is very understandable.

At the far end is a modern open theatre and performance area, where the Gjirokastra Festival used to be held. This was a very important international gathering of folk and traditional musicians, and a place where the rich and diverse musical traditions of Albania could be appreciated, now held in Berat. On the right, down a flight of steps, is a small café in one of the underground vaults, a preserve of traditional social life in the city dark, smoky, almost exclusively male, with a truly Balkan atmosphere of fellowship, political discussion and intrigue.

At the far end, the **garrison buildings** still have a small military presence, but there are no security restrictions and it is possible to look beyond the Ottoman clocktower to the breathtaking **views** southwards over the Drinos valley. On most days in the warmer months eagles and other birds of prey can be seen soaring on the thermals over the valley, a truly Albanian scene, with the great birds that dominate the national flag in harmony with the Alpine scale and grandeur of the landscape. Apart from the conflicts of earlier times, it is easy to imagine how the Italian and German motorised divisions must have looked as they rolled southwards down the valley towards Greece in the last world war, when, as in all previous history, the Drinos valley was of central military importance for northern invaders of the Balkans.

Return around the far side of the tower towards the museum. On this side the remains of the **aqueduct** can be seen (originally it was 10km long), and brought water to the castle from the Sopot mountain. It was built by Ali Pasha, and is shown on several paintings and engravings that have made the citadel famous, such as the work of Edward Lear. There were also remarkable bridges built across this gorge, such as the two-arched bridge that linked Shkembi i Ceribashit with the castle that was demolished in the Zog period, much to the chagrin of the local inhabitants.

Return to the museum and walk through to the end, near the original place of entrance. On request, the curator will show the modern *political prison. You follow through to the far end of the dark vaults under his direction, and climb wooden steps up to the roof of the museum. On the right, on the higher section of the roof, rows of cells can be seen; on the left, on the lower side, a prison yard. Originally built in Zogist times, the prison was expanded by the communists and the yard was said to be used as a place of execution, particularly in the early 1950s when Hoxha's political opponents, many of them dissident communists, were brought from labour camps such as Spaç and Burrel to be executed here. On other sides of the prison roof the dramatic views of the city and surrounding country can be enjoyed although the edges are unprotected and caution should be exercised, particularly on windy days. Return by the same route to the exit. A small gratuity should be offered to the curator if this visit is made.

Leave the citadel by the same route, returning to the central crossroads. Turn left into what is known as the **Mechite quarter** and walk down the slope past more Ottoman-period shops, after 300m the *mosque is on the left, at the corner of another small street leading up to the citadel. It is an elegant whitewashed 18C structure, begun in 1757, with a particularly fine minaret. The interior is dominated by a single dome, with fine ceiling decorations. A unique feature is the water pipe in the lower part of the minaret. It is a building that appeals for the austere purity of its outline. Shop premises were built into its lower structure. Like the other mosques in the city, it is fairly small, a sign of the large Orthodox population that has always existed in Gjirokastra. It was restored with financial help from the Turkish government in 1993/94. Before World War II, there were nine mosques in the town.

Facing you, at the end of this street, is a large modern building that used to be the communist party headquarters, to the right of it is a small building with a branch of the Albanian National Bank.

A very steep slope leads down the hill past the bank to some of the lower quarters of the historic city. Nearby is the church of **St Michael the Archangel**, the main Orthodox basilica in the city, originally contructed in 1756, then rebuilt after a fire in 1833.

Walk back towards the mosque a few hundred metres and a road leads up to the wooded hill that rises behind the Mechite quarter. Here, as elsewhere in the adjacent Dunavat, Pllaka, Cfaka and Manalat quarters, the variety, historic interest and beauty of the **Gjirokastra dwelling houses** can be appreciated.

The domestic architecture of the city is the finest preserved complex of buildings of its kind in the ex-Ottoman empire. Although the buildings of Berat are similar and have a particular charm, they lack the fierce and uncompromising quality of the Gjirokastra houses—their rough monumentality which so captures the atmosphere of this region in late Ottoman times. As a result of the uncertain political future of the city for much of the last phase of its history under Turkish rule, its status as a border town with an ethnically very mixed and often mutually hostile population, and the presence of a large number of rich *beys*, houses were also fortresses and their design reflects this dominant need. Different families were invariably 'in blood' or involved in protracted and violent quarrels over trade, women and land, and although banditry was a way of life, they also needed such collective security that the city offered against recurrent external threats from foreign powers. The latter half of the 19C was also a time of marked commercial expansion and of the growth of Albanian national feeling, and the owners could afford to find the best architects and workmen in the region and finance the construction of buildings that expressed the rich cosmopolitanism of the Ottoman culture but with a specifically Albanian architectural vocabulary.

There are many different examples to be seen, but nearly all conform to a basic plan of a whitewashed stone lower storey, with high walls, often with few or no windows, a fortified doorway, usually reached by external flights of steps and an upper storey or storeys of wood with overhanging wooden balconies. Intruders could be attacked by the inhabitants in several different ways. Within this general pattern of design there are tower houses, and houses with one side wing, or two. The genre appears to have developed originally at the beginning of the 18C, but many of the largest and most impressive houses, with twin wings, were built between 1800 and 1830. In earlier buildings, the ground floor was generally uninhabited and used to secure animals and goods in times of local strife, and for the women's activities, but this changed as the 19C progressed and trade rather than agriculture became the occupation of the owners. The first upper storey of what is usually a three storey construction has a balcony.

The best place to appreciate their structure and uses is to visit the **Museum of Material Culture**, in the Palorto quarter, in a small street descending the main hill, beyond the National Bank building. It is now housed in the building that used to be the Enver Hoxha Museum. It is a much less impressive and interesting collection than it used to be in its old surroundings.

Lower down this hill is the **Gypsy Quarter**, *Gropa e Hajdinit*, literally, the Evgjit's Hole. The **Bektashi Tekké of Gjirokastra**, built in 1727, and closed during the communist period, can be seen on the outskirts of the town in this direction, to the south of the Gypsy Quarter. It is an attractive two-storey building, but the surviving Bektashi community in the town is very small and its future seems rather uncertain. An important meeting was held here in June 1943 to try to establish a united anti-fascist front between the ethnic Greek Northern Epirus Liberation Front and the ethnic Albanian Balli Kombetar movement.

Leave Gjirokastra for Saranda by the Kakavia road, to Jergucati (18km). Turn right at the road junction here, and climb steeply via many tight hairpin bends through the **Muzina Pass**, across arid limestone country with remarkable views east towards the village of Glina and the Buret mountains. After 8km the road divides at **Muzina**, an Orthodox ethnic Albanian villlage. On the left, above the road, the

Church of St Nicholas, Mesopotani

*church of Shenmri, a very fine building undergoing extensive restoration. It is 28m x 13m, with an attractive cloister with four Romanesque arches, and a single apse. Local people believe it was built about 300 years ago.

The road runs across a flat plain, the **Vurgu de Delvina**, which was a marsh until the early 1950s. A small track, left from the village of **Bamatati**, leads to the ***church of Shen Kolli** (St Nicholas) at **Mesopotami**, a predominantly Greek minority village. It is near the site of ancient ***Phoinike**, and masonry from the ancient city is used in the foundations. Fine carvings of dragons and other mythological beasts can be seen, and parts of very high fortifying external walls, enclosing an area of about 2 acres. Many Mesoptani villagers are ethnic Slavs, but speak Greek. Remains of **Byzantine harbour walls** can be seen by the road near Krane village, a relic of times before the sea level changed here.

History

Phoinike was established as the centre of the kingdom of the Illyrian tribe of the Chaones. It became the capital of the kingdom of Epirus in the 3C BC, and is mentioned as a place of importance in the ancient world by Polybius and Strabo.

In 231 BC it was involved in the Illyrian offensive under Queen Teuta against the Epirote League. In 205 BC the peace treaty between Rome and Macedon was sworn here. Under the Roman Empire it continued as a small provincial centre, with many trade links with Saranda, ancient *Onchesmos*. Urban life continued in the Middle Ages, but declined under the Turks and subsequently Phoinike was abandoned, except for a few shepherds and rural inhabitants.

The site can be reached on foot across the fields from the road, on a low flat-topped hill 270m high that is easily recognisable. There are some visible remains on the acropolis which shows extensive foundations of ancient buildings, the most impressive of which are the walls of the central town treasury building and standing columns. Excavation of the site in the 1960s revealed the foundations of a Christian church, theatre, tombs and numerous commercial and domestic buildings. The modern village is a pleasant, rambling little community, virtually all Greek-minority people. About half a kilometre along the road, **Byzantine walls** can be seen, as garden boundaries, on the left. The **church of the Virgin** is worth visiting, a simple oblong building, suffering from serious subsidence problems. There is a small bell tower. on the north wall.

About 6km east of the Finiq junction is the town of **Delvina**, with about 7000 inhabitants, mostly Greek minority people. It has suffered economically from the closure of its food processing factory, and from migration to Greece. The site is interesting, between high cliffs and bare limestone ridges. There is a small ruined fort, dating from Ali Pasha's time. It was visited by Hobhouse on 1809, who noted the general prosperity of the region, and the large number of goats reared locally. Delvina was 'a clean town, peopled by Greeks, with 300 habitations'.

History

Delvina grew up around a Byzantine castle built in the 11C, possibly built on the site of ancient *Omphalon*. In Ottoman times it became a small trading centre, within the *vilayet* of Ioannina. Under Ali Pasha, after 1811, it bene-fitted from his development of Saranda as the port of Ioannina. A branch of the League of Prizren was founded in 1878. It was the birthplace of the distin-guished leader of the Istanbul Albanians, Sulejman Delvina (1884–1932). In the Second World War important battles against the Axis occupiers were fought in the vicinity.

After Delvina the road follows the river valley towards Saranda (16km), first crossing arid limestone uplands then coming into the narrow fertile coastal strip where olive cultivation dominates the agriculture. There are good views of Corfu across the straits.

Corfu Channel Incident

It was here, on 22 October 1946, that the 'Corfu Channel Incident' took place. The British warships *Saumarez* and *Volage* were struck by floating mines, with substantial loss of life, an incident that poisoned Anglo-Albanian relations for many years and led to the impounding of Albanian gold reserves held in the Bank of England in London until 1992. Accounts of the incident, and its many subsequent repercussions, are to be found in *The Eagle Spreads his Claws* by Leslie Gardner (Blackwood, London, 1966) or *The Corfu Incident*, by Eric Leggett (New English Library, London, 1976). Evidence has emerged in recent years to cast doubt on the Albanian origin of the mines concerned, and the highly partisan accounts of what happened that have dominated public and academic discussion of the incident in Britain and the United States may need reconsideration by future historians. But whether the mines were of Albanian or Yugoslav origin, the events led to the largest loss of British life since the end of the war with Germany, at a time when British public opinion was ill-prepared to cope with such losses, irrespective of the cause.

The International Court of Justice at The Hague found subsequently that the British case was legitimate and the refusal of Albania to pay compensation was undoubtedly the root cause of the later problems in bilateral relations. The Albanian case has always rested on the view that the political regime established after the liberation in 1944 had never been accepted or recognised diplomatically by the Allies, and that the British ships were intruding into Albanian territorial waters. As part of the background it should be borne in mind that at this time, in general, there were certainly a number of covert operations organised by Anglo-American intelligence agencies and Albanian émigrés who were trying to overthrow the communist regime.

It has been generally assumed that the Soviet spy Kim Philby, working within British intelligence, played a part in informing the communist regime in Tirana of what was happening, and was responsible for the failure of the émigrés' schemes. Other commentators have felt that the communist regime was secure by the late 1940s and early 1950s, and that the covert operations were incompetently organised and badly carried out and would have failed in any event. A somewhat politically-biased apologia for the covert operations has been written by Lord Nicholas Bethell in his book *The Great Betrayal* (London, 1984), published in the same year in the USA under the title *Betrayed*. In these disputes, as in many other aspects of modern Albanian history, it is likely to be many years before any reasonably full and objective account of many controversial events is possible.

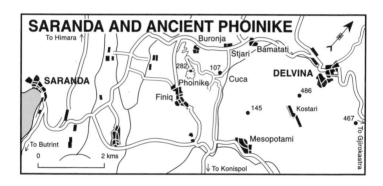

Follow the steep road down into Saranda (2km) past an electrical power installation and agricultural co-operative administration buildings, a military camp, then rows of pleasant small stone houses in olive groves.

SARANDA

Saranda (pop, 29,000), ancient *Onchesmos*, is an attractively situated port and seaside town. It has hotels, and it is fairly easy to find private rooms. Inside the seafront hotel is a teashop, restaurant and souvenir shop, all open to non-residents. This hotel lays on a very good folk music and folk dancing display for these visitors at lunchtime which is well worth seeing. The deep booming rumble of the Epirote clarinet, well played, is a sound that will haunt everyone who has ever heard it while visiting this part of Albania.

The town is built back from the pleasant small beach, fringed with palm trees. On the far side of the bay is the harbour and the modern town above the port facilities, with an unattractive collection of blocks of flats. The town has been used to foreign visitors for many years, and it can be a good place to shop for traditional Albanian artefacts. Day trips can be made by boat from Corfu (see Practical Information), although the service has become unreliable.

- **Hotel**. The *Butrint Hotel*, on the front, quite well modernised, but expensive. Better value is *Genc's Hotel*, by the bus station. Warm, clean and friendly, recommended. Bad B accommodation in Saranda can also be expensive, as much as $40 a night in the summer.

- **Medical care**. Policlinics (outpatients dept), tel. 222; District Hospital (emergency service), tel. 312; Dr Mico Xneferi (surgeon), tel. 445 (home); Dr Jaho Ballaci (internist), tel. 443 (home). A British financed children's hospital, St Luke's, is being built near the main hospital, and welcomes British visitors.

- **Police**. Tel. 350 or 293.

- **Buses**. From the central bus station in the upper town. To most southern towns, four times a day to Tirana. Local bus to Delvina every hour or so.

- **Marina**. Moorings are available in the central; harbour. Care needed over security at all times.

- **Greek Consulate**. In a mansion building about 200m from the hotel. Often closed.

History

Saranda has had several names in its long history. In ancient Greek it was called *Anchises Harbour*, in Roman times, *Onchesmus*, then *Agia Saranda*, 'Forty Saints', Later the Italian form *Santi Quaranta* became more commonly used. It was an important base in World War I for the Italian navy between 1915 and 1918. In this pre-war period, Albanians called the town *Pirro*. The port was called *Porto Edda* after June 1939 under the Italian annexation, to honour Mussolini's daughter Edda (see entry re Count Ciano p. 262). The population at the time was about 2000 people. The town of Saranda is only a few kilometres from Corfu across the straits, and the town has often been linked with the island in history.

Although originally developed by Greek colonists as the port for Phoinike, and mentioned by Strabo and Ptolemy, Saranda only really became a place of any importance in Roman times, as a stopping point on the sea route between Italy and Greece. Cicero, returning from the east, notes 'a favourable wind from Onchesmus'. It was occupied by Ostrogoth invaders in 551. Most of the remains from this period have disappeared, owing to changes in the sea level. It continued as a small port into Byzantine times, then followed the common pattern of decline of most Albanian coastal centres under the Ottoman occupation. Under Ali Pasha it became the port for the trade to Ioannina. It revived somewhat in the early years of this century, although malaria was a serious problem. Between the wars its principal export was dried mullet roe, to Italy. In the Second World War Saranda was one of the few places in the Balkans to experience an assault by a British landing force, when in October 1944, 40 Royal Marine Commando captured the port to prevent the evacuation of the German garrison on Corfu.

Under communism it was developed as a port and tourist centre, although the relentless patrols of the security boats designed to prevent Albanian refugees from swimming to Corfu were an objectionable feature for visitors. Nonetheless, some refugees still tried to escape; I have met an Albanian who served 18 years in prison, six years of which were forced labour in the chrome mines, for attempting this swim.

Saranda is a pleasant place to stay for a day or two, with long hours of sunshine at all times of the year, very mild winters and shelter from strong winds thanks to the surrounding **Eremece** mountains. The sunsets are particularly famous, when the island of Corfu seems to float on the surface of the Adriatic. The beach in the town is dirty. **Avoid**. There is good swimming off the rocks 1km south of the town. It is also a good base to visit Butrint (15km south; see below), where there is no accommodation. Taxis can be hired from the car park below the hotel.

There are interesting remains of the Roman period in the small town **museum,** among the shops above the front, which has been built around a mosaic which was discovered there. There are also some exhibits from ancient Phoinike displayed, principally a marble statue of a woman, and a bust of Artemis, dating from the 2C AD, and various lamps, coins and small artefacts.

At the end of the row of shops, beyond the telephone exchange, are the exposed **foundations of various Roman buildings**, principally a small early Christian **basilica**. Sections of the ancient city walls, dating probably from the 5C AD, can also be seen near the basilica, and in other places, such as the fragment of Roman masonry protruding from the centre of the beach. It is clear that systematic excavation in the town would lead to the discovery of Roman remains of major scale and importance, but there has been modest activity to date. There is also little in the town to remind the visitor of the '*Forty Saints*', each with their own church, that once existed. A very large new **Orthodox church** is under construction on the seafront. On the hilltop above Saranda, at **Kalive**, there are remains of Illyrian walls, made of large rough hewn blocks, dating from the early Iron Age.

BUTRINT

The main purpose of most visitors to Saranda is to visit ***Butrint: in Albanian, the site is also sometimes called **Buthrot**. This is one of the great, largely unknown, archaeological sites of Albania and of the whole Balkan peninsula. It is situated in remote countryside near **Lake Butrint**, south of Saranda, and is quite close to the

Lake at Butrint

border with Greece. At least half a day is needed, allowing time to travel from Saranda, about an hour each way. There are few facilities at Butrint, so it is wise to take your own food, drink and cigarettes. A major programme of excavations and site development started in 1994, under the auspices of the British School of Archaeology in Rome and financed by Lord Sainsbury and Lord Rothschild under the auspices of the Butrint Foundation which was established in 1994 with a donation from them of £500,000.

Travelling south by the coast road from Saranda, after 17km you reach the modern hamlet of **Ksamil**, ancient *Hexamilion*. In the communist period various experiments with shellfish farming were made here, mostly unsuccessful, and Lake Butrint, seen on the left as you proceed down the road, is beautiful but largely useless economically and few people live in the vicinity. By the northern boundary of the lake remains of the outer walls of the ancient fortifications can be seen, part of a defensive system that made ancient Butrint effectively an island. The first walls were built of very large blocks of stone in the 4C BC, and were rebuilt in late antiquity, along with square towers at each end. Proceed south from here, with the road hugging the low hillside above the lake.

In general all this region has been depopulated in the last two years by emigration to Greece. Although not suffering the same intractable public order problems as some parts of Albania near the Greek border, you should exercise caution, and avoid wandering around the countryside without reliable local guidance. The hillsides are rich in interesting flora and butterflies. There are proposals for mass tourist development in this area which give rise to great concern on environmental grounds.

History

The settlement of Lake Butrint lies on the outlet of a small river, about 4km from the sea. The lake, stretching about 8km from north to south, and 3km east to west, is navigable 5km from its outlet. The Vivari channel to the south is open to the sea. Diversion works to the Bistrica river have reduced its flow and added considerably to the salinity of the lake, adversely affecting the wildlife therein. This process has been assisted by diversions of rivers above Saranda for hydro-electric power, without regard to the ecological impact. It has, however, reduced the mosquito problem, now merely a nuisance but pre-war making Butrint a notorious malaria blackspot.

In Classical mythology, what was known as *Buthrotum* was supposed to have been founded by settlers from Troy. It was referred to by Virgil (*Aeneid*, Book III 292–293): 'Soon were the lofty peaks of Corcyra lost to view; We (e.g. Aeneas and his companions) coasted along Epirus, and coming to the Chaonian Harbour, we drew near Buthrothum, that hillcity.'

The ancient legend, revived by Teucer of Cyzicus, claims that having arrived at this site from Troy, Priam's son Helenus sacrificed an ox to ensure his safe entry to Epirus. The wounded ox plunged into the sea, swam into a bay and then walked onto a beach where it fell and died. Helenus took this as an omen and he called the place *Buthrotos*, meaning 'the wounded ox'. According to Virgil, Helenus was already established there, married to Andromache before Aeneas arrived. The events in the French classical tragedy *Andromache*, by Racine, take place at Butrint.

In reality the area was certainly inhabited from the earliest times. Excavation has revealed Neolithic settlement, communities based on fishing probably similar to those of Maliq, near Korça. These perceptions are likely to

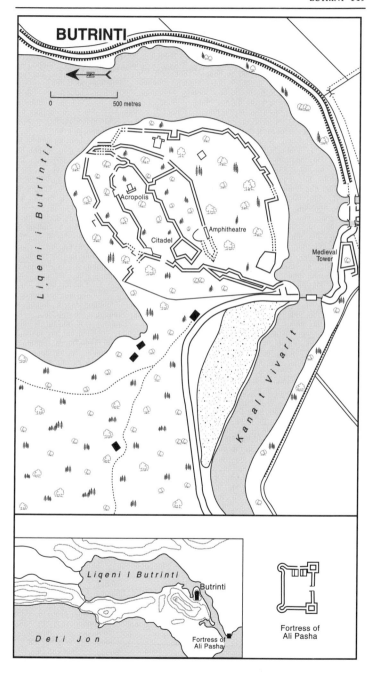

BUTRINTI

0   500 metres

Liqeni i Butrintit

Acropolis

Amphitheatre

Citadel

Medieval
Tower

Kanali Vivarit

Liqeni I Butrinti

Butrinti

Deti Jon

Fortress of
Ali Pasha

Fortress of
Ali Pasha

be reinforced by the very recent Neolithic discoveries (September 1992) of American archaeologists in a cave between Butrint and Konispol, 21km further south, near the border with Greece. Excavations there had begun in 1939, but were cut short by the onset of the Second World War.

After the Neolithic era, the area was a major centre of Illyrian settlement. An Epirote tribe called the *Prassaiboi* lived in the region. A substantial city and fortress was established as early as the late 7C BC. The top of the hill was circled by large blocks of unhewn stone. This was followed by colonisation from Corfu in the 6C BC. The precise extent of Greek and Illyrian influence in the foundation of the city is an academically controversial matter. The Greek colony was under the ultimate control of Corinth and was mentioned by the Greek geographer Hecataeus in the 5C as an Illyrian *Polis*. In the 4C BC the city was growing rapidly and the first promenade and temple were built. It soon became part of the kingdom of Epirus, and was governed by a Council of all free citizens, the *ecclesia*.

It became an important Roman town after the conquest and the break up of the Epirote League, and it was spared the destruction meted out to most of the 70 other cities of Epirus. In this period, it increasingly overshadowed Phoinike. In the time of Julius Caesar and Augustus it was a naval station and grain depot for Caesar's army. About 10 BC the main aqueduct, bringing water to the city from the Xara springs, was built. The aqueduct was about 3km long and is depicted on Roman coins dating from the time of Augustus and Nero. Butrint is mentioned frequently in the letters of Cicero, who, in a letter to Atticus, compared it with Antium. In the 4C the city walls were rebuilt, which by then enclosed a substantial town covering 11hectares with a theatre, market buildings and temples. This activity is thought to be linked to the interest of the Emperor Julian the Apostate in Epirus. Christianity was established at Butrint at a very early stage. The first bishop of the town was consecrated in 451, linked to that in *Nicopolis*, and Christian buildings dating from the late 5C have been excavated. The city successfully resisted the Ostrogoths who occupied Corfu in 551.

Urban settlement continued between late antiquity and the conquest of Butrint by the Norman, Manfred of Sicily, in 1081. It is mentioned as a city in the chronicles of George the Cypriot and later by Arsen of Corfu (876–953). The latter praised the fertility of the soil, local fruit trees and the mussels of the lake. In 1084 the town was plundered by Normans and partly burnt down. About the middle of that century it was mentioned in the guide for medieval merchants written by the Arab chronicler, Al-Idriz, as a prosperous small city with a market and many shops. In 1204 it became part of the Despotate of Epirus. A separate fortress, away from the central acropolis, was built in this period. Further fortifications were built by the Venetians, who maintained an important naval station at the mouth of the river for over three hundred years. It was taken over by the Turks, and then by Ali Pasha. The latter constructed a fort by the river estuary mouth. It was occupied briefly by the French under the Treaty of Campo Formio in 1797, during the Napoleonic ways.

In the later Ottoman period, the city was abandoned and vegetation covered the ruins. In 1875 the English traveller Dr James Bennet noted the primitive state of the village, then called *Bucintro*, which depended on olive cultivation. It was excavated by Italian archaeologists between 1928 and 1941, under the direction of Luigi Ugolini, which exemplified the frequent link between the ancient world and modern political controversy in Albania, when many important artefacts were removed from Albania to Italy in a process that mirrored the Italian annexation of the country. King Zog had given a very generous concession to the Italians in 1927. For many years after the Second World War, only Albanian archaeologists were allowed to work on the site. Following the visit of Lord Sainsbury and Lord Rothschild to the site in 1991, the Butrint Foundation was established in London to protect the site and promote archaeological research.

In July 1994 an agreement was signed between the Albanian Institute of Archaeology, initiating five years of excavations. In September 1994 trial surveys and excavations began, concentrating first on the area of the 5C fortress walls. The first results of these studies show that Butrint was much larger in late Roman and early Byzantine times than has hitherto been realised, with the remains of many villas in the vicinity, and what is believed to be the site of the ancient and medieval port has been found. Evidence of the wealth of the area in Venetian times is emerging. The director of the work is Professor Richard Hodges of the British School of Archaeology in Rome. The World Bank is currently considering proposals to make Butrint a national park.

Approach the site by the road, which turns left towards the acropolis, and park near the site entrance. Enter through a gate, where a small charge is sometimes payable, usually 100 lek. The path is marked by two small columns. The general aspect is of an ancient landscape with ruins of the sort beloved by the neo-classical painters of the 18C, with rambling creepers and other vegetation concealing a wealth of ancient masonry. Farm animals such as sheep and pigs are often found grazing within the site boundaries. The site is large and complex, with ruins from many different periods, and for the non-archaeologist or non-specialist student of the site, the easiest route on a first visit is to keep as close as possible to the perimeter, and walk around the walls and see the way the town and fortress developed as an island stronghold, and then to proceed towards the centre to see the finest of the ancient buildings. Some parts of the site, such as the central medieval fort, rebuilt by the Italian archaeologists between the wars, and containing the museum, are not at present open, but it is usually possible to enter the perimeter.

Turning right from the entrance gate, you follow the perimeter path past the ruins of a Roman bath and a Venetian tower, then a section of wall dating from the 4C AD. After about another 400m, you come to the remains of an early Christian cult centre, and then a bath formed in the shape of a cross, which may have been part of a medieval church. On the right there is a very fine view over the broadening channel leading back to the lake. You next follow a long section of outer wall, also from late antiquity, then walk through wooded glades towards the north end of the island. On the left, as the end of the path is approached, there are walls from a medieval chapel, near the point where interconnecting walls of the outer fortifications join. The inner wall dates from the 3C BC.

Turning left and following the path by the most northerly point of the island, much older **Illyrian walls** begin, dating from the 4C and 5C BC, built of Cyclopean-scale blocks. The original walls are thought to have been about 9m high here. On the right, there are very beautiful views across the lake, with a rich variety of birdlife. The area used to be famous for hunting, particularly of snipe, and Butrint is occasionally mentioned in 19C British sportsmen's memoirs in this context. Hunters based in Corfu used to make day trips for shooting in the Butrint marshes.

This path leads to the south west, around the edge of the island, from a tower. After a couple of minutes' walk, you will find a gatehouse in the walls and an ancient warehouse, later used as an early Christian burial place. Below the gatehouse is a well where brides used to draw lustral water, the **Well of Nymphs**. A Greek inscription indicating the use of the well can be seen on the wall. It reads: 'Junia Rufina, friend of nymphs'. Several different phases of construction of the well have been isolated, the earliest in the 4C BC. It assumed its final form in the 1C BC, when it was covered with a domed roof and decorated with paintings, one showing two peacocks and a parrot. The nearby gate entrance has a finely carved stone lintel showing a lion devouring an ox. The size and strength of the Illyrian masonry at the lower levels is comparable in the impression created at the great Mycenaean sites of Greece, such as Tiryns and Mycenae. Unusually, towers do not play much part in the Illyrian defences of the city.

Although the perimeter walk can be continued here to return to the entrance gate, this is a convenient point to enter the inner fortress. Across from the trees and scrub is the base of the acropolis, with the oldest fortification walls, dating from the 6C BC. This end of the **acropolis** is accessible, with an **early Christian church** in the centre, among the trees. It is the oldest Christian building in Butrint. In design it appears to be similar to other churches in Albania found at Elbasan, Phoinike and Byllis, with an arched roof and mosaic floors. It dates from the first half of the 4C. In the medieval period it was rebuilt, with the addition of a small chapel on the south side. The far end of the acropolis, where Venetian and Turkish cannon remain in position on the walls, is laid out as gardens around the central fort. This was 'restored' between the wars by the Italians but at the time of writing access to this part of the site is not possible.

Cross the acropolis and climb down towards the central complex of ancient buildings and join the central path through them. They are enclosed within the perimeter wall dating from the 3C BC. From the path, walking westwards towards the site entrance, you will find the remains of a large **Roman house**, dating from the 2C AD. Its centre was an open courtyard paved with flagstones, around which 12 stone columns rose from a plinth. Eight rooms surrounded the courtyard. Next to it is the stoa, an early building perhaps dating from the 4C BC. Next to the stoa is a finely preserved **Roman theatre**, rising against the rocky outcrop of the acropolis. The orchestra is often under water and in the spring is full of toads and frogs. The water is causing problems for the building structure. It was built in the 3C BC and extended in the next century. It is Greek in atmosphere and influence, a far cry from the great Roman edifices of the other coastal cities such as Dyrrachium. The 22 rows of seats would have accommodated about 2000 people. The audience reached the seats by means of six radiating flights of steps. The steep incline forced the builders to support the sides of the seating with transverse walls, supported by two lateral walls, giving the theatre a quadrangular form unusual at the time. Entry to the building was made by a corridor on each side. At the beginning of the 2C the orchestra pit and the stage were reconstructed. A number of statues were found here during excavations, including two animal statues, a head of Agrippa, Augustus's general, and most important of all, the finest Classical statue found in Albania, the so-called 'Goddess of Butrint', now exhibited in Tirana in the National Historical Museum. They stood in six marble niches.

Above the theatre was a 2C BC temple which was built simultaneously with the theatre and integrated into its foundations. Inside there is a foundation where the altar stood, and a stylobate in the east corner. In the 1C BC the floor was covered with a black and white mosaic made in geometrical patterns.

South east of the theatre are the remains of baths, dating from the 2C BC, four rooms, heated by under-floor conduits, and associated buildings. On the opposite side of the theatre to the stoa, below it, are the remains of the **Temple of Asklepios**. This temple was constructed in the 3C BC, and rebuilt in the 2C. Many small marble statues and votive offerings were found here, and are now exhibited in the museum. It is thought to have been fed from water flowing from a cave behind the theatre which was believed to have curative properties. Inscriptions found indicate that Asklepios was thought to be the protective god of the city. The temple was covered with an arched roof. The walls of both the naos, the sacred area, and the vestibule were covered with plaster and painted with frescoes. The front entrance was flanked by two windows. It was reconstructed using similar building techniques to the theatre.

The finest building on the site is the ****EARLY CHRISTIAN BAPTISTRY**, one of the most important and best preserved paleo-Christian monuments in the whole Adriatic region. This is reached by another path through the trees and undergrowth, not very easy to find, east from the theatre, across the 3C walls. Nearby are remains of a very large late Roman bathing establishment, the size of which illustrates the prosperity and importance of Butrint in that period. A votive inscription dedicated to Zeus Cassios, the god protecting mariners, has been found inside it, indicating the importance of Butrint as an ancient port.

The baptistry floor has very fine mosaics showing wild animals, which have been recently cleaned and restored by the British archaeologists on the site. Their style resembles others found in Epirus, at Nikopolis in particular, and would suggest a construction date in the first half of the 6C. In the centre of the mosaic is the tree of the Eucharist, a vase with a bunch of grapes, two small birds and two peacocks above them. Sixteen smooth granite columns support what would probably have been a wooden roof. Some archaeologists consider the baptistry is built on the site and used the structure of an earlier Roman bath building, within a town house, judging by the way the circular baptistry is laid out within square external walls, and from other archaeological evidence. It consists of a chamber on the north side and the main baptistry at the centre of which is the baptismal font from which eight lines radiate. The whole chamber is made up of three concentric circles. The visitor cannot fail to be impressed by the beauty and tranquillity of the place, where the natural surroundings so complement the beauty of the remains.

Return back towards the entrance gate through the woods. On the right is the **gymnasium**, which was built in the 1C and 2C. The main area, above the surviving row of steps, was both a place of physical and intellectual education in the city. A rectangular courtyard is surrounded by a series of rooms with mosaic floors. It is divided into two parts by a central basin in the form of a nympheum. The floor of the northern part is paved with rectangular slabs. Inside the nympheum are three circular niches faced with marble and mosaic. The floor of the basin is faced with marble of different colours in geometrical patterns. The north side was mainly used for gymnastic exercises, while the southern part was a rest and study area. The south-east rooms were parts of a bath house.

Return to the entrance gate along this path.

Some 500m from the car park are the remains of a medieval tower. On the opposite side of the canal, on the promontory above the sea, is a small **fortress** built by Ali Pasha in 1807, to protect the shipping lane from the French fleet. In Roman times there was probably a small bridge hereabouts.

The Treaty of Campo-Formio in 1797, and subsequent international agreements, gave France various Venetian possessions, including the Ionian islands. It was necessary for Napoleon to have good relations with the Albanian pashas, and after the Egyptian expedition, Napoleon made an alliance with Ali Pasha. The Porte in Constantinople declared war on France. A series of hostilities took place throughout Epirus in the following years, with the eventual result a triumph for Ali Pasha after the assault on Parga, in northern Greece. The French withdrew from the Albanian coast by 1814.

The central tower was originally a medieval structure, thought to date from the 14C. The fort can be reached by a small boat ferry (50 lek) and is worth a visit.

There are fine views south towards **Konispol** over the drained marshes from the 4m high walls, about 100m long. The land to the south is nowadays largely used for sheep grazing and horsebreeding. The animals are then sold in Greece, in a trade consistent with the original name of Konispol, *Konispolis*, from the Slav root, *kono*, meaning horse, and Greek *polis*, a town. The marshland drainage ditches are very rich in wildlife, reptiles, and wading and warbling birds in particular. They are threatened by the construction of golf courses under current development proposals.

In the centre of the fort is a small **Byzantine tower** with a red tiled roof. The interior resembles a tholos tomb. There are a number of small rooms for the garrison, with barrel vaulted roofs set into the walls around the triangular courtyard, a prison and storage areas. On the south west corner are the ruins of a **Venetian defensive tower** 8m across, reached by a tunnel from the interior. There are the remains of what are probably other small Ali Pasha period buildings below this tower.

There are pleasant walks south to the **church of Shenmri**, about 2km away, on top of a small hill near the village of **Vrina**, a small and very poor Muslim settlement. Some Kosova refugees are being settled in the vicinity. Vrina itself was established by the communists in 1958, as a Muslim Albanian village within a generally Greek minority area.

Pass a derelict ex-fish farm building 400m on the left, and walk south for about 45 minutes to the church. It was built in 1831 in traditional style, a sign of the relative prosperity of this area at the time of the War of Greek Independence. On the south side are the ruins of a smaller, much older church, probably destroyed in Ali Pasha's wars.

Near Vrina, in June 1940, the headless body of the Albanian Cameria leader Daout Hoxha was discovered. It was alleged by the Italian-controlled government in Tirana that he had been murdered by Greek secret agents. Hoxha was a leader of the Cameria struggle in the inter-war years and was a thorn in the side of the Greek government, leading armed men on raids as far south in Greece as Arta and Preveza. The Greek government claimed he was merely a bandit. The affair played an important part in the propaganda war between Greece and Italy leading up to the Italian invasion of Greece via southern Albania in the following few months.

A rough track south leads to the Greek border at **Quaf e Botës** (22km), but the border post is currently closed. The preliminary excavation results for the **cave of Santa Maria**, at Xarra near Konispol, on the Greek border here, indicate a site of considerable potential importance.

The Cave of Santa Maria site was originally excavated by Italian archaeologists before World War II, and produced the first evidence (in the form of flint tools and the bones of extinct ibex) that the Pavel River valley was occupied in the Upper Paleolithic period (before 10,000 BC). On terraces near the village of Xarra near Konispol, flints of the Middle Paleolithic period have been found. In 1992 a team of researchers from the University of Texas at Arlington and the Institute of Archaeology in Tirana began excavations in a large cave on the Saraqint Ridge above the town of Konispol. The site has turned out to be of considerable importance. It was occupied more or less continuously from the end of the Paleolithic through to the Neolithic Age (c 20,000 to 2600 BC) and has provided a deep and stratified structure of faunal remains which document the introduction of agriculture to Albania (c 6000 BC). The cave was also occupied sporadically in the Bronze and Iron Ages, probably in times of war and social disorder.

The border area here is sensitive and visits to this region are not particularly recommended, although there are no formal obstacles for anyone wishing to make them.

6 · Gjirokastra to Tepelena

34km on main road north, towards Vlora and Fier. Descend from Gjirokastra by a steep road to join the main route, then turn left and follow the Drinos valley for direct travel to Tepelena. For local excursions from Gjirokastra, see below. The road is generally good but often congested. There are frequent security checks near Greece.

This road passes through pleasant open fields along the Drinos valley. A visit to Tepelena can easily be made in half a day from Gjirokastra. In antiquity this region was probably more densely populated than it is now, and there are many small archaeological sites on the hills above the river, and evidence of ancient settlement, on both sides of the valley, dating from both Illyrian and Classical times. Short journeys can be made to all sites, from Gjirokastra, if there is insufficient time to visit Tepelena. Sites are not generally signposted and are difficult to find, often on remote hilltops in the case of the Illyrian hilltowns, and good local assistance is necessary, or prior study of detailed maps in the Tirana Archaeological Institute.

Many local people in Gjirokastra are proud of their rich local and regional heritage, and very knowledgeable about it and are pleased to help as guides, for which a small gratuity should be offered.

N.B. Visitors should bear in mind that the names of places or archaeological sites, used by those with a Classical education or Hellenistic background, are not the local names in use by ethnic Albanians in this region, and that much ill-feeling and wasted time can be avoided if you attempt to find out the Albanian names for destinations prior to departure. This particularly applies to sites which were originally Illyrian foundations, irrespective of later Greek or Roman influence. **N.B. The roads are more difficult than they may appear, and a four-wheel drive vehicle is strongly recommended.**

Leaving Gjirokastra, there is an Ottoman *han* on the left, and other Turkish buildings. The **han** is on top of a low hill, and at the time of writing only the exterior can

Ancient Antigonea

be visited. It is on the edge of the new town, next to a complex of modern flats. Other minor Turkish buildings can be seen in the vicinity. The *han* is an impressive building and it is to be hoped that it will be preserved and opened to the public at some point. It was a place for travellers to stay en route between Fier, Vlora and Greece on the caravan routes.

The *han* can also be reached from the main road, by walking up through the Partisan cemetery. A well preserved hexagonal **Ottoman military watchtower** is situated on farmland above the cemetery, although it is used as a domestic building, and cannot be visited. Take care with hidden entrances to modern underground tunnels. 2km from Gjirokastra is an army camp, 4km, a disused phosphorous mine, both on the west side of the Tepelena road. The road passes through thick deciduous woods, and the dense green vegetation of the river valley.

ANTIGONEA

The site of ancient *Antigonea, known in Albanian as **Jerma**, may be visited from Gjirokastra. The site is difficult to find, on a low hill, up a rough track off the main road near Gjirokastra. Cross the bridge to the east side of the valley, and turn right across the plain towards the village of **Azim Zemeti**. This is a very pleasant little place, named after a Partisan hero. There is a statue of him under a group of fruit trees. The road begins to climb steeply, and passes across very dry, stony, rolling uplands. There is a large Vlach element in the population here, and all along the east side of the Drinos valley, as well as members of the Greek community. The poor, deeply rutted road climbs towards the remote village of **Saraquinishta**. Ask directions locally here, as the site is difficult to find across fields. There is not a great deal to see, with many low walls, and some small standing columns, but if you have time it is worthwhile for the ****magnificent views of the Drinos valley**. A four-wheel drive vehicle is required for this journey in anything other than very dry weather.

History

Antigonea was founded in 295 BC by Pyrrhus, King of Epirus, and built during the next century on the site of an earlier Illyrian settlement. It was named after Pyrrhus's first wife. Excavations have revealed a marketplace, cemetery, domestic buildings and the foundations of a chapel dating from the 9C or 10C. The foundations of these and other buildings can be seen, along with some low-standing columns. The size of the dwelling house of which the latter were part indicates the wealth of the city in its early history. To the south-east of the site there was an early Christian church, from the 6C, where mosaics have been found. A very fine small bronze statue of Poseidon has been found at the site, now in the National Historical Museum in Tirana. These, and other artefacts, tend to indicate a connection with the sea and links with Amantia and the towns in the Bay of Vlora. Antigonea went into decline in the medieval period and was eclipsed by the rise of Gjirokastra as an administrative centre and military stronghold. In the resistance war against the Axis forces, these mountains were important bases for the Partisans.

This excursion can be conveniently combined with a visit to the site of **Melan**. It is reached by the track leading east from the main road near Grapshi village, which then crosses the Drinos and after 4km reaches **Glina**. Melan is off a track leading north from Glina, 2.2km towards Nepra Vishta. This was an ancient Illyrian settlement, 6km away from Antigonea, in the centre of the Drinos valley. It was built in the 3C BC with a military role in controlling the river valley. It was destroyed by the Slav invaders after Justinian had reinforced it in the 6C. Remains of the walls, which enclosed an area of over 7 hectares can be seen, and foundations of a 6C aqueduct. On a hill above the modern settlement of Vllaho-Goranxia there is an attractive small early 19C, Bektashi *tekké*, closed for many years under communism, but now being restored.

6km north of Grapshi, on the same side of the road, was the site of ancient *Hadrianopolis*, where there are the remains of a small amphitheatre. In Roman times it was called Hadrianopolis. Masonry from the buildings has been found in Gjirokastra. The ancient remains are about 1km east of the modern village, best reached across the Drinos river bridge 1km north of the modern village of Sofratika.

The main road to Tepelena runs north-west, 6km, to **Mashkullora**, a small village 3km up a track to the left. Illyrian tombs have been found here, in the vicinity of what was a prehistoric hilltop settlement, probably dating from the 6C BC. The modern concrete monument in the village commemorates the battle fought by local peasants from the area in 1908 against the Ottomans, led by the chieftain Cerciz Topulli.

4km north of Mashkullora is a small road leading west up the very beautiful narrow wooded Kardhiq river valley. 7km up here is **Prongjia**, where there is a small ruined fortress built by Ali Pasha.

After another 3km, the modern village of **Palokastra**, 2km up a track on the right. After the bridge at Kardhiq, turn left at the next crossroads, following the river, to the ruins of *Paleocastra*. In Roman times this was the site of an important stronghold, built between 313 and 311 BC, which controlled the road south from Tepelena. In the early part of the 6C a church was built within the ruins of the castle. Parts of the walls and foundations can be seen on the slope of the hillside near the modern village, along with more recent fortifications dating from Ali

Pasha's time. The site of the monastery of Cep, destroyed in the war with Greece in 1914, is nearby.

The journey is worthwhile in the summer months for visitors who wish to explore predominantly Greek minority villages living the traditional rural life of northern Epirus. It is best done on foot or on a donkey. Then the road passes through the village of **Kardhiq**, 4km. The inhabitants of this village had insulted Ali Pasha's mother when he was a small boy and he took his revenge over 30 years later by murdering most of them in 1811 and destroying a Turkish fort constructed by Sultan Bayzid. Above the village are the ruins of an outlying **fortress** built by Ali Pasha as part of his defensive system for Tepelena, 2km.

TEPELENA

The small town of *Tepelena (pop. 14,000) occupies a very important strategic situation, where the Drinos river joins the Vjosa, and has been a sought-after military strongpoint throughout the ages. The river flows through a wild, wooded **gorge**, and a stop on any through journey is justified, if only to see the riverside, where there is a pleasant café and restaurant. Although the food served may not be regarded as particularly appetising, the raki is of exceptional strength and quality. If a visit is made in the spring when the snow is melting, or after heavy rainfall when the river is in spate, the raging torrent through the rocks is particularly spectacular. The area is often subject to violent storms in the winter and early spring and the centre of the town is prone to flooding. Tepelena was the birthplace of Ali Pasha, or at least the village of Hormovë, nearby, and his **citadel** is well worth a visit. Although it does not have the physical scale and grandeur of Berat, Shkodra or Gjirokastra citadels, it has a unique atmosphere, savoured in the past by many visitors from the Anglo-Saxon world.

■ **Hotel**. One of the worst hotels in the country. **Avoid**.

History

The town of Tepelena lies on the left bank of the Vjose river, about 3km below its junction with the Drinos, on a rocky outcrop between the main stream of the river and the Bence torrent from Kurvelesh i sipërm. In antiquity the mountain above the river was known as the *Aeropus*. The valley is enclosed between high rocky spurs and the plateaux of Griba and Shendelli, but the north-west side is overlooked by the rolling Mallakastra country. 3km to the south-west is the source of *Uji i Ftohte* (Cold Water, in Albanian) a famous spring and healing centre.

The name of Tepelena means *Helen's Hill* in Turkish, the legend being that the place once formed an alliance with the neighbouring villages of Damesi and Dragoti under a local queen called Helen. In 198 BC the Roman consul Titus Quinctius Flamininus defeated Philip V of Macedon near the site of Tepelena, in an important battle fought in the *Aoi Stena*, the Aoos Narrows; Flamininus had only recently been appointed consul and was eager to make his mark against the Macedonians. He took over command of the Roman forces, bringing 9000 reinforcements with him from Rome. Philip's army was encamped on a number of strong points around the gorge. First, Flamininus met Philip to discuss a truce, but no agreement was reached. Then a bloody but inconclusive engagement was fought, after which a local shepherd led the Romans through the mountains above the gorge so that an attack on Philip's rear was possible, and the subsequent Roman victory. The Macedonian position covered the mouth of the Kelcyra gorge, ancient *Fauces Antigonenses*, from the flank, so the Romans could not advance up the Drinos towards Epirus.

Before the First World War, the town had a substantial ethnic Greek presence, making up about a third of the population. The modern town dates almost exclusively from 1920, when existing buildings were destroyed by an earthquake. In the same year 400 Italian soldiers surrendered to Albanian forces here. There is a local tradition that the town should never exceed more than a hundred dwellings or they will be destroyed. Although there was undoubtedly ancient settlement on the citadel site, and the Byzantines built a tower on the rocky outcrop where the citadel now stands, their existing fortifications were rebuilt in turn by the Turks in the 15C and then by Ali Pasha between 1809 and 1812. Tepelena was visited by Edward Lear on his Balkan travels, and he noted the devastated state of the buildings in 1847.

In January 1941 Greek forces made an assault on Italian positions at Tepelena but failed to take the town. After the Second World War an important forced labour camp was established by the communists close to the river, using an existing ex-Italian army camp. It was mostly occupied by Catholic nationalist prisoners from Shkodra and Miredita and became known as the '*Albanian Belsen*' for the brutal and disease-ridden conditions there. After a major cholera epidemic in the early 1950s, which resulted in the death of most of the inmates, it was closed. Many members of the Gjon Marka Gjoni and other famous northern clans perished there.

Ali Pasha

Ali Pasha of Tepelena was born nearby, the son of a local *bey*, descended from a *dervish* family which had been forced to leave Turkey the previous century. After members of his immediate family were murdered by the Ottoman rulers, he became an implacable foe of the Sublime Porte, and by combination of cunning, political skill and military expertise, managed to establish a vast domain stretching from Arta in Greece, in the south, to Berat in Albania, in the north. His fame spread far and wide throughout Europe in the Romantic period and he was visited in Ioannina and in Albania by numerous foreign dignitaries and travellers. His court was that of an Oriental potentate, combining great extremes of luxury and hedonism, and a cruel, tyrannical regime. As many as 600 women at a time passed through his harem. His political opponents were dispatched with summary vigour.

Lord Byron was the most famous of Ali Pasha's English visitors, describing his court thus, in *Childe Harold*:

The wild Albanian kirtled to his knee,
With shawl-girt head and ornamented gun,
And gold-embroider'd garments, fair to see;
The crimson-scarfed men of Macedon;
The Delhi with his cap of terror on,
And crooked glaive; the lively, supple Greek;
And swarthy Nubia's mutilated son;
The beared Turk, that rarely deigns to speak,
Master of all around, too potent to be meek,

Are mix'd conspicuous: some recline in groups,
Scanning the motley scene that varies round;

There some grave Moslem to devotion stoops,
And some that smoke, and some that play are found;
Here the Albanian proudly treads the ground;
Half-whispering there the Greek is heard to prate;
Hark! from the mosque the nightly solemn sound,
The Muezzin's call doth shake the minaret,
'There is no god but God!—to prayer—lo! God is great!'

Ali Pasha is thought to have been the model for the tyrant Giaffir in Bryon's
The Bride of Abydos, and for the pirate father of Haidée in *Don Juan*. In turn, Ali
Pasha admired Byron's 'small ears and curling hair and little white hands'.
His friend and fellow traveller Hobhouse has also left interesting descriptions
of Ali Pasha's court:

The court at Tepeleni, which was enclosed on two sides by the palace and
on the other two sides by a high wall, presented us at our first entrance
with a sight something like what we might have, perhaps, beheld some
hundred years ago in the castle-yard of a great Feudal lord. Soldiers with
their arms piled against the wall near them were assembled in different
parts of the square: some of them pacing slowly backwards and forwards
and others sitting on the ground in groups. Several horses, completely
caparisoned, were being led about, while others were neighing under the
hands of the grooms. In the part farthest from the dwelling preparations
were making for the feast of the night; and several kids and sheep were
being dressed by cooks who were themselves half armed ... we saw the
court Fool, who was distinguished by a very high round cap of fur; but,
unlike the ancient Fools of more civilised monarchs, the fellow is obliged
to confine his humour to gambolling, cutting capers, and tumbling before
the Vizir's horse when his Highness takes a ride.

Later in the 19C the antiquary Colonel Leake described a ceremonial visit of
chieftains to Ali, at Tepelena, thus:

They all come attended with followers armed to the teeth, in numbers
proportioned to the power and rank of the chiefs. Their array in
approaching, and their introduction to the Vizir, afforded some fine
pictures of feudal life which carry one back in imagination to Europe in
the tenth century; for the Turkish conquest of Albania has not merely
prevented this country from partaking in the improvement of the rest of
Europe, but has carried it in manners some centuries further back than it
was at the time of the conquest.

The fate of Ali Pasha and Tepelena and the regime he created, was ultimately
inextricably bound up with the fate of the Ottoman empire. After the death of
its founder, the domain of Ali Pasha had no political future, the Ottomans
were still strong enough, after the Napoleonic period, to prevent the emergence of rulers of independent pashliks with Ali's independence. But he has
left a lasting heritage in the minds of many Albanians and northern Greeks, of
the possibility of a local Epirote regime, unencumbered by loyalties to distant
and expensive capitals such as Athens and Tirana, which would unite the
people of the mountains of southern and northern Epirus, irrespective of

what some Greeks and Albanians still see as arbitary and ill-informed decisions of the Boundary Commissioners in 1913 after the Second Balkan War.

An important meeting of the Young Turk movement was held in Tepelena in February 1909, aiming for the unity of Albanian nationalists and the Young Turk revolutionaries in Constantinople.

Citadel of Ali Pasha at Tepelena

The **citadel** is approached by a path from Rruga Ali Pasha in the centre of the modern town, or paths up from the gorge, which are steep and dangerous in wet weather. The main interest of the walk is the magnificent view over the gorge, woods and surrounding countryside, and the 300m drop into the river. Most of the amenities of Ali Pasha's time, such as the extensive gardens laid out to a sophisticated design by Italian gardeners, have disappeared and the walled enclosure is filled with a jumble of small late Ottoman and inter-war houses and gardens. Although Tepelena was Ali Pasha's home town, it was always very much secondary in political importance to his central stronghold at Ioannina, and the fortress, over 400m long and 180m broad, is an austere ruin. The polygonal towers at either end are the most impressive testimony to his fortifications, and the military importance of Tepelena at that time. Ali Pasha's crest can be seen above the stone lintel in the east gate above the gorge. An attractive rope and wood suspension **bridge**, built by Ali Pasha, crosses the river below the citadel. One of the five small stone towers supporting it has collapsed.

2km south is a fine view of the two rivers converging in the narrow gorge, the beginning of what was known in antiquity as the *Fauces Antigonenses*.

Either return to Gjirokastra by the same route, or carry on north west to Vlora, 68km, and to Fier, 74km.

IV VLORA AND THE CENTRAL LOWLANDS

7 · Tepelena to Fier and Lushnja

From Tepelena the main road towards Memaliaj, 8km, has a good asphalt surface, but is often congested; then to Greshica, 44km, Ballsh, 59km, Patos, 84km, and Fier, 93km.

This route follows the valley of the Vjosa river north-west towards the coast and the industrial centres of Fier and Patos, then strikes inland across the drained marshlands north of the city to the regional centre of Lushnja. On the way the important archaeological sites of Byllis and Nikaia can be visited. The journey down the river valley is through attractive countryside for most of the way, and although Fier is not a particularly interesting city in itself, it has a good small museum and it is adjacent to the great ancient centre of Apollonia (see Route 8).

Leave Tepelena towards Memaliaj, with the high peaks of the Shendellia mountains on the right. The river valley broadens out below Tepelena, with a wide flat gravel bed that in some places is over 2km wide, with many small divergent streams and stands of trees and bushes growing in picturesque disorder. The road clings to the hillside on the right bank of the river. After 11km, you arrive at the small village of **Qesarat**, after which the road leaves the valley and turns inland. The view back up the valley is very beautiful, with the river running between gravel islands and stands of poplar trees, reminiscent, in the view of one recent traveller in Albania, of the young Tigris in eastern Turkey, particularly if it is in spate. After travelling for a time over hilly uplands, via Bejar, Ballsh is approached, the main centre of the Mallakaster region. The landscape changes rapidly from untouched rural woodlands and grazing country to a profusion of small oil derricks, with 'nodding donkeys' lifting the oil, although pitch and heavy oil can be seen coming to the surface naturally in many places.

> For those with particular interests in minerals, geology or the oil industry, a visit to **Selenica** is worthwhile, 30km from a junction on the road 3km from Greshica. This road crosses the Vjosa river near Rexhepa (11km), then winds through reclaimed marshland to Selenica (31km). Bitumen has been mined here since antiquity. An oracle existed in ancient times which pronounced on all matters except death and marriage, with the priestess being inspired by inhaling air and gases from the bitumen deposits that come to the surface. Ali Pasha rented the mines from the Porte in Constantinople, paying 10,000 piastres a year for them. In 1868 the concession was given to Ismail Kemal Vlora, who sold it to an English company in 1875. Later in the century, it came under French ownership, then it was sold to Italians in 1922. The town of Selenica is a centre of Vlach language and culture in this region.

Ballsh is now a rather insignificant small industrial town, but was much more important in both Classical and medieval times. In the medieval period it was known as *Glavinica*, and was the seat of a bishopric. In the town the remains of a large early Christian church have been discovered, 22m long and 17m wide, under the road in the Gjirokastra direction. Although full excavation results have not been published, preliminary reports indicate that the first phase of the church was built in the first half of the 6C, with two later phases of construction following, ending in the building of the apse in the 11C or 12C. To the north-east of the church a cistern has been found. Masonry from Byllis was used in the foundations, including material from the Greek island of Euboeia. The medieval town grew from the Classical site of Byllis and the neighbouring town of Nikaia (Klosi). Rrapo Hekali, leader of a 19C rising against the Turks, was a native of Ballsh.

The modern Albanian villages of **Hekali**, 6km from the main road, reached by a left turn off it (unsigned), 2km before the outskirts of Ballshi, and **Klosi**, 5km from Hekali, stand on the site of ancient towns. At Klosi Illyrian walls from the late 6C and early 5C BC can be seen, about 20 minutes' walk from Byllis, but most visitors will want to concentrate their attention on the latter, as it is a fine, compact hill site, with much to see. Turn off the main road in this direction and walk about 1.5km to the base of Gradishta hill, then up the hill to the site of ancient Byllis.

The ruins of the walls of Klosi are about 2km on the eastern side of the modern village.

BYLLIS

Byllis was originally built as an Illyrian stronghold to help control the Vjosa valley. It became a town by the 3C BC, and was surrounded by a protective cordon of hilltop forts at Gurzezë, Margelliç (see below), Rabie, and Matohasanaj. Its greatest period of influence was in the 4C and 3C BC, although masonry dating from the 6C BC has been found. Pliny, writing in the 1C AD, calls it a *colonia* and one of the several Latin inscriptions found here mentions a public road leading to the *Colonia Byllidensium*. Restoration works have been carried out on the older monuments. Byllis remained an important centre of trade throughout the Classical period, with buildings from as late as the 6C. It became a bishopric after the Council of Ephesus in 431.

The site is entered through remains of the external perimeter walls, if approaching from the Nikaia direction; the walls run along to the remains of a tower on the north side, with the ruins of various urban buildings straight ahead of you. Outside the inner walls, dating from the refortification of Justinian, are the foundations of a private house; inside these walls are a theatre, agora, stoa, part of a stadium, and other Classical buildings, and the foundations of two 6C churches. In antiquity the walls were nearly 3m thick and 9m high, with eight defensive towers, and it must have been a formidable stronghold, but it was unable to withstand the Slav invaders, despite Justinian's addition of six more towers to the inner defences.

The **theatre** is the most impressive remaining structure. It was built in the middle of the 3C BC and reconstructed in the 2C and 3C AD. With 20 rows of seats, it could accommodate 7000 people, and is Greek in inspiration and atmosphere. The structure incorporates elements of Illyrian masonry dating from the 6C BC. To the north of the theatre are the remains of a **Roman stoa** and of an **early Christian church**, to the south remains of another stoa.

Across the site to the north are the foundations of another early church, dating from the 6C. A large mosaic found in the narthex has fish and other marine scenes on it: a smaller mosaic in the naos has animal designs. It was built using local limestone in the first half of the century, on a design showing architectural influence from Constantinople. The floor plan shows the influence of other early Christian

Ancient Byllis

churches in Epirus, such as those at Butrint and Phoinike. Beyond the church are the ruins of a tower dating from the time of Justinian. On the south wall is an inscription recording that during the reign of Trajan the Roman soldier Valerius Maximus repaired a road nearby.

10km beyond Ballsh is the ancient Illyrian town of **Margelliç**, above a modern village with the same name, reached by a right turn from the main road. It was a centre of Illyrian ceramic production. Follow this road to Patos.

Patos has little to delay the visitor, a polluted town with oil and chemical industrial complexes, and many social and economic problems. There is some cotton growing in the fields near the town. Follow the road towards Fier. About 6km north of the town is an impressive new Orthodox church by the roadside.

FIER

Fier (pop. 74,000) is a predominantly industrial city, having grown from a pre-war market town with a population of only about 2000 people. It was then almost entirely Orthodox. It is built by the Gjanica tributary of the Seman river, and is surrounded by reclaimed marshland. With nearby Patos (pop. 13,000), it is the centre of the oil, bitumen and chemical industries in Albania, and a convenient place to stay to visit the major Classical sites at nearby Byllis and Apollonia. The population is predominantly Muslim. Main roads from the central square lead south to Vlora (35km), and east to the oil and chemical town of Patos (8km). Beyond Patos is the important tobacco growing area centred on Roskovec.

■ **Hotel**. The *Hotel Apollonia*, in the town centre is usable but not of a very good standard. Private rooms are becoming available.

■ **Taxi** and **buses**. Available from the main square. Drivers are familiar with the route to Apollonia, which is about a 20 minute drive. Negotiate a price before-hand, especially if the driver will wait while you see Apollonia. US $20 is a reasonable figure.

History

The history of Fier is inextricably bound up with that of the oil, gas and bitumen deposits nearby, although the modern city was founded by the Vrioni family, *beys* of Berat, as a market town in the 18C. A stone bridge was built over the Gjanica river in the 19C, greatly assisting in the growth of the town, as hitherto winter travel in the area was more or less impossible due to flooding.

The presence of asphalt and burning escapes of natural gas in the vicinity was recorded as early as the 1C AD. Dioscorides, in *Materia Medica*, describes lumps of bitumen in the adjacent river Seman, and also the concentrated pitch on the banks of the Vjosa river. Strabo, writing in about AD 17 states:

> On the territory of the people of Apollonia in Illyria there is what is called a *nymphaeum*. It is a rock which emits fire. Below it are springs flowing with hot water and asphalt ... the asphalt is dug out of a neighbouring hill; the parts excavated are replaced by fresh earth, which in time is converted to asphalt.

He was almost certainly describing the seepage at Selenica (see above; 22km south, near modern Vlora), modern exploitation of which began in the mid-19C. In antiquity the bitumen was important for caulking ships. As far as it is possible to establish the fact, there seems to have been little exploitation of it between the end of the ancient world and about 1800. Output rose to about 7000 tonnes a year by 1914.

During the 1914–18 war, Italian army officers reported a seepage of heavy oil near the village of Drashovice, and in 1918 a little oil was raised. Between the wars the oil industry expanded, with the main operators being the Anglo-Persian Oil Company (modern BP) and various French and Italian companies. There was intense competition between the different foreign interests in this period, with the French in 1923 refusing to agree to the appointment by the League of Nations of a British financial adviser to the Albanian government because of controversy over the oil concessions. Under King Zog, the fields were gradually taken over by the Italians, with production rising to over a million barrels a year by 1939. The oil workers were prominent in an uprising against King Zog led by Arben Cerova in August 1935. A group of rebels marched from Fier to Lushnja, where they were overwhelmed by government forces. (All the oil is of a heavy type, of specific gravity from 0.930 to 0.990 or more, containing 3–4 per cent sulphur and about 40 per cent asphaltic residue.) Since the war the fields have been further developed, but are now becoming depleted and their equipment is very antiquated. There are various exploration programmes in train to try to find oil and gas offshore, involving American, German and British multinational companies, and to modernise the onshore fields while it is worthwhile to do so.

Most of the Turkish town of Fier has disappeared, with virtually nothing left of the bazaar. Apart from one or two large houses that belonged to local *beys*, such as the Vrioni building now used to house the local library, the museum, and the **Orthodox church**, containing masonry from Apollonia. There is little for the visitor to see of interest in the town itself, although there are some pleasant avenues lined with pine, eucalyptus and orange trees. The late Byzantine remains of the church at Ardenica (12km along the road to Lushnja), and the small Fier museum, are worth visits and can be suitably combined with a trip to Apollonia. A very large new Catholic church is being built on the town outskirts, although the Catholic population of the town is very small.

The main interest of the **Fier Museum** are the exhibits from the nearby Classical sites of Apollonia, Ballsh and Byllis. In some cases the originals are in the National Historical Museum in Tirana, and copies have been made for this museum. The exhibits in the rooms on the ground floor include fragments of metopes from a Dorian building at Byllis, an Illyrian shield from the 3C BC, grave reliefs from the 2C BC (original in Tirana), grave reliefs from Apollonia, the Bust of Eros from Byllis, 2C BC. The central room contains fragments from a marble relief of a girl's head, from Apollonia, 2C AD, a sphinx, 2C BC, a Roman statue of a woman, from Apollonia, 2C AD. Adjacent are other fragments from Apollonia, masonry from the theatre at Byllis 3C BC, and in glass cases, various small artefacts from Apollonia, and photographs of early excavations at the site. In the room displaying local popular art, there are wood carvings of iconostases from the 18C and 19C, pottery and examples of locally woven textiles.

To the Monastery of Shenmri, Ardenica

Leaving Fier by the main road north towards Lushnja, cross the large open expanses of reclaimed marshland. The communist regime attempted to establish productive state farms on land such as this, but with the end of that system most of the machinery has been stolen or abandoned, and a quite substantial proportion of the population has emigrated. The drainage systems were set up with forced labour and in its absence are falling into disrepair. By and large, much of the land is not cultivated at all at the moment, and in some places is reverting to marshland. Under communism, Fier region had been the most important producer of bread grain in the country, and the decline of agricultural production in regions such as these has been economically very damaging.

Follow the main road to **Mbrostar**, where there is a turn to the north-west running across flat land towards the coast and the salt lake at **Karavasta** (23km). Keep to the main road for about another 8km, then follow a track to the left towards the monastery on a low wooded hill.

About half-way up the track, you will notice the entrances of **modern concrete tunnels** leading into the hillside. It is possible to walk into them and to see that they are empty. They were built in the early 1970s and examples can be found throughout Albania. Enver Hoxha believed then that the country would be subject to nuclear attack from the superpowers, the Soviet Union and the United States, who were conspiring together against Albania, and that civil defence works of this kind would offer the population some protection from the ICBM warheads that he expected to rain down on Albania. Local farmers often use them as livestock shelters nowadays. Return to the road and follow the track up to the monastery. There are many Vlachs among the local population here.

The *Monastery of Ardenica is protected by high walls and is entered through wooden doors. The gatehouse dates from 1474. Immediately on the right in the entrance tunnel is a door leading to a cellar with an olive oil press. The church standing in the central courtyard was built in the time of the Despotate of Epirus, at the beginning of the 13C, and is profoundly Greek in atmosphere and inspiration, a sombre, dignified greystone building among cypress trees on its lonely hilltop. The surrounding cloisters housed the monks, guest-rooms and rooms for economic and trade activities, and resemble many contemporary buildings in mainland Greece.

Much of what remains of the **church of the Virgin Mary** was built in the 18C, an inscription on the wall noting that it was reconsecrated in May 1743. The bell tower was rebuilt in 1925. It escaped major damage in the anti-religion campaigns of the 1970s, and attractive fresco paintings can still be seen, dated 1744, the work of the famous painters Konstantine and Athanas Zografi of Korça. They show scenes from the Old and New Testaments. The picture of **San Michele e Transito della Madonna** is outstanding. Some restoration work would be desirable.

The narthex lies to the west, with an open entrance hall to the south of it. In the east wall of the church, and in different places in the outer walls, masonry fragments from Apollonia can be seen, showing how the stone from fallen buildings in the ancient city was used in the construction of the church. There were also fragments of Greek and Roman gravestones and funerary monuments on display, but in the difficult security situation in this locality, they have been removed for safekeeping. Edith Durham visited the area at the turn of the century and noted:

> Tall men in dazzling white fustanellas, dark blue leggings, crimson waistcoats with two bands of silver chains crossed on the breast, and white coats with hanging sleeves embroidered in black; women in long-skirted sleeveless coats striped diagonally with scarlet—brilliantly aproned and a-dangle with coins—who flashed and glittered like parrots in the sunshine.

The ownership and control of the monastery are currently in dispute between the Orthodox church and the Albanian government, and in 1995 important ikons belonging to the monastery were still held in state custody. It is possible to stay overnight in the monastery rooms.

Return to the main road by the same route, passing through Kolonja (2km), then to Lushnja (32km from Fier).

A small monastery used to be attached to the Church of Shenmri in **Kolkonda** village, 3km north of Ardenica, named after St Kozma, one of the first Christian martyrs in Albania. In it was preserved an important Codex recording wedding contracts in the Myzeqe area, of considerable historical and ethnographic importance.

Return to the modern road, built during the war to replace a track that was prone to serious flooding. The Illyrian settlement of **Babunjas** was excavated near **Gradishte**, 26km north of Fier, along a track to the left of the main road.

Lushnja is a typical middle-sized industrial and commercial lowland town, with antiquated industries, poor housing, high unemployment, potholed roads, and on first glance it is difficult to imagine that anything of fundamental importance to Albania could have happened here. But in 1920 the Congress of Lushnja was held in the town and it rejected the policies of the National Assembly which had been put forward at the Versailles Peace Conference and voted for complete national independence. As Prince Wilhelm of Wied had not yet abdicated, a 'Council of Regency' was set up, with Muslim, Catholic and Orthodox members and this led to the foundations of the modern political structure of Albania being laid, with the capital moving to Tirana, a young tribal leader, Ahmet Zogu, later to become King Zog, being put in charge of public order, and the forces of the Italian occupiers driven back to *Valona*, modern Vlora. In August of that year Italy recognised the 'regency', and withdrew from Albania, apart from a military base on *Saseno island*, modern Sazan island. It is generally claimed that this was because of the valour of the Albanian national resistance, which was certainly a major factor, but the very high incidence of malaria, then 70 per cent hyperendemic in this region, must also have played a major part in the Italian decision to abandon colonisation plans. The English traveller Joseph Swire visited the town in the late 1920s and observed:

> Humble houses, mostly single storey, cluster round a cobbled market place or slink away down muddled alleys; and on the shop-front shutters which, when lowered, become the shop-front counters, sit the tradesmen cross-legged among their wares. On a butcher's counter a ram contentedly chews away his last hours, and turkeys gobble everywhere. Most townsfolk are dressed in nondescript clothes; but the peasants come in wearing woollen capotes, heavy and brown, with open sleeves and hoods: baggy brown woollen trousers narrow at the ankles, red socks and *opinga*. Some wear *xhurdini* like the Tirana plainsmen, and most wear dark blue high necked waistcoats and coloured sashes. Head wear, white and woollen, varies from the fez-like to the polo cap or close fitting skull cap of the north. As elsewhere in the Muslim lowlands women are rarely seen and are always veiled—they shuffle along like lame black crows.

In recent years, Lushnja has played a prominent role in the movements that led to the end of the one-party state, and was one of the first cities to elect a majority of non-communist representatives to local and national government bodies.

> 9km south-west of Lushnja, on an isolated area of reclaimed marshland near Lake Karavasta, is the village of Gradiste. This was established in the early 1950s as an important centre of forced labour. Political prisoners, most of them supporters of King Zog or the Balli Kombëtar nationalist movement were interned here and made to work for many years as labourers on the land drainage projects. Many of the prisoners came from the northern highland region, or the city of Shkodra.

24km east of Lushnja, along a poor road leading up into the hills of the Dumre region, in the direction of Cerriku and Elbasan, is the village of **Belsh**. 1km out of the village, on an exposed hilltop, is the ancient site of **Gradishte**, originally an Illyrian fort and hilltop settlement that was taken over by Greek colonists as a small town. It then grew considerably in Roman times as a trading centre with the proximity of the Via Egnetia. A **Temple of Aphrodite** was built on the side of nearby Lake Seferani. Terracotta votive objects have been found in the lake.

From Lushnja, the road continues north to join the modern Via Egnetia at Rrogozhina (17km), with flatlands to the left, the low Gjuzaj hills to the right, then on to Kavaja (34km), Durres (53km) and Tirana (89km).

8 · Fier to Apollonia and Vlora

From Fier, to Apollonia, 12km, taking the road towards Plazhi i Semanit, then a left turn along a track after 6km at Pojan, then another left turn in the village to Apollonia archaeological site—track condition fairly good, returning by the same route to Fier. To Vlora, 35km, on a good asphalt road south via Novoselë, 12km.

This route enables the visitor staying in Fier to visit the great archaeological site and museum of Apollonia, a few kilometres away to the west in a beautiful open rural landscape near the Adriatic Sea, and to travel south on the main coast road, crossing the Vjoses river, towards the important port of Vlora, ancient *Aulon*. A visit to Apollonia should be included in any journey to Albania, if at all possible, as it is the most accessible and well documented major Classical site in the country. It can, if necessary, be seen in a round trip lasting a day from Tirana, if an early enough start is made, although to enjoy the beauty and interest of the site properly more time is needed, and an overnight stay at Fier is recommended.

APOLLONIA

Apollonia is easily identified from the track by the sight of a large Byzantine building, the **Church of Shenmri**, standing on a low hill, on the beautiful open plain between the sea and the Kryegjata valley. It stands on part of the ancient site, the remainder of which stretches over a wide area to the north and north-west of the church. As you approach, the track runs up to the summit of the hill; parking is allowed on the open space below the church. On the left-hand side of the track, remains of ancient perimeter walls and foundations of Roman buildings can be seen. There is no charge to visit the site, which is entered through a small iron gate to the left of the parking area, a small charge, a dollar at the time of writing, is paid to the attendant if you wish to see the church, museum and monastic buildings.

History

With *Dyrrachium*, Apollonia was one of the two most important ancient Greek colonial settlements in Albania. It was founded in 588 BC on a hill near the sea, and near what was then the course of the Vjosa river, by settlers from Corfu and Corinth. At that time, before the great changes in land formation and the Adriatic coastline caused by an earthquake in the 3C AD, the harbour of Apollonia could accommodate as many as one hundred ships. The site is generally thought to be on the southern boundary of a native Illyrian settlement, being mentioned in *Periplus*, a sailor's account of the Adriatic written around the middle of the 4C BC, as a Greek city. It was near the territory occupied by the Illyrian tribe of the Chaonians. The original foundation may have been attempted in order to establish a stronghold on the frontier between these people and the Hellenised inhabitants of Epirus to the south. The colony was said to have been named *Gylaceia* after its Corinthian founder, Gylax, but later changed its name to that of the city of the god Apollo.

Archaeological investigations have revealed that for hundreds of years the Greek and Illyrian inhabitants of the site appear to have lived in separate communities. Aristotle took Apollonia as a model in his analysis of oligarchy, the ancient philosopher being unable to find any element of democracy whatsoever in its political organisation, with descendants of the original Greek colonists controlling the very large Illyrian serf population. The economic prosperity of Apollonia grew on the basis of trade in slaves, and the local rich pastoral agriculture, with coins having been found as far away as the Danube basin. In the years from 214 BC onwards the city was involved in the war between the Illyrian Taulantii and Cassander, the king of Macedonia; and in 229 BC came under Roman control. In 168 BC, its loyalty to Rome was rewarded with booty after the defeat of Genthios. In 148 BC it was integrated into the province of Macedonia. For 200 years it was of central importance in the Roman effort to colonise the east and may have been an original terminus of the Egnatian Way.

In the civil war between Pompey and Julius Caesar it was a vital stronghold for Caesar. In 45 and 44 BC, Octavian, later to become the Emperor Augustus, studied for six months in Apollonia, which by then had established a high reputation as a centre of Greek learning, particularly the art of rhetoric. It was in Apollonia that Octavian heard the news of Julius Caesar's death, in 44 BC. It was noted by Cicero, in the *Philippics*, as *magna urbs et gravis*, a great and important city. Strabo mentions a Fountain of Cephissus near the gymnasium at Apollonia.

Under the Empire it remained a prosperous centre, but began to decline as the Vjosa silted up and the coastline changed after the earthquake. The hitherto fertile hinterland of the city began to turn into malarial swamp.

Apollonia was an early centre of Christianity in the region, with a bishop attending the Council of Ephesus in 431, and the Council of Chalkis in 451, but the continual increase in the area of swamp surrounding the city led to Vlora becoming dominant in the region and by the end of antiquity Apollonia was largely depopulated. The earliest mention of the site was made by Busching in 1764, and it was described by Pouqueville and Leake in the early 19C. Some preliminary excavations were made by Austrian archaeologists, Prachniker and Schober during the First World War, and a French team continued their work between 1924 and 1938, directed by Leon Rey. In 1944 parts of the site, especially the walls around the acropolis, were damaged by German troops using the fortifications as a source of building stone. After the Second World War work started again in 1948 by Albanian archaeologists led by Hasan Ceka and Skender Anamali. A substantial area of the site remains unexcavated to date, although some work is in progress.

Entering the site through the small iron gate, you walk towards the central group of ancient religious and mercantile buildings. In spring, this part of the site is particularly beautiful thanks to the profusion of wild flowers here. Tortoises are also very common. Passing the foundations of Roman houses to the left of the path, you see the **bouleuterion**, an elegant and compact building from the Hellenistic period whose façade with six marble Corinthian columns was restored in the 1960s. Most of the marble architrave is original. The building measures 15m by

Bouleuterion at Apollonia

20m and the columns stand 9m high. The interior behind the columns is a U-shaped room, surrounded by marble-faced brick walls. A Greek inscription on the architrave states that the building was constructed by Quintus Villius Crispinus Furius Proculus, in honour of his deceased brother. His identity is unknown.

Excavation in the interior of the building has revealed that it was used as the office of the imperial administration in the city, in particular for the official concerned with administration of the imperial cult ceremonies. The date of the inscription is also unknown, but the building as a whole is thought to date from the second quarter of the 2C AD. The use of concrete in the restoration has been a controversial matter with some experts, but there is no doubt that as it stands it is a beautiful and evocative structure that brings many images of the prosperous ancient city to the mind of the contemporary visitor.

Immediately beyond the bouleuterion is the **odeon**, a small Roman building dating from the 2C AD. It seats about 600 spectators, and the steps have been restored to allow it to be used for modern concert performances. The two buildings are thought to have formed the edges of a small square, and the remains of buildings on either side of the odeon were probably used in connection with the imperial cult, or for some other religious function. The view from the top row of the seats offers a fine prospect of the sea and the coastal plain. To the right of the odeon are the remains of a **small stoa**, and a small square building that formed the foundations and lower walls of a **Roman bath**. Between the odeon and the bouleuterion are the foundations of four large columns.

To the left of the odeon is the finely preserved *large stoa, an impressive oblong building in front of an earth bank. It is about 75m long, with a twin series of marble columns running from north to south, with 17 insets for the display of statues. The lower floor had a perimeter of Dorian columns, while the upper floor was supported by Ionic columns. It dates from the 3C AD and is an outstanding example of late-imperial stoa design and construction, and evokes perfectly the mercantile atmosphere and wealth of the ancient city.

To the west of the stoa is the **theatre**, a large Hellenistic structure dating from the 2C BC, but in a poor state and in need of restoration. It could accommodate about 7500 people. It has only been partly excavated. It appears to follow Dorian

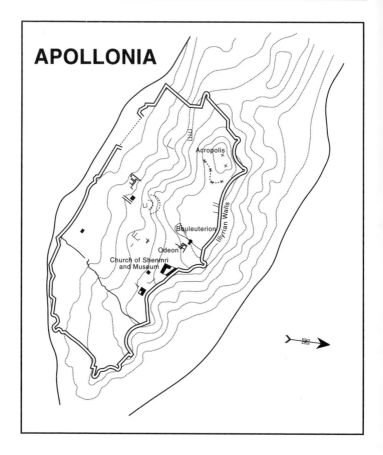

Greek design concepts, and shows little trace of Roman or native influence. It is the largest theatre of this period to have been found in Albania. To the west of the theatre is a length of Roman street, and the foundations of a large Roman house with a mosaic floor. Other foundations of Roman domestic buildings can be seen to the south of the theatre.

Behind the stoa, it is possible to climb over the earth bank through brambles and other undergrowth, and over the remains of a Byzantine wall that was built across the site running north–south behind the stoa, to the original **acropolis**, which can be seen rising in the distance. To reach it involves walking across a flat area about 500m wide, partly covered with grass, partly with undergrowth. The acropolis has no visible ancient remains, and has been vandalised by civil engineering works constructed by the Albanian military in the Hoxha period. The regime was obsessed with the possibility of Anglo-American invasion from the Adriatic and used the acropolis as a base for anti-aircraft artillery and bomb shelters. Despite this unfortunate recent history, it is nevertheless well worth the walk, as the view is outstanding from the top, and it is possible to imagine the original foundation of the city. Very little of this side of the site has been excavated and much of the ancient city lies near the surface, and some illegal digging has taken and is still taking place. The area is thought to have been occupied largely by mercantile buildings during the Roman period, the masonry from which was removed and used to build houses and agricultural buildings in the medieval and modern periods in the nearby villages of Mbrostar and Pojan.

Below the acropolis to the north-west are the remains of the nympheum, known in antiquity as the **Fountain of Cephisus**. This was supplied with water from a dammed spring at the base of the acropolis. It is in a good state of preservation, largely thanks to being covered with debris after an earthquake in the 4C AD. The water from the spring, after being contained in a structure 70m long, was piped into a large central basin surrounded with five Doric columns. It is generally thought to have been built in the 3C BC.

Returning across the site by the original route, to the east is a **small acropolis**, 1.27 hectares in area, with a few olive trees growing on it. This was the site of a temple dating from late antiquity, probably dedicated to Apollo or Artemis, the foundations of which have been excavated and can be seen. Excavators found some resemblances to the Temple of Assos, in Asia Minor. The acropolis itself is thought to have been one of the first parts of the site to be occupied, with the wall on the east side having foundations that are thought to date from about 600 BC, and indicate Illyrian settlement. The wall here was about 3m thick. In the 4C BC, the city is thought to have spread to the south and south-west of this acropolis.

Re-entering the central complex of buildings, you pass through the base of the entrance tower to the old upper city, and a monument to Apollo. Climb up the slope to the south side of the odeon, and immediately the massive masonry of the ***perimeter walls** of the site are in front of you. A walk around the walls in this direction towards the church of St Mary is a rewarding experience, as they are on the whole in a well-preserved state and there is a wonderful view over the valley east of the odeon. On the far side of it, tunnel entrances constructed for nuclear defence purposes in the early 1970s can be seen in the hillside. After a short walk to a corner tower, turn towards the church and follow the walls south. In total they are about 4km in length and were constructed in different stages, with the first large-scale fortification of the city undertaken in the 4C BC and with later construction in the 3C and in the time of the Roman monarchs. At the base of the walls a short walk from this point is a monument to Apollo, dating from the 3C BC.

After walking in this direction, climb up to the entrance in the walls at the base of the ***Monastery and Church of Shenmri**. This is one of the most interesting and beautiful Byzantine buildings in Albania, and it also contains the **Apollonia Museum**, although at the time of writing much of it is not open, for security reasons, as there have been some serious thefts and most of its treasures have been removed to vaults in Tirana for safekeeping. A few statues can be seen under the monastery cloister's roof.

The monastery and church in general are thought to date from the first part of the 13C, although there has been much learned discussion about the dating of different phases of construction, and all authorities agree that substantial rebuilding has taken place in later periods. Masonry from ancient Apollonia is incorporated in the walls, in a way reminiscent of the original Athens cathedral, in Plaka. The surrounding cloisters were inhabited by the monks, and their cells and a variety of domestic and agricultural buildings can be seen around the perimeter.

The church stands in the middle of the fine open courtyard, with some ruined Ottoman period buildings on the north and north-west side. The south-west bell tower was built in the 20C, between the two World Wars.

The church is entered through an exonarthex, with the columns supporting the roof carved with fantastic animals that are very similar in style to mythical beasts found in Gothic churches in Western Europe. Some scholars believe they are a sign of cultural influence in the area from the Norman kingdoms in Sicily in the early medieval period. In the centre of it is the base of an ancient column, with a circular hole cut in it that gives access to a large underground cistern below, the main water supply of the monastery. On the west wall of the narthex itself is a fresco of Emperor Andronicus II Paleologus, and Emperors Michael VIII and Michael IX. The fresco is thought to date from about 1281/82. The exonarthex was not part of the original church building, and was probably added about a hundred years afterwards, in the 14C.

The interior of the church is very beautiful and a strange shape, with a slightly oval dome over an interior that is not oblong but built in the shape of a parallelogram. The exterior of the dome has twelve sides. To the north is the sacristy. Most of the paintings were made in the 18C and 19C and show a variety of biblical scenes.

It is possible to obtain overnight accommodation here, in the old monastery buildings.

Return from the site to **Fier**, then at the central crossroads in the city take the road south towards Vlora (35km). It is possible to continue along the road west from near Pojan village on the way back to the sea at Plazhi i Semanit, but it is near the end of the canal linking the Seman river with Fier with the sea and bathing is not particularly recommended. The canal was an important component of the land drainage schemes in this region that were important in the early stages of the communist period.

Leaving Fier, you pass a large fertiliser factory and power station to the left, the road following the railway line south. After 3km you reach the small hill village of **Cakran**, where prehistoric remains have been found, indicating a middle Neolithic settlement that concentrated on the production of pottery in underground kilns. In 1978 a large hoard of Greek and Roman coins was also discovered near here. Another 4km brings you to **Levan**, on the edge of the vast **Myzeqe** area of drained marshland.

History

The area of Myzeqe is named after the Muzakaj feudal family, who controlled it between the 13C and 15C. It consists of river alluvium, and until the 1920s was a huge, marshy, lowland area. In the early Middle Ages it was called *Savra*, and was an important part of the economic hinterland of Vlora. In 1510 a member of the family, John Muzakaj, published in Naples a work of seminal importance for the history of medieval Albania, his *Historia e genealogia della casa Musaccia*. Until the First World War, the area was occupied by an exceptionally backward and repressed tribe called the Lales, who suffered from the hyperendemic malaria of this region and were subject to appalling treatment by the Turkish *beys*. Many Lales people welcomed the Italian occupiers as a result, but found their hopes dashed when their land was seized to make way for Italian settlers. When they, too, were soon decimated by malaria, Mussolini set in train the first stages of the land drainage programme that was accelerated under communism. The area was settled after the Second World War by Kosovar refugees, and Cams from northern Greece. There is also a sizeable Vlach minority in the general vicinity.

Follow the road through the village and across the plain, a vast largely featureless landscape that has suffered depopulation since the end of communism. The road crosses the Vjosa river, 4km, and runs towards Novosela, past salt pans, with the railway now on the right-hand side of the road. The **Liq. i Nartës** is seen on the right after Novosela. After 16km, a small road to the right leads to the village of **Narta**, a centre of grape cultivation, and beyond Narta, a track runs along the south side of the lagoon towards the tiny village of **Zvernec**. On an island nearby is the 13C Byzantine **monastery of Narta**, surrounded by woods. It is not possible to reach it at the time of writing.

History
Zvernec has been inhabited from the earliest times, and prehistoric remains have been found in the vicinity. It stands on an isthmus called *Treportat*, Three Gates. It was a prosperous port in ancient and early medieval times, before the Narta lagoon silted up. In the Middle Ages it was known as *Spinarica*, when it was held for a time by the Angevins from Sicily, then was captured by the Hohenstaufen emperors in the 13C. It became a small port but it declined at the end of the 14C, when it became part of the Despotate of Epirus. It was destroyed by the Turks in 1417.

Continue 5km to Vlora; see Route 9.

9 · Vlora to Himara and Saranda

From Vlora, 92km south by the coast road via Orikum, 18km to Saranda, and Himara.

VLORA
Vlora (pop. 88,000) is a large port and naval base, the centre of the Liab people's region and with Fier, the administrative centre of the oil and bitumen industry. Sazan island, in the Bay of Vlora, is the site of important defence installations. The hinterland of Vlora contains many interesting ancient sites, some of which have been excavated, some of which have not, and substantial areas of drained marshland. In the early Middle Ages it was an important Byzantine city, and the hub of the Emperor's Adriatic Sea defence system. Before World War II the hills surrounding the city were known for their Dervish *tekkés*.

Vlora is a city with many social problems, very high unemployment and a growing presence of organised crime. Cannabis growing is common in the vicinity. Visitors are not recomended to stay the night in Vlora without local contacts to assist them.

■ **Police**. Tel. 23 27, 21 45 or 22 07.

■ **Medical care**. Policlinics (emergency room), tel. 22 00; District Hospital (emergency service), tel. 21 13; Dr Pellumb Daxhiu (surgeon), tel. 35 42 (home).

■ **Hotel**. *Hotel Adriatic*, adequate but very expensive for what is offered. Some new B hotels have opened recently. Private rooms are available in houses along the seafront. Swimming here is not recommended.

History

In antiquity, Vlora was known as *Aulon*, a name given by early Greek settlers. In the Middle Ages it was often called *Avlonya*. The small city founded, from *Avlon* (channel), minted its own coins, and held territory in the hinterland as far as the Vjosa (Aoos) river. In the civil wars of the Roman republic it supported Caesar's forces. It is mentioned by Ptolemy in the 2C AD and, like Durres, became an early Christian centre. It grew in importance as Apollonia declined following the change in course of the Vjosa river after a great earthquake at the end of the 3C AD. By the 5C it had a bishopric. With the decline of the Eastern Empire, it became an unimportant fishing village, reappearing in history in the 13C when in 1258 it was taken by the Norman, Manfred of Sicily, and used as a base for his attacks on the Byzantine Empire. From 1266 to 1372 it was held by Charles of Anjou, but was then recovered for Byzantium by Emperor Andronicus II. In 1345 it was taken by the Serbian Tsar Stefan Dushan, then by the Balsha feudal lords who eventually sold it, with most of southern Albania, to Venice in 1417. It was soon taken by the Ottoman Turks, but was recovered by Venice in 1504, and again in 1690. It was an early centre of Jewish settlement in Albania, with 609 Jewish households existing in 1519–20, mostly refugees from Spain. It became a flourishing commercial centre until it was taken by Ali Pasha in 1812, after which it went into decline and became a refuge of pirates. In the late 19C and early 20C it began to reclaim its importance as a port.

On 28 November 1912 Ismail Qemali, a local *bey*, proclaimed an independent Albania in the city following the Congress of Vlora, and so it became the seat of the first independent Albanian government. It took in large numbers of destitute refugees from other areas of the country during the First Balkan War. Under the secret Treaty of London in 1915, Italy was given Vlora and an area of land around the city including the important military stronghold of Sazan island, then known as *Saseno island*. The synagogue, unique in Albania, was destroyed in the First World War. On 11 June 1920, 3000 peasants fought a battle with Italian soldiers which led to the subsequent withdrawal of all Italian troops from the area in September 1920. In the spring of 1924, forces opposed to King Zog set up a revolutionary headquarters in Vlora after the assassination of Avni Rustemi.

The town grew in the inter-war period and, like Durres, benefited economically from King Zog's projects to improve water supply and sanitation. Before then, it had been the single worst area for malaria in the whole of Albania, with the studies made by L.W. Hackett in the 1930s showing the disease in Vlora as hyperendemic, with some of the highest spleen enlargement and malarial parasite infestation figures ever recorded in medical literature. In 1939 it had about 70,000 inhabitants, two-thirds Muslims. In the Second World War it was an Axis naval base and was proclaimed a 'Hero City' for its outstanding contribution to the Partisan resistance movement against the occupiers. A fine description of newly liberated Vlora is to be found in *The Adriatic Sea*, by Harry Hodgkinson.

Under communism the port was leased to the Soviet Union as a submarine base, and played an important part in the conflict between Enver Hoxha and

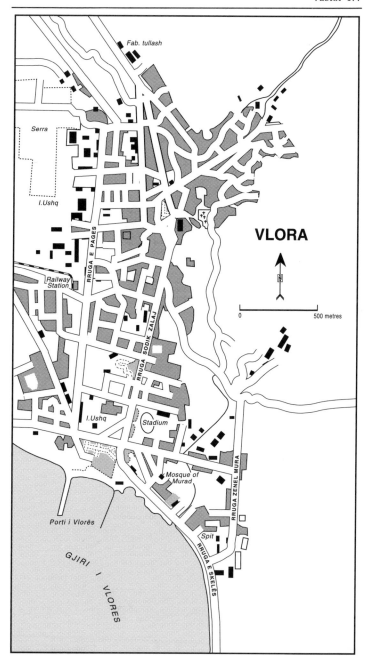

Fab. tullash

Serra

I.Ushq

RRUGA E PAGES

Railway Station

RRUGA SODIK ZALAJ

VLORA

0   500 metres

I.Ushq

Stadium

RRUGA ZENEL MURA

Mosque of Murad

Porti i Vlorës

Spit

RRUGA E SKELËS

GJIRI I VLORES

Khrushchev in 1960–61, as the Soviet Union had made very considerable investments in the naval facilities here, and objected strongly to the loss of them as a consequence of Albania taking the Chinese side in the split in the world communist movement. The Soviet Union threatened to occupy Vlora with Soviet troops in April 1961, and cut off all Soviet economic, military and technical aid to Albania. The threat was not carried out, largely as a result of the simultaneous development of the Cuban missile crisis. But in many ways, the place has never really recovered its former prosperity from that time onwards. Under Hoxha it was an important recruiting centre for the *Sigurimi*, the secret police. Vlora has grown in importance as an agricultural centre, with very large-scale planting of olive and fruit trees, and as a centre of the food processing, oil and bitumen export industries.

Vlora can be explored on foot, but distances are quite large and at the moment visitors are advised to have some form of transport and/or local assistance near at hand in case they run into difficulties. Drive into the centre of the town from the Fier road, descending through very attractive large olive plantations. After an urban fringe of small houses among the trees, the road passes blocks of flats and comes into an open area, with a mosque on the right, surrounded by a small garden. Most of what remains of old Vlora is in this area. Before World War II, this was the old city centre. On the opposite side of the road are the remains of the original Turkish residential area adjoining the bazaar. Some attractive small and medium-sized Ottoman houses, with ochre-painted walls and trailing vines and bougainvilleas, can be seen here.

Cross the road to the **Mosque of Murad**. This was built between 1542 and 1557, and is an evocative, peaceful small building, an island of quiet, with a wooden entrance hall, and a fine dome and minaret. The whitewashed interior is being restored, although the prayer hall is in use. It was designed by Mimar Sinan, the great architect who lived in Istanbul and designed a number of mosques in Turkey while in the service of the Sublime Porte.

Sinan was born in about 1500, in the region of Topoyani, in central Albania. He studied ancient Greek, mathematics and engineering techniques, and became the founder of classical Ottoman architecture. He became the Sultan's architect in 1538 and died in July 1588.

The great fort of Vlora built by Süleyman the Magnificent in 1531, of an octagonal character with ten defensive towers, each 18m high, has all but disappeared. It was built using masonry from the ancient settlement of *Treport*, but it was demolished and used in harbour construction in 1906.

Proceed down the wide avenue towards the seafront. On the right is a very large oblong concrete building which used to be the regional communist headquarters. In front of it is the empty plinth that used to support a colossal marble statue of Hysni Kapo, a local man who was one of Enver Hoxha's closest associates and became foreign minister, and secretary of the PLA central committee, in the 1950s and 1960s. He was particularly influential in the split with the Soviet Union in 1961. His memorial was demolished by rioting crowds in 1991.

On reaching the seafront, turn left towards the Skela district, and drive about 500m. On the right, above the beach, is a small 19C house that is now a café. On the wall is a **plaque** noting that it was where Ismail Qemal proclaimed the independence of Albania on 28 November 1912. It is a pleasant place to have a coffee and admire the beautiful view over the Bay of Vlora. Note that your car should be parked on the concrete park adjoining the beach, where it can be seen at all times. Then follow the road in the same direction, out of Vlora proper, with a pleasant beach fringed by pine and eucalyptus trees on the right, and attractive wooded hillsides on the left. There is normally one bus a day between Vlora and Himara. At the time of writing it leaves at 15.30.

In the bay, **SAZAN ISLAND** can be seen, where most of the Albanian naval facilities are situated. In the past it was known as *Saso* or *Saseno Island*. The island is about 4km x 5km, and has a rhomboid shape. The interior is dry and hilly. It has always been of strategic importance in the Adriatic, and was occupied by Italy before the First World War. It was first granted to Italy by the secret Pact of London in 1915. After it became officially Italian under the Treaty of Tirana in 1920, it was fortified by Italian military engineers. At the south east corner of the island they built a lighthouse. There was a small civilian population pre-war, most of whom had to leave under communism. In the 1950s it was an important Soviet submarine base. A few people have begun to return to the island recently. There is also activity on the island by United States military advisers to the Albanian government.

A road leads from here running east back through the town towards Tepelena, 69km. It is a good asphalt route, and is the way to the archaeological site of **Amantia** (31km) which is an interesting excursion. Excavations have revealed some particularly fine Illyrian sculptures, which are in the Tirana museums, and the remains of Illyrian, Hellenistic and Roman buildings, including a unique stadium.

Follow the Tepelena road out of Vlora, through **Drashovica** (10km), climbing from the coastal plain along the valley of the Shushices river which rises in the Gribes mountains to the east. To judge from this, and other local place names such as the nearby village of Vodica, this was an area of Slav settlement in the Dark Age invasions (*voda* means water in Slavonic). 5km from Drashovica, beyond the modern village of Veliqot, is the large hillfort of **Zharra**. It was an important Illyrian stronghold between the 6C and 3C BC, and seems to have continued as a small settlement in Roman times. It can easily be seen as a flat-topped hill 1km south from the main road.

Continue another 8km to **Kota**, where the road crosses the river, then bear left, and drive another 7km, to **Vajza**. *****Amantia** is on a bare conical hilltop to the left of the main road, about 4km after Vajza.

The site is reached by walking up a dirt track from the main road near Ploça village. It can easily be identified from the road by a large limestone block on top of a rather bare and eroded hillside.

History
Amantia was a typical Illyrian hilltop settlement, with an original walled enclosure about 500m long and 60m wide. The walls extend for 2200m. It was established about 350 BC, probably by members of the Taulantii tribe. A large fort was built with two gates and two defensive towers to the north. It occupied an important defensive position above the Vjosa river valley to the east, and on the road to the coast and the Bay of Vlora. It appears to have

grown into a prosperous and influential urban centre quite quickly, in contrast to some of the Illyrian sites in the north where a more primitive rural culture remained dominant.

The work *Coastal Passage*, attributed to Scylax, links it closely with ancient *Oricum*, in the Bay of Vlora. It was among the earliest Illyrian cities to mint its own coins. It was included in the Epirote League in 230 BC. After the period of Greek colonisation it came under the influence of Apollonia. In the Roman period it declined in importance and was bypassed by the Egnatian and Candavian Ways, although it remained a small urban centre and in early Christian times was the seat of a bishop. It is thought that it may have been abandoned by the end of the 6C AD.

The *stadium is about 100m below the site to the south-east and is the principal monument. Excavations have revealed that it was used for athletic contests including running races, boxing, javelin and discus throwing. It is 55m long and 12.25m wide. There are 17 tiers of seats on the west side, eight tiers on the east side, that could accommodate about 4000 people. A number of Greek inscriptions have been found on some stones. The stadium was constructed in the 3C BC and remained in use until the 3C AD. It is the only well preserved ancient stadium in Albania.

Walking up from the stadium, in a north-west direction, you come to the south-east side of the fort, with remains of low walls visible below the small acropolis. Turn left and walk along the walls to the south-west, after about 200m are the foundations of a temple of Aphrodite, then after about another 100m, a particularly well-preserved section of **Illyrian wall**, built of polygonal shaped masonry. The skill and sophistication of the construction technique is a sign of the advanced culture of the city in Illyrian times. Turning right here, and crossing the site to the north, you come to the foundation of an early defensive tower.

About 100m down the hillside, below the section of Illyrian wall, are the remains of a small early Christian church and an ancient temple. The remains of the temple are very badly damaged and it has proved difficult to establish what it was. There are column bases for Dorian columns at the east and west sides. It is thought it may have been built in the 2C BC, rebuilt in the 1C AD, while the church was constructed in the early 6C. The copious use of marble in the church suggests that a relatively wealthy small community must have existed here at that time.

13km north-west of Amantia, 1km off the main road to Vlora, is the village of **Mavrova**. This is believed to be the site of ancient *Olympe*, a small settlement that was subject to Amantia.

Return to Vlora by the same route.

After about another 500m or so towards Himara, the road, which has followed along just above the beach, enters a short tunnel, at *Uji i Ftohte*, 'Place of Cold Water'. On the right, just above the entrance to the tunnel, ***Enver Hoxha's holiday home** can be seen, a modern concrete structure built into the cliff over the sea. Some of the acrimonious arguments with Nikita Khrushchev recorded in Hoxa's book, *The Khrushchevites*, took place here. The dictator was very fond of Vlora and used this strucuture to entertain many famous guests and foreign political leaders. The house has now been turned over to public service use. 200m above it, on the left, is another similar structure, that was the holiday home of Mehmet Shehu, Hoxha's number two for many years until his fall from power and subsequent murder in 1981. An air of curious calm and domesticity surrounds the vicinity now, after so many years when its privileged inhabitants were feared by the general population. This shows what the communist system could offer its leaders, just as the remains of the forced labour camps at Spaç and elsewhere illustrate the pain of its victims. There is a pleasant clean beach beyond these houses to the south.

Near here, in the 1920s, in the village of Krip, was the house of Nexhmie Zaimi, author of *Daughter of the Eagle*. When it was published in England in 1938, it was the first autobiography of an Albanian woman to be translated into English. It is an interesting, evocative memoir of inter-war social life in and around Vlora. It also contains a unique description of transhumance by Sarakatsan shepherds in Albania at the time.

Follow the road on, until the turn for **Kanina** (6km from Vlora). Take the track (poor, rutted) leading up the hill to the left from the main road to the modern village (2km) where **Kanina fortress** can be seen. Kanina was originally an Illyrian hilltop settlement and at many periods in its history formed part of the defensive system for Vlora. In antiquity it was closely linked with the inland city of Amantia, controlling its sea trade. It particularly prospered in the Middle Ages, when Vlora was in decline, and Kanina became the centre of a settlement that was to all intents and purposes independent. The Emperor Andronicus II gave the town trading rights in the 13C, when it was the seat of a bishopric for a time.

Remains of the walls dating from various periods can be seen behind the village, with some large blocks of Illyrian foundation dating from the 4C and 3C BC, and evidence of rebuilding in the time of Justinian (6C AD) and Byzantine, Venetian and Turkish masonry constructed afterwards. Kanina declined after the 16C when Vlora re-established its former importance. Although the remains of walls are of a common pattern found throughout Albania, the excursion is worthwhile because of the spectacular views, over to Sazan island and along the coast towards Mali i Flamurit (826m) on the promontory at the south-west side of the bay. It was originally built by the Italians as a military road in 1939.

Follow the main road south towards Orikum (12km) and Himara (73km). On the way to Orikum there are some pleasant pebble beaches lined with peach orchards, with unspoilt agricultural land behind them; but although a good place to sunbathe, swimming is not particularly recommended, as the detritus of Vlora can become trapped in this end of the bay.

Opposite the beaches, on the far side of the bay, the **Karaburun peninsula** forms a rocky arm of landmass extending into the sea and has always played a role in Vlora's history as a secure Adriatic port. It is 16km long, and 4km wide. In Turkish it was called *Karaburun*, the Black Cape. It is virtually waterless and a windy, desolate place, used only by shepherds. There are many caves, in some of which ancient inscriptions have been found. Being so remote, and difficult for the Axis occupation forces to police, it was an important landing point for British liaison officers attached to the Resistance in the last war. It is now free of previous military restrictions and can easily be visited. There are beautiful views of the Adriatic from the hilltop.

Continue 12km to **Orikum**, ancient *Orikos*, which was founded in the 5C BC by Greek settlers from Euboea. Scymnus claims that this occurred after the Trojan War. Excavations carried out by Islami in the early 1980s indicate that Orikos must have been founded, at the latest, by the second half of the 6C. It quickly became an important trading post and by the 3C was minting its own coins. Later, as

Dyrrachium and Saranda grew in importance, it went into decline but remained a small urban centre. It was attacked and held for a while in 214 BC by Philip V of Macedon. In the Roman period it was used as a naval base by Caesar in his wars against Pompey. Remains of walls and a small theatre seating 600 spectators dating from the 1C AD can be seen. In the 2C it seems to have gone into decline again, after an earthquake. In the Middle Ages it was called *Jericho*, when it was used as a port by Angevin princes from Sicily. The name may have been linked to Sephardic Jewish settlement in the Bay of Vlora that was taking place then, or to ancient Jewish communities here, noted on by the Roman historian Flavius Josephus. Under Ottoman rule it was called *Pashaliman*, the 'Port of the Pasha', then *Palaestro* by the Italian occupiers. A modern Albanian village with that name is 3km west of Orikum. The modern settlement is a quiet, pleasantly situated little place at the end of the bay, with fruit and olive growing the main activity of the inhabitants. You will notice that some inhabitants speak Greek; Orikum is on about the northernmost fringe of the part of Albania partly occupied by the Greek minority.

3km from Orikum is the little Byzantine church, of **Marmiro**, an attractive small building on a low hill. To visit it, follow the road west towards Pasha Liman, from Orikum, crossing the Tzvorei river by a large bridge. Marmiro is on the far side of the village, above the road. Park about 4km from the bridge and approach the church on foot, by a track up the hillside.

The road turns inland here, across the Plain of Dukat, through orchards dominated by peach cultivation, and begins to climb towards the twin villages of **Dukat i Ri** and **Dukat**. The English 19C artist Edward Lear spent some time in Dukati, then known as *Dukades*, on his Albanian journey in October 1848. He noted the shepherds, their

> ... huge morose dogs, like wolves and the women of the village, many clad in male attire and the the oddest looking creatures I ever beheld. Worn and brown by hard labour in the sun, they have something pensive and pleasing in the expression of the eye but the rest is unfeminine and disagreeable.

After Dukat, 12km from Orikum, the road begins to climb steeply, with magnificent views towards the ****LLOGARA PASS**. The Llogara area is a national park, and is probably the most dramatic and beautiful unspoilt seascape and cliff scenery left along either coast of the Adriatic. The tops of the **Çika mountains** are bare limestone, the slopes are wreathed in natural pine forest and drop sheer into the sea. In the distance, Corfu can be seen, to the south-west. The highest point of the Pass is 1050m, there is a small stopping place and monument to the national liberation struggle. Accommodation can be found nearby. 5km down the other side of the pass is the village of **Palasa**, with many Greek minority inhabitants. Julius Caesar landed on the coast below Palasa in the Roman civil wars. Until recently this was a closed military area. A stay in the **Llogara Tourist Village** is recommended. This is an admirable ecotourist development opened by the Albtourist Enterprise Co. in 1993. There are 13 wooden houses with 44 beds. Each house has two double rooms, WC, and shower. There is a bar and restaurant nearby (tel. Vlora 23783/23794).

5km further on, the road descends steeply in a breathtaking series of hairpin bends to **Dhérmi**, a small village above which are the highest peaks of the Çika range, 2051m. The three churches of Dhérmi are worth visiting, in a village with mostly ethnic Greek inhabitants. Shen Maria (St Mary's), a small building dating from the 13C and 14C, with very fine frescoes indeed, painted in the 16C; it was seriously damaged in a storm in 1995 and requires urgent restoration work; the Church of Ipapandi, with frescoes dating from the 17C and 19C; and the little church of Shen Stefani (St Stephen). The ethnic Greek inhabitants call their village *Drimades* (from Greek Drymades, oak woods), and it is a centre of the *Vorio Epirus, enosis* movement, campaigning to have this region of Albania re-incorporated into Greece. There is an attractive old Turkish fountain by the side of the main road as it clings to the cliff where the people gather in the evenings. Many slogans, calling for *enosis*, can be seen here and elsewhere in this region. Dhermiu, and other similar villages in this area, preserve many features of traditional Greek village life that are sometimes difficult to find in Greece itself nowadays. It was visited by the Swedish writer Jan Myrdal in the late 1960s when it was a workers' holiday settlement where even senior party members, or foreigners, were not allowed to stay here. According to a local dignatory, 'A central committee member tried to stay here once and we didn't make an exception. Tourists and bureaucrats can bathe at Durres or Sarande. Dhérmi is for the workers.'

The road follows on 13km, through a small half-ruined village called **Vuno** (in Greek, *'the hill'*), that was the victim of a devastating fire during the last war. Vuno was a centre of communist political organisation in the region, and at one time two of the eleven members of the PLA central committee came from this tiny place. In the distance, at the bottom of a precipitous cliff, Himara can be seen, the largest settlement on the coast between Vlora and Saranda. The road descends a series of steep hairpin bends to the coast; great care is needed, the edges of the road are usually unprotected and are not in a very good condition. The mountains are referred to as bare and sterile by 19C travellers, and the reforestation programmes of the communist period have been ecologically successful.

Himara is a pleasant little seaside town with a fine beach that makes a good stopping point after the arduous journey from Vlora. There are cafés and restaurants along the seafront. The town has a mixed Greek- and Albanian-speaking popula-

Church of St Panton

tion. The coastal district is called **Spila** and is of much more recent origin than the upper town on the hillside, built there because of the good water supply and security against pirates. The upper town should be explored, with its interesting narrow streets and churches. Agios Nicholas and Agios Spyridon both have good frescoes. The latter was damaged by a storm in 1995 and requires urgent restoration work. Above the town is a partly-ruined medieval citadel.

History

Himara is named after the ancient Greek word for a ravine. Early Greek settlers from Corfu came here and a small city was established, while the surrounding area remained in the hands of Illyrian tribes. Philip V of Macedon attacked the city in 214 BC, and it was a Roman base after the first Macedonian war in 167 BC. The steep cliffs above and along the coast from Himara were known in antiquity as the *Acro-Ceraunian mountains*, and were famous for the dangers they caused to mariners. Julius Caesar, when overtaken by a storm near Himara when he was sailing to join his army in Italy is said to have given his sailors courage by the words, 'Fear not, for thou carriest Caesar and his fortunes.' The poet Horace refers to them as *infames scopulos Acroceraunia*.

The town became an early Christian centre and by the 9C had a bishop. In the 10C it was overrun by the Bulgarians. In Byzantine times it was called *Chimarae*. It was taken by Mehmet the Conqueror for the Turks, but in 1570 they were expelled by the Venetians. The Turks soon returned, and like most Albanian coastal towns, Himara fell into decline under their rule. In 1797 Ali Pasha of Tepelena ordered an attack on Himara, in retaliation for the town's support for the Suliotes, and nearly 6000 unarmed civilians were slaughtered. He captured it, in 1810, to lose it soon afterwards, and recapture it in 1816. After his rule the area suffered severe depopulation. It formed a separate Greek Orthodox episcopate until 1833. It then became part of the Pashalik of Valona. At that time it was much larger in population than it is now. In the later period of the Ottoman rule, Himara enjoyed a considerable measure of practical independence from central authority. The town and its six surrounding villages, with a population of about 20,000 people, paid a tribute of 16,000 francs a year to the Sublime Porte in Constantinople. Government in the locality was based on the archaic system of *demogeronties*, with eight village elders dispensing justice. The area became a centre for Albanian emigration to France and the USA at the end of the 19C. In 1912 the Greek government sent gunboats to Himara to attempt to prevent the incorporation of Himara district with the new Albanian state. In 1923 the League of Nations noted the large Greek-speaking population of the area, about 6000 persons. In 1927 the Protocol of Himara was signed between the Albanian government and the Himariots, in recognition of the privileges of the town. In the 1930s the town was at the centre of the controversies over Greek language education in the Zogist period, with the Zogist gendamerie putting down anti-government riots in 1932 when Greek language education was terminated.

In the wartime resistance the town was a base for the 'Northern Epirus Liberation Front', then the Partisans after the ethnic Greek Front had been destroyed in fighting with collaborationist Balli Kombetar elements and Axis forces. In 1946, 13 members of the Greek minority from Himara who refused to join the Albanian Democratic Front were executed in Vlora. In the last two years, emigration has resumed, mainly to Greece.

Leave Himara by the coast road, continuing south. The road winds 23km through beautiful mountain and coastal scenery to **Borsh**. It lies in a gorge made by the river **Shushicé**. Below it is the seaside village of **Shkalla**, whose name indicates its ancient Greek origin, from the word meaning steps, or promontory. It is now a small rundown seaside resort. Above Borsh can be seen the ruins of the citadel of **Sopot**, which was built in Ottoman times on ancient foundations and acted as a military control post on the coast road. Along the coast to the immediate north is the exquisitely beautiful **Bay of Porto Palermo**, where the ancient settlement of *Panormus* was sited. In the 18C and 19C the village had some importance as a small port. 8km south from Borshi is the village of **Pigeras**, the birthplace of the assassin Vasil Laçi, who tried to kill King Victor Emmanuel III of Italy in Tirana in 1940. Then after 7km, the village of **Lukova**. The road passes through very large terraces, planted with olive trees.

This area was the scene of 'Terraces of Lukova' agricultural project in the late 1960s, where about 75,000 young people from all over the country worked as 'volunteer labourers' to construct the olive and citrus plantations. It was a central feature of Enver Hoxha's imitation of aspects of the Chinese Cultural Revolution, where young people became 'Red Guards' and were sent to learn from peasants in the countryside. More than 650,000 trees were planted in the vicinity of the villages of Lukova, Sasaj, Piqeras, Perparim and Ninica, on the western side of the Konjak-Lavan-Shendellia hillsides. Roads and irrigation works were also constructed. In most cases the terraces are no longer cultivated, owing to labour shortages and depopulation caused by emigration to Greece.

The road follows on, under **Mount Lugji** to the left (763m), and drops gradually towards Saranda, and the plain of Rrezoma. There is a good view of the acropolis of ancient *Phoinike* from here.

5km to the east, above the Plain of Vrina, known in antiquity as *Kestrina*, is the Illyrian site of **Çuka of Ajtoj** (10C BC). It is worth visiting to see the impressive Illyrian gate, and remains of low walls.

Continue to Saranda, through rather empty and depopulated countryside.

V BERAT TO KORÇA AND THE MORAVA MOUNTAINS

10 · Berat to Korça via Përmet

Berat, by very poor track over the mountains south to Leskoviku, 140km, Erseka, 184km, to Korça, 184km. Four-wheel drive vehicle recommended, but not absolutely essential in summer months.

BERAT
Berat (pop. 71,000) lies on the right bank of the river Osum, a short distance from the point where it is joined by the Molisht river. It is a remarkably preserved Ottoman city, with a wealth of beautiful buildings of the highest architectural and historical interest, including what many people consider to be the finest large medieval citadel in the Balkans. The pine forests above the city, on the slopes of the towering Tomori mountains, provide a backdrop of appropriate grandeur. The Osumi river has cut a 915m deep gorge through the limestone rock on the west side of the valley to form a precipitous castle-rock, around which the town was built on several river terraces.

> According to legend, the Tomor mountain was originally a giant, who fought with another giant, Shpirag, over a Berat girl. They killed each other, and the girl drowned in her tears, which then became the Osum river; it is a typical Albanian folk story, with its tragic and bloody resolution. Mount Shpirag, named after the second giant, is on the left bank of the gorge, above the district of Gorica. Berat is known to Albanians as *The City of a Thousand Windows*, a similar epithet to that sometimes applied to Gjirokastra, *The City of Two Thousand Steps*, and has a mixture of Orthodox, Muslim and Vlach inhabitants. It was proclaimed a 'Museum City' by Enver Hoxha in June 1961 and it is a UNESCO World Heritage City.

■ **Hotels.** There are a number of hotels in Berat but the best are the *Hotel Berat*, on the banks of the Osumi river, on the right-hand side of the road as you enter the town from the Fier direction and the *Manga Lemi* hotel. It is becoming easier to rent private rooms, which are much cheaper.

History
Berat was inhabited from prehistoric times; stone tools found indicate settlement from the Bronze Age (2600–1800 BC). Mount Tomor has a strong tradition of pagan religious ceremonies, some of which may have involved human sacrifice to the local god, said to be an aged Albanian chieftain whose spirit had entered the mountain and was venerated for his miraculous works. The vicinity was the centre of the Illyrian kingdom of the *Dassaretes*, with walls dating from the middle of the 4C BC when a stronghold was built to control the river valley. It was then taken by the Roman invaders under Apustius in 200 BC in a campaign against the king of Macedon that was described by the

historian Livy. Apustius had been dispatched by Sulpicius to lay waste the Macedonian frontier. It was renamed *Antipatra*, although in later Roman times it became known as *Albanorum Oppidum*. According to Livy:

> The legate Apustius arrived at Antipatrea, the city standing on a narrow gorge. First, he summoned the rulers to talks and tried to persuade them to give the city to the Romans, but they rejected his words, because they had confidence in the might of the city, in its walls and in its position. He eventually attacked the city by force of arms and captured it. After killing all the inhabitants over sixteen years of age, he allowed the army to plunder the city, put it to the torch and destroyed the walls.

The Romans built a subterranean conduit to the river to ensure a water supply during sieges, and that assisted greatly the development of the citadel as a virtually impregnable stronghold in later ages. Berat was rebuilt by the Emperor Theodosius II in AD 440, the walls refortified, and renamed *Pulcheropolis*, after his sister Pulcheria. After the Slav invasions of the 7C, it was captured and renamed *Beligrad*, the White City, from which the name Berat derives. It was held by the Bulgars between 860 and 927 and 969 and 1018, and then was retaken by the Byzantines, becoming the seat of a bishopric in the 9C, and being refortified with great skill and investment of resources by the Emperor Comenos in 1205. After coming under the Despotate of Epirus, it was captured by Catalan adventurers for the Angevin kings of Naples in 1270, after a desperate siege lasting over a year. Subsequently it fell to Tsar Stefan Dushan for Serbia in 1345, following a peasant rising in 1337 which had displaced the Byzantine ruler. The feudal lords of the Muzakaj family and the Balshaj family subsequently took control of the region, and established a realm stretching from Kostur (modern Kotor) in Montenegro in the north-west to the Shkumbi and Vjosa rivers in the south. In 1417 it was occupied by the Turks. At this time it had about 4000 inhabitants.

Berat held out in important battles against Skanderbeg in 1455, thanks to Turkish reinforcements of 40,000 men. Its governors afterwards became leading functionaries in the Ottoman court at Constantinople. It was taken by Ali Pasha in 1809, with a force of 5000 men who received military advice in the siege from an English officer, Colonel Leake. According to Hughes, the contemporary historian:

> By him the siege was pressed with so much vigour and the bombardment was kept up against the citadel and town from the opposite heights, whilst the garrison and inhabitants were so terrified by those newly invented instruments of destruction, the Congreve Rockets, under the direction of an English officer, that Ibrahim Pasha was obliged to capitulate upon condition of retiring with his suite and treasures to Valona.

It was subsequently retaken by the Turks, and refortified, using in part cannon that Lord Nelson had given to Ali Pasha. In this period, the region around Berat was known as 'the granary of Albania'. Curzon, in his *Visits to Monasteries in the Levant*, describes how he saw a Turkish force leave Ioannina in 1834 to go to the relief of Berat. In 1847 another English traveller, John Spencer, found the Turkish governor expecting an attack by Albanian peasant rebels, and an exodus going on from the lower town, including 'the old and the young, the sick and the infirm, the suckling babe and the cat of the fireside'.

Berat survived intermittent local rebellions as an Ottoman stronghold throughout the 19C. The Albanian Leagues of 1879 and 1914 were active in Berat and in the latter part of the 19C both Greece and Italy attempted to increase their influence here, the former by the establishment of schools and churches. The city fell to Albanian nationalists in June 1914, then was taken by Greek irregulars three months later. In early 1916 they were evicted by Austro-Hungarian troops who in turn were driven out by the Italian army in July 1918 who held Berat until 1921. The area was very important in the Partisan struggle against Axis occupation and the communist dominated Provisional Government of Albania was formed here in October 1944. Mount Tomor remained an important centre of popular religious tradition until recent times, with a tradition of oath taking, by both Muslims and Christians. Until the end of the one-party state, the city had remained a centre of communist support, with many still strongly adhering to the ideas of Enver Hoxha. The city is the administrative centre of Berat region, which includes the oil city of Kucova (formerly *Stalin City*). The main industries locally are agriculture, tourism, textiles and oil.

The **Old Town** of Berat lies below the citadel and is best explored on foot. The citadel is only accessible from the south-east side. At least a day is needed to see the main sights of the city properly, although if time is short it is possible to drive up to the citadel entrance by car and have a walk around the top and see the outstanding views. The citadel access road runs from a left turn off the main road into Berat from the north. Otherwise leave the hotel by the main entrance and walk across the public gardens alongside the river, then cross the main road, towards the Leaded Mosque, beyond the bus station and a partially demolished statue of Enver Hoxha, about 500m away across the main square. The river is wide, with attractive clumps of trees and bushes growing on the gravel banks between the many different rivulets.

The Christian population mostly lived in and around the citadel in Ottoman times, hence the location of the mosques in the lower part of the city. The remains of the small mosque within the citadel area was for the use of the Ottoman garrison. There was a small Greek population at Berat for many years, and a Jewish ghetto. The city spread down the garrison hill in a number of different phases of building, although at first sight most of the houses and public buildings seem to have been constructed at the same time and in much the same style. A great impetus for the growth of the town was the earthquake at Durres in 1776, which led many people from that city to move to Berat.

The **Leaded Mosque**, *Xhamija e Plumbit*, was one of the earliest constructed in the city, and in this part of Albania, with work beginning in 1553 and finishing in 1555. It is an elegant structure, with a particularly fine minaret and a large white-washed entrance hall where fragments of ancient statuary are displayed. It was founded by Izgurli Skuraj, a local feudal *bey*. Restoration work is in progress at the moment, and at the time of writing full access to the interior was not possible, although the fine windows of coloured glass and the very beautiful dome can be appreciated.

Walk back towards the street at the base of the citadel. On the left, is the **Mosque**

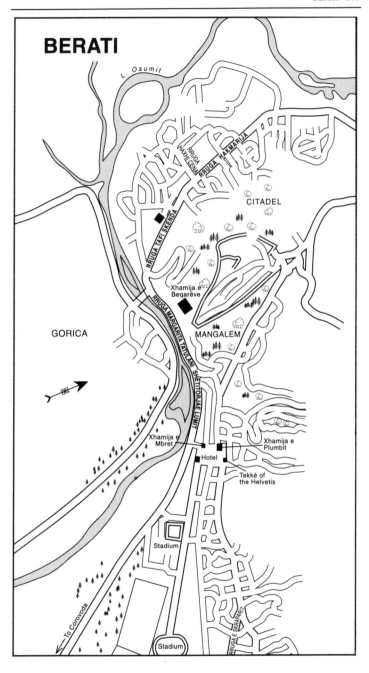

BERATI

L. Osumit

RRUGA HAHLI CENAJ

RRUGA HAKMARIJA

CITADEL

RRUGA TAFI SKENDA

Xhamija e
Beqarëve

RRUGA MARGARITA TATULANI

GORICA

MANGALEM

SHETITORJA E LUMIT

Xhamija e
Mbret

Xhamija e
Plumbit

Hotel

Tekké of
the Helvetis

Stadium

To Corovoda

Stadium

of the Bachelors, *Xhamija e Beqareve*, which used to house the Exhibition of Berat Material Culture, but is now in the process of returning to religious use. Next to it are a series of commercial art and souvenir shops, newly established under privatisation. The architecture of the wooden buildings housing them is very attractive, showing typical Ottoman styles of shops at the end of the last century.

The Mosque of the Bachelors was built in 1827 and is mainly noteworthy for its wall paintings, which are similar in style to those of the Mosque of Etem Bey in Tirana, with beautiful representations of plants, flora and domestic buildings, evoking a static, idealised dreamworld of the Albanian rural landscape. The mosque is named after the Albanian word for bachelor, *beqar*, and it was built originally for the use of the unmarried shop assistants in the town below the citadel. In a small garden below this mosque is a dignified small bronze monument in the socialist realist style to a Partisan heroine, Margarita Tutalani (1924–43). Further along the street is a damaged but still attractive Turkish fountain and rows of shops, such as barbers and grocers.

Between these two mosques, in the centre of the old urban area, is the **King's Mosque** (*Xhamija e Mbret*), the oldest in Berat, built in the reign of Bayazid II (1481–1512). It houses a small archaeological museum displaying local artefacts, at the time of writing closed but scheduled for re-opening soon. It has a very fine ceiling. Near this mosque is the **Tekké of the Helvetis**, built in 1790. It is also closed at the moment but the exterior and portico are well worth seeing. Under communism there were plans to make it a luxury hotel, but these came to nothing and the city authorities have not yet decided on its future use. The portico is very attractive, with five arches leading to an inner covered courtyard. The ceiling is finely carved and painted in complex patterns of colour. South of the *tekké* is the very ugly modern concrete building that houses the art gallery. Most of the old permanent exhibition of paintings on political themes in the socialist realist style has been removed.

> Near the *tekké* was the **grave of Shabbatai Zvi**, a Turkish Jew living in Berat who in the 1660s declared himself to be the Messiah, and began a movement that led to hundreds of thousands of impoverished European Jews trying to follow him in an attempted emigration to the Holy Land. The Ottoman authorities put him on trial for disrupting the Imperial Peace, and he was imprisoned for a time in Constantinople. The sultanate then forced him to convert to Islam and exiled him back to Albania where he lived out his last years. Documents suggest that Zvi eventually returned to Judaism. After his death his tomb was taken over as a Bektashi shrine and remained that until until 1967.

The old city is divided into a number of quarters, like Gjirokastra, with numerous dwelling houses of outstanding beauty and architectural quality, in a maze of narrow winding alleyways that evoke perfectly the urban atmosphere of the late Ottoman world. The English Albanologist Swire stayed here in the late 1920s and described Berat, thus:

> Here in Berat we stayed with Major and Mrs Dodgson (of the gendarmerie), who lived in a shady whitewashed house high enough on the slope to catch any lagging breezes which favoured this hot valley. Its wide-flung windows overlooked half the town, letting in only human and animal noises for wheeled things could not approach very near; but that night the animals made up for the

machines and there seemed to be legions of dogs and cocks in the town. A dog barks, his neighbour takes up the cry, and then from all over the town others of his clan join in—and having the last bark seems an affair of honour with these wretched creatures. But the Albanian cocks are worse. They have two peculiarities. They crow at all hours of the night; and they crow as if suffering from violent colds in their throats—and worse still, draw out the eerie, creaking, final note for upwards of a minute! For these qualities they are highly valued, particularly as wedding gifts (and the longer the crow the more valuable the cock), for they have great power against evil spirits.

There are numerous routes leading into the old city from the base of the citadel. A good one to follow, although it does not lead right to the top, is up the alley to the left of the Mosque of the Bachelors, then following the steep and intricate paths up the hill in the Mangalem quarter, the original bazaar area of the city, giving the visitor the impression of entering a labyrinth; this quarter was renamed the '13 September' quarter under communism but has now reverted to its old name.

The ***DOMESTIC HOUSES OF BERAT** are similar in general design and ambience to those of Gjirokastra, with semi-fortified lower floors, often window-less, whitewashed walls and overhanging balconies, usually with finely-carved wooden decorations, and overhanging eaves. In general they are smaller and gentler in their impression on the visitor than the fierce, block-like Gjirokastra buildings. This can be seen as a reflection of the different social and economic position of the cities in 18C and 19C Albania, where Berat was a relatively secure and prosperous city compared to the frontier town ambience of Gjirokastra. As a result, there is perhaps more variety among the Berat houses, some having a separate terrace, some with one wing, others with two, and perhaps most characteristic of the city, a bewildering variety of beautifully designed and carved bay windows and wooden balconies.

Many of the ground floors are built into the solid rock below and behind the houses, and have wells in the lower floors, or cisterns to collect rain water. High walls, entrance gates and very heavy doors are formidable in scale and strength and offer major obstacles to any intruders. A walk in this city is the high point of many people's holiday in Albania. Return by the same route and walk to the bridge.

Over the other side of the river Osum is the **Gorica quarter**, again a place returning to its former name after being called the 'Partizani' quarter between 1944 and 1991. The name indicates early Slav settlement, meaning 'little mountain' in Slavonic. This should be visited, as the outlying houses here are much more similar to the fortress-like designs of Gjirokastra, a sign of the less impregnable situation of this side of the river. There are good views up and down river, and over to the citadel. The bridge is an attractive 18C construction, now unfortunately modified by modern additions.

The hill above Gorica is **Mount Shpirag**, known locally as *Mali me vija*, the striped mountain, after the indentations on its rocks. On the sides of it is a separate fortress, at the top of which are **Illyrian walls** dating from the 4C BC, which may be part of the ancient Illyrian city of *Dimale*. Although they are modest in scale, many visitors may well feel the journey up to see them is worth making; given the general inaccessibility of most Illyrian fortresses in Albania, Gorica and Mount Shpirag offer a relatively easy and trouble-free location to view remains from this seminal period in Albanian history. There are also extensive remains of walls dating mostly from the early Ottoman period, and a café that was opened in 1981, an attractive modern building surrounded by pine and cypress trees.

The mountain was an important Partisan base in the last war. It was visited by Colonel Billy McLean, one of the British Liaison Officers from SOE in Cairo attached to the Albanian resistance. In his memoir *The Anglo American Threat to Albania*, Enver Hoxha describes him in typically abusive terms:

> McLean once made a visit to Shpirag. We appointed Koço Tashko as his interpreter. He had gone down from there to observe the positions at Kucova. When they returned, a frightened and indignant Koço came to me and said:
> 'Find another interpreter for the Major, Comrade Enver, because I'll not go with him again. Do you know what he did? He stood on an exposed hill, wearing his red sash, and looked all round with his binoculars. If he goes on exposing himself in this way, the Germans will kill us one day.'
> 'But why did he put on a red sash?' I said.
> 'To show he is an officer', said Koço.

The rough track leading up from Gorica is only really suitable for four-wheel drive vehicles. Return to the main town back over the bridge, and walk round the base of the Mangalem quarter, round past the Mosque of the Bachelors, to the bottom of the road leading up to the citadel.

CITADEL OF BERAT

The ***Citadel of Berat is one of the great historic monuments of the Balkans; a vast, imposing fortress dominating the Osum valley. It is remarkably well preserved considering its long and turbulent history. Within the citadel complex are important churches, domestic buildings, an icon museum and a ruined mosque. The magnificent views of the surrounding country are breathtaking in their extent. The citadel was built to a roughly triangular plan, following the contours of the top of the hill, and is only accessible from the south-east. Viewed from below, that side of the citadel almost seems to be part of the hill, a human extension of a great natural fortress that has offered control of the Osum river valley in all periods of history. It is approached up a broad, well-paved road, dating from the late Ottoman period. The hour-long walk can be strenuous, particularly on a hot day, and you may prefer to try to find a taxi. Visitors with cars can park at the top. Above the winding road on the left are attractive hanging gardens which on a hot summer day waft the scent of coriander everywhere, and olive groves line the outskirts of the city to the right.

The entrance gate is reached at the top, with a roughly paved courtyard outside it. The tower, a brutal-looking square structure would be an ideal set in a film of one of Shakespeare's darker tragedies. Just inside the entrance, after walking up the path to the left, is the **Church of Shen Todri**, St Theodore, with very fine frescoes by Onufre the Great, a 16C Albanian painter. It is a small building with an exterior polygonal apse. It was built on the foundations of an older church and most of what can be seen dates from the 16C. The paintings of the Virgin with outstretched arms, the Church Fathers and of Christ and the Angel Gabriel are particularly fine. St Theodore's also contains some icons, of Christ Pantokrator, from the 16C, John the Baptist, from the 17C, Virgin Mary with Child, 19C and St Theodore in a struggle with a dragon, dated 1741.

The citadel at Berat

The citadel was always famous for its churches, with no fewer than 14 hidden within the walls of the fortress. They were severely damaged, in many cases during the anti-religious campaigns of the 1970s. In 1975 Gardiner comments that they were:

> ... all dark and constricted, all musty with stale incense, the ghosts of liturgical choirs, tarnished silver vessels, icons and swinging lamps and a junk heap of glass droplets from wrecked candelabra; all pretty much alike in the gloom.

With the advent of democracy, this sad state of affairs is beginning to be remedied, and you should expect to find workmen on site involved in restoration work which may limit access, although not very many tourists visit Berat at the moment and great goodwill is shown towards visitors. The restoration work is often in itself very interesting to watch, in any case.

The inner entrance tower contains masonry blocks dating back to the original Illyrian fortifications, which were constructed in the 4C and 3C BC. An outer perimeter wall with 24 towers encircled the top of the hill. The high central tower on the edge of the inner fortifications is also Illyrian in origin. The outer walls that can be seen today date originally from the reconstruction of the citadel under the rule of Michael Comnenos, under the Despotate of Epirus, between 1204 and 1215. The central north tower was reinforced then, and the walls running above the river Osum extended to the south-east, and the outer entrance gate built. In the 16C further refortification was undertaken by the Turkish conquerors, and under Ali Pasha modifications were made to enable the fortress to be defended with modern artillery. Follow through into the inner bailey area.

In the centre is the **Church of Shen Maria** (St Mary), which also contains the Onuphre Icon Museum. The church was built in the late 18C and completed in 1797. It is a typical construction of the Ottoman period, with a three-domed basilica. It is richly decorated inside, with depictions of animals, John the Baptist, St Nicholas, the three Church Fathers, John Chrysostomos, St Basil and St Gregory. The richly carved wooden iconostasis dates from 1806, and was carved by the Berat master carver, Stefan.

On the north and west sides of the church is the *Onuphre Icon Museum, which was opened here in 1986. It contains some of the finest examples of religious art in Albania, and should be visited if it is open. It is named after the great 16C painter of the Albanian school, Onuphre.

Room 1, facing the entrance, displays one of the most beautiful icons in the museum, a work by Onuphre in which the Virgin Mary is shown holding the infant Jesus on her right arm, enclosed by metalwork beautifully decorated with geometric and natural motifs. The style developed in Albania at this time was closely related to the icon painting school developed in Byzantine art in the time of Emperor John Paleologus, and the work of the Albanian painters drew on, and developed, a tradition already 200 years old. An icon representing Tyron and Stratiliate is exhibited at the entrance to the naos. The two warrior saints are shown dressed as soldiers and kneeling in prayer. The room also contains objects made for liturgical use and ornate Bible covers made by the Berat master Agathangjel Mbrica. A particularly fine example shows the life of the Prophet Isaiah.

Room 2 is a large space with many icons exhibited in it. On the left is an icon 'Candlemas' from the citadel Church of the Annunciation. It is a complex, elegant, richly-coloured composition. The western side of the room is taken up with several other icons representing the Annunciation. Another outstanding icon in this room is that of the Virgin; made in the 17C, it is heavily influenced in style by the contemporary icon painting school on the island of Crete. It has a delicate style, and very fine colour gradation. Icons of St Michael and St George of outstanding interest are also found in this room.

Upper Room. Most of the icons in this room, reached by the central wooden staircase, are from the citadel church of St Demetrius. The finest is perhaps the icon of St Nicholas, attributed to Onuphre, or the icon of John the Baptist, by the same artist. At the end of the room is an interesting icon giving a picture of the citadel and town of medieval Berat in the background, an example of the work of Cetiri. Textiles and small metal objects are also displayed in this room.

Across the inner fortifications area, behind St Theodore's, are the three small churches of St Nicholas, St Constantine and St Helena, and St Mary of Blachernae. Behind the latter is one of the large cisterns built to supply the citadel with water during sieges. The very small *St Mary of Blancherne** has very fine frescoes by Onuphre's son, Nicholas, that were painted at the end of the 16C. In their good state of preservation, and in their outstanding artistic quality, they are perhaps the finest examples of their period in an Albanian church, showing Biblical scenes and scenes from the life of Christ. The painter signed his work in 1578. The **Church of St Nicholas** also has interesting frescoes, and there is evidence of an earlier church dating from the 6C. An inscription on the door indicates that the church was completed in 1591. **The Church of St Constantine and St Helena** is a little later, being completed in 1644; the frescoes concentrate on scenes from the martyrdom of Christ.

If you walk along behind the churches, following the road lined with very old houses that runs inside the ramparts, magnificent views can be enjoyed over the walls.

N.B. The masonry of the Berat walls is often insecure, and the drop on the far side of the walls is often sheer; great care should be exercised when exploring.

On a small hillock within the fortifications is the **Church of the Holy Trinity**, dating from the late 13C and early 14C and having interesting frescoes. It was well restored in the 1960s.

The inner walls are now in front of you. These are built on Illyrian foundations with later Byzantine and Turkish rebuilding. They enclose the heart of the old fortress. Near the entrance are the ruins of the **White Mosque**, and a variety of domestic and military buildings. On the far side is a large cistern. After walking in the inner citadel, walk to the outside of its walls and proceed southwards. The ruins of the **Red Mosque** are found outside the walls near the south-east tip of the fortress. It was built in the latter half of the 15C for the use of the Turkish garrison and is one of the oldest mosques in Albania. The **Church of St George**, 500m in this direction, has been turned into a tourist pavilion, where it is possible to have a coffee and enjoy the magnificent views of the Tomor mountains to the east. The building dates from the 14C.

Below the café, continue to the south-east, below a ridge outside the perimeter walls (a difficult climb, take care), where you will find the **Church of St Michael**, dating from about 1300. It is notable for the combination of 'European' building techniques with a Byzantine style of architecture. It was particularly badly affected in the anti-religious campaigns and is undergoing restoration.

Return the by same route to the city across the citadel and down the hill into the old city.

THE ROAD FROM BERAT TO KORÇA VIA PËRMET

This road offers the more intrepid visitor with a car, or with the use of a car, the opportunity to drive on one of the most unspoilt mountain routes in southern Albania, from Berat via Përmet to near the Greek border, then turning north-east after the town of Leskoviku (140km), through Erseka (184km), with quite outstanding views of the Grammos mountains and the Kuq mountains, to Korça (224km).

N.B. It cannot be emphasised too strongly that substantial portions of this journey take place over poor mountain dirt tracks that will put considerable strain on both drivers and vehicles. It should not be attempted on your own, or outside the dry months of the year, or without adequate preparation, and without generous supplies of petrol and at least a day's supplies in the car. It is not advisable to travel if thunder-storms are forecast. Having said that, the route crosses one of the last expanses of truly remote mountain country in Western Europe, and by comparison with some Albanian mountain routes, a four-wheel drive vehicle, although desirable, is not essential. A minimum of seven hours should be allowed for the whole journey, although if difficulties are encountered it can take much longer. You should not assume that petrol can be obtained anywhere en route although generally supplies are available at Permet and Erseka.

Leave Berat by the bridge over the River Osum, through the Gorica quarter, and turn left, following the right-hand bank of the river southwards. The road becomes a dirt track and begins to climb slowly through woods and fruit tree plantations, then quickly enters thick dark pine forest, with stunning views across the Osumi valley towards the **Tomor mountain** range in the distance. After 4km, the track divides, take the right fork, the left goes to the village of Bilca (3km). The highest peak of the Tomor range is Mount Partizan, renamed after 1944 to commemorate the heroic role the tough guerilla çetas of the Berat region played in the struggle against the Axis. The view back towards the Berat citadel is also spectacular, and it is often possible to see birds of prey soaring on the thermals above the town, castle and river valley in the warmer months of the year.

Despite the height of the country the road runs through, there is a surprising amount of fertile agricultural land in the region, with the grapes of the Shkrapar hills to the south-east being used to make some of the best raki in Albania. You will pass very unspoilt mountain villages and small farms, more prosperous than those of the northern and central mountain regions, but also more Westernised, in cultural terms, and traditional costume is not often seen in this region. The road continues through the rolling uplands, with a view of the little town of **Polican** far away down in the river valley to the left. This town is a centre of armament manufacturing in Albania, with an underground factory in a nearby hillside. Albania manufactures a copy of the Kalashnikov rifle, hand-guns, ammunition and a light mortar. Polican was the subject of anti-government riots in the summer of 1992, after having been more or less a closed city for the 50 years of communism. In the hills to the right, above the road, evidence of early Illyrian settlement has been found, near the source of the Molisht river.

After Terpan (25km), the land becomes poorer, with barren stony hilltop fields, and the road quality deteriorates, with many hairpin bends, and precipitous drops. A side road up the mountainside from Polican joins this track, leading towards Kelcyre. The road approaches the border of the Berat administrative district, and enters the Tepelena district, with magnificent views south towards the high mountains of southern Albania, the **Trebeshina range** in particular. Tiny remote villages cling to the slopes, with houses scattered like a child's toy houses on a staircase, clinging to the barren hillsides. **N.B. Extreme care is needed in this section**.

The road follows on above the treeline, through low scrub. You will notice that many of the mountains suffer from marked land erosion, a result of the combination of overgrazing with the heavy rain of the Albanian winter and early spring. The road in this section is very potholed and subject to landslides in wet weather. The track winds slowly southwards, clinging to steep hillsides, across a landscape that has rightly been called the 'Tibet of Europe', where the only human activity that can be seen is the solitary shepherd tending his or her flocks, against the background of a landscape of dramatic beauty and Olympian scale, with the great cloud formations ever changing above the severe mountain peaks.

After Buz, the road begins to drop quickly through the mountains towards the valley of the Dëshnica river, a tributary of the Vjosa, running southwards off the Trebeshina mountains. Passing a strange conical-shaped mountain, topped by a radio mast, the journey becomes easier from the point of view of road conditions, and joins the Dishnic valley at Ballaban. It then runs 12km along the river bank to the Permet district and the pleasant small riverside town of **Kelcyra** (pop. 3945).

History

Kelcyra was an Illyrian village in the 4C BC, part of the tribal pattern of settlements organised around hilltop forts in the Trebeshnit mountains. In Roman times the gorge was an important transport route, and a small settlement grew up. In 1272 it was mentioned in medieval chronicles under the name of *Klausura*. It came under Arberesh rule in 1335. After 1431 it took part in Skanderbeg's Albanian League against the Turks. Kelcyra was the home of one of the Albanian heroes of the Spanish Civil War, Musa Fratari, who fought with distinction in the Battle of the Ebro. He was shot by Fascists in 1938. The town has always depended on the high quality of local fruit and grapes for its economic prosperity and it is a centre of raki manufacture.

The visitor with a little time to spare can stop in Kelcyra and see the ruins of the **Turkish fort of Kelcyra**, an Ottoman stronghold that was built as the residence of the local *beys* to enable them to control the river valley, above the west bank of the river on Mount Trebeshina. It probably used to be an imposing structure, but this river valley was bitterly contested in the battles between the Partisans and the retreating Axis forces in the Second World War, when the fort was largely destroyed. Ever since Roman times, control of this road has been important in securing military control of southern Albania.

The road here improves considerably, and runs 18km asphalted towards Përmet, through the sheltered valley, rich with many Mediterranean plants, a sign that you are approaching the Vjosa valley. On the right, above the beech and ash woods of the valley, are the peaks of the **Dhembël mountains**, that above Permet reach a height of 2050m. The river is very beautiful, particularly after heavy rain, with a rushing torrent running through large rocks. After 8km, a left turn leads northeast up a track to the mountain village of **Frashër** (17km), on the northern headwater of the Lengarice tributary of the Vjosa river. It is on a small pass, *Qafë e Dellenjes*, that leads to remote countryside in the upper Osum valley.

History

Frasher is named after the three Frasheri brothers, Abdyl, Naim and Sami, 19C intellectual founding fathers of Albanian nationalism and the *Rilindja* movement. Their writings, as poets and ideologues, and their political role, in organisations such as the League of Prizren, were of fundamental importance in the assertion and definition of Albanian identity during the final crisis of the Ottoman Empire and the struggle for national independence. They are also commemorated by bronze statues in central Tirana. Their tomb is in the park behind the central University building. The population of the village is a mixture of Muslim and Orthodox, with many inhabitants of Vlach descent.

A restored house in the village is being made into a museum for the Frasheris and it is hoped that in the future the semi-derelict Bektashi *tekké* nearby will also be restored. Continue to Përmet (7km after returning to the main road south).

PËRMET

Përmet (pop. 5804) is soon reached, a rather nondescript town, but in many ways the spiritual heart of Albanian communism, if it could be said to have had one. It was very deeply involved in the anti-Fascist struggle and as a result was completely burnt down by the Germans in 1943/44 and all the buildings are modern. Much of the population of the surrounding mountains is of Vlach descent.

A British SOE liaison officer, T.W. Tilman, DSO, MC, was attached by SOE in Cairo to a partisan brigade in the Second World War in this area of the country. Passing through Permet in August 1943, he noted the damage the area had suffered in the Balkan Wars of 1911–12, and other recent conflicts:

> There was no sign of the war until we reached the town of Permet; but of past wars there were many, for in this troubled country there are few places free from scars. The village of Frasher, for example, which we passed had been ravaged by the Greeks in 1914 in company with 150 other Albanian villages; and on the highest mountains one would find stone sangards and heaps of spent

cartridges fired by the Greeks in their campaign against the Italians. Përmet itself had suffered in that campaign, and had recently been burnt again by the Italians as a reprisal for some partisan action. It was now garrisoned by Italians who occupied newly built barracks.

■ **Hotel**. In town centre, clean, basic.

■ **Post office.** Long distance telephone calls can be made from the kiosk in the central Post Office, in the town square.

History

The town is first mentioned in 15C chronicles, although there must almost certainly have been an ancient settlement on the site. It grew as a small Ottoman administrative and trade centre, and was an early supporter of the Albanian nationalist movement in 19C. It was a centre of resistance to Greek irredentism at the end of that century. The nationalist assocation *Bashkimi* (Unity) was formed in Permet in 1909. The 6th Partisan Brigade was formed here by Enver Hoxha and Mehmet Shehu in 1943. On 24 May 1944 the anti-Fascist Congress of Liberation was held here, always known in Albania as the Congress of Permet, which laid the political foundations for the communists taking undisputed power in the autumn of that year.

The Congress is commemorated by a socialist realist monument in the town centre by Odhise Pashkali. A small museum, principally devoted to the national liberation and resistance movement, is currently closed. On the sheer cliff of the mountain behind the town, the *Guri i Qytetit*, the Town Rock, there are the ruins of a medieval fortress.

3km south of Permet is Leusa, with an attractive Orthodox church, with good frescoes by Onufre.

The road follows south 27km along the Vjosa valley, through beautiful country-side, and below the great **Nemërçka range** that towers over the road on the right-hand side, before turning sharp left 14km before the Greek border, towards Leskoviku (39km from Përmet). A track continues towards Greece, but there is no road at all over the border and crossing into Greece is not possible here. **N.B. The paths that can be used to walk across the border have been the scene of violent incidents in the last two years between Greek and Albanian security police, and Albanian illegal emigrants. Avoid**.

There are police control posts at several points along this road, particularly between Leskoviku and Erseka, and you should be sure your documents are in order and carry them with you at all times. If you are using a hired car, you should make sure that the driver's car ownership documents are also in order. Although the visitor has nothing to fear from the Albanian security personel, it should be pointed out that it is not unknown for the driver of your vehicle to need a few dollars in hand to pass these controls smoothly.

As the road (good quality asphalt) approaches Leskoviku, it enters a wild and remote landscape, and very large uninhabited pine forests. After 16km, **Leskoviku**, a strange marooned old town, with some attractive small derelict 19C *beys'* houses and a large Orthodox church. It used to be an important town under the Ottoman Empire, but the Boundary Commissioners' decisions in 1913 deprived most of the local landowners of their land, now over the border in Greece, and it has never recovered. It is ironic that it was during the Commissioners' stay in Leskoviku in October 1913 that the decisions were taken on this land, leading to the Protocol of Florence in December 1913 when the current Greek-Albanian border was established. The French war correspondent René Puaux left a description of the town as it was when Crown Prince William of Weid arrived there in 1913:

> the enthusiasm became delirious. Armfuls of flowers were thrown at him, the Prince kissed the Gospels, listened to the addresses delivered in Greek and Turkish while in the front rows of the crowd, both men and women, broke through the line of troops and threw themselves upon the Crown Prince, kneeling in the dust to kiss his feet, his knees, his sword, his hands.

Leskoviku is well-known for its local wine and raki. There appears little else to do in the region, other than grow grapes, make good drinks, and consume them. After Leskoviku, the road enters the **Barmash Pass**, remote and more or less uninhabited, clinging to the wooded hillside on the left while the vast mass of the ***GRAMMOZ MOUNTAINS*** appears to the south-east. Snow-covered for much of the year, the awesome Grammoz mountain wall divides Greece from Albania, remote and with a harsh climate, the last stronghold, in this part of the Balkans, of wolves, bears and jackals. A few villages can be seen in the lee of the mountains, as the road winds towards Erseka, but generally the climate and inhospitable environment have prevented much in the way of human settlement. The defeated Democratic Army of the Greek left in the civil war retreated down the mountains here in the aftermath of their defeat in the Battle of Grammoz in 1949. Vlach shepherds are often the only people the traveller is likely to meet nowadays. In the past this was an important Vlach area, but in the inter-war period many moved to Romania. In the Barmash Pass is the tiny roadside village of **Borova**, scene of a massacre by the Germans in the Second World War, where all the inhabitants, including women and children, were shot in reprisal for their support for the partisans.

After 12km is the little town of **Erseka**, capital of this region, which is the most thinly populated in the whole country.

History

Erseka was a very small market in late Ottoman times, on the road from Korça to the Adriatic. It grew as a very small town in the 18C to its present size of about 3700 inhabitants. In 1909 the Albanian nationalist association 'Unity' established an office here. It was important in the Second World War as a sector of battle between the Greek forces of General Papagos and the Italian invaders. The Greek defences were based on the heights of the Morava mountains. It was liberated in July 1944. Under communism it was a centre of the food industry. The area around the town is known for its hunting in the winter, of wild boar in particular. Many wolves live in the vicinity. It has a cold winter climate with bitter north winds.

In 1938 it was visited by the English traveller Nigel Heseltine who noted its importance as a small market town:

> Gradually we drift into Ersek, where the market is. Noisily they put their horses and their donkeys together in an enclosure on the edge

of the village, and advance, searching for acquaintances. In the centre of the village is an open space. Women dressed in black have spread melons, peppers, and embroidered rugs, but the crowd is round the stall of cheap imported shaving-soaps and safety-pins. Most of the men have their umbrellas up, here and there a *hodja* with his beard and different clothes, goes among the people or sits in a doorway smoking. There is considerable clamour but no excitement. In the evening many of the men will get drunk in the numerous inns with big bottles of *raki* on the counter. Already the only street is full of mud and ruts.

The town has serious social problems, and stopping in Erseka is not recommended. Unemployment is very high, and the atmosphere poor.

After Erseka, the road carries on in the same direction towards Korça (44km) through the *Qafa e Qarrit*, Oak Tree Pass, with extraordinary views of the Grammos range, and Mount Cukapecit (2523m), then the lower *Mali i Kuq*, the Red Mountains, above Floq. It crosses the **Plain of Kolonja**, an empty region that was the floor of a primeval lake and now forms the upper valley of the tributaries of the River Osum.

After 33km, a left turn leads 14km past a small lake to **Vithkuq** (pop. 3501), a hilltown that was the birthplace of Naum Veqilarxhi, a friend and collaborator of the Frasheri brothers in the *Rilindja*. The town has a history, ethnic make up and economy similar to that of Voskopoja (see Route 11), in that it prospered in the 17C and 18C as a rival to Korça, but was destroyed in wars between the *beys* and has struggled on as a small, predominantly Vlach, farming centre. It has three churches which are worth visiting because of their architectural quality, and in one of them, **St Peter's**, there are very fine frescoes by Zographe. It was an area of strong support for the partisans during the war, and communism after it, with the *Qamil Panariti* brigade of the partisans inflicting heavy losses on the Italian occupiers in battles in 1943. British SOE officer David Smiley describes a celebration there after the inauguration of the Brigade in 1943, in his memoir *Albanian Assignment*:

> The Vlachs roasted whole sheep on spits, and eaten in a pilaf they tasted delicious; there was plenty of raki, chianti, and beer; the celebrations finished with a good deal of singing.

Follow the road back to the main road and then continue 18km to Korça (see Route 11).

11 · Korça and environs

From Tirana, via Elbasan, 55km, Pogradec, 89km, to Korça, about 144km. **N.B.** *From Greece, via Kapshtica border point, 34km. See Route 9:* **note difficulties with frontiers and other security considerations in this area.**

Korça (pop. in 1984 58,000, now probably about 50,000) is the regional capital of south-east Albania, occupying a central position on the open flatlands of the Plain of Korçe, but dominated by the Morava mountains to the east. It is an interesting, historic, relatively sophisticated town, with rich cultural traditions and some interesting buildings from the Ottoman period, including one of the most important mosques in Albania. While cold in the winter, being nearly 610m above sea level, the region has a healthy climate, good water supply and is very productive agriculturally.

Although Korça was a fountainhead of the Albanian nationalist movement, the population in and around the city is very mixed, with ethnic Greeks, Vlachs, Slav-speakers and Roma all in evidence. It is near the ruined 18C city of **Voskopoja**, now an important Vlach centre. There are many interesting small villages in the vicinity, some of which have Orthodox churches of great historical, artistic and architectural interest. The nearby coal mines at Drenova have been worked since Ottoman times and are of considerable economic importance. The area has been affected by heavy migration to Greece in search of work in the last two years, and although the local economy has made some progress, many difficulties remain.

■ **Buses and taxis** from outside the *Illyria Hotel.*

■ **Police.** Headquarters, tel. 29 19 or 26 96; Police Station, tel. 20 00.

■ **Medical care**. Central Policlinics (out patients dept.), tel. 22 22; District Hospital (emergency service), tel. 29 72; Dr Ahmet Dulollari (surgeon), tel. 29 31 (home); Dr Namik Kasimati (cardiologist), tel. 26 86 (home).

■ **Hotels and restaurants**. Finding reasonable accommodation in Korça can be difficult. The *Illyria Hotel*, near the old bazaar, is the easiest place to stay, but it is in poor condition, having changed little since 1990. The staff are unhelpful, and restaurant dirty. Some rooms smell. It can be very cold in winter, sleeping bag recommended. The water supply is often a problem, as elsewhere in the town. **Avoid**. The *Hotel Tourist* is very bad indeed, with squalid sanitary arrangements and insect infestation. **Avoid**. The old **Han of Elbasan** in the market is being reconstructed as a hotel but is not yet open (see below). Private rooms rented are a better prospect.

There are a number of good new cafés and bars, but not many private restaurants as yet. The *Restaurant Mbledhja e Beratit* has a good reputation. It is difficult to find, in a small back street beyond the museum, ask directions locally. Korça region Merlot wine is excellent.

History

The Korça region has been inhabited from the earliest times, with neolithic remains found indicating continuous occupation of the site of the city for the last 6000 years. The *Bakri*, or copper epoch, lasted from 3000 BC to 2100 BC and saw considerable cultural advances, followed by a Bronze Age culture lasting until about 1000 BC. In the Iron Age cultural influences from Greece became very strong. There are a large number of unexcavated archaeological sites in the region, many of which are believed to be of the same period as the Mycenaean culture in ancient Greece.

The area was important in the spread of Byzantine Christianity in Albania, and a church was established in 898. A town here called *Coviza* is mentioned in medieval documents in 1280. The modern town dates from the end of the 15C, when Iljaz Hoxha, under the command of Sultan Mehmet II, developed Korça. The Ottoman occupation began in 1440, and after Hoxha's heroic role in the siege of Constantinople, in 1453, he was awarded the title 'Iljaz Bey Mirahor'. For a long time it was rivalled by Voskopoja, but with the destruction of the latter in the late 18C, Korça achieved a pre-eminence it never subsequently lost in the region. It was an important stopping point on the caravan routes and at one time there were no fewer than 16 *hans* in the city. In the 19C it became particularly prosperous, and a centre of the growth of Albanian national consciousness. In 1887 the first school teaching in the Albanian language was established, and in 1891 the first Albanian school for girls.

The region was in turmoil during the Balkan Wars and suffered serious losses of buildings and population, coming under particular pressure from the activities of the Greek irredentist movements of the time. Korça was occupied by Greek forces on 6 December 1912. It surrendered to the Boundary Commissioners shortly afterwards, but was then retaken by Greek forces on 10 July 1914. The English Albanologist Edith Durham was forced to leave Korça at this time, describing the situation thus:

> The pro-Greek gang at King's College started a story that I had had to fly for my life from Korcha because they all wanted to be Greek and I had tried to stir up Albanian trouble. The truth being that I and Nevison, who was there as a correspondent, made a forced march of three days—two nights sleeping on the bare ground—across the mountains to Berat at the urgent request of the Albanians. Berat being the nearest station from which a telegram could be sent, uncontrolled by the Greeks. Nevison drafted the telegram to the Council of Ambassadors in London begging that no attention be paid to the Greek account of a meeting asking for Greek rule. This meeting having been a forced one held with Greek bayonets. This telegram saved Korcha. The Greek governor made everyone paint their shops blue and white. And after the hideous cruelty of the Greeks when they raided south Albania in 1914 ... I have no use whatever for Greeks. I can never forget the crowds of refugee women and children dying and starving under the olive trees around Vlore ... . The matter was never bothered about. But it was, I believe, part of the whole Sarajevo crime plot. The Greeks and Serbs were working together to take Albania. They meant to drive out Wied. And it was they who planned the rising against him. While I was still at Vlore, the Serbs sent a message they would attack Vlore and that as they had France and Russia on their side, Vlore had better surrender. But the Austrian attack on Serbia stopped that. (Letter to H. Hodgkinson 11 Jan. 1939.)

During the First World War, the region was occupied by Austria-Hungary, then again by the Greeks and then by French troops in 1916. An autonomous republic of Korça, known to Greeks as *Koritsa*, then set up was overthrown as a result of Greek entry into the war on the side of the Allies; its President, Thermistokli Germenji, was shot by firing squad in Salonika. French occupation ended in 1920 but cultural influence continued, with the Korça French lycée playing a formative role in the life of the communist dictator Enver Hoxha, where he was both a pupil and teacher. In 1929 the inhabitants of Korça were active in the agitation for Prince Wilhelm of Wied to return to Albania as monarch.

During the 1930s the labour movement grew strongly in the city, and the underground Korça group of communists (some of whom were ethnic Yugoslavs) became the nucleus of the Albanian Party of Labour, under the leadership of the Albanian Comintern agent Ali Kelmendi. In 1936 a demonstration of the unemployed was brutally repressed by the Zogist police, and the Korça liberal newspaper *Bota e Re* was banned by the government. The Korça region was bitterly fought over by Italian invading armies and Greek defence forces in 1940–41, with heavy losses on both sides. In the war the city was a very strong centre of the partisan movement and the resistance to Axis occupation, and a demonstration against the occupation was fired on by German troops in 1943. The city was a bastion of popular support for communism for many years after the war. The already existing furniture, carpet and snuff industries were complemented by the building of a major coal-fired power station and engineering factories. The surrounding regional district is the second largest in the country, after Shkodra, and takes up about 8 per cent of the country, with 188 villages and three towns. Before the war much of the region was marshy; on the reclaimed land agriculture is concentrated on the production of grain, tobacco and sugar beet. The Orthodox Cathedral was an important historic building that was completely destroyed by Enverist militants in 1968.

A visit to Korça takes about a day, if the museum and the most interesting parts of the city are visited, and at least another day is needed for excursions outside the city.

Leaving the central hotel by the main entrance, on the left is the *Old Bazaar* area, most of which was demolished in a brutalist redevelopment scheme in the 1970s. The quarter had previously been damaged by serious fires in 1822, 1858 and 1879; and according to inscriptions on the walls, the oldest house standing today dates from 1870. Korça had been a great place of importance for the Ottoman caravan routes and at one time there were no fewer than 16 hans in the city. All that remain are the 'Han of Monastir' and the 'Han of Elbasan', impressive, solid Turkish buildings that were used by carpet and textile traders. The *Han of Elbasan* is being restored as a hotel, with an impressive dedication to the original architecture. It is an old Ottoman building of great charm and dignity. It was built in the early 18C with a very attractive wooden upper gallery and stone paved internal courtyard. With the advent of a market economy, large numbers of small businesses are beginning to re-establish trade in the area and it can be a good place to shop for food and souvenirs. A single street of run-down but attractive Ottoman-period shops remains. In the centre of the new trading area is a Turkish stone column.

Beyond the Han of Elbasan is the original **Ottoman Market Square** and associated streets of market buildings. It reached its height of prosperity early in the 19C. This is a wonderfully impressive complex, but in general is in a pitiful state and it is far from clear what its future will be. Many of the semi-derelict houses are currently squatted in by Roma. As it is unique in Albania, and probably in the Balkans more generally, it is to be hoped that the essential international support and material aid for its restoration will be forthcoming before many important buildings are lost, such as a beautiful arched gateway that collapsed in 1994. **N.B. Security in these streets is often poor**.

Turn left and walk up a slope through the edge of the market towards the mosque, the *****Xhamija e Mirahorit**, reached in its surrounding garden through a small side road leading off the bazaar area. This is one of the most architecturally important mosques in Albania, dating from 1494, the earliest example of a single-domed building that has survived. At the time of writing reconstruction and renovation works are in progress, financed by the Turkish government, but it is generally possible to gain access. It has a plain white interior, dating from the 19C, with attractive wall paintings of Mecca and Medina, and a sense of calm and dignified religious life. The minaret on the south-west side was seriously damaged in an earthquake in the 18C. The garden in which it stands has been disfigured by entrances to underground shelters, built to 'protect' the population against the nuclear attack on Albania that Enver Hoxha feared in the late 1960s.

Returning to the hotel, and turning right into the main street leading towards the centre of the city, up a slight hill, you pass by a number of administrative buildings, including the first **public library** to be established in Albania. Then, on the left, is a large square building that housed the first school teaching in the Albanian language, established in 1887 by Naim Frasheri, then nearby the first girls' school in the country, opened in 1891.

In 1966 the writer Dymphna Cusack, in her memoir *Illyria Reborn* recalled meeting one of the original pupils of this school:

> I was introduced to a frail old lady in deepest black, Efigenia Pendavini, who told me in a quiet voice how she had gone to the Girls' School of Servasti Qiriazi, a remarkable woman who opened the first Albanian School against much opposition. People used to call us faithless and throw stones at us, but we never gave up. That school worked hard to unveil women. We used to put on plays—with girls playing boys' roles. I remember particularly The Merchant of Venice and William Tell. Oh, what a lot of trouble there was about that. The Pasha's wife said it was subversive!

You come to a large open oblong area, on the left of which, on the opposite side of the road, is a modern building that used to be the communist party headquarters. Nearby was the site of the important historic **Cathedral of St George**, dynamited in the anti-religious campaigns in 1968. A new building is under construction. In the centre, over the road, is a group of very attractive Ottoman-period buildings. In the centre of them is **Korça Museum** (Director Mr Petraq Damko) and the offices of the local archaeological institute. The museum is officially closed, but if one of the institute staff is there it is usually possible to gain access. On the lower floor, outside the main door, there is a large pithos and part of a mosaic floor, while upstairs there are several glass cases in two main rooms displaying objects found during archaeological excavations in the Korça region.

The museum is in a very attractive Ottoman house, built mostly of wood, and is

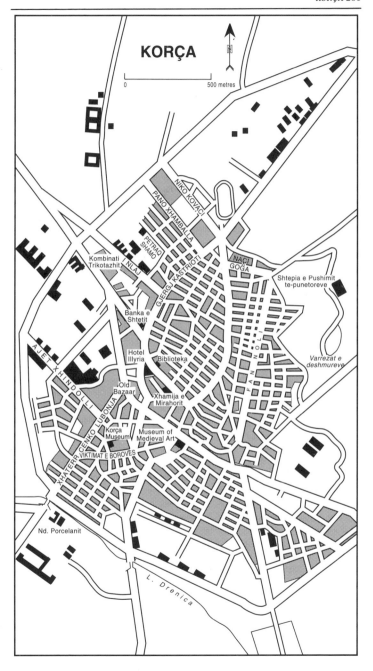

KORÇA

0   500 metres

NIKO KOVAÇI

PANO XHAMBALLA

PETRAQ SHAMO

Kombinati Trikotazhit

NLAJ

GJERGJ KASTRIOTI

NAÇI GOGA

Shtepia e Pushimit te-punetoreve

Banka e Shtetit

Hotel Illyria

Biblioteka

AJET XHINDOLLI

Old Bazaar

Xhamija e Mirahorit

Korça Museum

Museum of Medieval Art

XHATERR CENKO ÇUBONJA

VIKTIMAT E BOROVES

FAN LI NZ

Varrezat e deshmureve

Nd. Porcelanit

L. Drenica

well worth a visit, even if you have no special interest in archaeology. The collections are mainly from the prehistoric period and include pottery, weapons and artefacts from Maliq and other sites in the region. The most valuable items are in vaults in Tirana for safekeeping and cannot be seen. The inter-relationship of Greek and Illyrian culture is a principal theme of the exhibits.

Near the museum are other well-preserved **houses** from the late Ottoman period when the town was prospering from trade in the region, and a walk around here is well worthwhile, with the dominant style of domestic architecture reflecting the use of stone for the lower walls, often with copious use of arches, and timber for the upper floors. There are many beautiful inner courtyards.

In this part of the town there used to be an important **Bektashi tekké**, the *tekké of Melcani*, which is believed to have been destroyed by a fire during the war. It was visited by the British writer Patrick Leigh Fermor when he was attached to the Greek forces in Albania in 1940. It was of particular interest as the dancing was accompanied by self mutilation of the face with nails, a Shi'ite practice.

> Patrick Leigh Fermor (1915–), the author of *Mani* and *Roumeli*, was British Liaison military officer in Albania in this period along the long front between Korça, Agyrokastro and Tepelena. The war was slow moving for much of the time, with activity limited to sniping and the exchange of mortar fire. The Greek troops often sufferred from frost-bite. An American officer active in the Korça area at the same time was Colonel William 'Wild Bill' Donovan, then of the Office of Strategic Services. He was later to become the founding father of the modern Central Intelligence Agency (CIA), in his work for the US government after World War II.

2km east of Korça is the modern village of **Barç**, reached by a track across the plain near Dishnica. A large late Bronze Age tumulus was found here, 41m in diameter, containing nearly 200 graves. Burials continued over a period of three centuries until about 850 BC. The earlier burials contained jewellery, gold and bronze ornaments, and Devoll ware pottery.

THE ENVIRONS OF KORÇA
Some of the villages around the city make delightful excursions, particularly for those with an interest in or some knowledge of Balkan history, Orthodox churches and art, and/or ethnography. As they are generally on or near the Plain, rather than in the mountains, it is possible to reach them without too much difficulty by taxi from the city, and without a four-wheel drive vehicle being essential. The area has seen many movements of population, local wars, invasions, early examples of ethnic cleansing and foreign occupations in its history, and all these events have left their mark on the composition of the population. It is, in general, very mixed and the visitor will meet an extraordinary diversity of people within a small geographical area. While Albanian is universally understood, in some quite small villages it is possible to hear as many as four languages spoken in a community of a few hundred people.

> In the 19C the area was famous for brigandage, and was the scene in 1884 of the epic adventure of the British and Foreign Bible Society missionary Gerasimos Kyrias, who was captured by bandits near modern Zvezda, on the edge of the Thate mountain north of the city, while on a journey from *Monastir* (modern Bitola, in Macedonia) to Korça. He lived with them in the

mountains near Korça for six months, recording his experiences in a book *Captured by Brigands*, an illuminating record of the chaotic social conditions of the time. He describes a meal with his captors, reflecting the primitive, Homeric world of the *çeta*, thus:

> That day Shahin ordered four of his men to go down to where a flock of sheep was grazing, and catch four of them for mutton, saying, 'Keep your eyes wide awake, and choose lambs.' They ran and brought them. They were quickly butchered and skinned. Some went and cut spits, tressels, and crotches, some gathered brush for making fire, others made ready a place, and were rejoicing that they would have roast meat to eat.
>
> Having skinned them, they ran a spit through them, wrapped the internal fat round them, and tied them up with the entrails, the contents of which they had squeezed out, for there was no water to wash them. They set the crotches in the ground, and put the spits with their carcasses on them, and four men turned them. Others collected the viscera, sliced them, slit the large intestines, and cleaning them with their hands, put all on a spit, and made a great delicacy. Another took a stomach, and emptying it, threw in a handful of salt, and clapped it on the coals. He took it when well roasted to one side and ate it, lest a comrade should snatch it from him. This fellow had put a kidney, and its suet, too, on the coals, and guarded it. Before it was well cooked, he took it from the coals, and put it straight into his mouth lest it should be snatched from him...
>
> While the meat was roasting, shepherds, and others hungry for meat came round, and did not go away empty. The piece of meat given them they considered as given from the brigands' own property, and counted it a great favour. They said the latter were benefactors, and did not believe they were eating something stolen.

A visit to the hilltown of ****Voskopoja** (21km) should be part of every visit to Korça, although the road to the place is not very good and unless the arduous journey is undertaken in dry weather, a four-wheel drive vehicle is recommended.

Voskopoja, or *Moskopolis* as it was known in Greek, is one of the most evocative and atmospheric places in this part of the Balkans, with Orthodox churches of the highest architectural and historical interest, remarkable fresco paintings, and the remains of a small urban settlement that until the mid-18C was one of the most flourishing and prosperous cities in the region. It was destroyed by internicine wars in the late 18C, and has declined to a small village and centre of pastoral agriculture that is largely inhabited by Vlach shepherds. The region is still a stronghold of the Vlach language and culture. Some local students go to Romania for their higher education.

To reach Voskopoja, take the small road west out of Korça past the power station and head into the countryside over the flat plain to the village of Poshtme, 3km, then carry on along a track towards Goskova, turning left up a steep track through forest towards Voskopi after about another 3km. The road is a poor, deeply-rutted track and great care is needed. Follow the track through the woods, climbing steeply via hairpin bends until a plateau is reached, then the modern village of **Voskop** in the distance is reached after about another 6km.

Church of St Christopher

POLENA

From Voskop, it is possible to make an excursion along farm tracks to the interesting Orthodox village of ***Polena** set at the bottom of a hillside beyond the Dunavec river. The name is of Bulgarian origin. It was originally a much more important settlement than it is now, and the large old village occupied the upper slope of the hill, where the inhabitants had moved in the 17C to escape the Turks. In Ali Pasha's time some of the people moved to Oher and Krushova in Macedonia, to escape his wars. It was a centre of the anti-Axis resistance, supporting Mehmet Shehu's First Partisan Brigade, and the old village was largely destroyed by the Germans in a reprisal raid in 1943. The modern village dates from 1947, but parts of it were destroyed by an earthquake in the 1960s.

Polena was famous for its five churches and in the 18C its prosperous economy must have been linked with that of Voskopoja. In 1975 the people resisted pro-atheism gangs by ringing the church bell until they retreated and spared the building. If the track up from the top of the village is followed there is a steep climb for about 800m up the hill, to the top, with very fine views over the plain. On the rise, on bare overgrazed grassland, there is the tiny **church of St Christopher**, which has been restored and is in use. It is a minuscule building, about 4m x 2m, on the brow of the hill, with an impressive bell hung in a tree nearby, and a humble, bare interior with a few candles and a dollar bill lying on a minute wooden table. There are the foundations of other buildings in the vicinity, and the pavement of what appears to be part of an Ottoman or medieval road. There are very good views down over the Plain of Korça. Christian burial continued in the adjacent cemetry until the late 1950s.

Return to Voskopi by the same route.

VOSKOPOJA

Carry on through Voskop, towards ****Voskopoja**. The road is very poor and great care is needed. The pine forests here are being attacked by an infestation of caterpillars which are causing widespread damage. After about another 10km, at the head of the valley, old Voskopoja is seen, set in open fields and deciduous woodland, at an altitude of 1115m. The plateau was an important 'drop zone' for British officers parachuted into southern Albania in the last war from Special Operations Executive in Cairo, and the area generally was the scene of bitter fighting between the Albanian Partisans and the Axis occupation forces. Nearby Vithkuq was the headquarters of the legendary First Partisan Brigade under the leadership of Mehmet Shehu.

Voskopoja now is a strung-out rural settlement, with some stone-built farm houses mixed with modest peasants' houses, churches in varying stages of repair, sheep huts and other farm buildings. On the outskirts is a concrete memorial to members of the 4th Partisan Brigade, who died fighting the Axis in the area in November and December 1944. Bronze plaques record the names and villages of the dead.

The local flora and fauna are very rich, particularly the wild flowers in fields below the village.

History

Voskopoja first appears as a place of any importance in medieval chronicles in the 14C. It was then known by the Greek name of *Moschopolis*. It was taken over by the Ottoman invaders in the 15C and developed as a trade centre. It grew rapidly, and was particularly prosperous after the Venetian expansion in the Balkans, acting as an entrepot between Venice and Constantinople. Merchants from Vlora had large interests in the town, and business connections existed in places as far away as Saxony, Budapest, Constanza, Trieste and Poland. By the middle of the 18C as many as 50,000 people may have lived in the vicinity, and 30,000 in the town itself. It was the second largest city in 'Turkey in Europe' after Constantinople. The first churches were constructed in the 17C. In 1720 the first printing press in the Balkans was said to be established, and in 1760 books in Greek were being printed. The writers Theodore Kavalioti and Theodore Haxhifilipi lived here. At this time there were about 22 churches in the town. Between 1741 and 1751 a school was in operation. But the wealth of the city aroused the jealousy of the Turkish *beys* in the surrounding parts of the Balkans, and between 1769 and 1789 various military expeditions were mounted against Voskopoja, and many Christians were murdered or expelled from the town and their houses burnt down.

The town declined rapidly as Korça grew as the regional capital and it suffered further serious damage to its buildings during vicious inter-communal fighting in the region during the Balkan wars in 1911–12, in the conflicts over control of Korça during and after the First World War, and most of all in the battles between the Axis troops and Partisans in 1943–44. In 1914 there were still 24 churches standing,and 2200 Greeks in the population, served by Greek-speaking priests and Greek language schools. In 1916 the area was occupied by the Austro-Hungarians. After this Voskopoja played a full part in the national independence movement under the leadership of the patriot Sali Butka.

The visitor entering Voskopoja immediately notices what appear to be incongruously well-paved Ottoman streets running between run-down farm buildings and small churches in the village. In the centre of the village is the ****Church of Shenkolle**, built in 1721, the finest Orthodox church in this part of Albania, and also often the only church in the village it is possible to visit. It is locked up all the time: the curator is called Mr Apostolis Zguri; local enquiries will usually locate his whereabouts. The priest is Mr Tomas Samera (speaks some Greek). Most of the inhabitants of the place today are Vlachs, and one of the many pleasures of a visit is to experience the culture of this minority people and hear their ancient language spoken. At the far end of the village is a very small taverna, with exquisite raki made from local plums, where you can be sure of a warm welcome. Other good cafés have opened recently.

The Vlachs

The Vlachs are a predominantly pastoral people who live in scattered communities in northern Greece, Romania, Macedonia, Albania, Bulgaria and regions of ex-Yugoslavia. Known by themselves as *Aroumanians*, by the Greeks as *Koutzovlachs*, by ex-Yugoslavs as *Cincars*, they speak a language descended from Latin. It is generally believed that they are descended from remnants of the Roman legions stranded in the Balkan region. In 1914 the English scholars Wace and Thompson estimated that there were about half a million Vlach speakers scattered over the Balkans, although the German Vlachologist Weigand in 1888 had estimated numbers at only 373,520. Vlachs have migrated to the cities in recent years, and have tended to lose their linguistic identities, but in Albania they have experienced less cultural repression than in Greece, and the language has survived in many isolated communities. Vlach villages in Albania, as in the northern Pindus mountains in Greece, tend to be found at the heads of valleys, near a good water supply. Vlachs have some distinctive physical features, being usually short, dark and with widely set dark eyes, by comparison with most Albanians.

Church of Shenkolle

The **church of Shenkolle** immediately strikes you as belonging to a community of a much larger size. The historic church stands behind a rebuilt 20C bell tower (1936) that was damaged in the last war. It is mainly notable for its remarkable fresco paintings, depicting over 1000 figures over the whole church, including a beautiful but damaged series of paintings under the arches of the exterior. An inscription on the west wall of the church records that it was built between June 1721 and September 1722. It was decorated by the famous painter David Selenica during 1726, with two assistants from his family, Konstantin and Kristo. Paintings on the south wall show events in the life of St John, on the west wall the Crucifixion, with the entrance fresco showing scenes from the Apocalypse, in the style of the Korça painters Konstantin and Athanas Zografhi. A number of outstandingly beautiful 18C icons can be seen near the altar. The cloister paintings are in very urgent need of protection and restoration.

The eight other churches in the village are generally locked up or are used for agricultural purposes. St Michael's church is on the north-west side of the village up a gentle hill. Although is empty, it is possible to peer inside through a small hole in the rear wall. St Mary's is built to the same general plan as the church of Shenkolle, but has suffered considerable damage over the years. The iconostasis is in a fair state of preservation. Two other churches in the village are the church of St Athanasius and the monastery of St John the Baptist. The former is said to have paintings by the 18C artist Constantin of Berat.

The two other surviving churches that are most interesting and accessible are the *Church of the Holy Trinity and the **Church of Shen Thanasit.

The 18C Church of the Holy Trinity is in open fields on a small hillock to the north east of the centre of the village. It can be reached along village roads, well paved from the original 18C urban development although often very muddy in wet weather. Walk about a quarter of a mile past a cow shed with the characteristic very small dark brown cows of the region. The **church** can be seen behind a very fine **belltower**, with two storeys of Romanesque arches. It is in a poor state of repair, and requires urgent restoration. The church is a large oblong building, with a dark interior that is usually locked up, although it is sometimes used in the winter for animal shelter. There are horses kept nearby, although their temper is aggressive and untrustworthy. It is a very beautiful, evocative place, with something of the atmosphere of Wordsworth's reflections on Tintern Abbey, deep clouds over the distant deserted hillsides, and the incessant call of the cuckoo. Return to village by the same route.

The **Church of Shen Thanasit is in the lower central part of the village, and is a low building with one surviving cloister. It was seriously damaged in fighting nearby in the Second World War when it was used by the Italians as an ammunition store. The interior is much better preserved than that of Holy Trinity, and there are some finely *frescoes covering most of the interior walls. The screen is skilfully carved in the local style, but requires restoration. The remaining cloister wall on the portico has six broad Romanesque arches, and was built in 1712. The roof is supported by eight very large limestone columns, which look as though they could have come from some earlier structure on the site. The cloister was restored about 15 years ago. A visit to this church is a moving experience for anyone with a sense of history of the region, and the lost glories of Voskopoja.

The condition of this wonderful building, and several others in the village, must give rise to great concern, as the local inhabitants have no resources to conserve their buildings, and a good case could be made for urgent international help for the village.

Return to Korça by the same route.

*Boboshtica is another village near Korça with outstanding ecclesiastical monuments. Oral tradition maintains that it was founded by Polish soldiers left behind from a Crusaders army. It is reached by taking the main road south-west in the direction of Erseka for about 4km, then a track to the left for about 3km. It lies on the south side of the Plain of Korça in the lee of the Kuq mountains.

Drive into the centre of the village, with its many small whitewashed houses, all full of character and in the summer covered in vines and surrounded by fruit trees. The village is well known for its mulberries. Many of the inhabitants are of Slavonic race and speak a dialect of Bulgarian, although Vlachs and Greeks also live here. Park by the small crossroads and walk west down the main track towards the two very small churches of the village, St Demetrius and St John. Both have interesting frescoes, and have been well preserved over the years. **St John** is tiny, only 10m long and 6m wide. It is thought to have been built in the 13C. The very fine frescoes on the narthex walls show scenes from the life of St John. In the apse the paintings are of the Virgin Mary and the Church Fathers. Near the entrance is a famous icon of the patron of the church, John the Baptist. Various restoration and rebuilding works are thought to have taken place at different stages in the history of the church, although the exact dates are unknown. Some work may have taken place in the second half of the 15C, after the Ottoman occupation, while some of the paintings are thought to date from the 17C.

St Demetrius is also a tiny, isolated church at the far end of the village, a Christian building set against the background of the Plain with its vast skies and the sometimes sombre background of the Kuq and Morava mountains, a truly austere landscape. It was constructed in the 17C and its frescoes were also painted at the same time. They show the life of the saint, the Crucifixion, the Martyrdom of St Lazarus, Saints Constantine and Helena with Christ, and on the north wall by the entrance the entry of Christ into Jerusalem, the Crucifixion, the Virgin Mary and the Vision of St Peter of Alexandria.

Return to Korça by the same route.

Mborje is a small village on a hillside 5km south-east of Korça and has a small church of outstanding beauty, the ***Church of Christ's Ascension***, *Kisha e Ristozit*. The village is best reached by a steep road out of Korça itself, past a disused brewery, near the road that goes to the Drenova coal mines. It is best to ask for local directions, as the track is difficult to find. Above the village Illyrian walls have been found, on the north side of Mount Morava. The name of the village is of Greek origin, from *emporion*, and indicates that it was probably a market town on a Byzantine trade route running across the mountains between Greece and the Plain of Korça.

The church is reached by following the steep central street to the top of the village. It is usually locked up—ask locally for the key holder. It is a small, dignified building on the left-hand side of the road, set in a small garden. Many of the village houses are very attractive, and it has the atmosphere many northern Greek mountain villages used to have.

The church is built of alternating courses of brick and stone, with a very tiny inner church, a cell-like room a few metres long, with a minute dome, that evokes the atmosphere of early Christianity. The **fresco paintings** are of quite outstanding quality, in rich dark colours, with the portrayal of the entry of Christ into Jerusalem among the finest examples of Christian art in Albania. An inscription indicates that the church was in existence by 1389 and most authorities date the beginning of construction at about 1300, by analysis of the type of building techniques, particularly the way timber is used in the construction of the walls. The frescos on the west side of the outer wall date from the 17C.

From this village it is possible to visit **Drenova** nearby, mostly inhabited by miners from the coal mine in the hills above the village. It is a pleasant, quiet village, where many of the men also emigrate to Greece as migrant workers in the construction industry and in agriculture. The coal from Drenova is mostly used in the power stations at Korça and at Maliq nearby. Above the mines is the **Drenova National Park**, a large section of which was reserved for use as a hunting ground by the party leaders under communism. The forest is rich in game, pheasants and wild boar in particular. There is an important **fossil bed** near the coal mine, called *Fusha e Pare* (First Field).

N.B. Approaching closer to the Greek border from this direction is not recommended.

Return to Korça by the same route.

12 · Korça to Quaf e Thanës

From Korça, 86km north-east to the border with FYROM at Quaf e Thanës, on a generally good road via Maliq, 13km, and Pogradec, 40km.

This route enables you to explore this beautiful region of south-east Albania, adjacent to the borders of ex-Yugoslav Macedonia and Greece. The main attraction is the outstanding interest of the **Prespa** and **Ochrid** Lake complexes, both part of a UNESCO World Heritage environmental area, and the surrounding mountains which even by Albanian standards are remote, and largely unknown to Western visitors. The region has few visible monuments from the ancient world, compared to some parts of the country, but was of considerable importance in the medieval period, in the genesis of Slav Christianity, and in its spread northwards from the Balkan peninsula, and beyond. The population is one of the most ethnically mixed in all Albania, with Vlachs, Slav-speakers, ethnic Greeks and Roma all much in evidence. Generally speaking, inter-communal relations in this part of Albania are good, and you will enjoy meeting the diverse populations of the region, but great care is needed in exploring areas near the borders.

Leave Korça by the road for Maliq and Pogradec, travelling north out of the city. The road crosses the **Plain of Korça**, *Pellgu i Korçes*, over wide open countryside with occasional stands of poplar trees to the left; to the right, low hills rise to the Thate mountains in the north-east. The skies are wide and all embracing and may remind visitors from North America of the Mid-west. There are many relatively prosperous villages dotted around the plain, and the area in general has not endured the privations that other parts of the country have suffered in recent years. The deep and fertile soil and the warm summers, make it one of the most agriculturally productive areas of Albania, and the proximity to the cultured city of Korça has provided many amenities for the inhabitants.

If time allows, a visit to a village is well worthwhile, with their compact groups of houses where animals and people live in close proximity but without primitive squalor, and with a rich traditional rural life that may perhaps remind the visitor of the atmosphere of English novels of the 18C. **Shamoll** is a good example, where the population is almost all ethnic Albanian apart from a few Vlachs. It is in the middle of the plain, reached by a right turn onto a dirt track for Bulgareci, 4km from Korça, then followed through **Bulgareci** village another 3km approximately to Shamoll. It is interesting to see how the great plain is being divided into small plots through the privatisation process, and how what in many ways is traditional 19C Balkan peasant agriculture is being restored after the period of collectivisation. The dirt roads across the plain are not good and should only be attempted by non-four-wheel drive vehicles in the driest weather. Particular care needs to be taken of the deep drainage ditches and canals by the side of the track.

You will note that most villages have kept a consistent ethnicity, in that Shamoll, say, is predominantly Albanian and Muslim, whereas the villages on the hillsides, such as Bulgareci, have kept both their Slavonic names and a predominantly Christian Slav population. In this sense, the settlement patterns arising from the original Slav invasion of the Balkans have been retained here, with the pastoralist Slavs occupying the higher land with their sheep and goats. In this region of Albania, it is normal for ethnic Albanians to refer to *Slavophones* as '*Bulgarians*', even if in fact they are ethnically '*Macedonian*' in that they speak a Slavonic dialect that is similar to that spoken in the western regions of ex-Yugoslav 'Macedonia' rather than Bulgaria itself. Equally, some villages speak a dialect that is closer to Serbian. They are likely to be descended from people who settled here when the Serbian Empire extended to Lake Ochrid, in the time of Tsar Stefan Dushan in the 14C, although a very few people can be found in the region who settled here as remnants of the retreating Serbian army that came to Albania in 1916. Return by the same route to the main road.

After 12km, the small town of **Maliq** is reached, the centre of what was the Maliq marsh area until the 1950s. This very large wetland area revealed substantial evidence of neolithic and Bronze Age settlement when it was drained, in one of the mass labour force operations belonging to the early stages of communist land reclamation. Artefacts from both periods, mostly primitive stone tools and early ceramics and metalwork, can be seen in the Korça museum (see Route 11). Many examples of the characteristic Illyrian long-necked pottery vessels were found, and examples of fishing and wool spinning equipment. The excavation was particularly important for the evidence revealed about the Copper Age in the Illyrian cultures, with kilns used to make artefacts being discovered in a lake village built on wood piles resembling an ancient Irish *crannog*. Illyrian walls have been found on the hills above the plain, although without evidence of permanent internal settlement, and it appears they were only used for protective purposes during times of war and invasion. During the Hoxha period, archaeologists were forced to conclude that these places were where the 'Illyrian ruling class' lived, while their peasants were subject to massacres by invaders on the plain below, an example of the politicisation of archaeology and distortion of academic enquiry under communism.

The region is now the centre of the Albanian sugar beet industry, and the modern town of Maliq has grown up around the refinery. Many local inhabitants are Vlachs, especially in the hill villages near Maliq. **Bozdovec** is known for the very cold water from the Bear's Head waterfall, and for its wild strawberries. A local tradition is *Paçe*, a kind of lamb stew eaten at breakfast-time. 2km south east of Maliq is the village of **Vloçisht**, which was established in the spring of 1948 as the main forced labour camp in south east Albania.

> Under the communists, by the end of 1949 there were estimated to be about 10,000 political prisoners in Albania. In early 1948 the prisons of Tirana, Elbasan and Durres had been emptied and the inmates formed into forced labour battalions at Vloçisht. Most were professional people and many were from northern Albania, including several Catholic priests. They worked on the construction of the Dunavec canal to drain the marsh, so the flow of the Dunavec river was channelled into the river Devoli and Lake Prespa. Hundreds died in conditions of extreme brutality and privation, some, including Father

Josif Papamihali, head of the Roman Catholic church in Korça, were buried alive for infrigements of camp discipline.

From Maliq, a road leads from the town centre to Plasa (10km) and there joins the branch road from Korça to the Greek border control at Kapshtiça, passing through Bilisht (23km). In Italian times, Kapshtiça was known as *Capeshtize*.

11km to the south west of Bilisht is the village of Trestnik, scene of fierce fighting between Greek and Albanian troops in August 1949, when, after the Battles of Grammoz and Vitsi in the Greek civil war, Greek troops followed retreating columns of the Greek Democratic Army into Albania. The Greeks refugees were attacked from the air by RAF Spitfires and shelled by a Greek army artillery brigade.

4km from Bilisht, along a dirt track leading towards Prespë e Vogël, is the village of **Tren**, lying below a steep rocky cliff, *Pamje e Shkëmbit të Spilesë*, Spile Rock. Excavations here in caves in the rock face in 1966–67 revealed evidence of Iron Age settlement, of the Maliq II culture, with bones, ceramics and small artefacts being found. Early Iron Age paintings were discovered on the rock face near the caves, of horsemen with dogs in hunting activities, the earliest works of art that have been found in Albania. Ceramic remains indicate trade links with Greece during the Geometric Period. This area contains some beautiful and remote wooded countryside adjoining the south-west shore of Lake Prespa.

5km south of Bilisht is the modern village of Kuç. Important Illyrian works of art were found in Illyrian tombs excavated at **Kuç i Zi** nearby, including bracelets and bird-shaped amulets which indicate the advanced development of metallurgy in the Korça basin in the prehistoric period. The tribes here are thought to represent the most southerly extension of the Glasinac-Mat material culture. The two tombs contained five swords, spears, arrows, knives and choppers.

The Illyrian tumuli of the Korça basin are among the most important in Albania. The tombs indicate the process of social development from the Neolithic to the early Iron Age period. The tombs near Barç and Kuç i Zi villages were excavated between 1967 and 1975. All belong to the large type of Illyrian tombs, reduced in size over the centuries by damage from agricultural and forestry work. Their height ranges from 1 to 2.5 metres and their diameter from 14 to 43 metres. The inner architectural elements were made of stone, and covered a total of 347 graves, indicating the prosperity of the rich tribal groups occupying the Korça plain. The most common burial method in the tombs was for the aristocratic corpse to be placed in a crouching or lying position, with the knees drawn up. Cremation is very unusual. The tombs have been found to contain both native Illyrian and imported ceramics, the latter from Greece, of the Mycenaean and Geometric periods. The local characteristics of the metalwork and pottery place the tombs within the manufacturing patterns of the Devoli culture. The potter's wheel was introduced in this region in the 6C BC. Ceramics of the Devoli type have been found in many parts of the western Adriatic, including the coast of southern Italy, indicating the extensive trade relations the Korça tribes enjoyed with distant regions.

The ruling dynasty in this region are thought to have constructed a complex of fortifications leading to the Korça plain, including Symize and Bellevode to the west, Bilisht to the south and the Tren area in the east, which in turn controlled the Wolf's Pass, *Gryke e Ujkut*, leading to *Prespes se Vogel*, Little Prespa Lake.

LAKE PRESPA
**Lake Prespa is one of the most remarkable natural phenomena in the Balkans. The border between Greece, Albania and FYROM meets in the centre of it. With Lake Ochrid, 30km to the north-west and part of the same water system, linked by underground channels, it forms an area of outstanding natural beauty and ecological interest. The water is extraordinarily clear, reflecting the magnificent scenery and surrounding mountains of primitive, rugged grandeur. The area is the last stronghold of the Dalmatian pelican and many other rare birds, plants and animals, and is managed under the auspices of UNESCO, which has designated it a World Heritage Site. But it is a wild and forbidding region, with bare limestone peaks and sombre uninhabited forests on the Albanian side of the lake, the home of bears, jackals, wolves and lynx, and there are virtually no facilities of any kind for the visitor. In the last four years, the level of the lake has been dropping, the ecology is threatened, and a scientific enquiry has been established to investigate the causes.

Two parts of the Prespa-Ochrid lake complex lie within Albanian territory, the tip of *Prespa se Vogel* (Small Prespa), near the village of Treni where the end of that lake becomes swamp and marshland, and about one-sixth of Lake Prespa proper (*Prespa se Madhe*), which covers 290sq km, about 15km to the north. On the east side there is the solid wall of the Perister mountains, on the west, in Macedonia, the vast limestone mass of the Galicica range. On the west side, the mountains drop sheer into the lake and road construction is difficult. As it is nearly 1000m above sea level, it is very cold here in the winter, and the shallow Lake Prespa has been known to freeze over, although Lake Ochrid does not. In the summer the lake is a natural paradise where frogs, insects and fish teem in the brilliantly clear waters, and holidaymakers can relax on the shingle beaches. The low cliffs surrounding the lake have many small caves, often full of bats. There are forest paths around the lake.

N.B. Walkers should bear in mind that it is easy to get lost and that the area is adjacent to two very sensitive borders. There have been recent shooting incidents and fatalities involving refugees. The security forces of all three countries have considerable difficulty in controlling illegal population movements, and are not inclined to tolerate border violations. Tourists should carry identification documents at all times in this area, and also be aware of the revival of banditry since the end of communism.

From **Gollommoboç**, a hamlet in the centre of the west shore of Lake Prespa, a small wooded island can be seen, **Golemgrad**, very near the point where Greece, Albania and Macedonia meet. This island was given as a gift to King Alexander of Yugoslavia by King Constantine of Greece before the war. It can be reached by boat from **Psarades**, on the Greek side of the lake. The region was seminal in the foundation and spread of Slavonic Christianity, with the Cyrillic alphabet being invented at Ochrid to the north by St Clement. The inhabitants of the lakeside villages nowadays, in all three countries, are still generally of Slav descent, although there are also many Vlach pastorilists, especially in Greece.

In the caves around all the lakes, there are remarkable **rock churches and medieval rock icons**, although these are also most easily reached from the Greek side of Lake Prespa where boats are available. Just over the border with FYROM, between Lake Prespa and Lake Ochrid, is the outstanding monastery of St Naum, which was ceded to Yugoslavia by King Zog. St Naum was a contemporary of St Cyril and St Methodius, the founders of Slav Christianity. In Albanian waters is another small island, **Maligrad**, with a 14C church with good frescoes. At **Trestenit** village is a cave with early 12C frescoes. The area around the smaller of the Prespa lakes was an important Byzantine city in the Middle Ages.

The best way to approach the Albanian lake shore is to turn north from the Korça-Kapshtica road at **Plasa**. Follow a reasonable dirt track across the flat plain, and cross a small river by a wooden bridge. Pass through maize fields and stands of poplars, and begin to climb after 3km to the narrow **Zvezda Pass**, the *Quaf e Zvezda*. The road deteriorates rapidly here, and becomes a very poor track leading across empty hilly grazing land, heavily depopulated by emigration to Greece. It winds downwards towards **Lagthiza** (17km), a small upland village. Lake Prespa is visible to the east. Turn right at a road junction here, the main track continues on to **Kallamasi** (23km). The track down to the lake is so bad here, it is better to leave the vehicle and walk. After 2km, the lakeside village of **Liqenasi** is reached, an attractive fishing and farming community of about a thousand people. Nearly all inhabitants are ethnic Slavs and speak a dialect of Bulgarian. They also call their village *Zaroshte*. There is a large empty church in the village, inside a courtyard. It is just beginning to return to religious use, but requires extensive restoration. It was used as an agricultural building under communism. The size indicates the large rural population the area must have supported in the Middle Ages.

There are also two very interesting small churches in the vicinity, both reached by following the road east through the village, along the lakeside, towards Greece. The *****church of St George** is on a small hillock on the far side of the village, a low oblong building 9m x 17m with a bare whitewashed nave supported by eight columns. There is a small graveyard nearby. Note the traditional farm buildings and wattle animal pens. The wooden plough is still in use. Neither church is open at the time of writing, but both are in the process of restoration, and appear to be of the late Byzantine period. There are good views across the lake towards the FYROM mountains, and towards the very beautiful village of **Psarades**, in Greece. Psarades used to be called *Nivica*, before the Greek civil war. To the south there are beautiful wooded hillsides, with pine and juniper most common. In the Greek civil war the headquarters of Markos Vafiades' *Democratic Army* was hidden in these woods. The area is known for hunting hare and rabbits. Return to the main road by the same route.

Another road leaves Maliq in a north-westerly direction for the coal mining town of Lozhani (19km) to cross the south-east mountains via **Strelca**, arriving eventually in Gramsh and Elbasan, but most of the route is very poor indeed and is not suitable for conventional vehicles after Strelca (21km). At the time of writing, the road is blocked by landslides. **AVOID**.

The main road continues north-east through magnificent country towards the mountains surrounding Lake Ochrid. After crossing the pass near Stropcha, the road descends to the lake and the town of Pogradec (35km from Maliq).

Pogradec has one of the largest mines in eastern Europe, with a giant lead-iron-nickel complex in the side of the mountain 2km to the north of the town, and is the terminus of the railway running to the coast at Durres. But this industrial importance should not prevent the visitor enjoying the beauty of Lake Ochrid; compared to the very remote terrain around Lake Prespa, it is a more accessible landscape.

There is an interesting small museum in a house on the opposite side of the main street from the hotel, with Greek and Roman gravestones on display in the garden outside, and locally-found small ancient artefacts inside (closed at time of writing).

The main mosque in the town centre has been rebuilt with assistance from a Birmingham-based Islamic Relief Organisation in the UK. It is called the **Mosque of Ebu Beker Essiddiku** and is large and architecturally undistinguished. A new **Orthodox church** is being constructed near the lakeside. An important historic church on the site was burnt down in the anti-religious campaign in 1968. There is a pleasant street of renovated Turkish buildings running south west into the centre of the town from the main square, with some good cafés and shops. A good bet is the *Kristlindja café* near the top end. The owner is very welcoming.

■ **Hotel**. The *Pogradec Hotel*, a dull, cold and poorly managed concrete block but adequate for a short stay. More interesting, although primitive, the *Liqeni Hotel*, a small 1930s Italian building dating from King Zog's time.

■ **Transport**. Taxis and buses, 400m up from the lakeside in the street by the post office. The train from Tirana stops near the mine, about 1km north of the town.

History

Pogradec (pop. 20,100) has been inhabited since prehistoric times, with evidence of early man living by the lakeside in fishing communities common in the vicinity. In Illyrian times it was occupied by a tribe called the *Enchelei* (in Latin, the *Encheleae*, the 'Eel People'). There was a town called *Enchelanae* in the area, referred to by Polybius, although its exact location is uncertain. The tribe seems to have controlled a large area of territory in the Drin Valley. Greek sources record that these tribal rulers claimed descent from Cadmus. Excavations at the Illyrian hilltop fort above the modern settlement have revealed defensive walls dating from the 5C BC, followed by urban development in the 4C. Building methods used resemble those at Zgërdhesh, near Kruja. Ancient Greek villages were established by the lake, and in Roman times it took part in the pattern of settlement and economic activity centred on the nearby Via Egnatia and Ochrid town itself. The fortress appears to have been abandoned in the early Byzantine period. Pogradec means 'above the town', and is a Slav name, perhaps originating in the Serbian empire of Stefan Dushan when it became an important urban centre. In medieval times, it was a Christian centre comparable in importance to Mount Athos in the Greek world, with over 300 shrines and churches in the vicinity of the lake. Pogradec was then known as *Mokrea*.

The modern town grew up in the 18C, and was the centre of a rich agriculture based on wine and fruit growing. In the 19C it grew and absorbed the nearby small town of *Stavrova*. After the last war the mining complex was developed, with particular expansion in the early 1970s with the construction of the current ore reduction and transport complex under the direction of Chinese technicians, at the outlying place known as *Guri i Quq*, 'Red Stone', clearly named after the colour of the ferro-nickel ore outcrop. Coal mining, tourism and forestry are also important in the regional economy. There was damage to the historic buildings in fighting in the area after the fall of the French republic of Korça in 1921, and during the Greek-Italian hostilities in the area in 1940. The town was favoured by both King Zog and Enver Hoxha, who had holiday houses here, the latter in Rr. Okoma. Under Italian occupation, Pogradec was known as *Perparimi* ('Progress'). In the early stages of political change in the late 1980s and over the last two years, the town tended to remain a bastion of communism, until January 1992, when it was affected by serious food riots when a number of central warehouses were burnt down by angry crowds, many of them peasants from the surrounding countryside who had ridden into the town, drunk on raki. Pogradec was the home of **Lazgush Poradeci** (1899–1987), one of the founders of modern Albanian poetry.

Apart from the *Guri i Quq* mine there are other important mineral deposits in the vicinity at Menelisht (alumina) Carvenaka (ferro-nickel), Hamezi (coal), Pishkupasi (chromite), Verdora (coal) and Dardasi (stone quarry). Timber is cut at Alarup and Bimitza.

There is an attractive bronze statue on the lakeside by the hotel to the *'Chaiouski'*, the protective spirit of the Pogradec miners, a mythical spirit playing a flute, said in origin to be related to Orpheus. The town has a small Slav-speaking community and some members of the ethnic Greek minority. There is a well kept Partisan cemetery on the outskirts of the town on the Korça road.

Swimming near Pogradec is not recommended, until the World Bank-financed sewage scheme, currently under construction, is finished.

Zogist period house at Pogradec

LAKE OCHRID

**Lake Ochrid has a different character from the Prespa complex, being larger, less remote, and a centre of sophisticated urban life since ancient times. The lake covers 347sq km. It is believed to have always had an independent existence from Lake Prespa, even in Tertiary times, despite belonging to the same pattern of geological faults. It is the deepest lake in the Balkans, with a maximum depth of 310m. It was much larger in the Pliocene epoch, although it appears then to have been drained by the Black Drin flowing northwards from Struga into Macedonia in much the same way as it is today.

Unlike Lake Prespa, over the last 100 years the level of Lake Ochrid seems to have been rising, as sands deposited in the Black Drin as a result of human activities have limited its capacity to drain the lake. Lake Ochrid is very rich in fish, particularly a unique member of the trout family, which is delicious to eat and can often be bought cheaply from local fishermen. It is also found in Lake Prespa and in Lake Baikal in Siberia, a survivor of tumultuous upheavals in the primeval world that resulted in their entrapment in these lakes. In Ottoman times, there were special courier services to take the fish to the table of the Sultan in Constantinople. To date, the efforts of the Albanian authorities to prevent pollution of the lake from mining activities seem to have been successful, and a very rich variety of bird life, especially in migration times, can be observed from the town itself. Cormorants, grebes and wading birds seem to be particularly common.

The lake is the subject of a famous Slavonic song, *Biljana platno belese, na ohridskite izvori*—Biljana was bleaching her linen by the springs of Ochrid. There have been many discoveries of Illyrian hilltop settlements in the vicinity of the lake, in all three countries. The most dramatic was at Trebeniste in FYROM, where a great collection of Illyrian gold masks and jewellery was found in a necropolis, now on display in Belgrade.

Leave Pogradec by the lakeside road running north. There are many fine views as the road winds towards **Mëmëlisht** (6km), with a chromium mine in the hillside, then **Udenisht** (9km), a small lakeside village, then to **Lin** (27km), on a promontory stretching out into the north-west side of the lake. 8km from Pogradec is a small, attractive new Orthodox church on the lakeside, the **church of St Elias**, built on the site of an earlier church destroyed by anti-religion vandals in 1968.

Modern **Lin** is a charming unspoilt fishing village on the shores of Lake Ochrid,

New Orthodox church, near Udenisht

and, apart from its ancient importance, is well worth a detour to see the wooden and stone houses, and for the good sandy beach on the far side of the promontory. The site has been inhabited since ancient times, on the acropolis which protrudes into the lake on the east side of the village. Illyrian remains have been found on the upper hillside. Many inhabitants are ethnic Slavs. The village, and 14 others nearby, was Greek until 1921, when the Ambassadors Conference adjusted the 1913 borders of Albania.

To reach the archaeological site, until very recently in a closed military area and quite inaccessible, drive into the village until at the far end of the main street the road divides into two forks. Park here and walk up the right-hand dirt track past traditional houses with picturesque balconies. After 400m turn left up a steep track past a small military observation post and follow up the south side of the acropolis. At the top of the track are the ruins of a recently demolished modern military building, a defensive tunnel entrance, and the remains of restored ancient walls. In the centre is a 4C cistern, about 3m deep, and Roman and Byzantine paving. The walls are part of the remains of an *early Christian church, dating from the first half of the 6C. Eight fine mosaics were found here, with designs showing fish, water birds and bees. When it was built, Lin may have been an island. The foundations of the church indicate eastern influence from Syria and Egypt. It had a single apse at the east end, and conches added to the outer walls on the north and south aisles.

The **views from the acropolis over Lake Ochrid to the east, north and south are quite outstanding, with the distant FYROM towns of Struga and Ochrid cradled under the forbidding wall of the Galicica mountains. It is a particularly good place for ornithological observations of the rich birdlife of the lake.

Leave Lin, following the road to the north-west towards Përrenjasi, then turn sharp left after 1km and begin to climb up a steep series of hairpin bends towards Quaf e Thanës. The railway to Durres follows a tunnel driven through the mountain. After 3km you make another sharp left turn and a further short climb, with outstanding views over the treeless karst hilltops back down towards the lake, to reach the border post with FYROM.

Quaf e Thanës used to be one of the more convenient borders to use when entering or leaving Albania by road; there was usually less traffic compared to the chaotic conditions often encountered at the Greek border crossings. Unfortunately this is no longer the case, after the imposition of the border blocade of FYROM by Greece in 1994, congestion is often very bad for vehicles. It remains to be seen whether the recent agreement to lift the blockade will improve the situation.

There are generally taxis available on the Albanian side and assistance to hand, if required, and the crossing is within easy reach of the FYROM town of Struga (12km) if problems are encountered. Struga is an interesting place to stay the night, with some good hotels in the countryside. It is a majority ethnic Albanian town, and is becoming more so, as Albanians are leaving Ochrid town.

A taxi from Struga to Quaf e Thanës used to be easy to obtain and reliable, but social problems in Struga have made finding transport to and from Quaf e Thanës more difficult and expensive. Travellers using this route may need to pay for petrol separately in Struga, in dollars. A price should be negotiated with the driver before any commitment is made. The pass is high in the mountains and, bearing in mind the inevitable delays with border formalities, warm clothing is essential if using this route in winter. Travellers leaving Albania should report to the customs and passport control in the large building on the roadside just inside the Albanian border gate.

VI KRUJA, MATI AND THE CENTRAL HIGHLANDS

13 · Tirana to Kruja

By the north road, via Kamza, 9km, and Fushe-Kruja 11km, to Kruja, 25km. The road is good quality asphalt but it is often congested.

This is an interesting excursion from the capital which enables the visitor to see the historic citadel of the Albanian national hero Skanderbeg at **Kruja** itself (see Route 14), but also gives an opportunity to visit the Illyrian hilltop remains of *Zgërdhesh. This important site is one of the few relatively accessible Illyrian hill sites in Albania, and is set in beautiful countryside near Kruja.

Leave Tirana by the main road to the north-east. The road passes through industrial suburbs. After 2km, turn left at the road junction with the main road running from **Ferraj**, and head back west towards Kamza, passing through the village of **Babrunja** (2km). The road runs across flat farmland, most of which has been privatised and where the peasants who used to work on the state farm here are concentrating on growing fruit and vegetables for the Tirana market. After 9km is **Kamza**. This village is mainly inhabited by workers from the important coal mining centre at Valias, 2km from the main road, by a left turn from Kamza. Kamza was originally established as a forced labour camp, with many women and children among the inmates. Lignite seams that are known as the Tirana Basin are mined here, and there is also a coke and phurnacite plant. The mine was one of the most modern in Albania, with advanced technology using deep-freezing techniques to mine the water-logged lignite, although recent technical problems have reduced production levels somewhat and it may be closed. It is linked by a branch railway line to the main network. Much of the coal was used for industrial purposes. After 2km along the main road north there is a left turn for Rinas airport (11km).

Rinas airport is the airport for Tirana, and in practice the only airport available for civil aircraft in the country. (See Practical Information for flight information.) The construction period ended in 1958, with a runway 2760m long, and the installation of an air traffic control and meteorological centre, all built under the supervision of Soviet advisers. The airport is used for both civil and military flights, although the former predominate. About 80,000 passengers were handled during 1992, with 12 to 15 aeroplanes a day using the runway. Numbers have increased recently. It is also used as a base for the medical corps helicopters used to transport patients living in remote mountain regions to the Tirana hospitals. The surrounding agriculture concentrates on fruit growing, particularly peaches. The local farms were collectivised in 1956 but have now been returned to their original owners. A major redevelopment and modernisation of the airport is being planned under the direction of Siemens of Germany.

Continue along the main road to **Fushë-Krujë**, a large village, dependent on the nearby cement factory. It appears in 16C chronicles as *Ura e Zeze*, Black Bridge, after the Zeza, the Black River, which runs through the place. It has strong Kosova connections, being settled by refugees after the Kosova disturbances in 1945, and with a monument in the centre of the village to Qerime Galica, a Kosovar heroine who fought against the Yugoslav government in the 1920s and died here in 1927. There is a good view of the majestic range of the Skanderbeg mountains to the north-east, and of the Dajti mountains to the east.

Kruja village and the **citadel** of Kruja can be seen a few kilometres away to the north-east. To reach Kruja, follow the main road in that direction. (See Route 14 for information on Kruja.) For the important ancient Illyrian site of ***Zgërdhesh**, take the road directly east from Fushnë-Krujë, through houses and a small industrial district. Follow this road about 4km into the countryside, until a small track leading to the right off this road is met. It is possible to drive about 1km along this track before it is essential to walk towards the site, or a vehicle can be left parked near the road junction.

To approach the site follow the path until the modern village of Zgërdhesh is reached. Ask here for directions to the ancient site, where remains of Illyrian walls and fortifications can be seen. If in difficulties, find the stream about 500m to the east of the village, cross it, and the ruins are on the hillside to the east, at an altitude of about 400m.

History

The Illyrian city of Zgërdhesh is not mentioned in ancient literary or historical documents, as such, although many scholars believe that it was the city of *Albanopolis* mentioned by Pliny. Archaeological investigations have shown that settlement on the site at the base of the Kruja end of the mountain range began in the 7C or 6C BC, when an acropolis covering about 1.3 hectares was enclosed with walls. In a second construction phase, in the 4C or 3C BC, a much larger area was enclosed, covering over 8 hectares, with the walls totalling 1350m in length. A series of defensive towers was built around the perimeter at this stage.

The city seems to have flourished for 300 or 400 years before being largely abandoned in the 2C BC, and the inhabitants moved to Dyrrachium or Lissus. Some evidence of settlement has been found going up to the 6C, when Kruja came to dominate completely the surrounding district.

Much of the site of Zgërdhesh is covered in scrub and you are advised to wear boots or strong shoes. A visit is rewarding for the magnificent views across the coastal lowlands towards the Adriatic as well as the ancient remains. On a clear day there is a good view of the sea.

Approaching from the lower part of the hill, you first see the massive foundations and walls of three rectangular ***Illyrian watchtowers**, which are thought to have been built in the 4C BC. A protective earth bank appears to have been thrown up outside them, to assist the perimeter defenders of the fort. Follow the path up the hill on the right hand bank of the small stream, past a military camp and conscript training centre. On the path about 500m past the closed entrance track, at the base of the fort, there is an outstanding ***fossil bed**, where in blue lias many good quality fossils can be seen and collected. Ancient mussels are particularly common.

Behind the watchtowers are twin defensive walls, with earth packed in between. These outer defences run around the acropolis, at the lower end about 300m from the summit. Climbing the slope, you pass across what was the lower part of the town, with the foundations of various buildings of unknown use being visible, then up the slope towards the inner protective wall of the acropolis itself. On the left is a strong round tower and the inner wall, with an entrance through what would have been an inner gatehouse. This wall is about 150m long and has three defensive towers on the exterior at 50m intervals.

Just inside the entrance are the foundations of an **early Christian chapel**, a very small building indicating the continued occupation of the site in later antiquity, but also its greatly diminished importance.

The original city was built on the acropolis but there is little to see in the way of visible remains except a section of the eastern defensive wall, with a tower on the north-east corner. But it is a beautiful, evocative place, with many birds and butterflies and wild flowers to be found, and somewhere suitable to reflect on the world of the ancient Illyrians and what many visitors to Albania find is the essential mystery surrounding the original inhabitants of the territory.

Proceed to Kruja by the road north from Fushe-Kruja or return to Tirana by your original route. 17km from Fushë-Krujë via the village of Kikla is the hill village of **Mukje**.

It was at Mukje in August 1943 that the critical meeting was held between the leaders of the different wings of the Albanian national movement, the communist-dominated National Liberation Council and the rightist Balli Kombetar as well as independent nationalists such as Ihsan Toptani. It took place under pressure from the Allies who wanted to unite the Resistance and avoid a civil war in Albania. Both agreed to fight for a united ethnic Albania, including Kosova. Within days of the agreement being signed it was rejected by the communists over policy differences on Kosova. It has subsequently been claimed that Enver Hoxha gave in to Yugoslav pressure on the issue. The Yugoslav version of events can be found in *Struggle for the Balkans* by Svetozar Vukmanovic, Tito's emissary to the Albanian resistance movement, a seminal and absorbing if highly controversial book.

It is possible to walk to Kruja from the site of Zgërdhesh, which takes about an hour and a half, along sheep tracks.

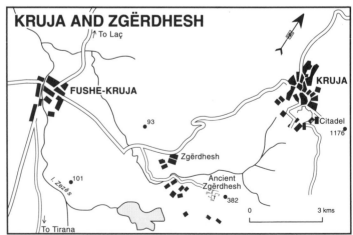

KRUJA AND ZGËRDHESH

To Laç

KRUJA

FUSHE-KRUJA

•93

Citadel
1176

Zgërdhesh

•101

Ancient
Zgërdhesh
•382

0   3 kms

To Tirana

14 · Kruja to Burrel, the Mati, and Peshkopia

From Tirana, via Vora, 16km, to Kruja, 17km, see Route 13; then from Kruja to Laç, 24km, from Laç to Burrel via Milot, another 49km.

KRUJA

Kruja (pop. 11,200) town is built around the foot of the steep castle rock, 610m high. The great castle, the citadel of the national hero Skanderbeg, is a shrine and monument to the aspirations of the Albanian nation. It is built at a height of 548m on an isolated spur of the limestone wall of the Kruja range, and has spectacular views of the surrounding region. It contains an interesting museum, and the well-restored bazaar and a beautiful Bektashi *tekké* are among the other historic buildings that should be seen. To the south and west of Kruja is the fertile plain of the Ishmit river, a tributary of which flows from the mountains near the town. There are fine views of the Skanderbeg mountains to the east, and across to the Adriatic coast to the west.

The journey from Kruja to Burrel enables a visit to be made to the **Mati region**, which was the heartland of support for King Zog and his son, the pretender to the throne, Leka. Mati is deeply traditional in its culture and politics, and an area of outstanding natural beauty. While road conditions are reasonable, the drive is arduous, and plenty of time should be allowed for the journey, and adequate supplies carried.

■ **Hotel.** *Hotel Skenderbeu.* Not particularly recommended. Some private rooms are available.

History

Kruja is thought to be named from the Albanian word *krua*, meaning a spring. The citadel was used by the Illyrian tribes centred on nearby Zgërdhesh (see Route 13), as early as the 6C BC, and may have become the main Illyrian castle in the area after Zgërdhesh was abandoned in the 4C. Objects from the Arberesh culture (6C–8C BC) have also been found. A local legend relates that 'the stones of Zgerdhesh were picked up and placed at Kruja'. There is no information available about the site during and after the Roman conquest of the Illyrians, and Kruja only re-enters history in the Byzantine period, when it is named in 9C church records as an episcopal see. The citadel was rebuilt in this period, and it remained a fortress under Byzantine control until the end of the 12C. The first Albanian feudal state, the Kingdom of Arber, was formed here around the year 1190, with Kruja as an important component part of its defensive system, under its leader, the Arberesh Progon. It appears to have been closely linked economically with Durres. It is mentioned as an important castle in the writing of the Byzantine chronicler Georgius Akropolitis, who in 1245 called it *Kroas*, and said it belonged to Gulam, the Lord of Albanon. At the end of the 13C it was taken by Charles of Anjou, who repaired the walls, after which it passed to the Thopia family.

In 1396 the Ottoman Turks occupied Kruja for the first time, but soon withdrew and did not reappear in the region for another 20 years. In 1430, an uprising against them started under the leadership of Gjon Kastrioti,

Skanderbeg's father, but the Ottomans crushed it. With the return of Skanderbeg to his homeland, a new phase in the resistance movement started. In 1450, during the first siege of Kruja, the castle suffered serious damage. With heavy cannon, the Turks managed to destroy the walls of the main gate, but did not take the central stronghold. The same heroic Albanian resistance was organised when Sultan Murat II returned with an even stronger army. The Turkish chronicler, Dursan Bey, who took part in the second siege, wrote of the event that 'the Albanians have been born to resist and disobey'. But in the end the Ottoman forces triumphed. A German chronicler of the 16C records that 'Only by starving out the defenders were the Turks able to take the strong and impregnable castle on June 16th 1478', ten years after Skanderbeg's death.

The town and citadel were laid waste by the Sultan's troops and renamed *Aksahissar*, the White Fort. The damage they caused was added to by the earthquake of 1617, which caused considerable depopulation. The remaining inhabitants converted to Islam soon afterwards. In local fighting between Turks and Albanians in 1832, the castle was further damaged. After this, the main part of the fortress was finally dismantled by Mehmet Reshid Pasha, as during the 18C and 19C the Turks had made some efforts to restore the defensive walls for limited military purposes. But their efforts did not affect the numerous local revolts against their rule in the later years of the 19C, of which the most prominent event was the Battle of Tallajbe in 1906 when 22 citizens of Kruja were killed. Some economic development took place after independence. In the Second World War part of the bazaar was destroyed, along with a residence belonging to the Toptani family. Kruja played a prominent part in the resistance to the Axis occupiers, with the 23rd Partisan Brigade based in the mountains nearby, and Kruja was fought over in three bloody battles before its liberation on 20 November 1944. In 1968, on the 500th anniversary of the death of Skanderbeg, the city was proclaimed a 'Hero City' by the government. The main local occupation is olive growing and pastoral agriculture.

Kruja was the setting for Ismail Kadare's novel *The Castle*.

Driving up the hill towards Kruja village from the main road, the citadel is immediately visible, in a dramatic situation high on a spur of the mountains, with the almost vertical limestone wall of the Kruja mountains behind it, treeless, and with deep eroded gullies. The road climbs though olive groves into the outskirts of an attractive old village, with many small 19C houses. The English journalist James Cameron described it in 1963 as 'a strange and wandering little town clinging to the slopes of a majestic mountain, all red tiles and whitewash, rose bushes and open drains and streets of enormous cobbles.'

It is possible to drive right up to the citadel entrance, but preferable to park a kilometre or so further down the hill and walk up through the **bazaar*. Although small, really only a single street of shops, and having undergone extensive restoration, the wooden buildings are of a very high architectural quality, and contain the kind of pleasant mixture of cafés and newly-privatised small souvenir and antique shops that it is to be hoped will become much more common throughout the country. The bazaar used to house the Exhibition of Popular Culture in the communist period. According to von Hahn, the pioneer German Albanologist of the 19C, 'the Kruja bazaar, which comprises a narrow street of shops, partly covered, which leads up to the castle, has such an ancient air about it that it seems as if it has undergone no change since the time of Skanderbeg'.

Particularly noticeable is the quality of the wood carving and decoration, a local tradition since the 18C, and the wide overhang of the roofs over the stone paved gulley, a reminder of the frequently severe winter weather in Kruja. While the general design and appearance of the shops is profoundly Ottoman, they have a unique local quality, something that is also found in some of the interiors of the dwelling houses within the castle complex itself. The typical Kruja house of the 19C is a three-storeyed constuction, with a partly enclosed ground floor, animal sheds and storerooms, where the women spent much of their working day, and with the upper floors divided into male and female quarters.

Leaving the bazaar, walk up the slope towards the entrance to the citadel. On the left, near the entrance gate, is an elegant small 15C **Turkish fountain**, on the face of which is a carving of two lion-like animals. On the sides are a number of Turkish inscriptions dating from the 15C and 18C.

The ****CITADEL** is in the form of an ellipse, built in a perfect defensive position on a rocky limestone outcrop, following the hilltop contours, with nine defensive towers around the perimeter. It covers almost one hectare, and encloses a complex series of ruins and buildings from different periods in varying conditions of preservation, including churches, mosques, garrison buildings and about 20 dwelling houses. Some of these are only of specialist interest and the attention of the visitor will inevitably concentrate on the restored Citadel Museum and on some of the more interesting smaller buildings, most of which are on the lower slope below the museum. On the west side there are magnificent views over the coastal plain towards the Adriatic Sea.

The citadel is entered through a stone vaulted entrance tunnel. On either side are two protective towers. The central part of the right-hand tower was used as a cistern for storing rainwater. A tunnel entrance through the three exterior gatehouses follows. On the right as you emerge are the ruins of what was originally a powder magazine, later converted by the Turks into a prison, then the ruins of a mosque, on the right-hand side of the pathway. According to local tradition, it was originally a church that was made into a mosque as soon as Sultan Mehmet entered Kruja. Opposite it, a little way up the hill, is the imposing reconstruction of the citadel itself, which houses the ***museum**. This building was completed in 1982, and was designed by Pranvera Hoxha, daughter of Enver Hoxha. It is in essence a neo-medieval edifice, which although impressive in its way, and certainly dignified has, in the view of many visitors, a slightly unfortunate atmosphere, reminiscent in some ways of aspects of Sir Arthur Evans' reconstructions at Knossos in Crete. Although the architecture is sympathetic, in one sense, and in keeping with the surroundings, in others it is a fabrication, the manufacture of a particular sense of tradition that was undertaken in the last years of the communist regime. The iconography seems intended to suggest, at both a conscious and unconscious level, a lineal similarity between Skanderbeg and Enver Hoxha.

There is nonetheless much of interest for the visitor inside. The interior displays show the world of Albania in the time of Skanderbeg, with maps and visual display systems, documents of the period, portraits and drawings of the man, and items of his military equipment. Especially designed for the visitor with only a basic knowledge of Albanian history, the visual displays are very interesting and effective, the 'reconstruction' of his study less so. The large central hall is used to display banners of the main tribal leaders who fought with Skanderbeg against the Turks, and within the apse room is a very large fresco by Haxhi Bakalli of the Albanian struggle against the Turks. A copy of Skanderbeg's own helmet is on display, made from the original that is in Vienna, and interesting original prints and paintings of the hero, and books connected with his life. The upper floors trace the architectural history of the fortress, with a series of models, and are used to display a series of busts of the participants in the anti-Ottoman struggle. The top floor has a room devoted to Skanderbeg, European diplomacy, and a small library of books about the national hero.

Skanderbeg, the Albanian national hero, from a French 19C print

Skanderbeg

Gjergj Kastrioti Skanderbeg is the national hero of all Albanians, and was an outstanding leader in the struggle of the Balkan countries against Ottoman Turkish domination. He was born in 1405, and when he grew up the local independence of the Albanian feudal rulers from the Ottomans was becoming increasingly threatened. After the Ballsha period of anarchy and internecine war (1366–1421), the Ottomans, already masters of Macedonia and Serbia, captured Ioannina in 1431, and threatened Albania.

Skanderbeg's great grandfather Pal was a chieftain of two villages of the Kastrioti clan in the Mati valley. His father Gjon ruled an area stretching from the Mati to Dibra and built the castle of Juban at the junction of the Drin and Drinisa rivers. In 1415 he acquired from Venice the fortress at Kruja. In 1423 his four sons were taken by the Turks as hostages, and when he died, three of them were poisoned. The survivor, Gjergj, became a Muslim and entered the Ottoman army and so distinguished himself that he acquired the name of *Skanderbeg*, after Alexander the Great. In 1443, after the Battle of Nish in Serbia, when the Ottomans were defeated by the Hungarians, he raised a force of 12,000 men and massacred most of the Turks in Albania. On 1 March 1444 an assembly at Alessio hailed him as 'Chief of the League of Albanian People', and after his reconversion to Christianity he allied them with Hungary and Poland against the Turks. He failed, however, to gain the support of the militarily vital Serbian rulers and their troops, and his ally Vladislaus of Hungary was defeated and killed at the Battle of Varna. A series of intense campaigns against the Turks followed, when he was named 'Champion of Christendom' by Pope Nicholas V for his struggle against the Muslim invaders. Skanderbeg died in 1467 of fever while negotiating for Venetian reinforcements. His tomb at Lezha is venerated by all Albanians. But the northern tribes, led by the Dukagjin clan, never followed him and gradually Albania came under Turkish rule, with the fall of Durres in 1502 a key event.

Leaving the museum, climb up the hill behind it to the north-east extremity of the walls. Here is the **clocktower**, which is thought to be the only remaining part of a late medieval church. According to legend, it was Skanderbeg's own church, where he used to pray before renewing his vigorous assaults on the Turkish conquerors. After the Ottoman conquest it was partly rebuilt and made into a citadel clocktower resembling that of Gjirokastra in style and function. Near the clocktower is a bare flat area of rock to the north, which was used for the beacon fires that played an important part in Skanderbeg's defensive system. The adjacent walls on the north side have been rebuilt in the early Turkish period with loopholes for firearms, and Ottoman builders' seals can be seen in some places. This part of the walls was rebuilt following the serious earthquake of 1617, then partly destroyed after the Albanian uprising in 1832.

Walking towards the western side of the walls, you see a number of partly or wholly ruined monuments, within which are the restored **Turkish baths**. The exact date of their construction is unknown, but the use of Byzantine building techniques, with interlocking bricks, places them very early in the Turkish period. The restored building has very thick walls and contains early examples of ceramic water pipes. On the west side of the walls is a round tower known as the **Tower of Dollma**, by which is the small ****Bektashi tekké**. This beautiful little building, perfectly proportioned and only 10m square, was built in 1789. Outside it there is a small garden with the characteristic series of graves of prominent Bektashis, with stone models of their domed hats on top of the gravestones. The interior also contains graves, and is a charming whitewashed shrine. On the walls are examples of embroideries made by local schoolchildren expressing images from the Bektashi faith and its history. The *tekké* was closed for many years in the Hoxha period, and the local *Babas* persecuted. It is a moving testimony to the vitality of this sect, and its deep roots in Albanian society, that vigorous life has so soon returned to this exquisite *tekké* under democratic conditions.

Near the *tekké* are a number of domestic houses, in a charming situation; with their low roofs, tiny gardens and trailing vines, with an appearance and atmosphere that must have changed little since Ottoman times. In the last century there were said to be as many as 80 houses within the citadel walls, now there are perhaps half that number. A walk around the alleyways that divide them is very rewarding. One of the larger houses was turned into an Ethnographic Museum. At the time of writing it is closed. It is to be hoped that it will soon be reopened, as it is particularly known for the quality of its rich interior wood carving, carpets and other furnishings. At the bottom end of this complex you will notice a small church, with its cross hacked off, a monument to the vandalism of the anti-religious campaigns of the 1970s.

Leave Kruja by the same route and rejoin the main road (3km). Turn right and follow the road north, towards Laç, across lowland farmland country. Before the war the plain was marshy, but has been drained and is used largely for growing grapes for the wine and raki factory in the little town of Milot. After 16km, you come to the small town of **Mamuras**, then another 8km brings you to **Laç**. Approaching the town, on the left you see the derelict remains of the Chinese-built superphosphate factory, a monument to the failure of industrialisation under communism; a vast, highly-polluted ugly eyesore on the landscape. According to informed observers, the Chinese experts were unhappy at the prospect of building this factory here, but were overruled by Hoxha and his advisers. It was closed in 1990 but some production has now resumed. Asbestos pollution is a particular problem and the area of the buildings should be avoided. A left turn from Laç leads to the small Adriatic resort of **Patok** (9km), a run-down seaside place with few facilities. The beach is not very good, and subject to pollution from the nearby Mati river estuary. **Avoid**.

At **Milot** (6m) the main road meets the Mati river, with its very wide, flat gravel river bed. In the past it was subject to tremendous spates and flooding, but the flow has now been controlled by dams and generally there is only a narrow channel of flow. The bridge was built under King Zog, and originally called the *Giovanni Berta Bridge*, after an Italian fascist hero. It is 473m long. Turn right towards Ulza and Burrel, following the left bank of the river eastwards.

If the river is crossed here by the main bridge, the right turn along the opposite bank runs north towards Rubik (17km) and Puka (78km), through the wilds of the old **Mirdita tribal territory**.

Rubik is well worth a detour, as it has one of the most outstanding ecclesiastical monuments in central and northern Albania, the ****CHURCH OF SHEN NOUT**. It takes less than an hour to reach from the main Tirana–Shkodra road. Follow the road, good quality asphalt along the riverside, with very attractive views of the several streams rushing through the wide gravel riverbed if the Mati is in spate. Thick deciduous forest covers the opposite bank. Workers wearing traditional costumes are soon in evidence, with women collecting wood and men quarrying stone for roof tiles by the roadside. Mirdita is a very culturally conservative area,

Ottoman interior decoration

Catholic and strongly anti-communist, and sufferred greatly under Enver Hoxha. With democracy and pluralism, the old traditions have reasserted themselves, although the Roman Catholic Church has great difficulty in finding priests for the villages. Mirdita people tend to marry into other Mirdita families.

History

The remote region of Mirdite was the traditional home of the largest of Albania's Catholic tribes, which was actually composed of three smaller clans. A legend explains the origin of the name Mirdite. Once there lived three brothers whose father left nothing when he died but a saddle and a winnowing sieve. The eldest son took the saddle (*shale*, in Albanian), the next the sieve (*shoshe*) and the youngest went his way empty handed, wishing his brothers good day (*mir edite*). This ledgend gives the three clans—Shala, Shoshi and Mirdite—a common ancestor.

Under Ottoman rule the Mirdites were extremely poor and lived in a perpetual state of half-starvation because Ottoman troops were persistently making incursions into the heart of their valleys, driving off their flocks, burning their villages and compelling them to flee to the safety of the barren mountains. During the First World War Serbian troops entrenched themselves in the Mirdite region, which witnessed savage fighting. Following the establishment of the independent Albanian state, the Mirdite remained deeply distrustful of the new Tirana administration, suspicious of any government they thought may destroy their liberty.

In 1920, the hereditary chieftain of the Mirdite, Prenk Bib Doda was killed in an ambush resulting from a blood feud. Prenk left no son or heir, his cousin Gjon Marka Gjoni expected, therefore, to succeed him but found that Prenk had disinherited him owing to his unpopularity. Gjoni had apparently deserted the front in 1914. Prenk had subsequently bequeathed his property to all the Mirdite. The Tirana regime, never penetrating the northern highlands, was unaware of the internal intrigues within the Mirdite. In an attempt to secure the Mirdite's loyalty, Gjon Marka Gjoni was encouraged to participate in the new administration. Gjoni, however, considered his status within the Mirdite to be more important than any post offered him by the government in Tirana. Therefore, in April 1921, he refused the official post offered to him in the capital and hurriedly left Mirdite for Prizren to seek Yugoslav aid for his claim as Chief of the Mirdite. By helping Gjon Marka Gjoni, the Yugoslavs hoped to weaken and discredit the Tirana regime, and thereby to extend their influence throughout the northern regions.

Furnished with Yugoslav money, Gjoni returned to Mirdite to stir the clansmen against the Vrioni administration. This was not difficult, as the government had by now threatened to tax the whole country equally and the Mirdite had never paid taxes. Gjoni managed only to win over the Bajrak of Orosh, but the Yugoslavs from Prizren proclaimed a Mirdite Republic in Marka Gjonis' name and supplied him with arms. Marka Gjoni accused the Tirana government of being Muslim, with 'Young Turk' tendencies, and of intending to interfere with the religious liberty of the Catholic Mirdites. Knowing he had the support of the Yugoslavs, who had put funds, training and mountain guns at his disposal, Gjoni attacked the government troops. His force comprised some 2000 men, only a few of whom were actually from Mirdite, the rest were either Serb or Albanian irregulars. His rebellion, however, was shortlived as the majority of the Mirdites ignored his call to revolt. Within days government troops had captured the Mirdite capital, Orosh, and with 50 of his men Gjon Marka Gjoni was forced to flee back to Prizren. He died in 1925 and his son Djon, born in 1886, succeeded him as Kapidan of the Mirdite. Djon, who was far less ambitious than his father, withdrew into obscurity and the 'Republic of Mirdite' lived on only in Prizren, Yugoslavia.

Throughout the interwar period, the Mirdite continued to live in isolated communities in their inaccessible, roadless mountains, neglected and ignored by the Tirana administration. At the close of the Second World War, the victorious Partisans destroyed the palace of Gjon Marka Gjoni, as a warning to the highlanders that their patriarchal, feudal society was now at an end and would not be tolerated in the new Albania. Under Enver Hoxha's regime, outsiders, usually Muslims from the traditionally hostile Mati neighbours, or from Kukes, were moved to Miredita to try to control the indigenous population who remained staunchly anti-communist. Armed Resistance to communism continued sporadically until the mid-1950s. (Miranda Vickers)

After about 15km, the town of **Rubik** is visible, on this side of the river, below a very high isolated rock with a church on top of it, some 300m above the river. Beyond the rock is the modern town, an ugly industrial settlement that grew up post-war around the mine on the east side of the town. A geological institute has been built near it, linked to the numerous other mines in the Mirdita area. With a population of about 2000 people, the main Rubik employer is the copper refinery, originally established in 1938 by an Italian company.

The **church** is one of the most impressive monuments in Mirdita and is both very beautiful, magnificently situated and a romantic ruin redolent of the turbulent history of the region. There is no road or modern path up to the church, either

Rubik church

take the dirt track from behind nearby blocks of modern flats at the edge of the town, or cross the road opposite the snooker hall at the foot of the rock and scramble up the stream bed on the town side of the rock itself. At the top, you come to the fence of a closed military area, with a sign reading *Ndal! Zone Ushtarake!*. Turn sharp left up the side of the rock by this sign, avoiding the camp fence, where there is a path around the east side of the rock. There are magnificent **views** west down the Mati river valley.

On the right as you reach the top are the ruins of large **monastic and church administrative buildings**, with the church standing in an isolated position beyond them on top of the rock above a precipitous drop into the river below. Herds of goats often graze in the vicinity. There is a modern road bridge at the base of the rock, and an interesting **traditional four pier suspension bridge** for pedestrians some 50m upstream of it.

The church was built in the 13C, and completed by 1272, although it is very likely the rock was used for pagan ceremonies in earlier times. According to local oral tradition, it was built by people from the *Shoshi* tribe from the east. The building was linked with the growing diocese of Kostor (*Kotur*) in Montenegro which had been established in 1166. It is of the traditional Byzantine style of its time with a triform apse and a compact oblong nave, about 15m long and 5m wide, and linked stylistically with similar churches built in Skup (Skopje), Vau e Dejes, and Lezha. The building is generally locked, except on Sundays, but it is possible to get a reasonable view of the outstanding frescoes on the east wall behind the altar, showing Christ and local saints, through a gap in the west wall doors.

The monastery and church was seriously damaged during the Second World War, when the rock changed hands several times in the bitter fighting for control of the road between the Axis occupiers, and then in conflicts between various nationalist and Partisan resistance groups. In the immediate aftermath of the war there was also serious fighting between the communists and anti-communists in Mirdita, and it is easy to find spent bullet cases in the vicinity of the buildings. Many Mirdita people fled into exile in the United States as a result of the political turmoil. The platform on the rock below the main church, where there are low walls which probably constituted the foundations of a small shrine was used by the communists as a place of execution. The reconstructed west wall of the church was rebuilt in the aftermath of the war. The three storey-high ruined and sadly roofless monastic buildings are said to be about 150 years old. A bell has been suspended in the ruins of an old bell tower on the very top of the rock. As well as the Catholic majority, there is also a small Muslim population in the town, nearly all people forcibly moved there in Enver Hoxha's time, and used to spy on the rebellious Roman Catholics.

This road is of reasonable quality and is a practical, if arduous and slow, way to drive to the north-east. To reach **Orosh**, the historic capital of the Mirdita clans, follow the dirt track through the town about 2km by the railway line on the opposite side of the river and drive on across open rolling hills covered with scrub and dwarf oak towards Rreshen. After about 10km there is a road junction. **Note petrol and diesel supplies are often uncertain and difficult in this area**.

Follow the sign to Kukes. The road is good quality asphalt and follows across hilly wooded country with many hairpin bends and little sign of habitation or cultivation.

Orosh is now little more than a collection of picturesque ruins and modest modern houses after the destruction meted out in the tribal wars in the 1920s between King Zog and the northern tribal leaders, and the post-war feuds, but it is an evocative and atmospheric journey into the rich past of this region of Albania and is highly recommended.

Orosh was the scene of the wedding in the Gjon Marka Gjoni family house attended by British gendarmerie commander Colonel W.F. Sterling in 1928. Sterling described the *kulla* he visited as 'built of solid stone and designed primarily for defence. From the small windows, scarcely more than loopholes, one had a wonderful view over mile upon mile of narrow winding valleys and pine clad slopes, while behind the house were the sheer rocky crags of Mali i Shenjt, the sacred mountain, rising 6000 feet above the distant gleam of the sea'.

Colonel W.F. Sterling (1880–1945) was an associate of T.E. Lawrence (Lawrence of Arabia) and for a time an influental, if controversial British figure in Albania in the 1920s. After service in Palestine and Egypt he was appointed by the Albanian Ministry of the Interior in 1923 to reorganise the police force. He was replaced when he resigned as head of gendarmerie in 1926 by another British ex-army officer, Major-General Sir Jocelyn Percy. He was a close friend of the British Minister in Albania, Sir Harry Eyres, and his memoirs *Safety Last* provide a very interesting, if partisan and pro-King Zog picture of the country as Zog attempted to put down the rebellion of the northern tribesmen and create a modern Westernised state with British assistence.

The proponents of the Zog/Sterling/Percy policy have claimed that without public order, Albania could not develop into a modern state, while its critics have maintained that the British leadership of the gendamerie, with its authoritarian and colonial ethos, led to the imprisonment, exile and death of numerous honest Albanian politicians such as Bajram Curri (see Route 18), and restricted the development of Albania democracy.

After 44km, through largely deserted mountain country, with the road following the Fan river, is the right turn leading to the mine at Spaç, 15km down a steep slope. The **Forced Labour Camp** at Spaç was at the centre of the communist penal system, and concentrated on political offenders.

Inmates drawn from the estimated 32,000 strong prison population worked at the mining of copper pyrite, in a mine built in a series of terraces up the mountain side. At different times the numbers at Spaç varied between 1500 and 4000 people. Living conditions for the prisoners were appalling, with water being drawn directly from the river, frequent epidemics, very little food and no safety precautions in the mines. It was common for prisoners to attempt to break their own arms and legs to get off work. The severe winter climate in the area was used as part of the punishment system, with offenders being hung naked above the river imprisoned in a wooden cage. In May 1973 the prisoners staged a revolt and successfully took control of the mine. Many were executed in the aftermath when the security police crushed the uprising. The camp was closed in 1990.

Return to the main road, and follow it north for 53km to the junction with the Puka road. 30km from Puka en route to Kukes is the small mining town of Fushe Arrez. On the hillside above Fushe Arrez was the labour camp of Quaf e Barit during the communist period. It was notorious for its cold climate as a result of which many inmates died each winter.

After 6km, the Kruja–Burrel main road crosses the smaller river Shqopeti, running southwards into the Mati, in a picturesque gorge. At the village of **Shkopet** are the remains of two Illyrian citadels, built to control the river valley. Low walls of Illyrian masonry can be seen. Continue 21km along this road towards the dam and hydro-electric scheme at **Ulza**. The artificial lake holds 240 million cubic metres of water, but recent low rainfall has generally left the wide sand banks exposed above the lake surface.

BURREL

3km before Ulza, the road divides, and unless you wish to have a close look at the 150m high dam, and what used to be called the Friedrich Engels power station (maximum annual output 120 million kilowatts), take the right fork towards Burrei. The road runs through beautiful, rather deserted upland country, with woods and grazing land, then descends in a steep series of bends towards **Burrel**.

■ **Hotel**. Not recommended.

History

Burrel is the capital of the Mati region. Although always a small and nonde-script town in itself, it has played a central role in many of the struggles to establish central government authority in Albania, particularly during the turbulent years of the 1920s when King Zog was taking power, and after-wards became his favoured place to imprison his enemies.

The town (altitude 316m) is first mentioned in 15C chronicles as a stopping place on the caravan route from Durres to Macedonia, and continued as a market town for hundreds of years under the Ottomans. It was always very small; the official census figure in 1937 showed only 400 inhabitants. To all intents and purposes, after the First World War, it was only a garrison town and the centre of Zog's gendarmerie, and where he built his political prison (see above). The town was severely damaged in the Second World War when, after the rising in 1943, it had been seized from the Italian occupiers by Mati tribesmen. It was later recaptured by Italian reinforcements. After taking the town they set fire to every building in revenge, and left the place a gutted ruin. The prison was taken over and modified by the communists, who made it into an important component of the forced labour system, notorious for the severity of the regime inflicted upon the inmates.

It has an impressive new mosque under construction in the town centre, financed by Arab interests.

Ahmed Zogu

Ahmed Zogu later **King Zog**, was born at Burgayet in Mati in 1895, the son of Xhemal Zogolli, then tribal chieftain of Mati. Both his grandfather and his father held the rank of *Pasha* in the Ottoman system, and an ancestor had been a *Grand Vizier*. He was educated at the training school for army officers at *Monastir* (modern Bitola, in FYROM) and at Galata, in Istanbul. When the Balkan Wars broke out in 1911, he was studying there, but he returned to Albania immediately, and started organising military resistance against the Serbs, who had burnt to the ground his family home at Burgayet. He was present when the independence of Albania was proclaimed in 1912 at Valona by Ismail Qemal Bey.

The Mati tribe who live in the surrounding region was one of the most important tribes in northern Albania and was Ahmed Zoghu's power base. In the 1920s there were about 40,000 people in the four branches of the tribe, and about 5500 armed men could be raised in times of political conflict. Predominantly Muslim, with traditionally bad relations with the Christian tribes of Miredita to the north, the Mati tribe occupied a large area bounded by the upper left bank of the Mati river, to the north by the Karice tributary of the Mati river, to the east the watershed between the Mati and the Black Drin, and to the west by the Skanderbeg mountain watershed. The Zogolli (from Turkish, *oglu*: 'son of') branch, from which the King came, was the most important, with the *saraj* residence (from Turkish, *serai*: residence) of the *bey* fortified on a low hill outside Burrel between Lis and Burgayet. The *kulla* tower houses were about 15m high and built with thick stone walls for defensive purposes during the protracted blood feuds that tended to dominate social life in the area until Zog's time, and have never been eradicated.

In the early struggles against the Italian occupation, in 1919, Zog occupied Kruja. During the war he had spent much of the time in Mati, establishing himself as a young military leader and the Mati as a haven for disaffected nationalists. He then put himself at the head of the nationalist movement after the Assembly of Elbasan. In March 1920, during the Adriatic Question crisis, he occupied Scutari (modern Shkodra), after the Italians withdrew, and was appointed Governor of Scutari. After the Congress of Lushnja, he became Minister of the Interior, when a *besa* was proclaimed throughout the country and all blood feuds were to cease and a process of nation building to begin. It is widely alleged that he arranged for the assassination, in Paris, of Essad Pasha Toptani, the Serbs' chief supporter in Albania, and began the process that was to lead him to undisputed power in later years. A key element was his programme to disarm all civilians, where he achieved some success in the south and central Albania, but it was strongly resisted in the north, where *adet*, custom, glorified holding personal arms. He had to crush Bajram Curri's insurrection in the north (see Route 18). He fled into exile under Fan Noli's government, only to return as King of Albania in 1926. On 27 April 1938 he married Geraldine Apponyi, a Hungarian aristocrat, in a lavish wedding. Among the wedding gifts was a scarlet supercharged Mercedes Benz, sent from Berlin by Adolf Hitler. He reigned until forced into exile in London by the Axis invaders at the beginning of the Second World War. He lived first at the *Ritz Hotel*, then in Lord Parmoor's house in Buckinghamshire. He remained in exile under the communists, dying in Paris on 11 April 1961. His widow, Queen Geraldine, lives in South Africa. His son, Leka, is currently pretender to the throne. The party campaigning for his restoration is known as *Legalitate*.

The lack of good roads has tended to isolate this area, even from the limited programme of modernisation under King Zog and the subsequent Italian annexation. Under communism the region was a stronghold of opposition to Hoxha's regime and so received little in the way of investment.

Mati was a centre of the nationalist resistance to the Axis occupation, and the British-led SOE mission in 1944 worked closely with Abas Kupi, the anti-communist leader in the region, against the Axis occupiers and the communist-led Partisans operating from their southern bases. Many of the local tribal leaders had collaborated with the Germans and were disunited as a result of ancient feuds and personal jealousies, and were forced into exile as the Partisans moved northwards. The history of this period is highly controversial, in particular the role of British assistance in the Partisan victory, but the memoirs of ex-SOE British Liaison officers who operated in the north, particularly that of Lord Julian Amery, in *Sons of the Eagle*, offer fascinating insights into the period and much information about social conditions of the time, irrespective of political matters.

The road leads into an open square and wide main street. Burrel was a centre of opposition to the one-party state and many shops and public buildings were damaged in rioting in 1991. Some have been repaired, others have not. Drive down to the end of the main street to the **museum**. At the moment the museum is formally closed for reorganisation, but in practice it is possible to gain admission by ringing the bell. The upper floor is completely closed as, being the modern history section, it was dominated by communist propaganda, but the lower floor displays some interesting local antiquities, including Illyrian pottery, items from the Classical period and traditional textiles and embroideries. The costume of a *traditional Mati chieftain is very fine.

The **Political Prison** at Burrel is worth visiting, a grim one-storey building that was originally built in King Zog's time, after which it was taken over by the communist regime and became a centre of the forced labour system. It has recently been made into a museum. King Zog's Prime Minister Koco Kota died here, after the war. Before that it had been used by the Italian army as a horse stable for a time. In colloquial Albanian, the word *Burrel* has come to mean 'hell'.

It is on the south side of the town, and is quite difficult to find; ask for local assistance. The central block of cells is about 180m long, and the prison held about 150 prisoners. Each of the 28 cells is only about 6 cubic metres in size, and in winter the temperatures inside often reached –12°C. Prisoners were only allowed to use blankets to keep warm in the night hours. The seven external towers on the perimeter were used as the bases of the armed guards. A series of special punishment cells only 2m across can also be seen. Former inmates have described the extreme hunger that was their lot, with a meatless diet and only 650 grammes of bread and 70 grammes of beans a day to sustain life. In 1971, an additional ration of 10 grammes of sugar a day was introduced, and in 1990, when the then UN General Secretary Peres De Cuellar visited Albania, 5 grammes of tomato sauce and 7 grammes of cooking oil were added to the rations. The prison was closed down in 1991, under a penal reform directive of the national unity government, and is being made into a museum.

King Zog's *kulla* was near Lis, 8km east of Burrel. Restoration is planned.

Return to Kruja by the same route (90km). The road from Burrel does continue eastwards through Klos (18km) and Bulqiza (32km) to Peshkopia (75km), the regional capital of the Dibra region.

16km from Bulqiza is the town of Klosi, 15km south of which, by a mountain track, is the important Illyrian site of **Xiber**, on the slopes of the Murrizja mountains. It was one of the first major urban settlements found in this part of Albania, dating from the 4C BC, when a slave-owning society developed and associated urbanisation.

PESHKOPIA

Peshkopia (pop. 13,400) is the capital of the Dibra region. It is a medium-sized town with a few good Ottoman buildings, and is a good place to use as a base to explore the very interesting, if often remote and little-known Dibra region. It is possible to reach it by road from Elbasan (difficult), and by the lower road from Kukes (very bad in parts and only suitable for four-wheel drive vehicles), as well as the Burrel road. Until 1939, this was a particularly backward part of the country. The Italian occupiers' official guide notes the complete absence of hotels and usable roads.

■ **Hotels**. *Hotel Korabi*, centre of main street, acceptable, with very helpful owners, and decent food, but very basic and extremely cold and damp in winter. Sleeping bag and full thermals essential. It has been recently privatised and may well improve in the near future. It was built as the first hotel in this part of Albania in 1956, extended in 1983. Manager: Mr Astrit Aslemi,tel, 2481. Also *Hotel Diber*, in the main street nearer the old town, primitive, not recommended.

There are a number of pleasant **cafés** and small **restaurants** opening, mostly in the main street near the *Hotel Korabi*. Local cheese can be very good indeed, and raki made from plums.

■ **Weather. Visitors to Dibra should note that the weather can become very cold as early as late October, and winter can continue until early April. Snowfall can be very heavy in some areas, with a very high wind chill factor.**

History

Excavations in the town have revealed evidence of settlement by Illyrian tribes between the 4C and 2C BC. The local sulphur springs were used by the Romans. The town appears in written records as Peshkopia for the first time in the 15C. The name is derived from the Greek *Episcopi* (seat of a bishop), and indicates early Christian settlement on the site. Skanderbeg was active in the area when he returned to Albania in 1443, and started to organise his followers to fight the Turks. It was a minor regional centre and market town under Ottoman rule, always being overshadowed by the natural regional capital, Debar, since the First World War part of Yugoslavia. In 1938 there were about 1000 inhabitants. The Italian occupiers laid out the main street and planted it with lime trees in the late 1930s.

Since the war it has developed somewhat as an industrial centre linked to the mines in the region. Of these, the chrome mine at Bulqiza is much the most important, where production started in 1950. It was the scene of a bitterly-fought strike in late 1992, which was put down forcibly by the Berisha government after a prolonged hunger strike by the miners. Production has improved since 1993 and the mine now is the mainstay of the local economy, although numbers employed there are considerably reduced. Other industries in the region are timber, some foodstuffs, including raki production, wine and grape juice, and pastoral agriculture. Most inhabitants of the region are Muslim, with a highly conservative culture, particularly in family relationships and in religious practice. There are very strong traditions of popular music and dance in the region.

The small town is set in a narrow ravine, formed by a tributary of the Black Drin. It is surrounded by fruit tree plantations. There are some fine Ottoman houses set back from the main road in the centre of the town, and an open air market and if crossing into FYROM, it is a good place to change money. The money changers congregate in the street market above the river. It has some pleasant cafés and on the whole has avoided the vandalism and destruction in some similar sized Albanian towns that came with the end of communism. Generally speaking, the region has been successful both under communism and under democracy in securing its basic interests. The government villa, now used mostly by the European Union Border Monitoring Mission, is on a small hill behind the Ottoman streets. It is a typical communist building, with the odd suburban atmosphere of so many Hoxhaist constructions. There are very fine views from here across the town towards the Selishte mountains.

The main historic street is just up from the street market area by the river. Walk to the **mosque**, an unattractive fairly modern building currently being restored. It

Fortified kulla at Peshkopia

has a good limestone minaret clad with steel. It was used as a Young Pioneers' centre under communism, and had another building constructed inside it. This is currently being demolished. It is planned to reopen it for religous purposes in late 1995. There is a very small modern **hammam** in the mosque garden, and remains of some graves. There are some interesting very old houses with overhanging eaves opposite the mosque. Then walk about 100m up the hill and turn left along a paved Ottoman street.

On the right are a number of old houses, including a very fine four story yellow ochre painted ***kulla**, a Dibra tower house of a leading clan. Note the traditionally constructed garden walls of baked mud covered with wood shingle, and the paucity of windows. 400m further on is another similar very large house, built in 1899, with fine defensive corner lookouts, which was made into the first school in Peshkopia, and opened in 1923, and known as the 'Dibra Institutional School'. Parts of the house were burnt out in fighting in the town after the establishment of the communist regime and the owners imprisoned. There is a very beautiful garden and internal courtyard (private, not open to visitors).

Next to this house, on the top of the hill overlooking the town is the **museum**. This is a small square two storey building that houses exhibits recently moved there from elsewhere, mostly local artefacts, folk costumes and ethnographic material, and displays on the history of Dibra. This building was a clinic until recently. The base of what appears to be a Byzantine column stands by the front door, and there are other pieces of (?) medieval masonry lying about in the outskirts. It is closed for reorganisation at the time of writing, but a town museum official, Mr Gafur Zotu, tel. 2203, can open it on request. The **ground floor** has a small collection of Illyrian stone tools and weapons, the **upper floor** displays Roman coins and other small artefacts, Byzantine material (not accessible), Ottoman military material, local ethnographic material (not accessible). There are some interesting models of the domestic houses of the Dibra region, and the *Vizier's Bridge*, an Ottoman bridge drowned when the Kukes damn was constructed.

There is a good view down the river valley from this point, with the sound of rushing water from the river in spate dominating the town.

There are a number of interesting ecclestical and Islamic buildings near the town. The plain of Dibra is beautiful, with great open skies and very distant and evocative views to remote horizons. There is a charming new **Bektashi tekké** at Fushë Bulqiza (12km), on the road towards Tirana, in a beautiful and remote setting on the valley floor below the Allamani mountains to the north. It is built of wood and stone and contains the graves of four Dibra *Babas*. On the exterior west wall there is a painting showing the main Bektashi ceremony.

The villages east of Peshkopia between the town and the FYROM border are notable for their large number of mosques, an unusual feature of rural Albania, and a sign of the longstanding cultural links with the more strongly Islamic areas of Kosova and western Macedonia. The people of Peshkopia have a reputation for eccentricity and richly individual behaviour throughout Albania. Their folklore, preserved in *Folklor nga Dibra* (Tirana, 1979) contains unique ballads, riddles and songs from the medieval and Ottoman periods. In the folk music the *Zyrle* is an important instrument, a small horn resembling the Turkish *Zurna*.

19km to the south of Peshkopia is the village of **Burim**, with a notable small **mosque**, built in the 16C. The village is reached by a straight track from the main road leading to the border post (4km) at Blata e Poshtme with FYROM. The mosque may have been built on the foundations of an Orthodox church, and is a charming dignified little building, with a very fine prayer hall, and new minaret. It was renovated in 1993. The prayer hall floor is covered in sheepskins, and there are very beautiful patterns of rose decoration on the walls. The mosque embodies perfectly the atmosphere of the rural Islamic revival in Diber. It is possible to ask permission to climb up the minaret, which offers outstanding and unusual views over the surrounding countryside. There is an old **Muslim cemetery** around the mosque, quite large, indicative of the once much larger village community in Ottoman times. Traces of Neolithic settlement of the Starcevo culture (6000–4500 BC) have been found at Burim. Beyond Burim on the main road to Peshkopia (3km) is **Maqellare**, known as the '*Philosophers Village*' from the vigour of discussion in its streets and cafés.

4km from Burim towards Peshkopia, bisected by the main road, is the important late Roman fortress and urban centre of ***Grazhdani**, on a sharp bend. It may be the site of the late medieval Bulgarian settlement of *Svetigrad*. Exposed walls about 1m high and 2m wide can be seen running across farmland to the south, stretching for about 300m. On the north side of the road there is a very large enclosed area covering at least 6 hectares although the extent of the site is far from clear. Remains of a church and other buildings have been found here in preliminary excavations. The origin of the settlement was most likely to be in late Roman times as an urban centre on the small branch road of the Via Egnetia running north from Roman *Episcopi*, modern Peshkopia, up the Black Drin valley. The exposed concrete centre of the north walls, by the roadside, suggests very late Roman construction for that wall, although without extensive excavation much remains to be established about the history of the site. The site is likely to have been chosen for the good water supply running from the hills to the north, and it must have had a population of several thousand people based on the economic prosperity of this region in late antiquity. It appears to have been fortified in haste in response to the threat of barbarian invasions, judging by the poor construction of the outer walls, and it must have been overrun during the Slav invasions after the time of Justinian. It is an impressive, extremely evocative site set in lovely rolling countryside with views of distant mountains. **Gjinovec** is the main Christian village in the vicinity.

Dibra was an important area for the **anti-Axis resistance**, and British SOE military missions were active in the area in the last war. A good account of their activities can be found in *Albania's National Liberation—The Bitter Victory* by Sir Reginald Hibbert. Dibra was liberated by Hadzi Leshi's forces and units from Yugoslavia which had been operating in the Drin valley.

Also near Peshkopia is Kalja Dodes, Doda's Castle, the site of a British hospital development funded by Jersey Aid charity. The village was originally an Ottoman gendarmerie centre.

PESHKOPIA TO KUKES VIA THE BLACK DRIN VALLEY

This journey, which takes about a day, is one of the most scenic and interesting routes in northern Albania. It follows the route of traditional mule tracks alongside the Drin that have existed since antiquity. **N.B. The road is variable quality, paved and dirt track but has some very bad stretches indeed and a four-wheel drive vehicle and local guidance is needed. It should not be attempted in the winter or after very wet weather. Problems with rock-falls and landslides are common**.

Leave Peshkopia by the road going north, follow a winding route across fertile farmland and upland woods. There are many small farms, moderately prosperous, with walnut trees, and horse and cattle rearing. The asphalt road follows down into the **Drin valley** and along the north bank of the river, through **Muhurri** village ($km), with a new small mosque. The area is famous for apple growing. Then cross a wide bridge over the Drin onto a poor dirt track, which rapidly becomes very bad indeed. The Drin valley was laid waste by the Serbs in 1920. Note the rich bird life, with many crested larks and pipits. Portions of paved surface survive from Italian road construction efforts in 1936–37. The Drin is crossed and recrossed, to **Arasi**, past a newly re-built hospital. The countryside begins to open out, with the road clinging to a steep slope above the Drin, through the village of **Zall Dardha** (43km), which has a small café. A road from Zall Dardha to the left goes to the **Lura National Park**. There are about a dozen remarkable lakes which occupy glacial cirques at heights of between 1200m and 1500m. Then climb steeply for 2km, with a very dramatic view to the right up the valley of the river Shullan, which empties into the Drin, with a wide grey limestone valley floor.

On the north bank where the rivers meet is the tiny isolated village of **Kalasi**, surrounded by trees. The valley narrows rapidly here to a gorge, with wild and fantastic scenery, and the occasional village built at a dizzy height above the river far below. On the valley floor there are tiny lush green fields, to the largely aban-doned Christian village of Drajrezi, with a large ruined Orthodox church on the valley floor on the east side of the river. 1km further and the road crosses the Drin by a Bailey bridge, great care needed on the old wooden planks. The road leaves the river here and climbs into bare rocky uplands, to **Slavica**. There is ****magnificent mountain scenery** in all directions. After Slavica, it follows a preciptous road above the river, to where the river Imisht meets the Drin, great care is needed on this section as the road edges are very insecure, then winds through the hills to meet the better asphalt road at **Kolenjasi**. It drops down steeply to Kukes, past a deep chalk pit and other old mine workings. A track leads from Kolenjasi to the Dardanian camp. 21km south of Kolenjasi a very bad road leads to the **Citadel of Bushat**. As you come into Kukes town the large new mosque is on the right near the lake. It is an impressive blue and white building that dominates the lakeside. Mr Fatmir Kallabaku, tel. 230, is a useful local guide and transport adviser in Kukes town.

The border crossing into FYROM at Bllata e Poshtme is open to traffic. It is gener-ally quiet, and security is reasonable in the vicinity, although difficulties with smugglers can occur.

VII SHKODRA, LEZHA AND THE DINARIC ALPS

15 · Shkodra

From Tirana, by a good quality although often congested, road via Lezha, 37km, to Shkodra, 99km. From Montenegro, via Hani i Hoti border crossing and the main road south (37km).

SHKODRA (pop. 81,000), old *Scutari*, also known as *Skadar* in Serbian and as *Iskenderie* in Turkish, is the regional capital of northern Albania, and a very interesting city with a long and often turbulent history, arising from its strategic position on the Adriatic coast and the military importance of its great citadel, Rozafat Castle. It is the Albanian city which has always had the closest links with Italy, both in terms of trade and culture. It is predominantly Roman Catholic in religion, but with a substantial Muslim minority. But although this has given Shkodra a Western orientation, and made it in the past and present a centre of progressive thought and new institutional development, the hinterland is the remote, barren and primitive northern highlands, understandably called the 'Land of the Living Past' by Edith Durham, the English traveller of the Edwardian period. The unique atmosphere of the city stems from this contrast, where peasants wearing traditional regional costumes are still commonly seen in the streets, alongside modern vehicles and shops. Until the land drainage schemes of the post-war period, it was a notoriously unhealthy city owing to its proximity to the malarial marshes on the flood plain of the Drin and Buna rivers. It was then divided into three fairly clearly defined parts, the bazaar quarter, the old town, and the modern city. The old bazaar quarter was seriously damaged by earthquakes in 1894 and 1913.

Shkodra used to have a large number of politically-inspired museums, such as the Museum of the Shkodra section of the Albanian Party of Labour, which have now been closed, either temporarily or permanently. Visitors should seek local guidance on what is and is not open at any particular time. Shkodra was the subject of a famous set of early photographs of Albania, by the Italian photographer Marrubi, which used to be exibited in reproduction. It is to be hoped that the exhibition will be reopened.

The city has undergone many changes in the last four years, with a marked revival in its twin religious traditions and the renewal of links with Italy and the Roman Catholic Church. A very large new central mosque is under construction, indicating the hope of the Islamic revival in the city. Shkodra has been the focus of international controversy as it has been widely claimed to be the centre of networks smuggling fuel to Montenegro and Serbia in breach of UN sanctions. It remains, as always, a focus of the central concerns in Albanian life and identity, and visitors who develop serious interests in Albanian history and culture often find it the most interesting and stimulating city in the country, although rarely, it must be said, the most comfortable.

Although Shkodra weather can often be very pleasant in spring or autumn, summer visits are recommended, and the town should be

avoided by the tourist in the winter. It can be very cold indeed then, with thick fogs sweeping off the lake or freezing cold north winds blowing off the Montenegran mountains. It can be very wet at any time of year outside the middle of the summer, and wellingtons or Dr Martens boots are essential, as elsewhere in northern Albania, where paths and roads can turn into quagmires after storms.

Shkodra shares many climatic features with neighbouring Montenegro, very heavy rainfall in particular. Driving conditions on local roads can be extremely dangerous, particularly after heavy rain. In fog, driving must be avoided altogether. If work involves winter visits, or much travel or work outside, oilskins or similar weatherproof clothing are recommended.

Expeditions into the rural and moutain hinterland can be made from the city, but travelling conditions are frequently difficult, for a variety of reasons, and local advice and careful planning are required.

■ **Police**. Police Headquarters, tel. (0224) 21 21 or 31 31; Police station, tel. (0224) 32 32.

■ **Medical care**. Central Policlinics, tel. (0224) 22 22; District Hospital (information office), tel. (0224) 22 55, Surgery Dept., tel. (0224) 30 44, Dept. of Internist Med., tel. (0224) 20 97; Dr Ferit Hoti (surgeon), tel. (0224) 33 66 (home); Dr Ferit Hoxha (internist-cardiologist), tel. (0224) 22 24 (home).

■ **Bank**. In the old shopping area.

■ **Hotel and night life**. The *Hotel Rozafati*, off the main square, used to be a reasonable place to stay but is now in very poor physical condition and internal temperatures in the winter can be arctic. Sleeping bag and full thermal equipment essential. Food is poor. **Avoid at the moment although it is due to be privatised and may, or may not, improve.**

Rooms can be rented over the road at the *Big Café* which are clean, cheerful and much better value at US $15 a night. It is one of the oldest continually occupied cafés in Albania, with a history going back over 400 years to early Ottoman times. Whether the visitor stays there or not the *Big Café* is strongly recommended for the quality of the traditional music. There are other pleasant cafés opening all the time although restaurant choice is still fairly limited. The restaurant in the main street opposite the National Bank is reasonable.

In the winter premises close early and it is best to try to eat early in the evening.

History

In the past the city was generally known as *Scutari*. There have been many traces of prehistoric occupation found in the region. In Illyrian times the city was founded by the Labeates at the beginning of the last millennium BC, then taken over by the Ardiaean tribe in the 3C BC. In the 3C BC, the area was the seat of a powerful Illyrian kingdom founded by King Agron, stretching from Lake Shkodra to the Gulf of Kotor. They had a bad reputation for piracy, a fact that led to prolonged conflict with the Romans. Genthius, the last king of the Ardiaeans, and of the Illyrian kingdom in the region, was drawn into conflict with Rome by Perseus, King of Macedon and was defeated and taken prisoner by the Roman general Aemilius Paullus in 168 BC. The city was then assigned to the area of the Labeates, like Lissus. The Roman town that was established passed to the Byzantines, followed by a period of Slav occupation from 1040 to 1355. It was taken by the Venetians in 1396, who built the stronghold at Rozafa, on the foundations of earlier fortifications. In 1473 Rozafa was attacked by Süleiman Pasha and his Turkish troops, who lost 14,000 men in a protracted siege of the citadel. He was repulsed by Antonio Lauretano with Venetian and Hungarian help. In 1478 Mehmed Pasha returned to besiege the city with 250,000 men and after another long siege in which he, in turn, lost 30,000 men, took Scutari in January 1479.

Shkodra then became the centre of one of the largest *sanjaks* in the Balkans, and its rulers soon began to show marked independence from Constantinople. The first printing press in Albania was set up in Scutari in the 16C. The feudal lord Mehmet Bey Bushati became Pasha in 1757 and under him, and his second son, Kara Mahmoud Bushati, the Pashlik achieved great regional power and influence. The Bushati family became 'Heriditary Pasha'. Their rule extended into Kosova in the north-west and to Berati in the south. By 1796, Kara Mahmoud was known as the Prince of Albania after having turned the Pashlik into a virtually autonomous Albanian state, defeating the pirate kingdom at Dulcingo (Ulcinj) and the Montenegrins.

The first Albanian newspaper to be printed in Albanian, and Turkish, was published in the city in 1879. The city had also become an important commercial centre, with 40,000 inhabitants and was the largest city in Albania. The Jesuits and Franciscans opened schools at this time, under Vatican patronage. The first strike in the history of the Albanian labour movement took place here in 1901. In the same year, 8000 armed men held an assembly in the city where they decided to resist any attempt by the Turks to repress the Albanian national movement by force of arms.

During the Balkan Wars the city held out between October 1912 and April 1913 against a siege from combined Serbian and Montenegrin forces. The defence was led by Hussein Riza Bey until he was assassinated by Essad Pasha who then surrendered the town. Until July 1914 it was occupied by an international naval force under Sir Cecil Burney, then on 27 June 1915 the Montenegrins reoccupied it, followed by the Austrians in January 1916, and the French and Italians from November 1918 until March 1920, and by the Italians alone until the establishment of the Albanian Regency in 1920. In 1918 a Committee for the National Defence of Kosova was founded in the city, mainly composed of political exiles from the region, with the aim of uniting Kosova with Albania.

Shkodra was the birthplace of the poet **Migjeni** (1911–38), the founder of modern Albanian language lyric poetry. Migjeni was the pseudonym of *Millosh Nikolla*, a member of the Serbian minority community in the town. He studied as a child there at the Serbian language school and at an academy in *Monastir* (Bitola) in Macedonia. On his return to Albania he gave up his priestly vocation and wrote poems in Albanian and taught at the school in Vraka, a few miles north of Shkodra until his early death from tuberculosis.

In the 1920s the city was at the forefront of the 1926 revolt of the northern tribesmen against King Zog, when the local gendarmerie was murdered by insurgent forces. It was subsequently retaken by King Zog's mercenaries. In general the area suffered from the relative neglect of the north in that period, and under Zog became little more than a small market town used by local

Late Ottoman Shkodra

tribesmen on market days, although it began to prosper again as Italian influence increased in the 1930s. A college and museum were established by the Jesuits, and Roman Catholic education was expanded.

A communist group was founded in Shkodra in 1934. The city suffered badly under communism and played a prominent part in the democratic movement leading to the end of the one-party state in 1990–91. Four demonstrators were killed and 57 seriously injured in anti-communist disturbances after the parliamentary elections on 2 April 1991. A monument to the dead and other victims of persecution in Shkodra was placed near the cemetery of Rrmaj in Zall Kir in March 1993. Enver Hoxha himself always had a poor view of the Shkodra communists, writing as early as 1942 about the poor quality of the membership here, saying that they lacked 'a clear-cut political line, a definite organisational form, and a sound discipline and secrecy'. The last communist president of Albania, Ramiz Alia, was born in Shkodra in 1925, into a Muslim family. There is a large open street market held on Saturday mornings by the bridge below Rozafa Castle. It is a good place to buy a horse or donkey.

A visit to Shkodra for most visitors usually falls into two parts, with a walk in the town to see the old quarters and to visit the shops, and a visit to the citadel and its surrounding historic buildings.

From the main square, with its small park with good drinks and ice cream kiosks, walk north-east from the hotel along the main boulevard about 400m. A very large bronze monument to the liberation of the city occupies the central roundabout. On the left, on the opposite side of the road, is the park, on the right an attractive row of Ottoman houses.

On the north side of the park is an 19C clocktower, **Padget's Clocktower**, which was built by a 19C English Evangelical missionary, Lord Padget. This houses

*Shkodra Archeological Museum, one of the best provincial museums in the country. It is sometimes closed, but try the left hand door beyond the entrance gate and ask for the curator, Mr Mentor Kopliku (French speaker), or Mr Zamir Tafeleca, who are very helpful. The garden contains some interesting examples of Roman, Venetian, Byzantine and Turkish sculpture, especially a very large Venetian font. There are eight Roman columns from Rozafa Castle on the east path of the garden. The long grass and wild vegetation are a refuge for stray cats and kittens.

The **tower** is an interesting, rather eccentric building which is full of character and the atmosphere of 19C Shkodra. It was built by Padget as his home and as a base for Protestant missionary work in northern Albania in 1868. The upper floor is preserved much as it would have been in Padget's time and is well worth visiting. The fine wood panelled staircase leads into a large central meeting hall, with an upper gallery for women visitors. It has the feel of a large room in a 19C Oxford college, such as Keble College, with mock Gothic windows, dark wood panels and rows of chairs, but also of Albania in the time of the League of Prizren and in the late Ottoman world. Apart from the general ambience, there are some interesting works of **19C Shkodra popular art** on the walls, such as *Tregtar Shajaku* by Simon Rrota, *Les Deux Routes* by Kal Idromeno, a very fine carved 19C wooden chair, embroideries, and ethnographic charts.

The **Archeological Museum** is on the lower floors, reached by a separate entrance through the garden and housed in what would have originally have been the kitchens and domestic areas of the Tower. It is not very well lit but is well laid out and the exhibits are consistently interesting.

In **Case 1** on the **lower ground floor**, there are artefacts from the Neolithic and Bronze Age settlements in and around Shkodra, mostly axeheads and other small tools. To the left of the entrance, various statues and masonry from the Classical and Byzantine periods, including *Illyrian stone carved with runic characters. **Case 2** and **3**. Bronze Age artefacts, swords, spears, axes. **Case 4**. Illyrian and Celtic material from the Illyrian sites at Dedaj, Ivanaj, Marshej, Grizhe, Shtoj, Golem, Dobrac, Lac Qyrsac, Mali Kolaj, Gajtan, Beltoj. **Case 5**. Iron Age ceramics, spears, axes, part of a helmet. **Case 6**. Iron Age pins, ceramics, pots, jewellery. On the floor by this case, *very fine Illyrian stone statue of a godess. **Case 7** Illyrian material from 5C BC–2C BC, metalwork, a stone cult object, small statue of a female godess, Illyrian stone funeral urns, Roman tombstone from 2C AD. **Case 8**. Material from the time of the Roman/Illyrian wars 229–167 BC, ceramics and Roman sculpture. **Case 9**. Illyrian artefacts from the Roman colony 1–4C AD in stone and bronze. **Case 10**. Exhibits from the Roman province of Praevalitana 4–6C AD, glass, ceramics, jewellery, axes, terracottas. **Case 11** and **12**. Arberesh culture from 6C–9C AD from Koman, bronze artefacts, fibulae, axes, jewellery. **Case 13** material from medieval Shkodra and Sarda (*Sardium*) arrow heads, leather work, terracottas, jewellery. **Case 14** and **15**. Shkodra under Venetian rule, pictures and engravings from the Ventian period, painting of Skanderbeg in the popular style. **Interior rooms**. A very interesting collection of *historical photographs, subjects including the death of Bajram Curri, Luigj Gurakuqi, the 1920 Kopliku Rising, Fan Noli and his associates.

By the side of the hotel, surrounded by pink oleanders, opposite the mosque, is a very good life-size *bronze statue of Luigj Gurakuqi (1879–1925), patriotic intellectual who was responsible for the adoption of the Latin alphabet in Albania. He was an associate of Bajram Curri and Hasan Prishtina and was assassinated by Zogist agents in a Bari café, as part of the King's crackdown on northern Catholic opponents.

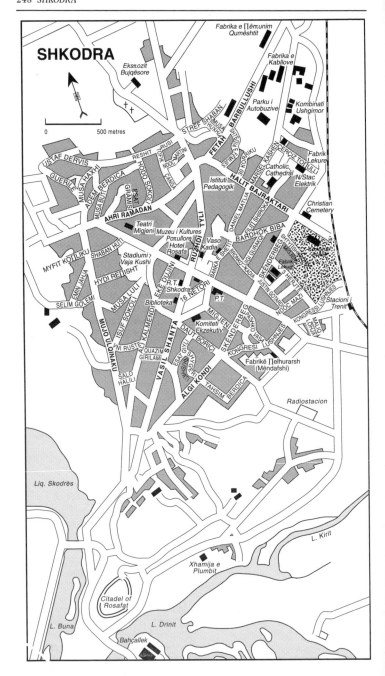

SHKODRA

0 ____ 500 metres

Fabrika e Πёπunim
Qumështit

Fabrika e
Kabllove

Eksπozit
Bujqësore

Parku i
Autobuzive

Kombinati
Ushgimor

STREF SHABAN

BARBULLUSHI

FETAH

USTAF DERVIS

RESHIT

RUSI

TOFIK

NDOC MARTINI

ÇANGA

HODO SOKOLI

MUSA BUTI

GUERILE

MUSA HAXHI

ADEM BERDICA

ESAT GRAMISH

AHRI RAMADAN

MUSA BUTI

30 KORçIKU

VARSEL KASHENI

CERÇIZ TOPULLI

Fabrik
Lekure

RALIT BAJRAKTARI

Catholic
Cathedral

N/Stac
Elektrik

Istituti
Pedagogik

DANIEL MATIJA

VASEL SHEFTI

UKE SHIROKI

BARDHOK BIBA

Christian
Cemetery

Teatri
Migjeni

Muzeu i Kultures
Poπullore

Vaso
Kadia

PRONGO KADIA

HYSEN GIRAKO

JUSTIN GOTARO

Fabrik
Lekure

Hotel
Rosafa

BANKA

RUZHDI TYLI

MYFIT KOTILIKU

SHABAN HUTI

Stadiumi
Vaja Kushi

EKE DUJINI

R.T.
Shkodra

SKENDERBEG

SHTJEFEN

HYDI REÇISHT

EMIN JAHJA

16 NETORI

P.T.

NDOC MAZI

KONGRESS LUSHNJES

Fabrik
Lekure

Stacioni i
Trenit

SELIM GOLEMI

MUSA LULI

JUSUF SOKOLI

Biblioteka

MIGJENI

SKENDERBEG

PASHO VASA

MUJO ULQINAKU

NI RUSTE

KALMENDI

VASIL SHANTA

Komiteti
Ekzekutiv

DAUT BORICI

KONGRESI

LUSHNJES

QUAZIM

GIRILAMI

ESAT GJYLI

GHYGRI

Fabrikë Πelhurarsh
(Mëndafshi)

SALO
HALILI

ALGJ KONDI

TAHSIM BERDICA

Radiostacion

Liq. Skodrës

Xhamija e
Plumbit

L. Kirit

Citadel
of
Rosafat

L. Buna

L. Drinit

Bahçallek

Across the road from the Tower the new ***Mosque of El Zamil** is being constructed. This is a very large and dramatic building which, when completed in early 1996, will be the largest mosque in Albania and one of the largest mosques in the Balkans. It is being built by the Saza Company with financial assistance from Egypt and Saudi Arabia. So far, it is possible to see very beautiful twin minarets with fluted stonework, and the construction of a single central dome covered with stainless steel. The mosque will occupy an area of 762m², and the surrounding gardens, at the moment enclosed by the builders with a high metal fence, 800m². It is built on the site of the Parruca mosque so-called after the Parruca district name for this part of Shkodra. It was demolished by the communists after being damaged in the Second World War.

> Among Albanian cities Shkodra has always had a reputation for the seriousness of its Islamic commitment. Before 1939 there were 35 mosques in the city. The Shkodra Islamic Centre is in the main street near the Partisan monument, the secretary is Mr Faik Hoxha, tel. 2081. Young men from Shkodra are being trained to become mullahs in the Lebanon, Egypt and Saudi Arabia. Islamic schools survived under communism until 1968, but at the moment there are only four imams in the city. An Islamic school has opened in 1993, with about 130 pupils.

Across the road in front of you is the building which used to house the Museum of the Party of Labour in Shkodra, which has been closed. It also housed for a time the regional offices of the Democratic Party. Down an alleyway to the left of this house is the headquarters of the Victims of Political Persecution organisation, an association of ex-prisoners under communism. Turn left and follow this street about 100m, and you enter the shopping area. This was very well restored in the 1960s, with the traditional character of the Ottoman shops being kept. There are small cafés and restaurants as well as numerous private businesses to be seen, some of the thousand or so private enterprises that have been set up in the city since the end of communism. Many commodities on sale are imported from Hungary, Bulgaria and Italy. There are also a growing number of private cars in the city, and economic activity is reviving in the copper wire and cable plant, the cigarette factories and the textile industry.

Shkodra is a particularly good place to shop for traditional Albanian musical instruments, traditional textiles, embroideries, folk costumes and wood carvings. This street used to contain the Exhibition of Material Culture of Shkodra, which displayed filigree work, weapons, fabrics, etc., but at the time of writing it is closed. A branch of the National Bank is in the street, which will change travellers' cheques.

On market days, usually Wednesdays and Saturdays, many peasants in traditional costume will be seen in the streets in this area, some bringing agricultural products to sell in the market, others coming with their donkeys to buy supplies. Shkodra has always been famous for the colour and interest of its street scenes, in the 1920s the Gordons, English visitors to Shkodra, commented:

> During the days that we waited making the necessary arrangements for the journey we frequented many of the cafés, sitting lazily with sweet coffee or with *rahatlakoom*, contentedly watching the people drift by us. Our favourite haunt was a small Moslem café near the central market-place and the pump.

Of women's costume there were at least eight wholly different varieties—the Christian ladies with their embroidered scarlet Venetian hoods, or their festooned lace veils and enormous pantaloons; the mountain brides with their swinging, flared, bell-shaped skirts, five-fingers'-wide ponderous silver marriage belts, and their never-easy knitting needles; the plainswomen with bobbed black hair, clothes of white, and vermilion; the madonna-like Miridita women in black; the poorer townswomen shrouded in wrappings of scarlet striped with white, even the Christian ones muffled up also and showing only a single eye; or the tall and stately women of Montenegrin origin from Vraka with their small pork-pie hats set amidst great plaits of hair above long, flowing coats of pale cerulean blue. The mountain women would carry their babes in wooden cradles strapped behind their shoulders, but one might often see any nursemaid of the town, her arms full of bundles, bustling along with the baby in its cradle balanced precariously on her head. The men could be grouped into four major varieties, though almost every mountain clan had distinctive embroidery patterns, so that an experienced eye could distinguish between them as easily as a Scotsman could tell the tartans.

For the **Catholic Cathedral**, walk back to the main square and ask directions; it is to be found south of Banka E Shtetit which used to be Enver Hoxha Street. It was the largest Catholic Cathedral in the Balkans. Construction began in 1856, and it was completed in 1898.The Body of Christ and the Virgin are venerated in a festival held on the third Monday in October. Under communism it was turned into a volleyball court and has been restored as part of the extensive activities of the Vatican in church restoration in Albania. Virtually all of the spacious 19C interior was vandalised in the anti-religious campaigns of the 1960s and 1970s, with the exception of the finely carved wooden ceiling. Steeply-banked rows of concrete seats were built inside so that spectators could watch the volleyball competitions.

Pro-atheism campaigns were conducted with particular ferocity in Shkodra, which had always been a deeply Catholic city and strongly anti-communist, and with the political background that, as in Croatia, some Catholic priests had actively collaborated with the Axis occupation forces in the war.

The building has now been well restored in the last two years, to produce a light, simple large interior, free from excessive decoration. A series of large Romanesque arches dominate either side of the nave. There is a fine wood sculpture of the Devil on the west wall, and Stations of the Cross in the conventional manner. The ****roof ceiling** has been beautifully restored by Italian craftsmen. To the west side of the cathedral is the attractive and very well restored **residence of the Archbishop of Shkodra**, an Italianate 19C building in the style of a Renaissance palazzo (closed to the public). It also contains the offices of the Caritas Catholic aid organisation. The local chairman of Caritas is Mr Gjon Marka Gjoni, of the famous northern clan. Caritas Albania have a British contact for Albania work who welcomes offers of assistance, Mrs Jane Englishby, 201 New Road, Porthcawl, Wales CF36 5HN. The CAFOD Catholic Aid organisation has a Tirana office in Rruga Kont Urani, No 17 (tel. 42630, Mr Tim Brown) near the residence of the British Chargé d'Affaires. To the east of the cathedral a new **church** is under construction, which will also include new office accommodation in the complex, on the site of a building destroyed in the pro-atheism campaigns 30 years ago. The current Archbishop is

Msg. Frano Ilija (tel. 3703). The Apostolic Nuncio, Ivan Dias, lives in the Vatican Embassy in Tirana.

If the street running north beyond the cathedral is followed, you reach the **Christian cemetery**, after about a kilometre. This is a pleasant walk down a street lined with attractive small Ottoman houses, and one or two have been turned into good quality small private restaurants. Near here is the **private house of the Gjon Marka Gjoni family**, a remarkable, theatrical Ottoman domestic building with a tower at the north end, behind high walls. The interior (not open to the public) is a veritable rabbit warren of different rooms, unchanged in atmosphere since the pre-war period. The wood pannelled rooms are outstanding. It is said to be about 250 years old, and to have once belonged to the Prenk Bib Doda clan.

The cemetery has some fine late 19C and early 20C monuments to leading Catholic citizens and families of the city. In the centre there is a small church, in process of restoration.

Opposite the cathedral is *****Rruga Branko Kadia**, a late Ottoman street of outstanding interest which leads back to the town centre. Cross the road and walk about 200m to the left, turn right, after about 100m on the right is a building that belongs to the Catholic Church, on the corner of Rr. Shejnaze Juka, with a small church and a very beautiful internal courtyard and cloister, originally constructed in 1865. It has a fine magnolia tree in the centre and many Romanesque arches. It was seized by the communists in 1947 and its priest shot in the yard after which it became a Young Pioneers club. It has been fully restored in 1993/94 and is now a monastery, opening hours for visitors by the doorbell.

100m further up the road to the left is the headquarters of the Democratic Party, in an attractive two storey building, and then a number of very attractive **large Shkodra diplomatic residencies** that were mostly built to be embassies in the late 19C prior to the final crisis in the Adriatic Question, and what Edith Durham later described as *The Struggle for Scutari* in her book on the subject. There are some good small shops, cafés and restaurants at the north end in very well preserved traditional buildings. At the north end it meets what used to be called Enver Hoxha Street, now renamed as Boulevard 13 Dhjetori 1990.

It is easy, here, to evoke in the mind the first visit of Edith Durham to the town in 1908, when as a young woman from Dorset, aged 32, alone, she set out on her committment to the Albanian people and their national liberation struggle. She would have sat in one of these cafés, with her Montenegran interpreter for the Albanian language, talking Serbian herself, a little arrogant, describing the Balkan warclouds that were gathering.

To visit the ****CITADEL OF ROZAFAT** (*Kalaja e Rosafatit*) and associated buildings, a short taxi ride is recommended, although it is possible to walk the 3km towards it, on the south side of the town. On the left is a small statue of the wartime resistance hero, Manush Alimani (1924–44). On the opposite side of the river over a small bridge is the Shkodra Gypsy Quarter.

The citadel is magnificently situated on a rocky outcrop of limestone 135m high above the point where the river Buna meets the river Kir. For most visitors, it has everything, in terms of romance and drama of its setting, that a large medieval castle in the Balkans could be expected to have. Below the citadel, and to the left of it, was the old bazaar quarter of the Ottoman town.

It can be approached by car up a steep winding road from the south side, with very fine Ottoman paving, although parking at the top is difficult. It began to take on military importance as early as the 2C BC, and never lost it until the First World War. There are spectacular views of the surrounding countryside from all sides, particularly of Lake Shkodra, the river Buna and the drained marshlands and flood plains of the rivers, and even if the visitor does not have time to make an exhaustive tour of the citadel, for which at least three hours is needed, a short visit should be made simply to enjoy the outstanding situation and to contemplate the scene of so many seminal events in Albanian history. Rozafat citadel was, in a general sense, quite impregnable, built on sheer cliffs, with its own water supply and secret passages leading down to the riverside below, and hence gave rise to some of the most blood-soaked sieges ever seen in Europe, particularly the final heroic defence against the Turks in 1479 after which vultures fed on the 60,000 unburied corpses lying on the surrounding battlefield. This cataclysmic event for the Christian world was the subject of Veronese's frescoes of 1585 in the Doge's Palace in Venice.

The name of Rozafat Citadel is derived from a version of the legend of the woman built into the castle wall, which is common in folklore in many Balkan countries. According to local folk stories in northern Albania, three brothers who were working on the construction of the castle found that the work they had done during the day was always demolished during the night. An old man who lived near the castle told the brothers that the Devil was acting against them, and the only way to frustrate his efforts was to wall someone up in the building as a human sacrifice to appease him. The brothers therefore decided to kill whichever of their wives was the first to bring them food on the following day, and to say nothing to any of the women about their murderous pact. But the two elder brothers did tell their wives about the plan, so the wife of the youngest, Rosapha, was the only one to come with food next day, and she was duly built into the wall of the citadel.

Shkodra Citadel is the earliest major building in the Balkans with a tradition of human sacrifice in its construction. The legend was classified by the 19C German folklorist Jacob Grimm as a characteristic example of a legend of *Immurement*. Elsewhere in Albania similar legends are associated with castles, and also with bridges in Albanian inhabited regions, such as the Saint's Bridge in Kosovo, the bridge at Arta in northern Greece, and Qine Bridge in Cameria. The Shkodra legend received its earliest exposition in Barleti's *Chronicle*, written in Shkodra in 1504.

From the approach road, you pass into a vaulted passage, entering the walls, which are about 600m in total length, and enclose an oval area, following the contour of the top of the rock, amounting to 9hectares and protected by eight towers. A massive **Venetian tower** is on the east side, to the right as the visitor enters. You enter the outer courtyard through a dark covered area, with a complex defensive system built in the early 15C. Excavations have revealed evidence of Bronze Age occupation in this area.

Turning left, you enter the main part of the citadel, with a very large open area enclosed by walls, dominated on the west side by the remains of **St Stephen's Cathedral**, which was turned into a mosque in 1479. The subsequently damaged minaret was added, on the south side, under the Ottoman occupation. The cathedral was built in 1319 and became the cathedral of the city. It is constructed in the Dalmatian style, and shows the extensive Italian influence on the city, even at that early time in its history. It is an oblong, austere building, with a single roof structure, although that has now disappeared and the interior is open to the elements. On the north side of the walls are substantial protective towers. The **spectacular views** on every side can be enjoyed from here, although visitors should take particular care to keep on the marked paths, where they exist, as there are several entrances to deep underground cisterns in this area, particularly on the north side of the cathedral, that were built to store water during sieges. They are often obscured by vegetation and can endanger life and limb. Similar care is needed with the walls themselves, where there are unmarked precipitous drops in many places, and much loose masonry.

To the west of the cathedral is a ruined building generally known as **the prison** (although it is far from clear if that was its original purpose), then the inner perimeter wall, which is entered through a narrow gate. To the left of the path opposite the cathedral is an ancient cistern and well entrance. Immediately to the left after passing through into the inner castle is a solid oblong three-storey building with very thick walls that was originally built as an **arsenal** by the Venetians, and taken over by the Turks for similar military storage purposes, and then for a short time as residence for the Pashas of Shkodra. It houses a café and a small museum of the castle but at the time of writing it is closed, although it is hoped that it will soon be re-opened. The views south from the walls this side are particularly spectacular, and on a clear day it is possible to see southwards to the citadel at Lezha towering over the flat coastlands and the Adriatic.

A visit to the citadel should be combined with seeing the **Leaded Mosque*, that can be seen beneath the walls and the group of Ottoman houses on the south-east side of Rozafa. It stands in isolation a little way from the houses, in what was a marshy area, surrounded by cultivated fields. It takes about 10 minutes to walk down to it from the citadel entrance. This was once the Old Bazaar area of the city, but was abandoned in the early 19C after earthquakes in 1815 and 1837 caused the river Drin to change course, flooding the district regularly, and making it uninhabitable. A small existing mosque on the site was substantially developed by the Heriditary Pasha Mehmet Bushati, of the famous 18C family, in 1773–74. The existing single-domed mosque was demolished, and the present multi-domed building modelled on the Great Mosque in Istanbul replaced it. It was damaged, although not that seriously, in the anti-religious campaigns, and has been restored. There is a charming outer courtyard, with arched arcades, and a white painted interior of great beauty and simplicity, with a single great dome in perfect architectural harmony with the small domes above the entrance hall. The mosque was the setting for serious violence in March and April 1991, during the first democratic election campaign held in Albania since the war, and paramilitary police fired on worshippers inside on 2 April 1991.

Opposite the mosque at the top of the track leading to it is a very fine **Turkish house** that was once a museum but has now been restored to its original owners. It is a very large two storey domestic building dating from the 18C (not open to the public). It may have been the home of an imam. The lower floor is occupied by farm animals, the upper floor is used domestically.

At the south west fringe of the town, on a roundabout, is a very large bronze **statue of Isa Boletini**, the Kosovar hero, in its way very impressive and evocative of the great days when the people of Albania were united in the struggle for Kosova.

Isa Boletini

Isa Boletini (1864–1916) was one of the first organisers and strategists of the movement for Albanian national independence in Kosova. He was involved in the League of Prizren at an early age, then in the League of Peje and the Young Turk revolt in 1908, and fought in the Balkan Wars with his *ceta* in 1911–12.

The Russian revolutionary leader Leon Trotsky wrote an animated account of the fighting involving Boletini's men in the Scutari region, based on his experiences as a war correspondent in the region 1912–13 during the Balkan wars. Boletini took part in the Treaty of London negotiations in 1913 and opposed the concessions to Serbia that were made on border and other issues. He was assassinated by a Montenegran nationalist on 23 January 1916 in Podgorica.

Mes Bridge

In the vicinity of the city a visit to the **Mes Bridge** is well worthwhile. This is a very fine late 18C Turkish arched bridge, 8km outside the town, on a minor road north-east towards the Dinaric Alps, via **Bardhaj** village (4km). It is an elegantly confident construction, with ten arches, 108m long, built over the little river Mes by the Pasha Mehmet Bushati. It is a tribute to the great technical skill of its builders that it has resisted the frequent torrential flows in the river after winter storms.

Illyrian citadel at Gajtani

Another interesting excursion is to the **Illyrian citadel at Gajtani**. This is on a hillside above the main road running south to Tirana, about 5km outside Shkodra. To get there, after crossing the railway line, take a left turn up a poor track towards the modern village of Gajtani. Ask for directions in the village; the site is up a steep track on the east side. Ruined Illyrian walls made up of dry-stone-laid, very large limestone blocks can be seen and an entrance gate. It is thought to be a very early Illyrian fort, probably built by the Labeates tribe, the original inhabitants of the area before they were displaced by the Ardiaeans.

For details of other itineraries in the Shkroda region, see Routes 16, 17 and 18.

16 · Shkodra to Lezha

From Shkodra (see Route 15), take the main road south, towards Tirana, to Lezha, 37km. This is a good wide asphalt road but it is often busy.

This route follows through the lowlands south of Shkodra, across drained marshland, to the great citadel of Lezha, and burial place of Skanderbeg, and the coast port of Shëngjin, a focus for many important events in modern Albanian history. Recent archaeological investigations in Lezha have uncovered impressive Illyrian remains which can be easily visited.

Leave Shkodra by the main road to the south, past Rozafat Castle on the left. On the right is a turn up a small road to the lakeside settlement of **Shirokë**, 3km. This is a small fishing village and holiday resort, and a good place for birdwatching expeditions.

In the centre of the village is a 1930s mansion that used to be **King Zog's holiday home**. The pink painted house lies on the left of the main road by the lake and is worth a short visit. In the communist period it was used as a children's home, called *Camp i Pushimit*, and it is still full of old beds and play apparatus. It is in a poor state of repair but there are impressive steps leading up the hill to the front entrance, with fine arches above a central balcony and the house itself is a good example of Italianate style of the period, and enables the visitor to conjure up the grandiose and pretentious atmosphere of the period of the Italian annexation. It is surrounded by some fine cypress and pine trees, although some have been vandalised and cut down. At the lakeside below there are some attractive walks, with good birdwatching for grebes, cormorants and many varieties of duck, and good rod fishing.

The road continues as a track towards the border with Montenegro. This and other tracks from the main road lead towards old border crossings which are not open to visitors or through traffic. **Avoid the sensitive border area**.

Continue along the main road for 2km, where it crosses the river Buna and goes through the village of **Bahçallëk**. This village was near the epicentre of the great earthquake (7.2 on the Richter scale) that affected this region on 15 April 1979, the most severe earthquake to affect Albania and Montenegro since the Second World War. Bahçallëk was totally destroyed and was rebuilt as a memorial to the earthquake victims.

> The earthquake of 15 April 1979 was one of the strongest recorded in the Balkans this century and devastated large areas of northern Albania, causing damage right across the northern mountain region, from Shkodra to Tropoja, on the Yugoslav border. Damage was recorded as far away as Zagreb in Croatia and Taranto in southern Italy. The consequences were very serious in southern Montenegro and Albania.
>
> About 35 people were killed in Albania, and 382 injured, 17,000 homes were completely destroyed and about 100,000 people were temporarily homeless, with 60,000 of them in the Shkodra district and 30,000 in the Lezha district. In the Shkodra district the earthquake completely destroyed 1911 houses, and almost everywhere the electricity network, telephone lines and water supplies were put out of action. A serious aftershock took place on 24 May, five weeks later. The devastation was used for propaganda purposes by Enver Hoxha, who stated in a speech at the time that:
>
> > It was a moment when our earth was shaken, our mountains were shaken, houses and villages were rased to the ground, everything was shaken, but not the Albanian. He stood firmly on his feet, as he had always done in the face of threatening storms, as he always has stood when enemies have tried to violate his freedom and the borders of his Homeland.
>
> The process of reconstruction was slow and expensive and was a marked economic setback for the region, particularly as 1979 was a year when the country was trying to complete various industrial construction projects that had been disrupted by the departure of the Chinese experts after a breach with Peking.
>
> Albania is very prone to earthquakes, with records of damage going back as far as the great tremor that hit the Dalmatian coast of the Adriatic in 1667, and doubtless many earlier seismic events of great severity have not been recorded. On average, an earthquake causing damage occurs every two years. In 1952, the first seismic map of Albania had been produced, showing the

existence of a number of zones of continual seismic activity, centred on Kepi i Rodonit, at the mouth of the Buna river, in the direction of the valley of the river Fan to Kukes, along the valley of the White Drin to the border with Yugoslavia, and then along a line stretching from Shkodra to Peja. The 1979 earthquake involved this latter area. In a pattern common to Adriatic coastal earthquakes, a compressional regime had been set up between blocks under the Earth's surface, between two faults, that of Ulqin-Virpazar on the south-east and Budva-Kotor on the north-west. During the earthquake, the western edge of this block was activated, which represents a zone of the Ionian-Adriatic deep faults.

From the main road a right turn leads (29km) to the coastal village and seaside resort of **Velipoja**, across fertile flatlands with many small farms. This was the territory of the Catholic Kastrati tribe, known as the 'Five Banner tribe'. They used to march behind these flags to Shkodra once a year to pay the Ottoman taxes on the Feast of St John. You then cross open and desolate marshland and low hills near the Montenegran border to reach Velipoje, which means 'Great Plain' in Slav. On the left is the Hill of Bakj Rrjoli, a strange wedge-shaped hill 545m high, after which the settlement is approached through a fine avenue of poplar trees. This is a run-down place, very bleak in winter, and not recommended for bathing, as it is very near the Buna river estuary. There are a number of blocks of flats from a communist workers' holiday settlement, and a bare and windy estuary beach. There is very good **birdwatching** on the sandbars and in the shallow pools. It is one of the outstanding areas for watching birds in the east Adriatic. There is also a good view across the estuary to Franz Joseph's Island where in 1892 the Hapsburgs established a naval station linked to the Powers later blockade of Shkodra. On a visit here it is worth taking a moment to reflect on the fact that this was once the **frontier of the Ottoman Empire**, a vital international boundary that ran across the vast and windswept reed beds.

Until the post-war land drainage programmes, most of the land in this district was heavily wooded or malarial marshland, and a rough track across swampy marshland was all that linked modern Velipoja, then known as *Pulaj*, with *Scutari*, modern Shkodra. It is worth noting that up until the First World War, conditions for Edwardian travellers in this area were so bad that the Hapag Lloyd steamers which took some of the first organised parties of tourists to visit Albania, in the shape of a few hours in Scutari, had to dock at Montenegran ports, travel overland in Montenegro to Vizpazar, at the far end of Lake Scutari, then take a steamer across Lake Scutari to the city. Travellers were recommended to buy 'oriental embroideries, silver filigree work and inlaid weapons' in the bazaar, the main attraction of their visit, although they were also taken to see 'the Albanian Acropolis', that is Rozafat castle. Those who find a visit to contemporary Albania arduous may find consolation in the memory of the rigours of travel in those pioneering days.

The **Buna river**, known in antiquity as the *Barbana*, and in Montenegro as the *Boyana*, flows out of Liqeni i Shkodrës from the south-west and is about 150m wide and about 3m deep along most of its course. Before the last war it was used for navigation for small vessels, of up to about 150 tonnes. In the disputes over the control of Albanian territory after the First World War, the control of navigation on the Buna between the sea and Lake Scutari was to be given to the League of Nations, with alternate Italian and Yugoslav control committees. This was seen by the Albanian government as a means of ending Yugoslav territorial claims on northern Albania. Yugoslavia had claimed that as the mouth of the Buna was often choked by sandbanks, and as a result flooded parts of Montenegro, so it should be included within Yugoslav territory.

The river now forms the border with Montenegro for about half its length. On the north bank there are salt flats. In the winter, it is subject to torrential flows and the mouth of the river, and its associated sandbanks, can change location somewhat.

The main road runs south across maize fields, towards the large village of **Bushat** (15km), which was the original home of the great *bey* family of the Bushatis, who from 1750 until 1831 were hereditary Pashas of Shkodra and ruled a vast sprawling domain in northern Albania that became a semi-independent state under the Ottoman Empire (see Route 15). It is now the headquarters of Mother Theresa's Missionaries of Charity organisation in northern Albania.

Mother Theresa
Mother Theresa is the most famous Albanian in the world today. The founder of the Missionaries of Charity Order, *Agnes Gonxha Bejaxhiu*, was born on 27 August 1910 of ethnic Albanian parents in Skup (Skopje), in FYROM. She became a nun, joined the order of the Loreto Sisters and taught for many years in India. In 1946 she heard the call of God to found her own order, while on a train journey. She visited Albania in 1990 and established her Order in the country during the following year.

After another 15km, a dirt track to the right leads to ***Shëngjin**, although it is easier to drive the full route to Lezha, then take the right turn towards the coast for Shëngjin, by the river bridge. This road winds through drained marshland towards the sea. Shëngjin appears to be an insignificant place now, with poor blocks of flats, farm animals wandering at will in the streets, and a small run-down naval base and harbour, but it has witnessed great moments in Albanian history. Most inhabitants are Roman Catholic. It is a grim, poverty stricken place with many social problems, and although there is no reason not to make a visit, you are not recommended to stay here.

History
Shëngjin was known in antiquity as *Nimpheum*. It was used by Julius Caesar as a naval base during the power struggle in ancient Rome, and mentioned in his literary works. It developed as the port for the Roman city of *Lissus* (modern Lezha), based on harbour works involving the construction of a small mole. Changes in the level of the coastline and the development of a huge area of swamp and marshland to the south of the town restricted its later development, and in the early Middle Ages it was little more than a small fishing village and occasional refuge for the pirates operating from the Montenegrin coast, until it became a centre for the trade of the Arberesh Progon in the 14C. It first appears in history called *San Giovanni di Medua* in a document written in 1313. It was developed somewhat by the Turks in the 19C, and with the end of the Ottoman Empire became a focus for Austro-Hungarian commercial activity and political intrigues in Albania and was renamed *San Giovanni di Medua*. It played a central role in the political exchanges which followed Austria's incursions in Serbia in 1908.

As a result of the development of the Central Powers' plan for the construction of the Berlin–Baghdad railway, as a means of penetrating Asia Minor and imposing their political control on the region, Russia envisaged an all-Slav railway, to run through Bulgaria with its Adriatic terminus at San Giovanni di Medua. It was captured by the Montenegrans during the Second Balkan War in 1912. Conflict over the little port was at the heart of the international tension between the Habsburg Empire and Russia, with Tsar Nicholas warning Serbia that Russia would not go to war with the Powers for the sake of a Serbian port on the Adriatic, itself part of a grand design to prevent the emergence of an independent Albania. Only the calling of the Ambassadors Conference in London at the end of that year prevented the crisis from plunging Europe into war.

The town was visited by Hon. Aubrey Herbert in his travels in Albania during and after the Balkan Wars. He commented thus on the appalling social conditions here, which in many ways were typical of the lowlands at the time.

> *Saturday, September* 6, 1913.—MacRury and I left, and arrived at night at St Jean di Medua, where we landed. Never have I seen a more horrible place. In the harbour were some sunken boats; on shore, the houses were tumbling down, miserable, decrepit, stinking. People crawled out of them like diseased animals; mosquitoes and flies hung in festoons from the roof of the place that pretended to be a café; along the road were thick slimy pools, which farther on became marshes—still, but for the movement of insects and water-beetles swimming about among tall bulbous plants, white, green and yellow. The very flowers looked as if they had their roots in corpses. Along the road were straggling trees, which the troops had tried to burn, but apparently they had not had vitality enough to catch fire. It was a place where a duck might have caught typhoid, a leech have developed malaria. I left MacRury on shore, for I did not want to get fever again; he soon joined me aboard swollen with mosquito stings.

When the First World War did start, two years later, San Giovanni came under the provisional administration set up by the Klementi tribal leader, Ded Soko. His rule was then replaced by the International Administration of Scutari, dominated by British military figures, after intrigues orchestrated by Ded Soko's long-standing enemy, the Miredita chieftain, Prenk Bib Doda. In 1915 and 1916 part of the remnants of the Serbian army which had retreated through Albania was evacuated from San Giovanni. Later in the war the port was occupied by Italy, in the crisis over the Adriatic Question, and was one of the last places to be evacuated when the occupation force retreated in 1920. In 1921 the port was occupied by Yugoslav irregulars, en route to attempt to take Tirana, in violation of League of Nations agreements. It became a centre of activity by the British representative in Albania, Sir Harry Eyres, who had a house on the waterfront. Originally a Lloyd's shipping agent, he worked underground for the British government as a spy before becoming the Diplomatic representative. In 1925, Italy sent destroyers to the port during the final crisis of Fan Noli's government.

Like other lowland ports, San Giovanni benefited from the Zog period and Italian annexation, and by the outbreak of the Second World War, harbour facilities had improved considerably, which were used mainly for mineral exports to Italy. The Italians dredged the silted-up canals linking San Giovanni with the river flowing from Lezha, and began a building programme. At the time, the resident population was tiny, perhaps only 200 people. At the beginning of the war, further expansion followed, with the two pre-war jetties being increased to seven. These naval facilities were taken over by the Albanian navy under communism. The port has been a centre for social unrest during recent years, with an attempt by a crowd of several thousand people to seize a ship and flee to Italy in December 1992.

It is worth driving to the centre of the town to see the **House of Sir Harry Eyres**. This is a simple whitewashed one storey building about 100m up the hill, behind blocks of flats in the centre of the town, on the right of the main street; it used to be the town cinema. The inhabitants hope to use it as a church in the future. Sir Harry Eyres was the first British diplomat to be resident in Albania, and took over the property in the 1920s after it had been used as the office of the Austrian Lloyd Steamer Agency. His main residence was in Tirana.

There is little of interest to see in the modern port but there is a long sandy beach on the south side of considerable tourist potential, and some attractive old Ottoman houses. Return by the main road towards **LEZHA** (pop. 8250); across the bridge and (7km) over the railway line you will see the ruined church containing the grave of Skanderbeg, above it the town of Lezha, and the fortress of Lissus on a hill about 305m high behind the town.

N.B. Lezha and Shëngjin have a history of problems with water supply. Visitors are recommended to drink only bottled water or to bring their own with them, particularly if there has been recent flooding in the area.

■ **Police**. Police Headquarters, tel. 201 or 202.

■ **Hotel**. The 'Hunters Lodge' Hotel (see p.222). Pleasant, wooded situation, but often not fully functioning.There is also a restaurant.

■ **Medical care**. District Hospital (emergency service), tel. 288 or 211; Dr Shyqyri Haxhia (surgeon), tel. 331 (home); Dr Ali Bushati (internist), tel. 376 (home).

History

Lezha was known in Classical times as *Lissus*, then called *Alessio* by the Venetians, then *Lesh* before the Second World War, and it was named Lezha after the war. The town is built along the banks of the Drin, below a bare hill, *Mali e Shelbuemit*, the Mount of the Ascension. The Drin used to be navigable here, and Lesh was a small port, before its main flow was diverted into the Buna, as part of inter-war land drainage schemes.

Lissus was an Illyrian settlement that was known in antiquity as a haunt of pirates. The earliest evidence of human settlement dates from the 8C BC, on the acropolis above the modern town. The fortress was built in the 4C BC, incorporating earlier 6C construction. It was besieged and captured in a brilliant feat of arms by Philip V of Macedon in 213 BC. He laid an ambush north of Acrolissus, which he then attacked, and when his men retreated pursued by the garrison of Acrolissus, the troops in the ambush were able to seize the citadel. It was an outstanding success for Philip V in his invasion of Illyria, although it is not known how long he held onto the area before it was retaken by the Illyrian king Genthius. Lissus was subsequently taken by the Roman invaders in 168 BC from Genthius and his fellow Ilyrian leader Perseus and was assigned to the area controlled by the Labeates, who paid tax to Rome. It was rebuilt by Julius Caesar after his Illyrian campaign in 48 BC, when it had been contested by Pompey and attained the status of a *municipium*. It remained an important regional fortress during the Roman and Byzantine periods before falling to barbarian invaders. In medieval Albania it was a stronghold of the Dukagjin family. From 1391 to 1449 it was a Serbian stronghold, then passed to Venice in 1493. It became an important fortress for Skanderbeg, who had formed the Albanian League here in 1444, and he was buried in the town on 17 January 1468. It was taken by the Ottomans in 1498 and burnt down, then refortified by Sultan Selim I (1512–20).

Under Turkish rule it became a small urban centre, market town and stopping place on the caravan routes. It did not particularly prosper in the early part of this century, and played little part in the independence struggle. In 1919 it was ceded to Italy in the Clemenceau Memorandum, in return for which the Yugoslavs were to be allowed to construct a railway along the Drin valley linking Lesh with Prizren, terminating at San Giovanni di Medua. The town stagnated under King Zog and in 1939 it had only about 1600 inhabitants. It was known then for its large bazaar. The nearby military airfield, the largest in Albania, was taken over by the United States in 1994, and is currently used to fly unmanned spy planes over Bosnia and Serbia.

The **Grave of Skanderbeg** is in the ruined Franciscan friary in an open grass area below the town, easily visible from the main road, enclosed by low ruined walls from the ancient city. The church is an impressive building, roofless, and contains only an altar upon which replicas of Skanderbeg's weapons are laid. The originals are in Vienna. Access to the interior is often difficult but this is not important as it is possible to see the interior at all times through gaps in the walls adjacent to the west doors if the entrance is closed.

What the visitor sees has little real relationship to the original 15C building, as after the Turks took the town they demolished Skanderbeg's original tomb and dug up the body, dismembered it and made charms out of the hero's bones. The church of St Nicholas itself was turned into a mosque. After many vicissitudes, it was rebuilt, as far as possible to the original plan, earlier this century, but was very seriously damaged in the 1979 earthquake and has had to be completely rebuilt. A bronze bust of Skanderbeg stands on the east side, by the sculptor Odhise Paskali (1903–85). An obelisk to the side of the church commemorates the rebuilding. But despite its lack of physical authenticity, it is a dignified and moving memorial to the great leader of the Albanian people against the Ottoman invaders, without the rather pretentious atmosphere which some visitors find permeates the museum at Kruja.

It is possible to walk around **ANCIENT LISSUS** by following the remains of the perimeter walls. About 2 hours should be allowed for this. The acropolis requires strong shoes or boots, as many paths are overgrown. There has been some damage to the walls in the last two years, and damage involving vandalism and thefts of wall stone for use as building material. Repairs and reconstruction to some parts are urgently needed. If there is insufficent time, you can easily confine yourself to walking along the flat area of the ancient city, in the vicinity of the church. This in any case includes the ****Illyrian gatehouse**, perhaps the finest monument of its kind in the Balkans insofar as it evokes the atmosphere of the urban civilisation of the Illyrians and dispels any image the visitor may have of the ancestral inhabi-

Ancient Lissus

tants of Albania as a wild, tribal people, whose only urban centres existed as a result of foreign, usually Greek, colonisation. The gatehouse is on the south-west side of the fort, and in fact is part of the south-west tower that guarded the lower side of the fortified town at the riverside approach. It is an unrivalled example of the system of ancient Illyrian military architecture, with sophisticated building techniques using huge stone blocks cut with great precision.

To reach the rest of the ancient settlement, cross the road in the lower town and climb the slope towards the acropolis. The walls begin on the south side of the upper town, and circumscribe the acropolis. The history of their construction is complex, and mainly of interest to specialists but broadly speaking settlement, and associated fortification, commenced on and around the acropolis in the 8C BC, using the steep slope on the west side as a protective wall, and beginning the construction of fortifications on the east side, with walls over 3m thick, in an oblong shape, with a defensive tower at each corner. In the 6C these walls were extended, followed by further fortification in the 4C, when the fort took its present shape, and the town of Lissus began to develop near the river Drin. The walls are 2150m in circumference and were about 5m high, and the fortified area occupies 22 hectares. Defensive towers were built at regular intervals.

A further phase of fortification was undertaken in Julius Caesar's time, which can be seen in the Latin inscriptions on the stone of the south-east tower, to one Gaviarius. Further building took place in late antiquity. The foundations of a Christian church have been found near the acropolis. In the 16C the Turks built a fort on the acropolis, which remained in use until late Ottoman times. Much of the masonry has disappeared, being used in the foundations of new buildings in the town itself.

2km north of Lezha on a hilltop are the buildings of the **Franciscan Convent of San Antonio**, which was founded in 1240. In 1832 it became the residence of the Franciscan provincial father. The medieval church was destroyed in 1918 by Hapsburg troops.

A track runs from Lezha south to the village of **Ishulli i Lezhës**, where Skanderbeg's grandson landed in 1501 before a battle against the Turks that was fought nearby, and to the Kune marsh region, which is a good birdwatching area, particularly for wading birds. Within it is **Count Ciano's Hunting Lodge**. This is now a restaurant and hotel, an attractive wooden building with an Alpine atmosphere and is a good place to have a meal en route, with attractive surroundings.

Count Galeazzo Ciano

Count Galeazzo Ciano was a senior figure in the Italian fascist regime of Benito Mussolini. He was born in Livorno on 18 March 1903. His father was an officer in the navy. He associated himself with the fascist movement in Italy at an early stage, and married Mussolini's daughter, Edda. He became Minister for Foreign Affairs in 1934, and played a central role in the annexation and subsequent invasion of Albania. He spent some time in Albania after the 1939 Italian invasion. He did not agree with the basis of the Axis alliance with Germany, the course of the war disturbed him, and he left the Foreign Ministry in 1943. He was executed by the Gestapo in Verona on 11 January 1944. His memoirs, published in English as *Ciano's Diary 1939–43*, are an invaluable source of information on Italian intentions towards Albania before and during the invasion, on King Zog's regime, and on how Albania was seen as a stepping stone for the fascist invasion of Greece.

His wife, Edda Ciano, (1910–95) daughter of the dictator Mussolini, who worked in Albania as a nurse on the Greek front, died in Rome on 9 April 1995. Her marriage to Ciano was stormy, and in response to his many affairs, she nicknamed him 'Gallo', the *Rooster*, in Italian. After Ciano's execution, Edda broke with her father, writing to him that 'You are no longer my father, I renounce my name Mussolini.' Saranda (see p.137) was named after her for a time in the 1930s, as *Porto Edda*.

Return to Tirana, by the main road south, via Laç, 42km, or north to Shkodra by the original route.

17 · Shkodra to Montenegro and the Albanian Alps

The round trip for this itinerary is 151km, if the whole route is followed, 17km on the main road north from Shkodra towards Hani i Hoti and the border with Montenegro, turning right at Koplik, 17km, then into the mountains via Dedaj, 29km, to Boga, 47km, to Theth, 71km, to Kiri, 114km, then returning to Shkodra, 151km.

A visit to Shkodra and the north would not be complete without at least a short excursion to see Lake Shkodra, and into the mountains to the north, the awesome peaks of the Dinaric Alps, with their brutal and severe grandeur, fully deserving the name of *Bjeshket e Nemura*, the Accursed Mountains. This route really requires a four-wheel drive vehicle to undertake it in full, although as far as Dedaj and Rapshiit is possible with a strong conventional car in dry weather. It covers land which inspired the seminal works on Albania written by Edith Durham and other English language ethnologists and travel writers, with Durham understandably calling it, in *High Albania*, 'the Land of the Living Past'. The countryside has an arid and desert-like quality, with vast open landscapes of treeless, waterless karst pavement and stony wilderness, all dominated by the great ranges of mountains on the border with Montenegro. The predominantly Catholic people live in a deeply conservative culture, often wearing traditional costume, and are rightly seen as a well spring of Albanian identity.

N.B. After Koplik, the road is a very poor dirt track that will test even the most robust vehicle. The route is not recommended at all if rain is expected. Four-wheel drive vehicle essential.
Leave Shkodra by the main road north towards the border with Montenegro at Hani i Hoti (39km). On the outskirts of the city is a very large Muslim cemetery. Before it was destroyed by the communists, there used to be a mosque here. After 1km is a small granite monument to the Gjirokastra-born nationalist hero Çerçiz Topulli.

Çerçiz Topulli
Çerçiz Topulli (1880–1915) was a southern Albanian hero of the *Rilindja*, the national revival movement of the 19C. He took a prominent part in the fighting against the Greeks in his own locality, then in the Young Turk revolts in 1908. He died in Shkodra in 1915 after being wounded fighting on the border with Montenegro.

The road is fairly good, asphalted, although often crowded with people and vehicles. It passes through a series of lowland villages, following a railway line, and enters an increasingly arid landscape, with the small fields littered with limestone boulders.

To the east of the road is the Slavonic area of **Vraka**. About 2000 Serbs and Montenegans live hereabouts, the last remnant of what was once a much larger Slav presence in the Shkodra area. Edith Durham considered that they were refugees from blood feuds in Bosnia and Montenegro. In 1990–91, many of them fled to Serbia, but resettlement arrangements often proved unsatisfactory, especially when the Milosevic regime tried to make them live in Kosova, and some have returned to their ancestral land. Edith Durham commented in 1909 that 'the men of Vraka live at the end of a gun—either end'. In the hills to the right, Illyrian burials have been found at **Goremi**. After 17km, you reach the small town and market centre of **Koplik**, a Roman foundation then known as *Cinna*. Koplik is a miserably poor little town, largely dependent on petrol smuggling, but has a new **mosque**. This is a very large ochre-coloured building, with a bright, airy prayer hall, financed by the Saudi Arabian government. It stands isolated in a muddy field, surrounded by decrepit little houses. To the east are the mountains of Montenegro, above Lake Shkodra. There is a good view of Mount Rurrulija, beyond which is the Montenegran port of Bar. The main road continues through the town another 18km to the border with Montenegro at Hani i Hoti. To the west is the Dukagjin country, home of one of the most famous and conservative Catholic clans. The great poet and scholar Martin Camaj, a Dukagjin, was born in the mountain village of **Temali** nearby.

Martin Camaj
Martin Camaj (1925–92) was the most prominent poet of northern Albania of recent times, and an internationally recognised authority on the Albanian language and grammar. He grew up in a Catholic family and was educated by Jesuits in Shkodra before fleeing the communists in 1945 and spending the rest of his life in exile. From 1970 to 1990 he was professor of Albanian Studies at Munich University. He was an expert on the Albanian dialect of southern Italy, and published a novel and several books of poetry, as well as an authoritative grammar of the Albanian language and a large number of scholarly publications.

As the road approaches the border, through open limestone grazing land studded with sink holes and scrub, and past rows of new petrol stations established by *Mafioski* interests in connection with fuel smuggling to Montenegro, it enters a security zone after the village of Bajza, 5km from Hani i Hoti. The road follows the Shkodra–Podgorica (Titograd) railway line. A concrete monument 2km from the border commemorates the opening of this railway in 1988. It has been closed since late 1991, as a result of the war in ex-Yugoslavia, and the requirements of UN sanctions. It was noteworthy at the time of its construction as marking a relaxation of Albanian economic isolation under the one-party state, and better relations with ex-Yugoslavia.

> A bilateral agreement covering the railway construction was first signed in April 1979, followed by a Protocol in April 1982, which was meant to authorise the beginning of construction work in July 1982. As a result of economic difficulties in Yugoslavia, and the differing value of the line to the two countries, construction work was delayed for a long time. The non-implementation of the agreement by the Yugoslavs caused economic difficulties in Albania.
>
> Police checks are frequent along this road.

THE ALBANIA–MONTENEGRO BORDER REGION

Visiting Montenegro from Albania is not particularly recommended at the time of writing, as life in Montenegro is dominated by the war in ex-Yugoslavia but there is no reason for the determined visitor familiar with Balkan wartime conditions not to do so. The Foreign Office strongly discourages crossing this border, or visiting Montenegro. Travel insurance may become invalid. Great care should be exercised in Montenegro and local contacts are absolutely essential to meet you the other side of the border. The train from Podgorica to Belgrade is a feasible route to Serbia from here but it has a bad security reputation. Avoid.

The practical border arrangments at Hani i Hoti are quite efficient, and it is usually possible to find a car to take travellers to and from Shkodra if the journey is southward. If the border is crossed going northwards, travellers should note that it is often necessary to bribe the border officials with dollars, by changing money with them at highly disadvantageous rates, and that the road linking the Montenegran border post with Podgorica (ex-Yugoslav *Titograd*, about 26km) is not suitable for large vehicles. Border guards can also be bribed to obtain transport. Visas are required to enter Montenegro and cannot be obtained at the border. See Practical Information p. 50.

Things were very different in 1935, in the time of Hon Theodora Benson's motor journey to Albania. Writing about the border arrangements here, she noted,

> The Albanian frontier with Montenegro was quite charming too. The chief officer shook us warmly by the hand, ushered us into his office, and not only gave us cigarettes but had coffee made for us. Perhaps he was a Moslem, perhaps only hospitable. He had a most beautiful picture of King Zog in his office.

It has been announced in June 1995 that a new border crossing linking Albania with Montenegro is to be opened. This will probably be the old road south of Lake Shkodra with the border point near Dajci village, to link Shkodra more closely with the predominantly Albanian-inhabited town of Ulcinje (pre-war *Dulcingo*, Albanian *Ulquin*) in Montenegro. It is not clear at the time of writing when, or whether, this will actually take place, or what the border arrangements will be. When UN sanctions against Montenegro are lifted, it will enable economic links between Albania and this diaspora community to grow rapidly. The Montenegran port of Bar, old *Antivari*, also has an Albanian population. It is known by Albanians there as *Tivar*.

The final section of the road follows the edge of Lake Shkodra to the border, through very beautiful and largely deserted countryside, with bare low hills to the east, and passing a small island in the lake surrounded by reed beds to the west. The lake here is rich in wading birds. The region has never really recovered from the savage fighting in the vicinity during the Balkan Wars, subsequent depopulation, and what many Albanian nationalists have seen as the mistaken delineation of the border with Montenegro and the Albanian communities there.

HOTI TO VERMOSH

This is a very interesting excursion along the road which follows the border with Montenegro and a four-wheel drive vehicle is not required for the first part, to Rapsh. It is an opportunity to see the outstanding Alpine scenery of the ***VERMOSH GORGE** using what is considered by many people to be the most severe and dramatic mountain road in Albania.

2km from the border is a small road on the right which leads to Hoti village, 3km, then is asphalted as far as Rapshi-Starja, 10km. A track runs north-east, roughly parallel to the border with Montenegro for a considerable distance, under Mount Bukovik (1155m), and into very remote country and the Dinaric Alps. The road is of good quality asphalt as far as Rapsh (12km) and subject to the border security situation, is recommended as a usable route to see the great gorge on the way to Vermosh. **At the time of writing there are no problems or restrictions for the visitor but the road has been subject to heavy security at times as a result of fuel smuggling to Montenegro in defiance of UN sanctions. AVOID AT NIGHT.**

Turning right from the main road towards Hoti, the road follows a flat plain to Hoti village across almost deserted but not infertile countryside. After 2km, on the left, is a large Roman Catholic church, set in isolated open fields. Hoti village itself has some good *kullas* and other old buildings.

The region is home to one of the historic tribes of northern Albania, the Hoti. In 1909, Edith Durham reported on their tribal structure, based on about 500 house-holds. At the time, they believed they had originally come to northern Albania to escape Turkish rule in Bosnia.

There is an impressive 1920s Italian house on the right at the far end of the settlement. The road then climbs steeply from the valley floor towards the border, across severe, bare, denuded hills, note the very fine *****view** back towards Lake Shkodra.

Hoti and the neighbouring Gruda tribal region were at the heart of the polit-ical crisis in 1879 between the League of Prizren and the Porte in Constantinople, where the territorial concessions made to Montenegro led to armed conflict in the border regions. In April 1879 the Powers, ignoring Albanian claims, gave Hoti and Gruda to Montenegro, and the Muslim areas of Plava and Gusinj were fought over, in what became known as the *Corti Line* decision. The issue was important in a wider context, as it symbolised the view of the Congress of Berlin that Albania was a geographical rather than a political entity.

The road follows through a largely deserted and depopulated landscape past a Catholic school to **Rapsh**, a pleasant strung-out reasonably prosperous village on the left. In Rapsh, and many nearby villages, traditional Austrian Catholic influence is reasserting itself. Most education and health needs are met by Austrian nuns and their charities. To see the Vermosh Gorge, drive through the village to where the asphalt road runs out and walk on the stony track 400m past the military post. The road then drops into a precipitous gorge, with hairpin bends winding down thousands of feet below to the valley floor.
This road is often closed by landslides and is only passable by four-wheel drive vehicles in good weather with local guidance. Not recommended otherwise.

The ***VIEW east towards Vermosh is truly stupendous, with fold after fold of bare mountains stretching to infinity, and the almost vertical limestone walls of the Vermosh gorge plunging thousands of feet deep to a narrow river bed. After 17km the track reaches Tamara, then a left fork leads to Selca, 10km, and 12km further to the Borolecit Pass, and 11km beyond the Pass to Vermoshi. A right fork leads 5km to Koznja, under Mount Surtes (1129m).

Returning to the main road, and driving back towards Shkodra, a short detour to the right here is very worthwhile, along one of the many dirt tracks leading from the main road, about 2km, to see *Lake Shkodra.

LAKE SHKODRA

Lake Shkodra, in Albanian *Liqeni i Shkodres*, in Classical times *Lacus Labeatis*, in Montenegran *Lake Skadarsko*, is the largest lake in the Balkans, covering an area of 368sq km, and it lies partly in Albania and partly in ex-Yugoslavia. It is about 40km long, from the north-west to the south-east, and about 15km wide for most of its extent. At the deepest point, it is 44m deep, but mostly it is much shallower, with a general depth of about 10m. It is fed partly from the Moraca river, and partly by underground springs from the nearby mountains, the largest of which is called *Syri i Sheganit*, the Eye of the Chestnut Horse. The Moraca rises in Montenegrin territory, with its tributaries the Zeta and the Cijevna, the latter rising in Albania where it is called the Cem. Its only outlet is the very short river Buna, which meets the sea south-west of Shkodra. Before the war, the Buna was a navigable channel for small ships, and played a part in the economic life of Shkodra, but is little used now. The edges of the lake are marshy, and it contains a great variety of fish which in turn supports a rich birdlife, particularly cranes, herons and many varieties of duck and wading birds. The Albanian border with Montenegro, running through the middle of the lake, is very sensitive at the time of writing, and although boats are sometimes available for hire from villagers by the lake side, any fisherman or birdwatcher doing so should stay close to the Albanian shore.

Beyond the marshes along most of the shores of the lake are low slopes of dry gravel, of very limited agricultural value, although near Shkodra there is more clay and a moister, more productive soil. Maize, tobacco, olives and grapes are grown in this area. The commonest fish in the lake is a kind of sardine, the *scoranda* (*Leuciscus alburnus*), in Serbian, the *ukljeva*, which is netted and sold commercially. The lake has little underwater vegetation except near its rivers, with the waters deficient in nitrogenous and phosphatic salts and little plankton. The bottom is rich in lime but poor in organic matter. Among the commonest aquatic plants are the white water lily (*Nymphaea alba*), the yellow water lily (*Nuphar luteum*), the water chestnut (*Trapa natans*), the hornwort (*Ceratophyllum demersum*) and the water milfoil (*Myriophyllum verticillatum*).

Return to the main road and take the turn for **Dedaj** in Koplik. On the left is the very large new **Alrahman Mosque** (see p. 263), There is a **Catholic church** in nearby **Ivanaj**, a very poor building which used to be an agricultural machinery shed. It has been sponsored by nuns from Austria, who, while no doubt engaged in good work locally, seem to be unfriendly and unhelpful to foreign visitors. They have provided a cross and seats; until last year the villagers had to sit on piles of stones during Mass.

The road almost immediately becomes a poor dirt track, with many ruts and potholes. The traveller is entering *Malcija te Mathe*, the *Great Mountain Country*, with the towering peaks of the Korriles range to the left, and the lower Velegikut range in the distance to the north-east. An **Illyrian necropolis** has been excavated 6km along the road, at **Marshej**. It was established by the Labeates tribe in the 7C BC. Remains of Illyrian masonry can be seen on the hillside to the left of the main track. The landscape to either side is flat, rocky and infertile, with the occasional shepherd sitting minding sheep, or if a woman, spinning wool by hand. This territory was referred to in the 1920s by the Gordons as

> the almost unpoached preserves of Miss Edith Durham, whose memory still lingers here. In the towns they have made her the godmother of some back street, but in the country, even in the none too retentive memories of the everyday people, they still call her 'Kralitza', or 'The Queen of the Mountains.'

Her work on this region, *High Albania*, is a classic of ethnographic and travel writing and should be read by anyone with an interest in Albanian culture, folklore or history.

Edith Durham

Edith Durham was born into a conventional English professional family in 1863. Her father's family were mostly distinguished in the medical profession; on her mother's side her grandfather William Ellis was a prominent economist and friend of J.S. Mill. Her travels in the Balkans did not begin until she was 37 years old, when, as a result of poor health, she was advised to spend time in the Mediterranean. She had trained as an artist and had become a well-known illustrator of natural history books. Her first journey followed the conventions of the time, being a cruise down the coast of the Adriatic but she soon began to travel for part of the year in the wilds of Montenegro and southern Serbia, and to spend much of the winter months back in England studying the Serbian language and Balkan politics and society. She was soon involved in the controversies about the Eastern Question, the future of the decadent Ottoman Empire, that were so important in late-Victorian and Edwardian political life, and she became an authority on the ever turbulent politics of the region. Her stance was often controversial, particularly her anti-Bulgarian positions.

In 1903 she finished writing *Through the Lands of the Serb*, and began to contemplate travel in regions of the Balkans that were still struggling to free themselves from Ottoman rule, the realms of 'the unspeakable Turk' as she liked to refer to the Sublime Porte and the Ottoman system of government. This led her naturally to Albania, elements of whose culture she was already familiar through her contact with the ethnic Albanian minority in southern Montenegro. Initially, her travels on behalf of the Macedonian Relief Committee took her outside Albania, and on her first visit in 1903, she really only got to know *Scutari* (modern Shkodra) well. This period resulted in her books *The Burden of the Balkans* and *The Struggle for Scutari*.

She returned in subsequent years to Albania, from her base in Cetinje, in Montenegro, and in 1908 set out on her journey into the northern highlands that formed the basis for her book *High Albania*, with its unique and profound insights into the poverty, violence and deep humanity of the life of the mountains, and her exploration of the workings of the blood feud. After this journey her health deteriorated, as a result of malaria contracted while staying in an Ottoman *han*, and she was never able to travel with the same freedom again.

With the outbreak of the Balkan Wars in 1911 and 1912, she was involved in relief work in field hospitals in Montenegro, and behind the lines at Podgorica. This work was repeated after the outbreak of the First World War, when after the Greek invasion of southern Albania, she worked in a field hospital at Vlora. In 1918, she became honorary secretary of the Anglo-Albanian Association in London. Her final visit to Albania was in 1921, which lasted only a month. She found Tirana distasteful, and detested the new political arrangements that had been established by the Powers. She subsequently continued her ethnographic work, and published a final volume called *Some Tribal Origins, Laws and Customs of the Balkans*. She remained a focus of attention and social life for the many exiles from King Zog's regime in London, and was on warm terms with Fan Noli, the exiled 1920s prime minister. She died in 1944. She was one of the very few English people to be warmly remembered in Hoxha's Albania, with the 1985 edition of the *Albanian Encyclopaedia* noting that 'until the end she remained a defender of the cause of Albania'. Many Albanian towns have a street named after her.

The Albanian villages in this region suffered more than most under communism, with their Catholic and fiercely anti-communist Gheg inhabitants being victimised in numerous ways. As a result, social conditions are particularly poor, and emigration has become a major problem. Serious malnutrition was only avoided in 1991 by the European Community food aid programme and many problems remain. Nevertheless, the villagers are bravely struggling to restore their lives, and welcome visitors, although foreigners should respect the extreme conservatism of social conditions in this area, particularly women's place in society. It should be borne in mind that until the last war, a woman could be bought or sold in this region for a price that was often less than that of a horse. It is still common to see a man riding along the road on a donkey, followed by his wife at a respectful distance behind, and burdened with goods. In Ottoman times it was the custom for a woman to walk nine paces behind her husband at all times. The story went that communism had reduced this margin to three paces. Manners are very formal, and often the guest will only talk to the oldest man in a family if invited into a household. Village democracy centres around the *Kryeplak*, the old man who is chairman of the village council of elderly men, an institution with roots in archaic society, resembling the ancient Spartan *gerousia*.

A good village to visit to see what is being done to restore life in the aftermath of communism is **Dedaj**, 12km along this road, and it is about as far as it is wise to go on a single day's journey from Shkodra, certainly without a four-wheel drive vehicle and adequate supplies. The village lies in the centre of the Thale valley, with small areas of fertile land on the valley floor, and very large areas of common grazing land in the mountains. Illyrian remains have been found in the vicinity, with evidence that Dedaj itself was an important tribal settlement. There are abandoned Muslim and Christian burial grounds on the outskirts of the village, indicating the much larger population the area once supported. The process of agricultural collectivisation under communism was particularly irrelevant and unpopular here, where communist officials tried to prevent the people from keeping even chickens and a pig on their private plots. With privatisation of the land, agricultural production is increasing, with the land on the valley floor being turned over to maize and tobacco.

A walk around the old village is a rewarding experience, to see the attractive small houses, made largely of wood, often painted in bright colours, the very tall dark-haired women, with hair plaited in the style of the northern mountains, wearing traditional dress with brilliantly coloured aprons and the men wearing the white Albanian fez, often wrapped with a dark blue scarf, making a picture that has changed little since Ottoman times. **N.B. Many people dislike being photographed, and the visitor should behave tactfully in this respect throughout this area of Albania, where belief in the evil eye is still widely held**.

Beyond Dedaj, the road goes north-east to Bogë (18km), and a further 24km to **Theth** and the grandeur of the Dinaric Alps—bare, jagged and awe-inspiring, a place where, as one French traveller wrote, there is 'a grandiose setting which is like the end of the world', under the highest peak in Albania, Mount Jezerca (2694m). Above Theth are the remains of a medieval fortress, at Dakaj.

At the moment this route is not really to be recommended for visitors, unless in a specially planned and organised party with an Albanian guide, although attempts were made to develop Theth as a mountain holiday centre under communism. Both road and social conditions are now very poor indeed. The area has very heavy rainfall, and the roads can become virtually impassable quagmires after a sudden storm, even for four-wheel drive vehicles. Landslides and rockfalls are also common problems. The intrepid visitor may, however, wish to undertake the journey, which can be completed in a round trip back to Shkodra (151km), following the road south after Theth, back to Shkodra via Kir. At least two days are needed for the journey; at the time of writing there is nowhere open to stay in Theth, Shala, or anywhere else en route, and travellers should plan accordingly.

This area has been immortalised in travel literature by the American writer Rose Wilder Lane, whose classic account of the excitement and danger of travel in this remote region, *The Peaks of Shala*, appeared in 1924. The Shala mountains are a severe and inhospitable range, even by the standards of this part of Albania, on the southern side of the Dinaric Alps, and Ms Wilder travelled there with her friend Betsy Cleveland, and Rrok Perolli, an official from the Albanian Interior Ministry. She describes how the area was a stronghold of the blood feud and the old clan system, with endemic violence between the Shala tribes and their neighbours, the Shoshi. Their position was complicated by the entrenched Serbian military positions in the mountains north of Thethi. The area had been a graveyard for the retreating Serbian army in 1916, when, decimated by typhus, it had marched into this part of Albania from the mountain passes with Kosova. A very fine contemporary account of the workings of the blood feud in this part of Albania can be found in *Broken April*, a novel by Ismail Kadare.

Return to Shkodra from Dedaj by the same route (29km).

18 · Shkodra to Bajram Curri and Kukes

By ferry boat, from Shkodra to Fierza, about 4 hours journey; Fierza to Bajram Curri, 23km. Or by road to Bajram Curri, to Fierza, via Puka and Fushë-Arrët, 131km. **N.B. This road is in a very poor state and is often impassable; the ferry is the only recommended method of travel on this route, see below. Bajram Curri to Kukes, by road, 125km. This road is poor and the driving very arduous, but the route is usable in spring, summer and autumn. A four-wheel drive vehicle is strongly recommended.**

This itinerary takes in the remote mountain country of north-east Albania, adjoining Kosova, and the beautiful valley of the Black Drin, with its series of great hydro-electric schemes that have transformed the economy and society of this region since the war. Kukes is an attractive mountain resort, where the White and Black Drin meet and set at the foot of the Vikut Mountains. Bajram Curri is at the centre of the remote Tropoja region, in beautiful countryside, with its many historic associations with the Albanian nationalist movement. Tropoja is the birthplace of the current President of Albania, Dr Sali Berisha, and there are numerous Tropojans in leading positions in government and public life, in the police and security apparatus, in particular. Two to three days are needed for this journey if the traveller is based in Shkodra and it should only be undertaken in the summer months.

Leave Shkodra by the upper road to the south, running towards the north bank of the Drin. The road passes through a poor area of the city, past the rubbish tip, and then enters attractive drained marshland, used for intensive agriculture, and winds over the flood plain. Bear left, towards Renc (3km), leaving the railway line; after 2km a track to the left leaves the main road for the Drin. Follow the main road to **Guri i Zi**, Black Stone, named after an ancient monolith standing in the middle of the village. On the hills above the village is the Illyrian fort of **Mazreku**, an important citadel of the Labeates tribe. Then you come to the village of **Juban** (3km), the birthplace of the leader of the 19C Albanian *rilindas*, National Renaissance, movement leader, Zef Jubani. After another 4km, the road crosses the Drin by a long bridge. On the opposite bank is the site of the ancient citadel of **Vig**. A fortress was built here by the Romans in the 4C AD to protect the road from Pristina to Lezha from the attacks of the Ostrogoths under Theodoric and the Visigoths under Alaric. Turn sharp left here and follow the Drin valley eastwards, along a winding road that follows the contours above the lakes of the lower Drin valley. Road quality is reasonable, with an asphalt surface, but there are risks of rockfalls in wet weather. After 36km, the road reaches the **Vau i Dejes** dam, a vast concrete wall that holds back the waters of the upper river. It was built between 1967 and 1971, and the complex has four hydro-electric turbines that can produce 600,000 kilowatts. An underground power station is set in the hillside. The electricity generating capacity was brought into operation between 1978 and 1985, and enabled Albania to become an exporter of electricity to surrounding Balkan states: 580 million cubic metres of water are stored behind the dam. The church at Vau i Dejes was built in 1361 by the Venetians and is one of the very few Gothic-style buildings in Albania. On an island in the artificial lake behind the dam are the remains of **Sarda**, a medieval ecclestical centre built on the site of the late 4C Roman fortress of Sardium that may have formed part of the same defensive system as Vig. The road runs across the base of the dam on a small bridge, then enters a tunnel 3km long— narrow, dangerous and unlit; great care needed—to emerge at the ferry station.

The **ferry** to Bajram Curri takes about 4 hours, on a roll on/roll off boat that will take about 20 cars and 100 passengers. An individual ticket for a single journey costs about £2, a vehicle ticket about £15, at current rates of exchange. Departures are currently in the early morning in either direction, on most days of the week; enquiries in Shkodra are essential to check on the up-to-date position. Tickets are bought in the ticket offices at either end. Early arrival is recommended, and a supply of food, drink, and cigarettes for the journey. At the moment, the boat returns to Shkodra from Fierza at 7 a.m. The excursion is well worth considering for those without the time, or inclination, to undertake the inevitably very arduous and sometimes expensive process of land travel in this region, as the ferry passes through a series of beautiful artificial lakes enclosed by high gorges which have much of the atmosphere of the Norwegian fjords. Travellers should plan carefully, though, if they intend to do this, as at the moment there is nowhere to stay at the upper Drin ferry terminus at Fierza. Passenger accommodation is limited, and unheated, and if the journey is made in the cooler months, warm clothing is recommended. In winter it can be very cold and wet indeed, with howling gales and violent rainstorms sweeping through the narrow defiles. There is now a reasonable café on the boat serving basic supplies of food and drink.

The whole course of the river Drin has been transformed since the war, by the construction of five dams, and hydro-electric power stations, along its course within Albania, from Vau i Dejes, to the junction of the White Drin and Black Drin at Kukes. Before the construction of these dams, the very heavy winter rainfall in this area used to produce serious and widespread flooding of many lowland areas, and contributed to the formation of the notorious malarial swamps along much of Albania's lowland coastline.

In 1930, a Shkodra newspaper commented that, 'According to local opinion the lighting of Shkodra with electricity, judging from the way this problem has been treated and its vicissitudes, is virtually impossible'. There was no electric power at all in Albania until 1927; the candle and the pine torch were used everywhere. In 1937, only ten towns had electric power, and it was a priority for the communist regime after the war to develop the large hydro-electric potential of the country, with the second largest exploitable potential in Europe, after Norway. Hydro-electricity is an important source of Albanian export revenue, although somewhat less than it was ten years ago, with the effects of UN sanctions on ex-Yugoslav industrial demand, ageing plant and many years of drought or relative drought.

The ferry arrives at **Fierza,** after the steady journey of the boat through the defiles of the river, with the steep slopes alongside covered with beautiful deciduous forest, and with little sign of human habitation along most of the route. Here is another great dam and power station, originally named the 'Light of the Party Power Station' when it was opened in 1978, now awaiting a new name. It had a generating capacity of 500,000 kilowatts, from water released to the turbines from behind the concrete wall 166m high. Evidence of Roman settlement has been found in Fierza village, and traces of a Roman road, which was presumably part of a route linking the road from Shkodra with the Kosova region. The ferry docks on an open quayside; there is a small café serving food and drink 300m from the terminus.

For Bajram Curri and the Tropoja region, leave Fierza across the bridge over the Drin, and follow the main road north past the very large remains of quarrying operations connected with the dam construction works. The road, asphalt good quality, winds along a pleasant wooded hillside northwards towards the village of **Bujan**, 8km. This was the birthplace of the hero of the League of Prizren, Mic Sokoli, who died in the struggle against the Turks in 1818, at the battle of Slivova. The house in which he was born is open as a small museum and is worth a quick visit, or at least a look at the exterior, even by those not particularly interested in the Albanian struggle for independence, as it is a very good example of a *kulla*, a northern tower house, with its characteristic fortified architecture. Those familiar with the tower houses of the Mani region of southern Greece will notice many architectural similarities, arising from the mutually antagonistic clan structure of both societies, and the absence of stable political authority.

North-west of the village are the remains of Illyrian walls from the citadel of **Rosuje**, which was built in the 4C BC to mark the frontier between the Labeates and Dardanian tribes. The excavations here in the 1950s showed continuous occupation of the site up until the Christian period, when it was abandoned in the face of barbarian invaders, probably Bulgarians.

BAJRAM CURRI

Continue another 8km along the road to Bajram Curri, the provincial capital of the Tropoja region. This is a run-down town, of about 10,000 inhabitants, but is the administrative centre of the Tropoja region since Tropoja itself was displaced in 1952. Social tension can be high here, and although most people are very welcoming to the visitor, the town is poverty stricken and visitors should be circumspect. It was renamed Bajram Curri in 1952, after the great Albanian nationalist Bajram Curri (1862–1925), having been previously called *Kolgecaj*. Tropoja was seen by the communists as a centre of opposition to their rule, and the whole process is indicative of the pattern of social change that was forced onto this region under the one-party state, where its reputation as a centre of opposition to the Hoxha regime led to wholesale and unnatural changes in its development.

■ **Hotel**. *Hotel Shkelzeni*. Of a fair standard, at the lower end of the oblong town square. The restaurant has much improved under private ownership and it is possible now to get a decent meal here. Rooms are habitable, but fairly primitive. The hotel is also used as the local mortuary, and on occasion corpses may be seen in the hall, awaiting funeral rites and burial. Local game is sometimes available in the winter.

It is also possible to rent a room in the government owned *Villa* currently partly occupied by the European Union Border Monitoring Mission, price about US $20 a night. Water supply is a serious problem both here and elsewhere in the town.

■ **Taxis** and **minibuses** to explore the locality can be rented from the side of an apartment block 1km south of the *Villa*. It is very difficult to hire four-wheel drive vehicles here, although they are essential for many journeys.

Bajram Curri (1862-1925)

Bajram Curri was an exemplary figure, who took a leading role in all the late 19C nationalist movements, from the League of Peja in 1898 onwards. He fought with his *çeta* against the Greeks in 1917, and routed Halid Lleshi's insurgents at Breza in 1920 during Esad Pasha's attempted pro-Serbian coup of that year. He then raised large numbers of armed followers for the struggle against Italian occupation. He was a great enemy of fellow tribal leader Ahmed Zogu, later King Zog, who sentenced him to death in 1922. He played a prominent part in the northern tribal unrest against Zog that led to many bloody encounters between tribesmen and police in the mountains during and after the 1924 revolution. According to tradition, Curri was eventually gunned down by Zog's police in the **Dragobi cave** (see below), in truly heroic circumstances, fighting his enemies to the last, a smoking pistol in hand, and with loyal followers from his *fis* surrounding him, but some revisionist historians have cast doubt on this, claiming that he committed suicide rather than surrender.

In the past, before the Balkan Wars, the First World War and the subsequent changes in borders, there were many close links between this region and Kosova, its natural economic hinterland. Bajram Curri himself was actually born in Gjakova, now in Kosova, and the economy of the region generally has always suffered from the effective closure of this border. Some legal cross-border trade resumed with the end of communism, but that has now ceased as a result of United Nations' sanctions against Serbia, although there is a large and growing smuggling trade. The local mining industry at centres like Kam has sufferred particularly in the last two years, in that ore mined there was feedstock for the Gjakova smelter. Political tension with Serbia is high, at the time of writing, and although the border can be approached (26km) at Quaf e Morines, and in theory crossed, the police will sometimes prevent people from attempting to do so, which is in their own interests as Albanian shepherds have been killed here recently by Serbian border guards.

Animal rights activists will find much to dislike in this region, with badger baiting and other blood sports being a traditional feature of male recreational life.

The town has some pleasant small cafés, and the large monumental bronze statue of Bajram Curri by Fuat Dushku is a very impressive monument. A small museum of his life is currently closed. Opposite the hotel is a small bronze statue, a memorial to Asim Vokshi (1909–37), one of the Albanians who fought on the Republican side in the Spanish Civil War, a native of Gjakova in Kosova. Otherwise, there is little to delay the visitor in the town, with the few Ottoman-period buildings in the town generally in a poor condition, and many blocks of run-down modern flats.

There are two outstanding excursions near Bajram Curri, one to ****Dragobi Cave** where Curri died, 15km along a track over the bridge of the river, and Valbona, and the other to Tropoja, 10km over the bridge in the opposite direction, towards Kosova. To follow the latter, take the road through attractive fruit tree plantations, which is the old road to Gjakova. ***Tropoja** is reached down a steep slope to the left, and is a **charming, unspoilt rural centre**, with very attractive Ottoman-period buildings around a small square, and many small farm houses on the outskirts. A good short walk can be had on the far side of the square, up a slope, where there is an outstanding view of the rugged peaks of this end of the Dinaric Alps, dominated by **Mount Shkelzen** (2400m). The outline of the word ENVER used to be seen on the upper slopes, a monument to the cult of personality of the dictator, built out of piles of stones laid by Young Pioneers in the 1970s. A house near Tropoja was the birthplace of the current President of Albania, Dr Sali Berisha. His family were traditionally shepherds in the area.

Sali Berisha

Dr Sali Berisha was born on 1 July 1944 in Tropoja into a Muslim family. In 1967 he graduated in medicine from the University of Tirana. In 1986 he was elected a member of the European Medical Research Science Committee based in Denmark, and developed his research into the field of heart surgery. He was an active member of the communist party for some years. On 12 December 1990 he was a founder member of the Democratic Opposition in Tirana, later to become the Democratic Party that took power in April 1992. He was first elected a deputy to the Peoples Assembly in the March 1991 elections. He became President of Albania after April 1992.

To reach ****DRAGOBI** and **VALBONA**, find a taxi in the town, preferably a four-wheel drive vehicle although this is not absolutely essential in dry weather. Follow the road out of the town towards the north east for about 2km, past attractive and moderately prosperous small farms to where there is a sharp left turn up a rise towards the gorge of the river Valbona. It is a poor stony dirt track that becomes very dangerous in wet weather, with severe landslides from the sides of the limestone gorge very common. Dynamite and bulldozers kept in Bajram Curri police station are used to clear the road when this occurs. You follow the path taken by King Zog's gendamerie in their final pursuit of Bajram Curri and his *çeta*.

The best time to make the journey is in late spring, when the melting snow from the Dinaric Alps to the north on the border with Montenegro turns the River Valbona into a wild surging torrent, with the frothing white water carrying rocks along its path. The road clings to the right side of the gorge above the river, with outstanding views of the snowcapped mountains to the north in Montenegro. The towering walls of the gorge are studded with clumps of trees and bushes, producing rock formations and patterns of vegetation of a truly Byronic character.

After about 2km, here is a superb **waterfall** dropping hundreds of feet into the far side of the river from a cave high in the gorge wall, and after 3km a derelict monument to a Partisan battle. After 4km, note '1908' carved into the rock above the river on the west bank, in commemoration of the strength of the Young Turk revolution in this area of Albania. On the right is a derelict settlement of workers holiday houses dating from the communist period. Cross a bridge and drive a short distance to reach****Dragobi** village.

Dragobi is a beautiful and evocative traditional northern village, with many wooden and stone *kullas* and other interesting buildings. It is situated on a wide patch of fertile land where the Valbona river valley widens a little, at the top of the southern end of the gorge, with dramatic views towards snowcapped Mount Gjarperi (2211m) to the north. The area was, and to some extent still is, a stronghold of the **blood feud**; note the absence of lower floor windows in many houses and the strong defensive measures in the building construction. On the left, on the outskirts of the village, are the remains of a large statue of Enver Hoxha which was dynamited by the villagers in April 1992 in celebration of the Democratic Party election victory. Attractive ash and beech woods surround some houses. Private agriculture is developing, with little fields laid out on the narrow area of fertile land adjoining the river bed. The area is populated mostly by members of the Ljuma clan.

The *Cave of **Bajram Curri** is in a high cleft in the rocks above the tree line to the left of the road north of the village, above an abandoned dwelling house,and it is not possible to reach it without a specialised expedition. The road follows on 13km further of similar dirt track through the gorge to Valbona, then 13km west to **Rrogam**, an isolated mountain settlement preserving many archaic features of social and economic life. It was the subject of a documentary *The Albanians of Rrogam* shown on British television in 1991 and made by Berit Backer.

Berit Backer

Berit Backer (1948-93) was a leading protagonist in the Albanian cause in Norway for many years. She was an anthropologist who was one of the first foreign academics allowed to work in Albania under Enver Hoxha's regime. She was later responsible for the establishment of the Albanian Helsinki Committee in Tirana, and was closely involved with the Kosova Democratic League in Scandanavia. She was murdered in Oslo in 1993.

Return to Bajram Curri by the same route.

BAJRAM CURRI TO KUKES BY ROAD

To reach Kukes (136km), a difficult drive is required, through very remote countryside on very poor roads, but the more adventurous traveller may feel it is worth undertaking because of the outstanding and dramatic beauty of the mountain scenery. There are two alternative routes.

N.B. Both require adequate preparation, a local driver or guide, a four-wheel drive vehicle and are much safer in the summer months.

(**I**). Leave **Bajram Curri** by the road to the south to **Fierza** (19km). Follow the road south-west, at first fairly close to the Drin, but then climbing steeply through remote forest country, past deserted copper mines. There are **magnificent views back towards the Dinaric Alps to the north**. The road clings to the southern side of the river, and winds through the forest in a seemingly endless series of hairpin bends. There is much to interest the student of natural history and ornithology in the forests. After about 60km, the road comes to a junction with the road for **Puka** and the wilds of Mirdita. Take the left turn here, towards Kukes, and follow a similarly remote and demanding track through pine and deciduous forests for another 60km, with little habitation along the way except isolated foresters' huts. The local houses are usually built of wood, with shingle roofs.

(**II**). An alternative route to, or from, **Kukes** is to follow the roads near the border with **Serbia**. This is not an inherently dangerous route, from the security point of view and road quality is not all that bad, apart from the last 15km, which are dreadful, following some reasonable asphalt stretches, as it was kept in repair under communism for defence purposes and for access to the **Kam chrome mines**. But it runs through many remote and largely deserted areas of upland and mountain, and mishaps with vehicles may cause serious difficulties.

N.B. Unaccompanied travel is not recommended. There is very little traffic or settlement in most places. The area lived by trading cattle with Kosova for centuries, and the closure of the border with Serbia after the First World War was an economic catastrophe from which it has never recovered. The main trade route ran from Shkodra to Djakova to Prizren in Kosova.

From Kukes, leave the town to the north, past the monument to Shote Galicia, the Kosovar heroine, and past old factories, on an asphalt road with very bad potholes. 3km to the west is the **Kalimash chrome mine**, mine buildings can be seen high on the exposed hillside. Note the grey chrome ore naturally occuring in stream beds by the road. Follow the road slope down to the **lake**, where the White Drin meets the Blàck Drin, a part famous for carp and perch fishing, then over a good modern bridge, and the road winds along a hillside through dwarf oak woods. The first village reached is **Muç Hasi** (4km), with some good Ottoman-period buildings in the lower village, entering the district of Kruma. Behind the village, fold after fold of mountains stretch to the horizon. To the left is a small lake. Continue through largely empty countryside to **Uranishte** (13km), a small town with a new mosque, a pleasant white oblong structure. The hills surrounding the village are deserted and covered with dwarf oak. Water is a problem in this region, in Ottoman times it was known as *Hasi i Thate*, the waterless place. Then pass through a very poor district of small farms. Has region was known as a stronghold of support for Bajram Curri and his *çeta*, the local saying going that 'the people of Has helped Bajram Curri, the people of Tropoja killed him.'

1km after Uranishte is a very fine ****kulla**, a massive and brutal-looking fortified tower house in trees about 500m from the road. Note the high door entrance in the walls over 20ft from the ground. Drop down to **Kruma**, with fine views towards the Pastevic mountains, then **Kamza**, 38km from Kukes. In the distance on the left above the road is the copper mine of **Kalimes**. Kruma is a rundown town with many social problems but has a fine new **mosque**, a large structure behind blue railings in the centre of the town built by funds from a Saudi Arabian foundation. It is in the modern style, with three very large windows on each side wall of the prayer room. Leave the town past a Muslim cemetery and a monument to Bajram Curri's 1925 retreat. Enter deserted uplands, with poor wet heavy land, then through very remote and largely abandoned grazing country, with a good view of the Dinaric Alps on the Montenegran border to the north. You can travel many miles here and see no sign of human life or habitation.

Then approach **Helshan** (62km), once the site of an Ottoman *han* on the caravan routes from Scutari (modern Shkoder) to Kosova, then into lonely forests used for foxhunting in the winter. Then **Kam** (74km) a desperately poor and depressed settlement around a now closed chrome mine, and enter the **Tropoja** district. The mine has suffered enforced closure as a result of United Nations' sanctions, hitherto being the source of feedstock for a smelter in ex-Yugoslavia. Barefoot children and signs of malnutrition are common.

Cross a river, then past a deep wooded gorge, with road-sides covered in attractive white and blue wildflowers and helibores, through the deserted and remote Bytyc hills, to **Paç** (92km) a nice little village on top of a hill with a new **mosque** and very good freshwater spring. There is a small café near the mosque. Note the traditional northeast building techniques with the house roofs covered in split wood shingle. The road runs through attractive deciduous woods, then becomes a very bad dirt track indeed, to the top of the **Quaf e Luzhës** (114km). The ***view** from the top of the pass is dramatic, with a drop of hundreds of feet into the valley floor below, and **Bajram Curri** town in the distance below the great peaks on the

Montenegran border. Follow down to the town (149km), onto the valley floor past fruit plantations, and the River Valbona, where there is a good place to swim near the bridge in summer although the water is very cold.

NB This last portion of this road is excruciatingly bad, with serious difficulties even for four-wheel drive vehicles.

To reach Shkodra by road direct, follow the Puka turn and drive 10km to Fushë-Arrëz, a timber and copper mining centre, then 15km to Puka, site of ancient *Epicaria*. Near Puka is the Qerret district. In this area is the village of *Koman* where the first evidence of the 'Koman' period of Illyrian culture was excavated in 1898. The concept of a 'Koman' culture has since been the subject of academic controversy. After another 35km, the road meets the main road, 15km south of Shkodra.

KUKES

To reach Kukes, continue travelling west from the Puka turn. The road improves somewhat as the Drin valley is rejoined, and eventually the large artificial lake below Kukes can be seen. It was filled with water in 1976, and Kukes is an entirely modern town now, as the original village lies below the surface of the lake.

■ **Medical care**. Policlinics, tel. 229; District Hospital (emergency service), tel. 221; Dr Osman Dafku (surgeon), tel. 364 (home); Dr Agron Loncka (internist), tel. 576 (home).

■ **Police**. Police Headquarters, tel. 321 or 221.

■ **Hotel**. Despite its remote situation, at the end of the new lake, about 2km from the town, and unpromising appearance, the hotel was once one of the best Albturist hotels in the country, with pleasant, helpful staff, a good restaurant and clean rooms. The local yoghurt, cheese and raki were of particularly good quality. Unfortunately this does not appear to be the case now, to judge from correspondence received. Water supply is a serious problem.Instead, try the *Hotel Gjalica*, near the town centre, for better, if very basic, accommodation and food.

History

Kukes has little to show in the way of recorded history. Illyrian tombs were found at Keneta, nearby. It was a small Roman settlement, a stopping point on a branch road leading eventually to the Via Egnetia, and a minor Ottoman market centre and trading post on the road to southern Kosova. Kukes was important for a short time in the political turmoil in the early 1920's, when in June 1924 Bajram Curri issued the call to arms from Kukes that led to the 'June Revolution'. By the end of the month the first government of Ahmet Zogu (later King Zog) had fallen, and he had to withdraw to Belgrade. He was replaced by the Democratic government of Fan Noli. Kukes only rose to any later prominence as a stopping point on the new road linking Shkodra and Prizren built by Italian engineers in the 1920s. The little town developed somewhat as the gendarmarie centre of King Zog's regional administration, but most development is modern and depended on the growth of the electricity industry and associated works. The Italian occupiers built an airstrip in 1937. In the last war the Kukes district was an important centre of British assistance to the Partisan resistance, with several officers from SOE Cairo active between 1943 and 1945. The artificial lake (area 12.5 sq. km) was created in 1976, engulfing the original small town. In recent times there has been substantial depopulation from this area, and conflict over government compensa-

New mosque at Kukes

tion for land expropriated from local inhabitants during the communist period to build electricity works. The border post with Serbia to the east is formally open, but using it at the moment is not recommended.

Kukes is the only centre of administration of a very large and remote area, stretching from Tropoja in the north to Dibra in the south, with few amenities, bad communications and near medieval conditions of life in some places. Illyrian remains have been excavated at Kolsh village nearby, and in another adjacent location, now drowned under the lake. West of Kukes is **Kalimash**, with its important chrome mine, a principal local employer. In the past there used to be a ferry service linking Kukes with Fierza, but it is not in service regularly at the time of writing, although it is hoped that it will soon be restored.

Kukes is a good centre for fishing and walking in the surrounding mountains, but many visitors may prefer to wait until social and political conditions in the area are more settled before attempting to do either. In bad weather Kukes can be dramatic, with huge threatening cloud formations over the Vikut Mountains, and the sparse streets of the little town and the lake, subject to violent gusts of the 'Bora' wind.

A large new mosque, the **Mosque of Salim Ben Mahfuz**, has been built on the lakeside, an impressive structure, with a north African feel, with blue crenellated concrete, an open terrace up a flight of steps, and a narrow portico. It was financed by the Egyptian Muafaq Foundation, and opened in 1995.

To the south east of Kukes is the **Shishtavec village region**, where most villagers speak Slav, in a dialect of Bulgarian. It is known as the *Gorë region*, its population the *Gorani*.

Return to Fierza by the same route, and take the ferry towards Shkodra, or drive back via Puka. Allow at least a day for either journey.

BIBLIOGRAPHY

There are a surprisingly large number of books in English which allude to aspects of Albanian life, some written in the remote past, others more recent, but few are exclusively about the life of the country. In the ancient period, **Illyria** was the site of some of Alexander the Great's first battles, recorded by Arrian. It is frequently mentioned in the works of ancient geographers such as Strabo, by Cicero, who owned land in Illyria, by the poet Horace, and by Roman historians, particularly Livy. Many of the most crucial battles in the power struggle for the future of Rome between Pompey and Octavian took place in Illyria.

In the **Ottoman period**, the country was chronicled in the normal course of official documents. But as the Ottoman archives in Turkey are still partly closed, much of what happened in Albania in this period remains obscure. Even if they were open, very few modern Albanian, British or American historians can read the Otttoman Turkish written in the Arabic script, in any case.

A few British travellers came to Illyria in the Middle Ages such as Syneon Sineonis, who visited Durres in 1322, and John of Newport, who fought against the Turks in 1457. Edward Brown, an English doctor, visited Albania in 1669. In Renaissance and Enlightenment Europe, little was known of the country, or written about it, so that it formed a suitably mythical and fantastic background for the events in Shakespeare's *Twelfth Night*.

The most typical reaction was the comment of the historian Edward Gibbon, who, when sailing down the Adriatic in the 18C and seeing the Albanian mountains, noted that 'within sight of Italy is less known that the interior of America'. Lord Byron's descriptions of southern Albania in *Childe Harold*, based on his 1809 visit, and remarkable as they are, were really all that most educated English readers had to guide them for a very long time, along with the record his friend Hobhouse wrote of his trip.

It was not until late in the 19C and in the Edwardian period that there were popularly available books in the English language that described Albanian life from the point of view of either the intelligent traveller or the academic investigator. A considerable increase in knowledge of Albania had by then taken place in Germany, where the work of the pioneer Albanologist Dr Johann von Hahn was of seminal importance. His *Albanesische Studien*, published in Jena in 1854, is a monumental work of scholarship and represented in many ways the first attempt to investigate systematically the Albanian language, ethnography and economy.

In the Edwardian period, in English, the work of Edith Durham was also of seminal importance, and in the inter-war period Joseph Swire's work was of similar value. A large number of interesting travel and ethnographic books were also published in this period. After the Second World War, and the establishment of communism, most writing about the country, from all points of view, pro and anti communist, has been dominated by political considerations, and needs to be read critically, and with great care, even if the topic is ostensibly non-political.

Germany remains a centre of Albanian studies in Europe, the South-East Europe institute at Munich in particular.

Ancient and Byzantine
The Peloponnesian War, by Thucydides
Life of Alexander, by Arrian

Geography, by Strabo
The Histories, by Polybius
Letters, by Pliny
Philippics, by Cicero
History of Rome, by Livy
The Kanun of Lek Dukagjin
The Byzantine Commonwealth, by Sir Dimitri Obolensky

Pre-1930

Childe Harold's Pilgrimage, by Lord Byron
A Journey through Albania, by John Hobhouse
Travels in the Levant 1848–49, by Edward Lear
Albania, A Narrative of Recent Travel, by Edward Knight
Albania Past and Present, by C.A. Chekrezi
Souvenirs de la Haute-Albanie, by A. Degrand
High Albania, by Edith Durham
Travels in the Morea, by W.M. Leake
Travels in the Ionian Isles, Albania, Thessaly and Macedonia during the years 1812-13, by Henry Holland
Travels in Sicily, Greece and Albania, by H. Hughes
The Spirit of the East, by David Urquhart
Excursions in Albania, by Captain J. Best
Travels in European Turkey, by Edmund Spencer
Turkey in Europe, by Odysseus
Pictures from the Balkans, by John Foster Fraser
A Ride Through the Balkans, by A.E. Conway
Some Tribal Origins, Laws and Customs of the Balkans, by Edith Durham
The Burden of the Balkans, by Edith Durham
The Struggle for Scutari, by Edith Durham
Twenty Years of Balkan Tangle, by Edith Durham
The Balkan Wars 1912-13, by Leon Trotsky
Guide to the Adriatic Coast, Baedecker
Two Vagabonds in Albania, by Jan and Cora Gordon
The Life of J.D. Bourchier, by Lady Grogan
The Sorrows of Epirus, by René Puaux
Safety Last , by Colonel W F Sterling
Inner History of the Balkan Wars, by Sir Reginald Rankin
The Peaks of Shala, by Rose Lane Wilder
Winter and Spring on the shores of the Meditteranean, by James Bennet

1930–39

To the Land of the Eagle, by Paul Edmonds
Balkan Holiday, by David Footman
Albanian Backdoor, by Bernard Newman
Albanian Journey, by Bernard Newman
Albania: The Rise of a Kingdom, by Joseph Swire
The Unambitious Journey, by Hon Theodora Benson
King Zog's Albania, by Joseph Swire
Albanien:Vergessenes Land, by Ivan Bernatzik
Dead Puppets Dance, by Philip Thornton
Scarred Background, by Nigel Heseltine

Albania-Guida D'Italia della C.T.I.
Mussolini's Roman Empire, by G.T. Garratt

Wartime
The Hollow Legions, by Mario Cervi
The Ciano Diaries 1939-43
Albania, Admiralty Handbook 1944
Sons of the Eagle, by Julian Amery
Illyrian Venture, by 'Trotsky' Davies
Struggle for the Balkans, by Svetozar Vukmanovic (General Tempo)
One Man in his Time, by Xan Fielding
Albania's National Liberation: the Bitter Victory, by Sir Reginald Hibbert
Albanian Assignment, by David Smiley
When Men and Mountains Meet, by H.W. Tilman
Albania's Road to Freedom, by Vandaleur Robinson

Post-war
Shqiperia Arkeologjike—Albanian Archaeological Institute, Tirana 1971 (with enclosed English translation)
Albanian Grammar, by Martin Camaj, Weisbaden 1984
Illyria Reborn, by Dymphna Cusack
The Eagle Spreads his Claws, by Leslie Gardner
With Pickaxe and Rifle, by William Ash
Albania, by Philip Ward
Albania—Who Cares?, by Bill Hamilton
The Albanians—A Modern History, by Miranda Vickers
Albania, by Harry Hamm
The Unwritten Law of Albania, by Margaret Hasluck
The Adriatic Sea, by Harry Hodgkinson
Albananien, by Guntram Koch
Albania, a travel record, by Pierre Courtade
Albanian Historical Folksongs, by P.J. Ruches
The Albanians: Europe's Forgotten Survivors, by Anton Logoreci
An Elusive Eagle Soars, by Robert Elsie
Albania, by Peter and Andrea Dawson
Albania and the Albanians, by Ramadan Marmullaku
Islam in the Balkans, by Harry Norris
On the Shores of the Mediterranean, by Eric Newby
Colloquial Albanian, by Isa Zymberi
The Jews of Albania, by Harvey Sarner
Selected Poems, by Martin Camaj
History of the Party of Labour of Albania
Albania Defiant, by Jan Myrdal and Gun Kessle
Albanian Stalinism, by Arshi Pipa
Socialist Albania since 1944, by Peter. J. Prifti
Albania, by Stavro Skendi
The Illyrians, by John Wilkes
The Vlachs, by Tom Winnifrith
Shattered Eagles, Balkan Fragments, by Tom Winnifrith
Albania—A Geographic Outline, Tirana, 1971
Albania—General Information, Tirana, 1984

The Corfu Incident, by Eric Leggett
Greece, Albania and Northern Epirus, by Edward Capps
Albanien, by Dardan Gashi and Ingrid Steiner
The Great Betrayal, by Nicholas Bethell
The Albanians and their Territories, Tirana 1985
Portrait of Albania, Tirana '8 Nentori' 1982
Geraldine of the Albanians, by Gwen Robyns
Albania—from Anarchy to a Balkan Identity, by Miranda Vickers and James Pettifer
Between Serb and Albanian—A History of Kosova, by Miranda Vickers
Albania and the Albanians, by Derek Hall
The Music of Albania, by June Emerson
The Search for the Eagle's Song, by June Emerson
Albanian Folktales and Legends, by Robert Elsie

Enver Hoxha's own writings are available in the Collected Works, the *Vepra*, no fewer than 71 volumes in the Albanian language, and in a six volume English abridgement, *Enver Hoxha Selected Works*. His account of Albanian–Greek relations, with many references to the problems of Epirus, is to be found in *Two Friendly Peoples*, Tirana 1985. A communist view of Hoxha's own personality and influence can be found in *Our Enver* by Ramiz Alia. The communist regime published numerous political documents in English, and a number of guidebooks. Not all of these are biased or useless, for instance, *Albania A Geographic Outline* contains a good deal of useful information about the geography, relief and geology of the country. Many are still on sale in Tirana kiosks, four years after the end of communism. But they should be read with great care, if at all, and the statistics contained in them are almost invariably untrustworthy if concerned with industry, agricultural production or politics. The best guide to Ramiz Alia's own thinking about the end of communism is to be found in *Une, Ramiz Alia*, Tirana 'Dituria', 1993.

The most reliable source of information on Albania in the UK is *Albania Life*, the quarterly publication of the Albania Society of Britain, available from specialist East European bookshops in London or from the Albania Society of Britain, 7 Nelson Road, London SW19 1HS, £8 annual subscription. Those interested primarily in aid projects should contact Friends of Albania c/o Ms P. Peacock, Peasacre, Thurloxton, Taunton, Somerset TA2 8RJ, tel. 01823 412 452. This organisation also publishes a newsletter, as does the Anglo-Albanian Society, 45 Linhope Street NW1. Oxfam, Adra Trans-Europe, and Feed the Children are the charities in the UK with most experience of work in Albania. A UK contact for the Butrint Foundation is Dr. John Moreland, of Sheffield University Archaeology Department.

A business guide *Albania-Information for Investors* is available from Albanian embassies in foreign countries. Material on Albania is published regularly by business intelligence agencies in the UK and USA specialising in economic and political analysis and risk assessment for businessmen contemplating investment in Eastern Europe. In the UK, Oxford Analytica, 5 Alfred Street, Oxford OX1 4EH and Control Risks Ltd, 83 Victoria Street, London SW1H 0HW are well known in this field, as are Kroll Associates in Switzerland and the USA.

A very useful business directory of firms operating in Albania, *Fax per Biznes*, is on sale in Tirana kiosks and hotel bookshops. It also gives telephone and fax numbers of all embassies and government ministries. Telephone directories are very difficult to obtain.

A UK expert on the Albanian mining industry is Nicholas Hunter MIMM, of Hunter Mining Consultants Ltd (UK 01225-336328, fx 01225-480887). Transport companies based in the UK with regular services to Albania include P&O Ferrymasters, London, United Maritime Ltd., Transargo of Billericay, Essex, Roeliling (UK) Ltd, I.S. Logistics of Birmingham, and R.J. International Freight Ltd of Cheshire. The views of the present government on Albanian political and economic developments can be found in *The Contract of the Democratic Party with Albania* (R.D., Tirana, 1995).

Kosova and FYROM
There are numerous books on Kosova. A good guide to the human rights problems faced by the Albanians there is *The Denial of Human and National Rights of Albanians in Kosova*, by Dr Alush Gashi, published in New York in 1992 by Illyria Publishing, Inc. Also *What the Kosovars Say and Demand*, Tirana, 1991, and *Serbian Colonisation and Ethnic Cleansing of Kosova*, Pristina, 1992. Serbian publications are obtainable from Serbian Information Offices in most European capital cities and in Washington DC, in the USA.

There is very little up to date or relevant literature on the Albanians in former Yugoslav Macedonia. See *Who are the Macedonians?* by Hugh Poulton (London, 1995) and *The Southern Balkans* (Minority Rights Group, London, 1994) for essential basic information.

The Greek minority and the Cameria issue
In the last two years there has been a considerable increase in the documentation available on the Greek minority and the Cameria problem, although inevitably much of it is written from highly partisan viewpoints and should be read very critically. In addition to older volumes such as *The Sorrows of Epirus* by Rene Puaux, and *Albania's Captives* by Pyrrhus Ruches, the Institute of Balkan Studies in Thessalonika has published *The Greek Minority in Albania—A Documentary Record (1921–1993)* by Basil Kondis and Eleftheria Manda, and there is a section on the minority in *The Southern Balkans*, Minority Rights Group, London, 1994. A very fine book of photographs, title in Greek (*On Epirus Earth*), was published in Athens in 1993 by Ekdoseis Asterismos, although the text contains many statements Albanians are likely to find highly objectionable, provocative, and inaccurate. Several books have been published in Tirana by Albanian writers putting the case for the Cameria people but none has yet been translated into English. There are numerous publications in the United States on the Northern Epirus issue, some in English, some in Greek. They are all written embodying highly controversial views of regional history.

INDEX

Topographical names appear in roman type; the names of people and tribes in *italic*, most important references are given in **bold**.